FIND A TRAIL or BLAZE ONE

A Biography of Dr. Reatha Clark King

as told to KATE LEIBFRIED

BEAVER'S POND PRESS

FIND A TRAIL OR BLAZE ONE: THE BIOGRAPHY OF
DR. REATHA CLARK KING © 2021 by Metropolitan State University.
All rights reserved. No part of this book may be reproduced in any form
whatsoever, by photography or xerography or by any other means, by
broadcast or transmission, by translation into any kind of language, nor by
recording electronically or otherwise, without permission in writing from the
author, except by a reviewer, who may quote brief passages in critical articles
or reviews.

Cover and interior photographs courtesy of the Clark King family and
Metropolitan State University Advancement Division

Book design and typesetting by James Monroe Design LLC
Edited by Madeleine Vasaly
Production Editor: Laurie Buss Herrmann

First Paperback Edition Published 2022
ISBN 13: 978-1-64343-700-2
Library of Congress Catalog Number: 2021908851

Printed in the United States of America
26　25　24　23　22　　5　4　3　2　1

BEAVER'S
POND
PRESS

Beaver's Pond Press, Inc.
939 Seventh Street West
Saint Paul, MN 55102
(952) 829-8818
www.BeaversPondPress.com

CONTENTS

A Message to You | *v*

Preface | *vii*

A Note on Racial Terminology | *x*

A Note on Sources | *xi*

CHAPTER ONE: Cotton Fields 1

CHAPTER TWO: South Georgia 5

CHAPTER THREE: Mount Zion 13

CHAPTER FOUR: Dirt Roads 21

CHAPTER FIVE: Dirty Spoon 28

CHAPTER SIX: Red Brick Walls 42

CHAPTER SEVEN: City of Wind and Fire. 64

CHAPTER EIGHT: The Nation's Beating Heart 88

CHAPTER NINE: To the Moon 102

CHAPTER TEN: The City So Nice. 117

CHAPTER ELEVEN: Moving On Up 125

CHAPTER TWELVE: On the Right Side of the Tracks 137

CHAPTER THIRTEEN: The School without Walls 154

CHAPTER FOURTEEN: In the Land of Lakes 170

CHAPTER FIFTEEN: Building Bridges 187

CHAPTER SIXTEEN: Driving against Traffic. 207

CHAPTER SEVENTEEN: To Grow a School. 220

CHAPTER EIGHTEEN: Foundational Shifts. 228

CHAPTER NINETEEN: Little Flour Mill on the River 242

CHAPTER TWENTY: Philanthropy in the Emerald City. 252

CHAPTER TWENTY-ONE: Reaching Wide. 265

CHAPTER TWENTY-TWO: A Living Legacy 285

Acknowledgments | 307

Appendix | 311

Bibliography | 321

A MESSAGE TO YOU

Dear Reader,

One of my greatest wishes is for you to recognize your own brilliance. You are a precious creation, a unique and wonderful individual, and I love and appreciate you, even if we have not personally met.

How do I know I love you?

Because I have traveled to all corners of our magnificent earth, have met thousands upon thousands of people, and have yet to meet a person undeserving of love. No matter your background, race, ethnicity, gender, socioeconomic status, or religion, you are a worthy human being and a treasured member of society.

There are those who find excuses to look down on others. They see flaws and shortcomings instead of aptitude and radiance. In my own life, many of my relatives felt self-conscious because they never learned how to read and write. Though I clearly value education and am proud of my degrees, I recognize that formal education is not the only mark of wisdom. Wisdom can be gained from farming the land or working in a factory. It can be gained from rearing children or learning recipes from our elders. Above all, wisdom can be acquired from truly listening to one another and learning from collective experiences.

Reader, it is possible (probable, even) that there are times when you feel unloved or unlovable. There are likely times when you feel as if the whole world is against you and nothing will ever go your way. Believe me, I've been there. I know what it's like to be told, "You can't." I know what it's like to be doubted and mistrusted because of who I am— because of my gender and the color of my skin.

But for every naysayer, I have had a dozen or more cheerleaders, supporters, and mentors. These special individuals are there for you, too, if you look for them. Open yourself to their guidance, let them into your life, and do your best to focus on their positive influences, instead of listening to your dissenters.

When you center yourself on life's blessings, it is easier to smile (even if you don't *truly* feel like smiling). And when you smile, you'll find that life softens its sharp edges for you. Doors open, and pathways reveal themselves.

Reader, I know you will face all manner of hurdles and hardships in your life. I know you will, at times, feel stuck or downright miserable. Take heart! The Lord will provide a way. He always does—you only have to open your heart, listen, and trust.

That doesn't mean you can sit back and let life's river sweep you downstream. Dare to stand up and work for what you want. From an early age, my family taught me the advantages of hard work, and it's a lesson I have never forgotten. Not every victory will come easily; some must be hard-fought and hard-won. I'm here to tell you to never give up. Believe in your dreams and believe in yourself.

You are a child of God, worthy of success and love. At the center of your being is a brilliant diamond. If you haven't unearthed it yet, it's time to start digging!

Blessings,
Dr. Reatha Clark King

PREFACE

Reatha Clark King has a presence. Her quiet confidence, her bridge-building congeniality attract others like sun-starved flowers to the light. She is warm and friendly and has developed the enviable skill of *truly* listening when others are speaking. Around Reatha, precipitous mountains are reduced to hills, and you begin to imagine that all things are possible. All you need is a dash of strategy and a heaping spoonful of hard work—the recipe Reatha used to rise from a girl working in the cotton fields of South Georgia to a doctorate-wielding chemist, academic, corporate executive, and philanthropist.

When I first met Dr. Reatha Clark King, I knew I was sitting across the table from a superstar. This was the woman who had contributed to NASA's Apollo 11 moon landing. This was the person who had rocketed through the ranks of academia, moving from associate professor to dean of academic affairs to university president in less than a decade (during an era when one could count the women of color who led accredited universities on one hand). This was the titan of philanthropy who had headed the General Mills Foundation, started numerous community-oriented initiatives, and served on the boards of a half dozen major corporations and *four times* as many nonprofit boards. This was the person who had delivered lectures around the world and had earned enough awards to wallpaper her entire home.

Reatha is more than a highly accomplished public figure; she is a quintessential American success story. As a ghostwriter, I've written about the lives of several accomplished individuals, but none sprouted from roots as humble as Reatha's.

Despite her impressive résumé and long list of trailblazing accomplishments, Reatha never acted like the superstar I expected. At the restaurant where we met, she greeted me with a hello and a warm smile (she would end our meeting with a hug), then proceeded to chat with every server, host, and maintenance worker in the place, asking how they were doing and "How's that new baby daughter of yours?" One man retrieved his phone and began showing her pictures of his family.

That's the kind of person Reatha is.

She's caring and kind. She thinks more about her grandchildren than her fourteen honorary degrees. She shines without paying any mind to her own brilliance.

Working with Reatha, I knew I could relate to her journey from both an insider's and an outsider's point of view. We're both career-focused women who have encountered discrimination and harassment due to our gender. We both come from rural backgrounds and were expected to chip in from an early age to support the family (though her young work life makes mine seem like a picnic on the beach). But despite our commonalities, I only know a fraction of Reatha's struggle. I'm not black; I wasn't raised in the segregated South. Try as I might, I can never fully understand the constant fear, the daily struggles, the pressing feeling that the world is rigged against you from the moment you take your first breaths.

Because my path has been different from Reatha's in many respects, I knew I had to make a concerted effort to ask a lot of questions, do research, and read mountains of books by and about people of color. I knew Reatha and I would have to walk in lockstep during the writing of this book, with her reviewing every chapter, every sentence, to make sure I was accurately capturing her voice and her journey.

But I needn't have worried. Reatha poured herself into this book, just as she has done with every project she has tackled, every grant written, every speech delivered. Now in her eighties, she still has the energy of an Olympic athlete and a mind sharper than cut glass. Together, we crafted her biography. She is the storyteller; I am the conduit.

On the day we first met, I couldn't have known how attached I would become to both Reatha and her story. She would become more than a subject, more than an interviewee. She would become a friend, a mentor, an inspiration. The woman sitting across from me in the restaurant—bright as a jewel in her floppy red hat and multicolored jangly jewelry—would become a guiding light for me, as she has been for so many others, while our city (and nation) clawed its way through some of the most difficult months in recent memory.

PREFACE

I am a better person for knowing Reatha, and I hope you, too, will absorb some of her brilliance through her incredible story.

Sincerely,
Kate Leibfried

A NOTE ON RACIAL TERMINOLOGY

After much thought and research, it was decided to refer to race in its simplest form. The terms "black" and "white" are used instead of African American or Afro-American (not all black people identify as African) and Caucasian. The term "person of color" is used occasionally to refer to a person who identifies as a race other than white. The lowercase versions of "black" and "white" are used for both races, not to cheapen racial identity but to put it on the same plane as terms such as woman/female, gay/lesbian/trans, and other identity-related terms that are not capitalized.

A NOTE ON SOURCES

All quotations are cited in footnotes with the exception of direct quotations given by Dr. Reatha Clark King to Kate Leibfried during interviews.

CHAPTER ONE

Cotton Fields

"Every great dream begins with a dreamer. Always remember, you have within you the strength, the patience, and the passion to reach for the stars to change the world."

—Harriet Tubman

Life started at four o'clock in the morning in Moultrie, Georgia. At that hour, when the streets were still dark and insects creaked out their predawn songs, twelve-year-old Reatha donned her overalls, grabbed the paper-bag lunch her mother had fixed, and waited. Soon, the farmer's truck would rumble down the dirt lane, kicking up dust as it stampeded through the early morning calm. Soon, Reatha and her sisters would pile into the truck bed and cling to the sides as the vehicle bumped and jostled down rutted country roads. Soon, she would be back in the cotton field.

The year was 1950, and Reatha was as familiar with the Norman family's farmland as the calluses on her fingertips. In this pocket of South Georgia, the Norman name was an old one, and the Norman properties swallowed mile upon mile of fields and forests. The arable land stretched out in a patchwork of mostly cotton and tobacco, with a few other crops[1] mixed in—watermelon, pecans, green beans, tomatoes, corn. Mrs. Norman lived in the Big House, as it was called—a tall white behemoth with the traditional pillars-and-porch aesthetic of antebellum

---

1. Refers to the small-scale production of growing one or more crops, often sold directly to consumers.

homes. But Reatha rarely set foot in the Big House. She worked in the fields of Mrs. Norman's bachelor son, Elmer, picking cotton or stringing tobacco.

The previous summer, when she was eleven, the field had been her babysitter. She would sit in the dirt, scratching out her ABCs with a finger or practicing her multiplication tables. Schoolwork was her escape; learning, her joy. She learned with urgency, the goal of "going north" always on her mind. The North held opportunity and the promise of life outside of manual labor. And the key to the North, it was said, was an education.

But even though her parents valued Reatha's and her sisters' educations, the two eldest Clark girls, Mamie and Reatha, still had to work. (Their sister, Dorothy, was still a hair too young to pick cotton, though she would ride along with them to the field in the wee morning hours.) Without their extra hands, the family would sink.

After Elmer Norman's truck deposited Reatha at the edge of the field, she would set about her work before the sun peeked over the tree line. She plucked cotton bolls at a frantic pace, always striving to keep up with her big sister, Mamie Lee. Mamie could pick at least two hundred pounds of cotton every day, which earned the family six whole dollars—a wage equal to their mother's daily salary as a maid in Mrs. Norman's enormous house. In time, Reatha could keep pace with her sister and bring in six dollars of her own, a vital contribution to the family.

Cotton picking is rough work. The Normans' fields of pillowy bolls stretched out for acres and acres (so white a northerner might mistake them for snow) and were mostly picked by hand in the 1940s and '50s.[2] A person working the fields would pick only the mature bolls—the cotton that was fully opened from its husk—and had to be careful to avoid the sharp spikes jutting from the plants. A cotton field may be harvested three or four times each season, so the pickers had to comb through the same territory time and again, shoving the collected cotton into eight- or ten-foot-long thick canvas sacks that rested over one shoulder and dragged behind them as they picked. The hostile cotton plants, coupled

---

2. The Model M-12-H mechanical harvester by International Harvester came into production in 1948 and rapidly grew in popularity. By the late 1960s, the vast majority of cotton harvesting was done by machine (Ganzel, "Farming in the 1950s & 60s").

with the pickers' lightning-quick pace, caused bloody fingers and aching shoulders.

By summer's end, Reatha's hands were as rough and dark as the bark of the surrounding oak trees. Despite the wide-brimmed hat she often wore, the sun would darken her face and neck, too. There was no avoiding it. Light skin was en vogue in Reatha's community, but there was little room for fashion in the fields. How could there be, when you had to don the same pair of overalls, day after day, until no amount of patches and thread would hold them together? How could you bother with fashion when your toes poked through your fabric shoes and the soles began to separate from the uppers?

Fashion was for church, not the fields.

So, overalls falling into disrepair and shoes growing tired, Reatha worked. When the sun rose to its zenith and its harsh rays scorched the earth and any exposed skin, the crew paused for lunch. This was high noon—Reatha's favorite part of the day. This was the time to huddle in the shade and rest a spell, to chat with Mamie while the pair of them munched on fried chicken sandwiches. Reatha's mother had a knack for fried chicken and could cook it just right, with the skin crispy and the meat melt-in-your-mouth tender. It was a family favorite, and the Clark family counted their blessings whenever they had chicken in the larder.

The high-noon lunch break, however, always ended too soon. All that cotton wouldn't pick itself, and there were dollars to be made, besides. The work would continue until about five o'clock in the evening, when the sharecroppers would weigh what they had reaped and hope they hit their mark. Reatha usually did.

She was a particularly motivated youngster. At age twelve, she was already preparing for her first year of high school. Her grandmother Mamie often said, "If there's anything worth doing, it's worth doing well," and young Reatha internalized those words, wove them into her moral fabric. The lesson of "doing well" applied to the fields as much as the classroom. Reatha would pick those two hundred pounds per day, come hell or high water. She would earn her six dollars.

Reatha came to know cotton picking intimately and understood why her days began at four in the morning. For one, the brutal Georgia sun made afternoon work even more grueling than it already was, and it was best to get underway before the sun peeked above the treetops. And for another, dew clung to the cotton in the morning, making it heavier. When you're paid by the weight of your harvest, every ounce counts.

In a world where white bosses constantly underestimated their black workforce, they surely didn't recognize the sharecroppers' weight-adding trick. These were the days before Dr. Martin Luther King Jr.'s leadership and the civil rights movement. These were the days before the *Brown v. Board of Education* decision desegregated classrooms and Rosa Parks refused to surrender her bus seat. Black subservience was taken for granted. Reatha remembers black men—black sons—being beaten, or worse, for just looking at a white person the "wrong way."

In a phrase, the odds were stacked against you if you were born with too much melanin. Reatha Belle Clarke,[3] however, refused to be shackled by expectations and oppression. She saw a path to freedom through education and hard work. She gained confidence through the support of her community, her church, her teachers, her family. She allowed learning to excite her; she dared to dream.

But even in Reatha's boldest dreams, she could not imagine how many lives she would affect and how many trails she would blaze. Twelve-year-old Reatha did not know her future work in thermodynamics would become integral to NASA's 1969 moon landing. She didn't know she would become a college dean or, later, one of the first black female university presidents in the nation. Nor could she have known she would become the vice president of a Fortune 500 company and the president of that same company's philanthropic foundation. Twelve-year-old Reatha didn't know she would visit dozens of countries, receive fourteen honorary doctorate degrees and numerous civic and business awards, sit on the boards of directors for major corporations, and quietly improve the lives of thousands of individuals through philanthropic and grassroots initiatives. She didn't know she would earn a reputation as a changemaker, a pioneer, a philanthropist, an innovator.

Twelve-year-old Reatha only knew that whatever she did, she had to do it well. She had to capitalize on the support of her community and prove she could make something of herself in this world.

She had to pick those two hundred pounds of cotton.

---

3. The *e* was mistakenly added to Reatha's surname by her grandma Mamie, who delivered her and filled out her birth certificate. It was later removed in December 1961, after she married N. Judge King.

CHAPTER TWO

South Georgia

"I have discovered in life that there are ways of getting almost anywhere you want to go, if you really want to go."

—Langston Hughes

On April 11, 1938, Willie B. and Ola Mae Clark welcomed their second daughter into the family. They named her Reatha, after Ola's brother Reece, and began to consider her future. She would receive an education, they decided, so that she might broaden her world and find work beyond the fields. Schooling would give little Reatha opportunities that they—who had a third-grade education between the pair of them—never had.

Willie B. and Ola Mae were loving parents who valued family above all else. They both hailed from large families and knew that the only way to survive in sometimes brutal, often unfair rural South Georgia was to stick together and help each other through thick and thin. Family togetherness was a theme in Reatha's childhood, her days filled with not only her immediate family but also a stream of relatives who would pop over for dinner or sleep on the couch for a week or two. From the moment she was delivered, Reatha was inundated with family visitors. Uncle Reece, her namesake, took one look at baby Reatha and said, "Ola Mae, that baby is *so* pink!" Thus, the nickname "Pinky" was born shortly after the baby.

Willie B. Clark was originally from Wilcox County in central Georgia. He was one of thirteen children and the second of only two boys. Raised as he was among sisters, his relationship with his three daughters was comfortable and intuitive. Reatha remembers Daddy, as she called him, as a big man with a good heart and a keen mind. Though he usually donned overalls and threadbare cotton shirts, when he dressed for church in his white linens, he was a striking man with a magnetic presence.

Willie's parents were young when they passed away. With few options in central Georgia, the thirteen siblings migrated south to the farming community of Pavo. There, they crowded into the home of some aunt and uncle and survived as any large, impoverished family did at the time: through dogged hard work and fierce loyalty to each other. Willie's older sister was the mother hen of the family (every large batch of siblings has one). She cared for her sisters and brothers, making sure they were fed and employed, and listened to their troubles.

Unfortunately, there was no time for school.

In those early days of the twentieth century, school was a luxury for children of color. Their hands were needed in the fields; their thoughts often revolved around survival and carving out the best life possible for their families and themselves. Because so many black boys and girls were denied the opportunity to read, they were denied information, and information is power. Information provides protection from swindling white bosses. Information lets people know their rights. Information is a bridge to healthcare, job opportunities, legal counseling, and essential public services.

In 1930, a full 20 percent of the black population in the southern United States was illiterate, compared to less than 4 percent of the white population in the same region.[4] Black schools were characterized by "inadequacy and poverty," and teachers were criminally underpaid. Almost all schools were housed in private buildings—churches, lodges, rural cabins—due to scant public funding. When Reatha was born in 1938, slavery had been abolished six decades prior, but change had not washed over America in a tidal wave. Instead, it took the form of molasses creeping from the jar. The Jim Crow South—characterized by laws and "etiquette" that mandated segregation—ensured separate but glaringly *un*equal access to schools, medical facilities, libraries, banks, restaurants, and even public lavatories. Unable to tap into well-established white financial and educational institutions, those in the black

---

4. Margo, *Race and Schooling*.

community were forced to do what they had done since the advent of slavery: use their limited resources, innovative thinking, and sheer willpower to make it as best they could.

In some parts of the country, black communities thrived. They created their own banks, lumberyards, trade unions, and laundry services. In Illinois, Annie Malone built an empire on hair and beauty products, becoming one of the first black female millionaires (if not *the* first). In North Carolina, Charles Clinton Spaulding presided over the highly successful North Carolina Mutual Life Insurance Company. However, in rural Georgia, opportunities were limited, and the grandsons and granddaughters of enslaved people did about the same work as their ancestors had done. They took to the fields, picking vegetables, cotton, and tobacco to feed, clothe, and satisfy the smoking habit of the nation. And those fields were rarely theirs.

From the end of the Civil War until the 1940s, a new, *legal* form of near slavery was popularized in the southern United States: sharecropping. Under this system, a landowner allows sharecroppers to work the land and borrow equipment in exchange for a portion of the harvest. This ties the sharecropper to the land indefinitely and leaves them at the mercy of the landowner's accounting—many crooked landowners would claim that the sharecroppers they employed owed them at the end of a harvest season for borrowed land, equipment, or seeds. Unfortunately, many sharecroppers were illiterate and unable to effectively dispute these claims. In early twentieth-century Georgia, two-thirds of field workers—both black and white—farmed land owned by someone else.[5]

Without even an elementary school–level education, Willie B. Clark had few options besides sharecropping. However, he was clever and diligent, and he ended up working for a family who did not exploit their workers as severely as many other landowners did.

In Pavo, Georgia, the Clark name came to be respected. The family was composed of honest, hardworking folks who were loyal and caring and regularly attended church. Willie had a voice like rolling thunder and would recite the scriptures with such vigor that he earned the nickname "Preacher." He took pleasure in singing hymns and traditional

---

5. Cobb and Inscoe, "Georgia History."

gospel spirituals at Mount Zion Baptist Church, a minuscule clapboard-clad building east of town.

What Mount Zion lacked in size it made up for in importance. It was not just a building but a gathering place, a refuge, and a community center. It's where people heard the latest news—both local happenings and national events. It's where, at the end of a long workweek, members of the black community were free to be their joyful, expressive, bright, brilliant selves. It was a place to sing and a place to celebrate. Mount Zion, like every other predominantly black church in rural America, was a weekly dose of oxygen in a world often polluted by racism and injustice.

Reatha recalls the care that went into preparing for church. Though the Clark family never had much, the girls always had Sunday dresses, which fell to their knees and were adorned with white collars and ruffles. The entire congregation endeavored to look their best on Sundays, wearing linen suits and dresses, heels and hats. Oh, the hats! Floppy brimmed, feathered, bedecked with faux flowers, or trimmed with ribbon—the Baptist women of those days adored their hats (and many still do today). "Cover your head!" was a common phrase, but it wasn't as simple as that.

There were rules—unwritten, of course, but rules nonetheless. "Don't wear a hat wider than your shoulders. Don't wear a hat that is darker than your shoes. If your hat has feathers, make sure they are never bent or broken. Sequins don't look good in the daytime. Easter hats should be white, cream or pastel—even if it's still cold outside. For a look that is both elaborate and demure, try a chapel veil."[6]

To this day, Reatha's church outfit only feels *truly* complete when she's wearing a hat.

Dressing up was a dignity. You could *be somebody*, if only for a moment. Society's portrayal of black men and women in the first half of the twentieth century was ugly and cruel. Newspapers didn't hesitate to print racist cartoons or advertisements. Television shows were white-washed, with black characters rarely appearing (and *never* appearing as the standard for a normal, American family). "We were assumed to be ugly, thick-lipped, and ignorant," Reatha says. "Dressing up for church fought those notions. In a way, it was an act of defiance."

---

6. Cunningham and Marberry, *Crowns*.

Another of the many roles black churches played (and still play) was to act as a matchmaker for young people. Where better to find your future spouse than at church? Besides, many black people in that time and place didn't have much of a social life beyond the church doors. There wasn't much money to spend on frivolities, and, more importantly, it was risky business being out after dark. True, some men dared to visit local bars or juke joints[7] in town, but participating in these activities could quite literally put their lives on the line. Reatha remembers her mother huddling with other women, sharing news about the police tossing someone's son in jail or beating someone's husband. In these situations, there was little to do but pray, hope, and pray some more. Reatha learned at a young age that going out after sundown was strictly prohibited. She didn't even question it. Nighttime was especially dangerous because that was when the local Ku Klux Klan group met and held rallies in the nearby forest. If a black person were to cross paths with a KKK member hopped up on hate and racist rhetoric, the encounter would surely end badly.

So, Reatha's family locked their door every evening and prayed (always praying) that the Klan would stay away and that the police would not come knocking.

Seven decades later, with the continued indiscriminate killing of our black and brown brothers and sisters at the hands of police, we are forced to ask ourselves the painful question: How much has society changed? As a nation, we have made visible progress toward racial equality in many areas, but why do racist mentalities persist?

As we do today, people of color grappled with these questions during Reatha's childhood. But they could not spend every waking hour pensive and worried. They needed a refuge, a safe space where they could celebrate with one another, laugh, gossip, and fall in love. They needed the church.

In the warm arms of the congregation, the black community could step beyond survival mode and *thrive*. The church became a haven for social life and budding romances. At innocuous events such as afternoon picnics and Bible study, young people could meet and fall in love,

---

7. Juke joints were establishments that offered music, alcohol, dancing, and/or gambling. Popular in the segregated southern United States, they were primarily black owned and operated.

free from the stressors of everyday life. Though Reatha never asked her parents where they met, there is little doubt in her mind they met at Mount Zion Baptist Church.

★ ★ ★

Reatha's mother, Ola Mae Watts, was born and raised in South Georgia. She attended school, but only until the third grade. Her parents needed her to support the family, and how could schooling possibly help with that? When a dozen hungry mouths need food, the long-term opportunities afforded by education are outweighed by the immediate need to survive. At least, armed with a few years of schooling, Ola Mae could read and write at a rudimentary level—enough to compose and read letters, which was an important skill in those days.

The Watts family was a big crew, brimming with love and loyalty. Ola Mae was the fourth child of eleven and was well loved by her siblings. She was an excellent listener and confidante, and years later, she would be the go-to sibling to host her brothers when they came home for their two-week military furloughs. With Ola Mae, the war-weary soldiers felt at home. At peace.

The Wattses were a well-respected family that had lived in the vicinity of Pavo for as long as anyone could remember. Pavo is a town so small that most people (including other South Georgians) will wrinkle their brow at the mention of the town's name and ask, "Where, now?"

The simple answer is "Fifty-five miles northeast of Tallahassee and a touch over two hundred miles south of Atlanta," but native Georgians may be able to pinpoint Pavo in relation to Moultrie (which lies about seventeen miles to the north) or Albany (fifty-five miles to the northwest). It's a land that revolved around agriculture and manufacturing—work requiring manual labor that, up until the Thirteenth Amendment passed in December 1865, was largely performed by enslaved people.

Ola Mae's grandmother, Lucy Mae Brinson, had been born in the nineteenth century when slavery was still a recent memory. Her descendants would live in the shadow of that abysmal time and would value their family members above all else, knowing that not so long ago, families were indiscriminately split up and sold off. Reatha remembers her great-grandma Lucy as a mild-mannered woman whom all her aunts and uncles treated with a respect bordering on reverence. She was the matriarch of the family—a woman whose long and often difficult life was mapped by the creases of her face and the calluses on her fingertips.

Lucy Mae's daughter Mamie was a strong, capable woman who walked through the world with the confidence and assertiveness her mother had never found. Her field-worked hands brought many children into the world, including her granddaughter, Reatha. Mamie raised her eleven children, including Ola Mae, to be respectable, humble, and churchgoing.

Despite a philandering husband (Thomas "Tom" Watts,[8] who died the year before Reatha was born), Mamie kept her head high and stuck to her values. She taught her children to be hardworking and diligent and to complete every task with pride and care. The Watts children, in kind, grew to be fiercely loyal to their mother and supported her in any way they could until the day she died.

Ola Mae took her mother's lessons to heart and performed her work duties as diligently as her Sunday prayers. Though the family grew up around farms, gathering vegetables and working the fields, Ola Mae found that she was well suited to domestic work. She began working as a maid for local white families and eventually landed the coveted position with Mrs. Norman in her sprawling Big House. With her fastidiousness, proper manners, and eye for detail, Ola Mae made a capable and trusted household maid.

Before she set foot into the Big House, however, Ola Mae was busy falling in love and starting a family. A striking woman with an oval face, smooth skin, and all the grace and poise of legendary singer Marian Anderson, she eventually caught the eye of young Willie B. Clark. Maybe he was attracted to her lovely singing voice, which rang through the rafters of Mount Zion every Sunday. Maybe he admired her piercing eyes and dark brows. Or maybe it was her serious but gentle demeanor.

Whatever the seed of their attraction, the romance between Ola Mae Watts and Willie B. Clark took root in the one-horse town of Pavo,

---

8. Reatha's grandfather fathered several children outside his marriage. The children of Thomas and Mamie Watts, including Ola Mae, accepted their half siblings and formed close relationships with them. Later in life, the Watts siblings and half siblings would all get together for large, jovial family reunions.

FIND A TRAIL OR BLAZE ONE

Georgia, and soon blossomed into a marriage with three brilliant little girls and a home of their own.

One of those little girls, of course, was Reatha Belle Clarke.

CHAPTER THREE

Mount Zion

"The outside world told black kids when I was growing up that we weren't worth anything. But our parents said it wasn't so, and our churches and our schoolteachers said it wasn't so. They believed in us, and we, therefore, believed in ourselves."

—Marian Wright Edelman

After Mamie Watts performed her midwife duties and delivered her squalling little granddaughter, she faced a predicament. A blank birth certificate sat in front of her, and she had never learned to read or write, beyond a few crude marks. But she did the best she could and (possibly with help) filled out the birth certificate with about 50 percent accuracy.

The baby's name was written incorrectly, morphing from Reatha Belle into Rueese Bell. A later iteration of her birth certificate would correct her first and middle name but would add an *e* to her surname, cushioning the five-letter Clark with an extra vowel. On another line of the original certificate, the baby's birthdate was marked as April 9th instead of the 11th and an *M* was penciled in for her sex instead of an *F* for female. It wasn't that Mamie Watts wasn't smart—she had a keen mind and a brand of household smarts not taught in the classroom—it's simply that she was never afforded the opportunity to learn her letters. The new baby in her daughter's arms symbolized hope and opportunity; the world lay before her little feet, and to access the world, she would need an education.

FIND A TRAIL OR BLAZE ONE

Young Reatha Belle Clarke didn't have to wait long until she would set foot inside her first classroom. At the tender age of four, she was enrolled in the first grade (there was no kindergarten) and followed her sister Mamie through the doors of a familiar schoolhouse: Mount Zion Baptist Church. During the week, the church served double duty as a one-room schoolhouse. The wooden pews would become benches and writing surfaces, the sermons swapped for lectures on grammar and equations. Reatha was comfortable inside the clapboard walls of the humble church. This was where her family went each week, dressed in their Sunday best. This was where they worshipped alongside about 150 other devotees, many of them close friends. Mount Zion was situated three and a half miles northeast of Pavo down busy Highway 122, and that stretch of road was well traveled by the Clark family. Reatha remembers the comfort and joy that would wash over her when the plain white church and steeple came into view. Nestled among pine trees and framed by neatly kept shrubbery, Mount Zion was a sanctuary and a beacon of hope.

It was the ideal place to start an education. Kids are better equipped to learn when they're placed in a comfortable, safe environment, and to Reatha, Mount Zion was the definition of comfort.

Every weekday morning during the school year, children ages four to fourteen thundered through the church doors, ready to learn their lessons from the school's one and only teacher, Ms. Florence Frazier. Ms. Frazier was a community icon. One part kind and empathetic listener, two parts determined motivator and cheerleader, she was the axis around which local education turned. She's what Reatha would now call a mentor, although that word wasn't commonly used in those days. With the patience and aplomb of a diplomat, Ms. Frazier would expertly wrangle the thirty-five or so students in her makeshift classroom, instructing the oldest and brightest to help the younger, less experienced ones with their studies. It wasn't long before little Reatha was selected to occasionally guide her peers in their lessons.

Reatha blossomed in the classroom. For her, attending school was a joy unlike anything she had ever experienced. Soaking in Ms. Frazier's lessons, her world expanded, and her perspectives and possibilities grew. Each morning, she would wake up early, eager to return to school. She would don a hand-sewn knee-length dress, carefully fold her socks down, and smooth her braided hair. With earnest, round eyes, young Reatha would watch Ms. Frazier with rapt attention as she went over the day's lessons. At night, she would practice or reflect on what she had learned—she didn't want to forget a thing.

Reatha's older sister, Mamie (named after their grandmother), was also a bright student, and the pair of them quickly caught the attention of Ms. Frazier. At church on Sunday, the teacher would tout the girls' achievements not only to Willie and Ola Mae Clark but to anyone who would listen. The Clark girls are bright, she would say, and they have the potential to make something of themselves.

Once Willie B. Clark learned of his daughters' achievements, he wasn't shy about singing their praises, either. "My girls are *smart*," he would say. "They're going to do great things. You wait and see!" Though his wife and daughters were too humble to gloat, the Clark girls couldn't help but feel a flush of pride at Willie's enthusiasm. Maybe they *were* going places. Maybe they *could* make something of themselves.

Once word got out that those Clark girls were sharp as the tip of a No. 2 pencil, the community showered the family with encouragement and support. Despite everything, they dared to hope—to dream that this younger generation would climb mountains that they themselves had been ill equipped to climb. Besides, a victory for one meant a victory for all. As Reatha puts it, "We were expected to lift as we climbed."

Lift a family.

Lift a community.

Lift an entire race.

The pressure of a people rested on Reatha's shoulders, but she was up for the challenge. She knew her family and her community had her back and would cheer her on from the sidelines as she climbed. The value of their encouragement is hard to measure. It motivated and inspired Reatha to do her best, be persistent in her studies, and strive for excellence.

Willie B. and Ola Mae Clark were already fervent believers in the power of education. Though the Clark girls occasionally had to miss class to help in the fields, their absences were relatively rare. Education, Willie and Ola Mae knew, provided a path away from manual labor. If their daughters could learn reading, writing, and arithmetic, they might eventually land jobs as teachers, secretaries, or maybe even nurses—occupations that women coveted in that era because they were among the only options available *and* they provided valuable services to the community. If Reatha became a teacher (which her mother encouraged her to do), she could return to Pavo after receiving her diploma and teach the next generation of black youth.

Reatha, however, began entertaining other possibilities and paths at an early age. During those early years in Ms. Frazier's makeshift classroom, she was influenced and inspired by the black entrepreneurs and innovators she learned about during Negro History Week. The precursor of Black History Month, Negro History Week was conceived in 1915 by Carter G. Woodson (a black historian) and Jesse E. Moorland (a prominent minister), who cofounded the Association for the Study of African American Life and History. It was a time to (rather briefly!) learn about the influential black people who helped shape and advance America.

As she and her fellow students learned about the giants of history whose shoulders they stood upon, one individual, in particular, caught Reatha's attention: agricultural scientist and inventor George Washington Carver. Captivated by the prominent scientist, Reatha learned about Carver's methods for reducing soil depletion and lessening the impact of blights through crop diversification. She learned that much of Carver's research had centered on the peanut (a crop he deemed a worthy alternative to the pervasive cotton) and that he devised a couple hundred uses for the humble legume, including incorporating it into soaps, dyes, medicinal oils, plastics, and gasoline.

Learning about George Washington Carver opened a door for Reatha that she had always considered locked and out of reach. Black people could be scientists, and not only that, they could be scientists who made a real impact. Yes, Carver had been a man, but his accomplishments excited Reatha and planted the seed of an idea in her mind: She might not have to become a teacher or nurse. Her feet might traverse a different path.

Buoyed by Ms. Frazier and the Mount Zion community, Willie and Ola Mae continued to press their daughters to study diligently and become as educated as possible. They didn't have to press hard. Both Mamie and Reatha were enthusiastic pupils who gobbled up their lessons and practiced their multiplication tables in the fields during summer recess.

Mamie Lee, born two years before Reatha, on September 3, 1936, quickly became Reatha's role model. As the eldest daughter, Mamie was dutiful, serious, and endlessly caring. She never hesitated to make sacrifices for the family—even joining the military in the middle of her college years so she could send a little extra cash to her struggling mother each month.

Mamie, like her sisters, had inherited Ola Mae's good looks and her round, thoughtful eyes. Neat and precise, she always strove to be her best, whether she was working a math problem or perfecting her handwriting. Reatha respected her and treasured any advice she had to give. "When she spoke," Reatha says, "I listened."

From a young age, Mamie became an ambassador for the family. Ola Mae felt perpetually embarrassed about her own lack of education and would send her eldest daughter to represent the family in a variety of matters, from buying household goods to engaging in conversation with other families. Periodically, older folks in the community would call on Mamie to help them fill out their Social Security forms, and she became a valuable asset to those who so desperately needed the benefits they were owed. When bill collectors knocked on the Clark family's door, young Mamie was sent to answer their call and either pay the bill or tell the collector, "Sorry, we don't have it today." Though the Clarks tried to keep up on their debts, the times when they "didn't have it" were all too common.

It couldn't have been easy for young Mamie to face these older white men and either hand over the correct number of dollars and cents or send them away, but she did it without hesitation or complaint. She accepted her role with the sense of dedication and duty that would become a cornerstone of her personality throughout her adult life.

Born two years after Reatha, on May 12, 1940, Dorothy Ola Clark didn't take life quite so seriously as her older sisters. She was quick with a smile or a laugh and had the type of infectious, carefree personality that could put a person at ease in two blinks. She was cute and bubbly, and her nickname, "Dot," was the perfect match for her bouncy personality. The baby of the family, her role was that of an entertainer rather than an ambassador. Well loved by sisters and parents alike, Dot was doted on as the "family pet."

Dot grew into a striking young woman who was playful and talkative. While her sisters were buried in their schoolbooks, Dot would be primping or telling a joke. Though she wasn't much of a bookworm, she did understand the importance of obtaining an education and eventually graduated with a high school diploma, just like her sisters. She then studied at Fisk University in Tennessee but dropped out after two years to find a job and care for her daughter, Cynthia. Following the advice of her community, Dot eventually went north and landed in Washington, DC, where Mamie was working as a nurse.

Growing up with encouraging, loving parents and a close-knit, ever-supportive community, the Clark girls flourished. Though life was simple, and they didn't have fancy clothing or any possessions beyond a few raggedy cotton-batted dolls, they didn't feel poor. Who cared if their shotgun housing[9] was minimal and drafty? Who needed running water when you could fetch it down the street? What did it matter if their nicest articles of clothing were hand-me-downs from Mrs. Norman? Why pine over the choicest cuts of pork when ham hocks and pigs' feet were perfectly enjoyable? Besides, both Willie B. and Ola Mae were innovative and resourceful and knew how to stretch a dollar.

Ola Mae was *not* enamored with sewing, but she did it when necessary, or when she was lucky enough to pick up some scraps of material from her maid jobs. Like other mothers of the era, she would upcycle empty flour sacks—the ones made of colorful patterned cotton—into patchwork skirts or quilting squares. Occasionally, she would buy a Simplicity pattern and use it to sew a dress or a shirt. Ola Mae had a few siblings up north, and they would sometimes send hand-me-down dresses for the girls—a real treat for Reatha.

No matter how tight things were in the Clark household, the girls always had their field outfits, their everyday clothes, and dresses for church. Sometimes, the girls traded dresses, as sisters do, and that helped stretch their wardrobes even further.

When it came to fashion, the girls didn't have a lot of room to be particular. However, their mother did occasionally take them to a beauty shop in town to have their hair cut and straightened. A family

---

9. Shotgun houses are modest single-story homes that are only one room wide and two to four rooms deep. Because there are no hallways in shotgun houses, it is necessary to walk through each room to get to the next.

friend owned the shop and would style Ola Mae's and her girls' hair for a good price, but even so, the trips were rare. Usually, the Clark girls wore a few simple braids, lovingly plaited by their mother.

When the Clarks did have money to spare on hairdos, Ola Mae would march her daughters to the beauty shop and have them each take a turn in the salon chair, where her friend slathered potent chemical straighteners into their hair and divulged the latest gossip. Aside from church, the beauty shop was one of the only gathering places for young black women in 1940s South Georgia. There, they could exchange family news, catch up on local happenings, and hear murmurings about the war overseas. The men had their barbershops; the women had their salons.

Most gatherings, however, took place within the walls of the Clarks' home. After a long day of work, the family would crowd around the dinner table, say grace, and share a meal together. Ola Mae was just as resourceful in the kitchen as she was with a needle and thread. When the family had access to fresh meat, she put every part of the animal to use. Chicken liver, hogs' feet, rendered fat—it was all creatively incorporated into their meals.

Though the family had a handful of chickens, much of their food came from the Norman family's farm—a benefit of sharecropping the land. They were allowed to go into the fields and pick whatever was in season. Okra, collard greens, beans, tomatoes, corn, a variety of melons—the Clarks harvested what they needed and carried it home. When it came time to slaughter the Normans' hogs, the sharecroppers could claim the scraps. They became quite creative with putting rejected parts to use, dressing up tough or gristly cuts of meat with deep-fried batter or sticking them in a soup.

At the mercy of whatever they had in stock, the Clark family usually ate a diet high in fat, salt, and meat. In those days, education about healthy eating was almost nonexistent, especially in impoverished communities. You simply used whatever you had and made it palatable by dousing it in salt, breading it, and frying it in hot oil. Collard greens were boiled and then panfried in bacon grease or rendered fat. Okra and green tomatoes were fried. Cornbread was slathered in butter. This was traditional southern cooking, and though it was calorie dense and grease heavy, it was undeniably delicious.

Reatha's father was resourceful in his own way. From the beginning of his employment as a sharecropper with the Normans, he made a concerted effort to demonstrate his integrity and work ethic, thus reaping the benefits of their trust. He was clever with fixing machinery and was often tasked with fixing a broken plow or a defective tractor. There wasn't a piece of equipment he couldn't take apart and put back together. His mind was sharp, and he had a knack for puzzling out how machinery fit together, even if he'd never previously laid hands on it.

Willie's reputation as a hardworking handyman earned him a few extra dollars and some occasional reprieve from the fields. The Normans counted on him to complete any task they threw his way with efficiency and accuracy, and he never let them down. This trustworthiness was part of his moral code—something he endeavored to pass on to his daughters, along with humility, sincerity, friendliness, and a strong work ethic. As he used to say to Reatha, "Hard work never killed anybody."

Today, Reatha likes to tell her children and grandchildren that they inherited their intellect from her illiterate father. This isn't an insult; it's a commentary on the potential that Willie was never able to fully realize due to his lack of formal education. His brilliant brain was never able to truly soar because it was shackled by the chains of illiteracy. Though he rarely complained about it, Reatha knows how much this frustrated her father. Once, when she paid him a visit during his later years living in Florida, he said, "I think about you and the family every day, but I can't show it because I can't write to you. And I'll be damned if those people at the post office are going to take my money to do it for me!"

CHAPTER FOUR

Dirt Roads

"The whole world opened to me when I learned to read."

—Mary McLeod Bethune

America's black population has a long, complicated relationship with the nation's military. Though few parents want to send their sons or daughters to a battlefield, sometimes it's the best option among a profusion of subpar choices. During times of unemployment or underemployment, the military provides a steady paycheck. Even when segregation was still legal, black and white soldiers fought on the same battlefields and flew in the same skies.[10] In an era when education and leadership opportunities were sparse for young black people, the military provided a path to learning about the world at large and developing the necessary skills to lead, motivate, and collaborate with others.

Though black soldiers were subjected to racism and rarely served as officers (except when leading all-black units) in the first half of the twentieth century, they played a vital role in our nation's wartime history. Approximately 180,000 black men joined the Union Army during the Civil War, constituting a full 10 percent of its force. During World War II, the Army Air Forces recruited black men to train as pilots in the now-famous Tuskegee Airmen program. This talented

---

10. Although some black and white soldiers fought side by side during the Civil War and beyond (the US Navy, for example, was integrated during the Civil War), segregation in the military remained common until 1948, when President Truman issued Executive Order 9981 to abolish racial segregation in the US military.

group of pilots, mechanics, bombardiers, and support personnel flew on hundreds of combat missions and provided vital support for the Allied forces. To recognize their accomplishments, the US military presented the Tuskegee Airmen with several awards and decorations, including Bronze Stars, Air Medals, Purple Hearts, and at least one Silver Star.

Despite their integral role in the military, most black soldiers were designated as "enlisted," with little opportunity to climb the ranks and become officers. That changed somewhat as the twentieth century progressed (notably, Benjamin O. Davis Sr. became the first black general in the army in 1940), but racism persisted.

Despite its flaws, the military appealed to young black men who were short on employment options and desperate for cash. Reatha says that for her many uncles and cousins who enlisted, the paycheck and leadership opportunities were attractive, but the military was still considered a "place of last resort."

Still, when the United States jumped into World War II, many of Reatha's family members jumped with it. It may have been a temporary career path, but it was hard to turn up one's nose at a reliable monthly paycheck, regular meals, and a chance to see the world. Besides, the armed services often felt safer than civilian life. In the army, young black men didn't have to dodge crooked police or KKK members. They didn't have to worry about being out too late or looking at a white person a fraction of a second too long. Nor did they have to fret about being arrested and sentenced to work in the chain gangs that proliferated throughout the South during this era. All told, joining the military wasn't such a bad route.

With the lesson to "look out for your own" firmly rooted in their upbringing, many black soldiers would directly funnel their monthly paychecks back home. This was how Reatha's grandma Mamie could afford a new house on a five-acre lot and how Reatha, eventually, was able to purchase a dress for her homecoming queen inauguration at Clark College. Selfishness is not a survival tactic. Only through magnanimous actions can an entire family—and an entire people—rise and prosper.

When the United States plunged into World War II in 1941, Reatha Belle Clarke was three years old. For the next four years, her young life would be punctuated by one—or two-week-long visits from her uncles, who would stay in the back bedroom of the family's shotgun-style home (one of two bedrooms in the house) when they were on a military furlough or home for a family funeral. Reaching her uncles during the time of paper letters and telegrams was tricky, but the American Red Cross played an invaluable role in contacting them. A largely female force, the 1940s and '50s Red Cross was known for its "Donut Dollies" and first aid work, but emergency communication was another much-needed service it provided, its people sometimes traversing dangerous territory to deliver messages to soldiers. Reatha's family directly benefited from the Red Cross's work, and they never forgot it. These brave young women helped bring their uncles home when it truly mattered, and that meant the world to the family.

Reatha's uncles, married and unmarried alike, would seek refuge under the wing of their sister Ola Mae. Her house was a comfortable one—a place where they could rest, eat three square meals, and count on a listening ear, if the spirit moved them to talk. With their mother, Mamie, in a new home and their other siblings dispersed across the United States, Ola Mae's house felt familiar and welcoming to the Watts brothers. It felt like *home*.

It was a time, Reatha remembers, of constant houseguests and activity. The Clarks, along with Ola Mae's many sisters, brothers, and cousins and Grandma Mamie Watts, would always plan a homecoming celebration for the visiting soldiers. Food was the centerpiece of the celebration, and the family would gather around plates of sweet-smelling meats and buttery biscuits and fried vegetables. In those moments, it didn't matter that their uncle, son, or brother was heading back to the front lines in mere days. He was here now. And the family could celebrate his presence and enjoy each other's company for a brief, shining moment.

The war added a twist to young Reatha's academic path as well. Grandma Mamie built a new home (funded by her sons' military stipends) and moved nine miles west of Pavo to the equally minuscule town of Merrillville. She needed company, the family decided, and seven-year-old Reatha was assigned to move in with her.

At this point, Reatha had completed the fourth grade (grades were somewhat fluid in Ms. Florence Frazier's classroom, and the ever-encouraging teacher had allowed Reatha to leapfrog over second), and she would begin her fifth-grade year at the tender age of seven. She already knew how to read and write, which was a boon to the family and to Grandma Mamie. Mamie yearned to write letters to her boys (and read their replies) but was unable to do so on her own. Reatha became her scribe, transcribing her grandmother's words onto paper.

Illiteracy, Reatha realized, does not only stifle opportunities and disconnect people from vital information. It also creates distance between loved ones and manufactures isolation.

For two years, Reatha lived with her grandmother and attended school in nearby Coolidge. She performed household chores, wrote letters, and helped count out the correct dollars and cents at the local grocery store. In the mornings, she often woke to the smell of hot grits on the stovetop and the sound of her grandmother's rich voice belting out the melodies of traditional spirituals.

> *Swing low, sweet chariot*
> *Coming for to carry me home*
> *Swing low, sweet chariot*
> *Coming for to carry me home I looked over Jordan*
> *and what did I see*
> *Coming for to carry me home*
> *A band of angels coming after me*
> *Coming for to carry me home . . .*

Singing was a central panel in the tapestry of Reatha's youth. When she began working the cotton and tobacco fields at age twelve, songs helped pass the time, unite the pickers, and distract from aching backs and stinging fingertips. In church, singing brought life to Jesus's word and allowed the congregation to express their faith at the tops of their lungs. Music would also ring out across the fields near Grandma Mamie's home, where the chain gang men would sing as they split rocks under the watchful eye of an armed officer.

> *I've been working on the railroad*
> *All the livelong day . . .*

Reatha recalls walking down the long dirt roads with Grandma Mamie (she walked a lot in those days) and passing the imprisoned black men in their black-and-white-striped uniforms. Their shoulders were broad from ten—or twelve-hour days of backbreaking labor and their faces dark from spending day after day in the hot Georgia sun. Though these well-muscled, sun-darkened men were the very image that stirred up fear and mistrust in white America, Reatha wasn't frightened of them. They kept to themselves (no one dared ignite the wrath of the armed overseer), and Reatha knew, besides, that many good men had been sentenced to work in the chain gangs. These were the sons and brothers of local families. These were men who may have committed egregious crimes . . . but they may have only stolen a chicken or two to quiet their children's grumbling bellies. Or, as was sometimes the case, they may have committed no crime at all.

One day in early September 1945, Reatha and Grandma Mamie left their house and made their way down the familiar dirt road, past the chain gang. The sound of sledgehammers against rock mingled with the men's voices and the crunch of gravel beneath Reatha's and Mamie's feet. It was a day like any other, hot and sticky, and they were headed to Pavo's black-owned grocery store to restock a few kitchen staples. Grandma Mamie had donned her usual light-brown straw hat, whose wide brim shaded her cheeks from the fierce sun.

As they made their way past the chain gang, a pickup truck rumbled toward them, kicking up a cloud of dust. The car slowed, and Mamie recognized the white gentleman in the driver's seat. He pulled alongside them and leaned out the window, his smile beaming bright as the midday sun.

"Mamie!" he called. "Have you heard? The war is over! It's over. We've won!"

Joy wrapped itself around Grandma Mamie and illuminated her every feature. "Thank God!" she exclaimed, throwing her hands to the sky. "Praise the Lord! My sons are coming home!"

In today's ultra-connected world, it may seem strange to receive news of this magnitude in such a simple way, from the mouth of someone in the know. This oral delivery of the news, however, was not unusual in the black community in that day. Since many people did not know how to read—and, even if they could read, did not have regular access to newspapers—people talked and listened and picked up whatever tidbits of news they could.

Every now and then, a person would get their hands on a newspaper—the *Atlanta Daily World*, or maybe even the *Pittsburgh Courier*, the *Chicago Defender*, or the Kansas City *Call*. These papers were black owned and operated, some of them since the dawn of the twentieth century. They were a true source of pride and a vital information pipeline. When Reatha's family managed to get ahold of a newspaper, the literate family members would pore over it again and again, cover to cover, until the ink faded from the constant press of fingertips. But in a rural community like Pavo, black-owned newspapers were hard to come by. The more consistent news feed was found at church.

Church was fertile ground for catching up on both gossip and noteworthy news. When the sermon was over, people mingled and relayed whatever new bit of information they had picked up that week. The grapevine was alive and healthy, and its tendrils wrapped around all aspects of life: national news, local happenings, someone's son courting someone else's daughter, the latest trouble stirred up by white supremacists, opportunities for work up north.

Reatha remembers the constant buzz about the North.

"You can get good work up in Chicago."

"I hear some factories are hiring in New York and New Jersey."

"A cousin told me black and white folks use some of the same grocery stores and parks. Can you imagine?"

"From what I hear, a person with the right education could really make something of themselves up there."

Though the northern United States in the 1940s and '50s was certainly not free of racism, the South's brand of flagrant and sometimes violent racism was not as prevalent. As one man wrote in a letter to the *Chicago Defender*: "Dear Sir, I indeed wish to come to the North—anywhere in Illinois will do so long as I'm away from the hangman's noose and the torch man's fire. Conditions here are horrible with us. I want to get my family out of this accursed Southland. Down here a Negro man's not as good as a white man's dog."[11]

The North was viewed not only as less racist (though the bar was set awfully low) but also as a place of economic opportunity. Agriculture—one of the primary industries in the South—was suffering from blights of beetles and competition overseas, and mechanized pickers

---

11. Walker, *Keeping a Family Legacy Alive*.

were beginning to replace human hands. For many southern agricultural workers, it made sense to try their luck at factories or trainyards or on shipping docks up north.

Reatha heard the buzz about the North. She read letters from her aunts and uncles who had found work in Maryland and Pennsylvania. She heard her community discussing the opportunities, the civility, that lay beyond Georgia's borders. From an early age, Reatha's compass tugged north.

CHAPTER FIVE

Dirty Spoon

"Education is the key to unlock the golden door of freedom."
—George Washington Carver

It wasn't long after World War II ended that Reatha's parents separated and, eventually, divorced. Reatha was too young to understand fully why their marriage fell apart, but she had noticed the arguments growing longer and more heated. She noticed her father spending more and more time in the comfort of his bottle rather than in the company of his wife. The marriage did not end in violence—it dissolved gradually, with the mutual understanding that their rocky relationship would never be smoothed.

Eventually, Reatha's daddy left.

Always resourceful and confident in his ability to pick up whatever work crossed his path, Willie B. Clark headed to Belle Glade, Florida, a town due west of West Palm Beach whose motto was displayed proudly on its welcome sign: "Her soil is her fortune." This was sugarcane country and Florida's heartland. Though Belle Glade has gone through turmoil in recent decades—in the 1980s it had the highest rate of AIDS per capita, and in 2010 about half of the city's young men were convicted felons—when Willie moved there, it was a promising agricultural haven brimming with "muck," a thick, nutrient-rich soil ideal for growing sugarcane. Besides, his sister Dora lived in Belle Glade, so at least he'd be among family.

After Willie left, Ola Mae became the sole caretaker of the Clark household. She wasn't entirely alone (there were brothers and sisters to support her if she truly needed it), but she wasn't comfortable with taking others' charity—not when she had two capable hands, a sharp mind, and two feet that could carry her to work. So, just as resourceful as Willie, she sought work wherever she could find a decent paycheck. And the best paychecks were to be found in the North.

Ola Mae's aunt Lessie lived in Trenton, New Jersey, and worked at the Campbell's Soup factory, a stone's throw from the expansive Delaware River. With Lessie's guidance, several relatives had settled near Trenton and found employment at the factory. In the 1950s, it was considered one of the better places for people of color to find work. Ola Mae would live in Trenton and work in the factory for several years while her daughters stayed with relatives in South Georgia. She saved every penny she could and sent money home, all while dreaming of buying a new home someday—a *nice* home.

Before moving to Trenton, Ola Mae had moved her three girls to Moultrie, Georgia, a town of ten thousand people sixteen miles north of Pavo. Compared to tiny Pavo (population 706),[12] Moultrie—with its multiple black-owned restaurants and barber shops, movie theaters, and soda fountains—was a bustling metropolis. With her limited funds, Ola Mae had managed to find a house to rent in Moultrie's Dirty Spoon neighborhood. She detested the area's run-down houses, reeking outhouses, and unsavory activities, but what choice did she have? Until she could save enough money to move across town, the Dirty Spoon would have to do.

The house in Moultrie was a bare-bones setup, much like the Clark's family home in Pavo. No electrical wires hummed through the walls, no water flowed through pipes. At night, Reatha would study by the flickering yellow light of a kerosene lamp. If Ola Mae needed water for cooking, one of the girls would fetch it from an outdoor well.

On Saturday nights, the family would go through the routine of readying themselves for church the next morning. They would starch their clothing and iron out wrinkles with a heavy cast iron that they heated in the fireplace. "It took skill to use that iron," Reatha recalls. "You had to be careful not to scorch your clothes!"

---

12. US Census Bureau, "Historical Census Information."

Saturday night was also bath night, which proved to be a laborious process. Buckets of water were toted inside and dumped into the porcelain bathtub. One by one, the girls would scrub themselves clean, cleansing their bodies in preparation for cleansing their souls the next morning. It wasn't until Reatha was in high school that the family would live in a home with indoor plumbing and electricity—signs that they were moving up in the world.

Since Mount Zion Baptist Church was now twenty miles away, Ola Mae and the girls had to find a new church in Moultrie. The church was, of course, a cornerstone of daily life, and without it the family felt off-kilter. This is where they would develop a new set of friends, learn the news, and revel in their weekly respite. Ola Mae chose nearby Mother Easter Baptist Church, and Reatha and her sisters—admirably resilient and adaptable—settled in and began learning the names and faces of their fellow congregants.

The girls understood sacrifice and accepted that their mother had to do whatever she could to keep their family of four afloat. While Ola Mae was working in Trenton, they stayed with relatives and attended whichever school was most convenient. During this time, the girls studied at a few different schools in the area, including one in nearby Funston.

Rather than walk the handful of miles to Funston's schoolhouse, the girls received rides from a couple of big-hearted teachers (and fellow Mother Easter Church attendees): Reverend Thompson and Marie Jackson. These two placed their full faith in the Clark girls and, like Ms. Florence Frazier, did everything they could to encourage their educations. They became two more important mentors for young Reatha and helped bolster her confidence and provide motivation during a difficult transition period. With Reatha's parents in different states, Reverend Thompson and Marie were pillars in her recently upended world.

Over the next few years, the Clark girls bounced around schools in Pavo, Coolidge, and Funston. They excelled wherever they went and capitalized on the encouragement of their community. Those kind words and "rah rahs" were not wasted on Reatha. She dove into her studies with a sense of purpose, motivation, and devotion, always keeping her thoughts on the future and her path to the North.

In 1950, at the age of twelve, Reatha began high school at Moultrie High School for Negro Youth (MHSNY).[13] At the time, segregation was legal and widely practiced, and schools (especially in the southern United States) were designated as either "colored"[14] or "white." Adherents to the Jim Crow laws of the South proclaimed these schools to be "separate but equal," but it's doubtful anyone who was paying attention actually believed this claim. In southern states, "the average annual expenditure for a black student was $19 in comparison to $49 for a white student,"[15] and funding for buildings and equipment was even worse. Many black schools were forced to use hand-me-down textbooks from white schools, which were often dog-eared, outdated, or falling apart at the seams. Teachers in black schools had to deal with annoyances such as overcrowded classrooms and failing HVAC systems in addition to providing daily lessons to a student body whose attendance was often less than consistent, since many students' families relied on them to bring in a little extra income.

Moultrie High School for Negro Youth was, however, an exceptional black school. In 1942, it became one of seventeen schools to participate in an experimental program funded by the Rockefeller Foundation. Called the Secondary School Study, it was designed to "reexamine administrative, curricular, and instructional practices."[16]

The Secondary School Study was the brainchild of activist William A. Robinson. He believed black schools needed to embrace an attitude of "progressive education" that would involve experimentation and carving out new paths for black students, rather than following the curricula established by white schools. As he stated in a letter to the General Education Board, if black students were going to be educated, then teachers "must learn new ways of approaching their tasks and new reasons for their educational activities."[17]

---

13. Moultrie High School, located less than a mile from MHSNY, was a whites-only school until it was forced to desegregate in 1958, four years after the *Brown v. Board of Education* court ruling.
14. Though outdated and offensive today, *colored* and *Negro* were the most prevalent and socially acceptable terms for black people during this era.
15. Kridel, *Progressive Education*.
16. Kridel, "Moultrie High School for Negro Youth."
17. Kridel, *Progressive Education*.

MHSNY's interpretation of progressive education involved establishing longer course periods (sixty minutes instead of forty-five), hosting extracurricular activities, and developing a curriculum that revolved around civic and social issues. The school also encouraged students to help develop the curriculum and become active participants in their learning. With eight teachers at the helm and 165 students on board, MHSNY sailed into the relatively uncharted waters of black student education. At a time when people in black and white communities alike questioned whether black education was even necessary, the faculty at MHSNY dared to dream of better, brighter futures for their students.

Eight years after Moultrie High School for Negro Youth joined the Secondary School Study and embarked on its mission to improve its curriculum, Reatha Belle Clarke strode through its doors wearing a hand-sewn dress and freshly braided hair. She was not aware of her high school's role in the Secondary School Study, but she did feel the devotion of her teachers and the energy of the other students as they strove together to learn, improve, and raise up the entire race (no pressure!). This was a place of achievement—of teachers who challenged their pupils and of college recruiters who flitted in and out, urging students to attend this or that school.

Reatha's sister Mamie had done her best to prepare her little sister for high school by telling her all about the faculty and students. Some of these students, she said, come from "fancy backgrounds." They've never set foot in a cotton field or picked a tomato off the vine. They don't have to help their families pay bills. And then there are the teachers—they don't dabble in this or that subject. Oh no. These teachers are *specialized*, focusing only on science or math, sewing or cooking.

Twelve-year-old Reatha listened, wide-eyed, as Mamie described each teacher and their personalities. This teacher was strict, that teacher favored the boys. Armed with her sister's advice, Reatha began her first year alongside about three dozen classmates. Though nervous and more than a little intimated, she kept the confidence instilled in her by her community, her family, and the Florence Fraziers and Marie Jacksons of her life. She could succeed at anything she put her mind to.

And succeed she did. Despite the constant moves, pervasive poverty, and living under the wing of a single parent who was often absent for months at a time, Reatha beat the odds. When she stepped through the school entryway every morning, she immersed herself fully. She didn't think about her after-school jobs. She didn't dwell on her plain, patched dresses or complain about not having a few extra cents to see a picture show.

She was all business, and she would do precisely what the family expected—*needed*—her to do: acquire an education, go to college if she could, and obtain a degree that would enable her to earn a little more than her parents had. The degree would be in teaching, of course, and after college she would return to the community and educate the Pavo or Moultrie youth. That was the plan; there was no other.

Ever the serious student, Reatha plunged into her studies and emerged with perfect grades in every class. She was one of those students whom teachers would whisper about and, eventually, brag about to college recruiters. They saw something in their star pupil—the tenacity, smarts, and stick-to-itiveness that would take her places. But no one could predict just how high young Reatha would soar.

★ ★ ★

Though she was ever committed to her studies, Reatha's education was punctuated by work. Every day after school, she spent two hours earning money for the family. For a time, she worked as a maid in a local white family's house, but after her mother remarried, she spent most of her time in her stepfather's shop, painting broom handles.

Mozell Campbell was a kind man and a hard worker. He and Ola Mae met while working in the same broom factory, an operation based in Albany, Georgia. Ola Mae made the long commute from Moultrie to the broom factory every day—a round-trip trek of over seventy-five miles. Somehow, despite her exhaustion, she had the energy and willpower to start anew and remarry. Her union with Mozell marked the beginning of a new era of prosperity and security for the Clark women. Ola Mae, always careful with the money she earned, had finally pooled together enough funds (including loans from generous relatives) for a down payment on a house on the other side of Moultrie—the *nice* side.

The new house was equipped with running water and electricity; it stood in a decent neighborhood among a throng of hardworking, respectable families. The white clapboard home with the little porch out front wasn't large or ostentatious, but it was *theirs*. It was a sign that, as a family, they were making strides and moving on up.

Mozell settled into Moultrie and began a little broom-making operation—a franchise that branched off the factory in Albany, Georgia, where he and Ola Mae had met. Mozell had originally learned the trade in his hometown of Autaugaville, Alabama, population 459.[18] Broom making became his primary livelihood and a decent way to carve out a living without working the fields. He would bind the bristles, paint the handles, and attach the handles to the heads. After Mozell married Ola Mae, his work became the family's work.

Reatha and her sisters would often help in the broom shop, carefully dipping the wooden handles in paint and running them past a rubber scraper to remove the excess. It was an art form—dipping the handles just right to evenly coat them in blues, yellows, reds, and greens.

The broom business was about the only business Mozell knew, and he planned on building and selling brooms until the day he retired. Unfortunately, the parent company in Albany shuttered its doors in the mid-1950s, and the pension Mozell thought he had coming never came. The news was devastating. At his age, with a limited skill set, he couldn't exactly start over. And he certainly did not have the means to pursue legal action against the company. In the end, Mozell Campbell did what anyone in his position would do: he moved on, doing his darnedest to forgive and forget. He relied on his meager Social Security check and the kindness of family members for the rest of his days.

Reatha spent many hours during the school year in her stepfather's broom shop, but in the summers, she was needed in Elmer Norman's fields. When she wasn't plucking cotton bolls, she was stringing tobacco. The tobacco season was a feast for the senses—the soft sound of bunching leaves, the stacks of vivid green, the heavy aroma of curing tobacco stretching out for miles and covering the land in a heady blanket.

Tobacco harvesting and curing is a fussy and potentially dangerous business, however. Men would typically harvest leaves in late July and early August, hauling them to the curing barn by a mule-pulled sled. There, workers (usually women and children) would unload the sled and begin stringing the tobacco on long poles, which were designed to hang

---

18. US Census Bureau, "Historical Census Information."

across the barn in rows, reminiscent of layered yellow-green fabrics, dangling from garment racks. The poles stretched across the width of the barn and were also stacked on top of each other—a packed-tight grid of hanging leaves.

To arrange the tobacco *just so*, the women and children were divided into "handers" and "stringers." The handers bunched the tobacco and handed it off to the stringers. The stringers carefully tied the fragile leaves to the poles. Since stringing the easy-to-crumble tobacco leaves was delicate work, stringers were paid one dollar more per day than handers—a total of four dollars for the day's work. Reatha was a stringer.

After the tobacco was strung and the poles placed across the curing barn, the furnace attached to the barn was lit. The fire expedited the drying process, staving off the Georgia humidity by sucking the moisture from the air. Over the course of seven days, farmers would tend to their fires, gradually raising the heat. The dry air would cause the tobacco to yellow and become dry and brittle as paper. The barn essentially became a tinderbox—with a roaring furnace leaning against the wall. Unsurprisingly, barn fires were commonplace, and an entire harvest could go up in flames from a rogue spark.

Once the drying phase was complete, the fire was quelled and the barn doors were opened to allow the tobacco to rehydrate. Like the tobacco in their barns, the farmers could breathe easy. The most dangerous part of the process was done, and they could reap the rewards of the harvest.

Reatha remembers the end of the tobacco harvest as an exhilarating time. Tobacco appraisers, dressed in their brown suits and fedoras, would descend upon little Moultrie from far and wide, visiting each of the dozen or so warehouses and assigning values to the crops. After that, well-to-do tobacco buyers would stream in from across the region to bid on that year's harvest. Reatha would listen in amazement as auctioneers conducted the bidding with their rapid-fire calls.

This was the glamorous part of the process, with people bunched together in their nice clothes and expensive hats, listening to the auctioneer's chants. But Reatha knew how much work went into the harvest. She had felt it in her sore, stained fingertips and in the sweat trickling down her spine, forehead, chest.

The long, sticky days at the tobacco barn only solidified her impetus to escape the fields—to find another path forward through education.

★ ★ ★

High school inspired Reatha. As she stepped from her preteens into her teenage years, she felt herself climbing toward adulthood—toward higher education, a career, and the opportunities that lay beyond the confines of the rural South. Though most of her life revolved around her little community within her corner of South Georgia, she had had the opportunity to tiptoe into the world beyond. On two occasions, she had traveled to the "big city" of Atlanta on field trips arranged (and, she suspects, funded) by her teachers. Their bus would travel two hundred miles to the north, leaving the cotton fields and farmhouses in the dust as it rolled into a place that hardly seemed real to young Reatha. Those towering buildings, that bustling business district (black owned and operated), those sprawling college campuses—these were facets of a world far removed from her tiny agricultural pocket.

In Atlanta, Reatha's teachers introduced her to a treasure trove of possibilities, among which were six historically black colleges that would (gladly! eagerly!) open their doors to her. It was during one of these tours that Reatha first set foot on the campus of Clark College. Though she hadn't yet settled on a school, she couldn't help but be impressed by the campus's neatly manicured lawns and red brick buildings. Seeing students cross the quadrangle to get to their classes sent an electric thrill through her body—this haven of academics and opportunity could be hers. She, too, could be part of it.

During her last two years at Moultrie High, college recruiters stopped by the school regularly and made a point of talking privately with promising students like Reatha. The grapevine in academia is wide reaching and robust, and recruiters easily learned who was the cream of the crop through the murmurings of Moultrie's teachers and principal.

The recruiting process surprised Reatha. She thought she knew precisely where she was going after high school: she would follow her sister to New Orleans and attend Dillard University. It was an acclaimed historically black university that had churned out many exceptional graduates, including MHSNY's very own principal, George

Parker. Mr. Parker's influence, in fact, had encouraged Mamie Clark to attend Dillard, and it looked like he was about to snag another student with Reatha.

But before Reatha committed to Dillard, C. R. Hamilton, a Clark College recruiter and dean of men, made her an offer she couldn't refuse. The school would give her an $800 scholarship, along with an on-campus work-study job in the registrar's office. The scholarship would pay for a full year of tuition, plus room and board, and work-study would help with the rest. Before she had even officially applied to Clark, the offer sat on the table, hers for the taking.

She accepted Clark's offer (which topped every other offer she received) and set her sights on Atlanta. The Queen City. Home of Reverend Martin Luther King Sr.'s congregation at Ebenezer Baptist Church. Land of Coca-Cola and birthplace of Gladys Knight. Home of successful black entrepreneurs on "Sweet" Auburn Avenue.

Young Reatha, daughter of sharecroppers, was *doing it*. She was stretching for her dreams and claiming them, one by one. She would, against considerable odds, become the second person in her family, after her older sister, to attend college.

As Reatha climbed, so did other black Americans in all corners of the nation. The month before she graduated from Moultrie High School for Negro Youth, the US Supreme Court deemed racial segregation of public schools unconstitutional. The case of *Brown v. Board of Education of Topeka* dragged on from December 9, 1952, until May 17, 1954, with renowned lawyer and activist Thurgood Marshall acting as lead attorney in the fight against school segregation. Marshall would continue fighting for equal rights, representing case after case—an astounding thirty-two in total—in front of the Supreme Court. Eventually, he was awarded a position as associate justice of the Supreme Court, the first person of color to earn the honor.

Despite the Supreme Court's landmark decision in *Brown v. Board of Education*, many US states were reluctant to integrate, Georgia among them. Georgia leaders whipped up fear in white communities, predicting violence and immoral behavior in integrated schools. Among the segregationists was Georgia governor Herman Talmadge, who proclaimed he would do "whatever is necessary in Georgia to keep white children in white schools and colored children in colored schools."[19]

In the weeks and months that followed, Governor Talmadge continued to take a hard line against the Supreme Court's decision and openly discussed schemes to circumvent it, including promoting private schools for white students, requiring aptitude tests for black students to enter white schools, and allowing superintendents or school boards to place students in whichever school they deemed appropriate. He spoke to cheering crowds about his commitment to upholding Georgians' "accepted pattern of life" and their long-standing tradition of segregation. He declared that the new ruling did not apply to Georgia and made a scathing rebuke of the Supreme Court, saying it had "swept aside 88 years of sound judicial precedent, repudiated the greatest legal minds of our age and lowered itself to the level of common politics."[20]

Local newspapers, such as the *Moultrie Observer* in Reatha's very own town, supported Governor Talmadge by giving him a platform. The paper published his statements without questioning them, no matter how bizarre or blatantly racist. (Among the most delusional statements by Governor Talmadge to appear in the *Observer* were "Negros would suffer if segregation is abolished" and "No one is a better friend of the colored people of Georgia than the white people of Georgia."[21])

Though the *Moultrie Observer* played at neutrality and stopped short of explicitly declaring its support of segregation, the newspaper's position was obvious. Perhaps most revealing is its front page from May 17, 1954, the very day the Supreme Court ruled segregation unconstitutional. At the top of the page, a modestly sized headline read, "School Segregation Unconstitutional, High Court Rules," followed by a short article. Below it, in considerably larger, boldfaced font, another headline states, "Tom Williams Confesses Double Murder Here on Saturday Night."[22]

Tom Williams, as the article reveals, is black. The drama surrounding his "slaying" of Mr. and Mrs. Rowland is described in scrupulous—even indulgent—detail, reading more like a soap opera episode

---

19. "Talmadge Repeats School Defiance."
20. "Talmadge Text."
21. "Talmadge Renews Protest."
22. Paine, "Tom Williams Confesses."

than a news story. This article reveals (as would a string of follow-up articles taking up front-page real estate in the *Moultrie Observer* over the next several days) that Mr. Williams was hunted down by a mob of two hundred men and chased up a pine tree by "snapping" bloodhounds. Williams is described as "a frightened, slack-jawed Negro, wearing a torn denim jacket."[23]

Bigoted caricatures of black men like this one—slack-jawed, murderous—are the very ones that fueled white fear and distrust. And they were abundant. What's worse, those negative reports—the petty crimes, the occasional murder—were about the only news about black people that reached white readership. They didn't hear about church picnics and weddings and birth announcements. They rarely heard about black soldiers' heroics. In a deeply racist world, white-owned and white-operated media controlled the narrative and fed into the echo chamber that labeled black people as dangerous and lesser than.

The *Moultrie Observer* was a microcosm of the anxiety and indignation swirling around white communities in 1954 Georgia. In the weeks following the Supreme Court decision, people began speculating about the chaos that would inevitably accompany integration. They started to ask, "What's next? What other public spaces will be forced to integrate?" They worried that desegregating schools would open the floodgates and lead to lifting laws against interracial marriage as well as mandating integrated prisons, housing projects, hospitals, city-owned theaters, colleges, and golf courses, to name a few.

Although the southern reaction to *Brown v. Board* was not monolithic (many progressive and moderate southerners called for compliance with the new law), fear and uncertainty were still pervasive in both white and black communities. People were nervous about integration and the mayhem that might erupt. While white citizens feared violence and racial mingling (one minister from Arkansas warned parents about coed dances, shower rooms, and PTA meetings and wondered "whether black males and white females would enact 'tender love scenes' in school dramas"[24]), black southerners were simply afraid. The Klan, and those who adhered to its tenets, was pervasive in the South, and black citizens worried that integration would only poke the dragon.

---

23. Paine, "Here's What Happened."
24. Daniel, *Lost Revolutions*.

Working as an after-school maid, Reatha caught firsthand glimpses into white opinions about integration. One of the ladies for whom she worked would drive Reatha to and from her house, occasionally offering up unsolicited opinions as they rode together. "Mixing the races is a terrible idea," the woman said one day. "Those kids will tear each other apart like cats and dogs."

Despite her trepidation and outright fear surrounding integration, Reatha, like much of the black community, was energized and excited by the Supreme Court's decision. It offered a ray of hope—a symbolic gesture from the federal government that things would and could improve. A crack had appeared in the South's barrier to equal opportunities; maybe someday the whole wall would crumble. One could only hope. As Reatha says, "We never gave up on America."

Ever the optimist, Reatha was hopeful about her place in the "Land of the Free" and confident her education would take her wherever she wanted to go. She couldn't have known that the country was merely dipping its toes into the civil rights movement and would soon plunge headlong into fights for voting rights, integrated bus systems, and the abolishment of separate public spaces. She couldn't have known how fierce the struggle would be in the Deep South—with cities such as Selma and Montgomery, Alabama, and Albany, Georgia (a mere forty miles from Moultrie), rising up in nonviolent protest and being beaten down time and again by tear gas and nightsticks. She couldn't have known that things would change at a glacial pace in the South, but, by God, they would change.

All she knew was that the first of June was her high school graduation day, and she had a speech to prepare.

The overcast skies on June 1, 1954, threatened rain, but nothing could dampen Reatha's mood. Today was a day for celebration. For *hope*. Today, alongside thirty-five of her peers, she would receive her high school diploma. It didn't matter that the *Moultrie Observer* failed to cover—or even *mention*—the event. It didn't matter that the paper printed the name of every student in the white high school on the other side of town *and* dedicated a separate article to their career aspirations. Even if Reatha had been a regular reader of the *Observer*, these glaring discrepancies would hardly have surprised her. The only time people in her community made the papers, apparently, was when they committed a crime.

On that warm, overcast day, the only thing on Reatha's mind was her graduation, and the magnitude of it all. She stepped to the lectern in front of a glowing audience filled with fellow classmates and community members. Her sisters, mother, and grandmother and a handful of aunts and uncles smiled up at her, so joyful. So proud. She was the valedictorian of her class, just as her sister Mamie had been, and had graduated with a near-perfect grade point average. As she addressed the crowd, the future spread before her on the northern horizon. She would travel the two hundred miles north to Atlanta. She would continue her studies. She would grab hold of her destiny and wrestle it in the direction she wanted to go.

With her community, her family, and her education empowering her, sixteen-year-old Reatha was ready to take on the world.

CHAPTER SIX

Red Brick Walls

"Hold on to your dreams of a better life and stay committed to striving to realize it."

—Earl G. Graves Sr.

In early September 1954, Reatha waited for the cherry-red-striped Trailways bus. She sat next to her mother in the Moultrie bus station, surrounded by other black passengers who were forced to crowd together in the "colored" waiting area. Beside her, a wood-and-leather footlocker sat on the ground, packed with a few dresses, some toiletries, and a handful of school supplies—all her belongings neatly folded into a few square feet. The temperature was already climbing, and Reatha tapped her foot impatiently, waiting for the steel-clad bus to rumble into the station.

A thousand emotions roiled inside her chest. Would classes be difficult? Would other students befriend her or distance themselves from the *country girl*? Would she pine for home and her family?

Mamie had already completed her first year at Dillard University and had told Reatha tales of wealthy classmates who wore pretty *store-bought* dresses and didn't have to pay for their own schooling. These were the daughters of doctors and businesspeople, and many of them took college lightly, daring to sneak out of their dorm rooms after curfew to abscond with young men from nearby universities. Reatha and Mamie didn't dream of doing such things. The stakes were too high, and the family was counting on their educations.

When the Trailways bus lumbered into the station and creak-hissed to a halt, Reatha kissed her mother goodbye, paid her fare, and climbed aboard. She settled into a seat in the back, her mother's worried voice still ringing in her head: "Get on the bus, go to the back, and stay in your place. Don't move until you know it's safe to do so."

Her mother's fear was justified. In the deeply segregated South, it rarely ended well when a black passenger dared to challenge the system. The ride from Moultrie to Atlanta wasn't long—about four hours with a break halfway through—but it seemed like an eternity to a mother like Ola Mae, sending her sixteen-year-old daughter into the wide, unpredictable world without a soul by her side.

On the bus, Reatha hardly questioned her place. She stayed in her seat, only leaving it once during a pit stop in Americus, Georgia (where, of course, she used facilities cordoned off from the "whites only" area). Protesting the segregated bus system was *not* something people often did at that time. However, in only a year and a handful of months, that longtime obedience and complacency would be widely called into question. Black passengers had had enough.

On December 1, 1955, a weary but determined Rosa Parks refused to surrender her seat to a white passenger, triggering the famous Montgomery bus boycott. After a 381-day protest and a long courtroom battle, the Supreme Court declared segregated buses in Alabama unconstitutional.

On May 4, 1961—four and a half years after Parks refused to surrender her seat—the Congress of Racial Equality (CORE) and the Student Nonviolent Coordinating Committee (SNCC) would begin their Freedom Rides in the slow-to-change South to exercise their right to an integrated and safe public transit system. A mix of black and white students, they rode the Greyhound and Trailways buses between major southern cities, boldly sitting in the sections that were not traditionally reserved for their respective races. Slurs and rocks were hurled at the riders; they encountered mobs with lead pipes and even a firebomb. Yet they persisted.

But in September 1954, when Reatha was shuttled off to college, the thought of protesting the segregated bus system was far from most people's thoughts, including hers. That day, she was engaged in a different, subtler form of protest: pursuing an education. In the spirit of

Booker T. Washington, she was determined to shatter barriers for both herself and her community by studying hard, navigating the system, and maintaining her appetite for lifelong learning and self-improvement. In the 1950s South, Reatha's pursual of education was a hard-eyed stare at the many people who flippantly labeled young black boys and girls as lesser than and ignorant.

The Trailways bus bumped and rattled forward, heading out of Moultrie and up Interstate 75 toward Atlanta. Toward Clark College and everything it had to offer. Toward Reatha's future.

★ ★ ★

After the bus rolled into the Atlanta station, Reatha hailed a cab designated for black passengers and headed to Clark College. The school sat in a bustling pocket of west Atlanta, surrounded by city streets and concrete. Reatha made her way down the sidewalk, to the front entryway. Stepping onto campus, a hush fell over her—a calm that belied the college's urban location. With a collection of red brick buildings and walkways crisscrossing the neatly trimmed grass of the central mall, the atmosphere felt like nothing short of a fairy tale. Reatha admired the sophistication and grandeur of the campus, and she wasn't the only one who felt this way. In the 1957 Clark College yearbook, one of her fellow students waxed poetic about the campus:

"At once noticeable is the campus' verdant splendor—the leaves of ever-green grass, the neatly-trimmed hedges, the appropriately-dispersed trees, the flowers that bloom, and those which only threaten to do so. . . . Nature has, indeed, given Clark beauty . . . the sun shines on it; clouds descend upon it; the rain falls; and the BEAUTY increases from much to more, year to year."[25]

As she looked over the sprawling lawns of the campus, Reatha was overcome with the distinct feeling that she could be anyone and do anything. This was the feeling that would propel her through the next four years—a sentiment constantly reinforced by all the professors, staff, and classmates who believed in her.

Within the walls of Clark College, Reatha was immediately welcomed and shown to her dormitory. The school was careful in its

---
25. Norman and Johnson, *The Panther*.

preparations, and the staff knew which bus Reatha had taken and when she was expected to arrive. She wasn't some anonymous student; the faculty and support staff cared about her success and well-being. Over the next four years, the Clark professors and administrators would demonstrate time and again that they were personally invested in her future. Her success was their success.

Reatha's dorm room was nestled inside Annie Merner Hall, the women's first—and second-year dormitory, situated among a cluster of three-story dormitory buildings toward the center of campus. When she opened the door to her bedroom, she was struck by how *nice* everything was—kempt, in good repair, and more spacious than what she was accustomed to. She unpacked her footlocker, arranged her few belongings, and set out to explore the campus that would become her second home for the next four years. When Reatha entered the school's mess hall, the difference between her home life and her new life was thrown into stark relief. The food! Here, a student could select from any number of options—greens, fruits, roasted meats, pasta, hamburgers, and a whole array of dishes she had never before tried. She loved her mother's home cooking, but this—this was a whole different ball game.

As Reatha familiarized herself with her new home during Freshman Week, she couldn't help falling in love with one area of the campus in particular: the Clark College chapel. Housed in the Haven-Warren building alongside administrative offices, classrooms, and laboratories, the chapel was a cavernous space with high ceilings and a wide stage at the front. It was here that Reatha would spend every weekday morning alongside her fellow students, worshipping, listening to student presentations and guest lectures, and soaking in the dulcet tones of the Clark College Philharmonic Choir. Chapel attendance was compulsory, but Reatha didn't mind in the least. Nor did she complain about her nightly curfew. Students were expected to be in their dormitories by six o'clock sharp, unless they were studying in Georgia Smith Keeney Library.

Looking back on her years at Clark College, Reatha thinks of it as a holistic experience. It was a place not only for gobbling up knowledge but also for nourishing the soul and gaining confidence in herself and her capabilities. Several mentors took her under their wings, including the "dorm mother" of Merner Hall, Christine Mathis, who, Reatha says, taught her (and the other freshman women) how to behave with the sophistication expected of a college student.

All around her, Reatha found role models and mentors who looked like her. It was an empowering and formative time in her young adulthood. She says, "It was an incredible experience to see black people in charge of something important." They ran every aspect of the college, from the top down.

Attending Clark College expanded Reatha's perspectives in more ways than one. Never before had she been surrounded by classmates from such diverse backgrounds. They hailed from many different cities and states, practiced different religions (she even had a *Catholic* friend!), and were perched on different rungs of the socioeconomic ladder. They did, however, share a common race, and that was the glue that bonded the Clark students together. They had all dealt with racism, in some form or another, during their lives. They all understood the importance of collective advancement through education.

In this academic environment, surrounded by peers and professors who supported and cheered each other on, Reatha thrived. Though she was more than a little nervous to start her first classes (Was she prepared? Would her peers outshine her? Would she grasp all the subject matter her professors covered?), her trepidation quickly dissipated. Before long, it became apparent that she was consistently the smartest person in the room.

She began pursuing a degree in home economics, with the goal of eventually becoming a teacher. It was a practical choice, and it was what her family expected of her. She was almost guaranteed a teaching position somewhere in the vicinity of Moultrie or, at the very least, in nearby Albany. Besides, she was a capable cook and a passable seamstress, so majoring in home ec seemed sensible.

With her path clearly defined, Reatha enrolled in the required first-year courses, including inorganic chemistry. However, with the destructive force of potassium chlorate mixed with red phosphorus, Reatha's college chemistry class obliterated her former career plans.

From the moment she began studying molarity and atomic structures, Reatha fell in love with chemistry. The periodic table, stoichiometry, the transfer of electrons—it all made *sense* to her. There was an order to it, a logic. The practice of combining elements and compounds to create something entirely new felt just short of magic.

What was more, Reatha was good at chemistry. More than good, really—she was exceptional. Her high school introductory chem class had given her an inkling of her capabilities, but in the inorganic chemistry class at Clark College, she was truly given her first opportunity to shine. Her chemistry teacher, Professor Booker T. Simpson, recognized her potential immediately, and it wasn't long before the chair of the chemistry department, Dr. Alfred Spriggs, also had his eye on the promising young chem student. They urged her to switch her degree to chemistry and even consider pursuing a doctoral degree. Dr. Spriggs, in particular, was insistent that Reatha study chemistry. Although few female students in that era majored in the sciences (and even fewer went on to pursue PhDs), he had full confidence in Reatha. He encouraged her interest in research chemistry and backed her with his full support.

Professor Simpson and Dr. Spriggs were just two of Reatha's many champions and cheerleaders at Clark College. Even the home economics department chair encouraged Reatha to pursue a degree in chemistry. She recognized that if any of her students could walk this path, Reatha could.

Propelled by her teachers' enthusiasm and praise, Reatha couldn't help but be excited by the brand-new future that was unfolding before her. Before setting foot in general chemistry, she hadn't even considered chemistry a viable career path. Women were supposed to become teachers, secretaries, or nurses. Sometimes librarians. But a chemist? Who ever heard of such a thing?

Even though Reatha was shepherded and encouraged by her advisor and mentors, she knew the path forward would not be an easy one. To become a research chemist, she would have to pursue an advanced degree from a science-oriented institution. She would have to continue her schooling for several more years after college . . . and find a way to pay the tuition and room and board. At that point, no one in her family had ever graduated from college, let alone pursued a doctoral degree. Reatha was not naturally rebellious, and her decision to study chemistry felt like both an act of defiance and a risk. Would any graduate schools let her in? And if they did, what then? How could she possibly afford tuition? After she graduated, would she be able to find work as a research chemist? And what, oh what, would her mother think?

Reatha fretted so much about Ola Mae's reaction that she put off telling her until it was absolutely necessary—a conversation she managed to delay until well into her third year. In the meantime, she quietly traded her pincushions and needles for graduated cylinders and goggles and forged ahead with a renewed sense of purpose. Despite her many reservations about switching her major to chemistry, Reatha was *excited*. She loved chemistry, she excelled at it, and she had the full support of her professors. She would do this, she decided. She would step forward with a bold heart and steeled nerves and let God take care of the rest.

★ ★ ★

As engrossed as she was in her studies, Reatha had to consider the practical matter of paying for her undergraduate degree. Her scholarship only covered her first year, and the $800 annual tuition (including room and board) wouldn't pay for itself. She had no savings to tap into, and her mother was in no position to help foot the bill. That meant it was up to Reatha to make her own way and earn money through her twelve-hour-per-week work-study job. Every paycheck she earned was funneled directly to her college tuition. She never held a dime of it in her hand.

For her work-study job, Reatha was assigned to the registrar's office, where she spent countless hours sitting behind a typewriter or filing papers into cabinets. But the job wasn't entirely mundane. Reatha was entrusted with tracking and maintaining student transcripts, which occasionally put her nose-to-nose with the FBI. The men (always men) in gray suits would saunter into the registrar's office, place their badges on the counter, and ask to see a particular student's transcripts.

Reatha would comply with the agents' instructions and hand over copies of the requested files. Presumably, these were transcripts of students who had applied for government work that required an in-depth investigation. At the time, the civil rights movement was gaining momentum and McCarthyism[26] was in full swing, so the agents were trying to weed out any "radicals" or Communist sympathizers.

Aside from working with the occasional man in gray, Reatha performed typical office duties with the same attention to detail she brought to the classroom. Her efforts earned her $0.35 per hour, or $4.20 each week. It doesn't take a mathematician to recognize that her meager salary was not nearly sufficient to cover Clark College's annual tuition. Though her ever-thoughtful relatives would occasionally send her a card with a crisp five-dollar bill tucked inside, none of them were wealthy enough to single-handedly fund her schooling.

There were times, in fact, when Reatha simply did not have the money to cover her semester classes. Her circumstances were not all that uncommon at Clark College, and the school had a system in place to deal with students who were late on tuition payments: they were not allowed to take their final exams without express permission from the college president, Dr. James P. Brawley.[27]

In addition to being Clark College's president, Brawley was a Methodist minister—a dual role that made sense given the close ties between historically black colleges and universities (HBCUs) and Christian churches. After the Civil War, churches (some, not all) were among the few institutions that intentionally set aside resources to educate formerly enslaved people. Though educating an entire populace was a major endeavor, these humanitarian-minded churches believed this was a task too important to neglect.

In 1866, the Board of Bishops of the Methodist Episcopal Church met and decided to throw its full force behind educating the four million people who had been enslaved and were now unemployed and trying to find their way in an often hostile society. In conjunction with the Freedmen's Aid Society, the United Methodist Church established "70 schools

---

26. Named after US senator Joseph McCarthy, McCarthyism was an aggressive campaign during the 1950s to prosecute alleged Communists, who were considered traitors to the United States. Many of the accusations were unfounded or exaggerated, and the campaign is often likened to a witch hunt.

27. The official rule in the Clark College student handbook governing student examinations did not allow for any exemptions from the college president. It was written in all caps in a single line: "ALL EXPENSES FOR THE SEMESTER MUST BE PAID IN FULL BEFORE THE STUDENT MAY RECEIVE A PERMIT TO TAKE SEMESTER EXAMINATIONS." President Brawley's exemptions were a covert act of kindness.

in the South and Southeast for Blacks between 1866 and 1882."[28] Eleven of these HBCUs remain, including Clark College (now Clark Atlanta University) and Dillard University (Mamie's alma mater).

The Methodist Church was not the only denomination to invest time, money, and human resources into educating formerly enslaved people. Quaker and Baptist churches were also among the earliest supporters of black education. Two years after the Civil War ended, the Springfield Baptist Church in Augusta, Georgia, founded an all-black school in its basement. This school, originally called Augusta Institute, would eventually become Morehouse College in Atlanta. One century later, Reatha's husband-to-be would graduate from Morehouse College, and a few decades after that, their youngest son would also become a Morehouse alum.

At Clark College, with its deep Methodist roots, President Brawley maintained the long-standing close-knit ties between the school and the church. He held his Christian faith close to his heart and was a living example of forgiveness and charity. Reatha remembers him as a kind-hearted man with an unshakable belief in the capabilities of his students.

Because Reatha often had trouble scraping together her tuition money, she had to pay the president more than a few visits over the years to request permission to take her final exams. President Brawley was well aware of Reatha's sterling academic reputation and would always allow her to proceed with her exams without a fuss. Sometimes he would see her approaching his door and call out to his secretary, "Approved. Let her go ahead with her exams." Other times, he would beckon Reatha into his office, and they would chat about her studies, the school, and occasionally the president's own financial hardships. Reatha remembers one occasion when President Brawley confided in her, "There have been times when the school hasn't had enough money to pay our professors' salaries."

Such was the reality of predominantly black colleges. They often did not have the same kind of financial backing as the nation's long-established predominantly white colleges. They did not have a large pool of wealthy alumni to lean on for major donations. Like Reatha, Clark College faced constant financial struggles and was accustomed to living on a razor's edge.

---

28. Hawkins, "Echoes of Faith."

Reatha's financial difficulties, however, would have been even greater if she hadn't chanced upon an unprecedented opportunity toward the end of her first college year: working as a maid for a wealthy family in Upstate New York.

★ ★ ★

Reatha caught wind of the job opening from Clark College's dean of women, Phoebe F. Burney. Burney informed her that a few families near Pawling, New York, were interested in hiring live-in maids for the summer and had reached out to Clark College for recommendations. As an excellent student with a calm, steady demeanor and a proven work ethic, Reatha was an ideal candidate.

Once the offer was extended, she accepted it in a heartbeat. The position would pay twenty-five dollars per week—a windfall in her world—in addition to providing free room and board. What's more, she would have the opportunity to see a new and exciting slice of the country, a place that seemed to exist in a different world entirely: New York. Home of the Empire City. Heart of the North.

After wrapping up her first-year classes, Reatha tucked her belongings into her footlocker and boarded a train in Atlanta bound for New York City's Penn Station. She had been assigned to work for Harvey and Lois Dann, performing household chores and caring for their three children: Mary, Tyler, and little Harvey Jr. At the time, she hardly questioned the family's motives for hiring an impoverished black college student from the South to work as their family's summertime maid, but since that time, she has occasionally reflected on their decision. Surely the family could have hired a maid from Pawling, or nearby Poughkeepsie. Surely they didn't have to reach a thousand miles to the south to find a suitable candidate for the job. The reason for hiring her, Reatha now suspects, was to make a political and social statement in addition to offering Reatha far better work than anything she would have found back in Moultrie. The Danns lived in a community teeming with Quakers and progressives, known for their reformist thinking and distaste of racial segregation. At a time when the civil rights movement was heating up, this was, perhaps, the Dann family's way of throwing their hat in the ring and offering much-needed support to communities of color in the southern United States.

But sitting on the rattling passenger train, a brown-paper lunch sack on her lap, Reatha didn't think much about the Danns' reasons for hiring her. She was too busy watching the scenery flit by and steadying her jangling nerves. This was, by far, the farthest she had ever been from home. Never had she placed so many miles between herself and her sisters, mom, grandmother, aunties, and uncles. Never had she strayed so far from her community, her church. The Deep South.

At Penn Station, she grabbed her luggage and exited the train. On the platform, a neatly dressed light-skinned woman stood, hands cupping her mouth as she shouted out to disembarking passengers: "Reatha! Reatha Clarke!"

Reatha crossed the platform toward the woman calling her name. When Lois Dann saw her, she stopped hollering and greeted her with a smile brimming with warmth. "Hi, Reatha. Welcome to New York."

For the rest of the summer, and for four summers after that, Reatha tended the Dann household. She cared for little Harvey and the other children, cleaned, and eventually cooked. (Oh, the recipes of rich folks! Reatha had never heard of many of the dishes she would learn to make, let alone cooked them.) The children were challenging at times, and Reatha had never witnessed such temper tantrums. When she was growing up, her parents and grandmother had zero tolerance for outbursts. Reatha and her sisters quickly learned that back talk and sass had no place in the Clark household. Unfortunately, little Harvey and his siblings had learned no such lesson.

Eventually, she learned how to quell the tornadic tantrums and always kept a cool head and an even temper when correcting the children's behavior. It wasn't long before she became a trusted member of the household and a fixture in the children's lives. Lois Dann was especially kind to Reatha and would plan little outings for her in New York City every Thursday, on Reatha's day off (Reatha refers to herself during that time as a "Thursday maid").

These outings had a tremendous impact on young Reatha. Never before had she had the freedom to wander around a big city, with no responsibilities and no one to answer to. Never had she experienced the thrill of a giant northern metropolis—let alone the incomparable New

York—in which people of all races, colors, and creeds bustled along the sidewalks with hardly a glance at one another. It was a place spinning in a different universe than southern Georgia. Here, you could dare to keep your shoulders up and your head high. Here, you could fill your lungs and practically taste the opportunity.

Each week, Mrs. Dann would drive Reatha to the train station and pay the fare for her seventy-five-mile trek to New York. "You simply *must* see the Statue of Liberty," she would suggest. Or climb the Empire State Building. Or walk through Times Square. Each week, she helped plot Reatha's itinerary and gave her a few dollars to spend in the city, along with her charge card. "Buy whatever you'd like," she'd say. "Anything that catches your eye." Reatha guarded the charge card with the care of a mother hen protecting a golden egg. She never used it, not once, but simply having it in her purse introduced her to a level of trust and regard she had never dreamed possible between a wealthy white woman and the daughter of a black sharecropper.

In Pawling, where the Dann family lived in their stately colonial-style house, Reatha found a place nearly as foreign as the skyscrapers-and-subways landscape of New York City. In the family's parlor, Mr. and Mrs. Dann would often host sophisticated soirées or welcome distinguished individuals. Among the more famous guests were radio legend Edward R. Murrow and motivational author and minister Norman Vincent Peale, both of whom spent their summers in Pawling. These celebrities were the first in a long string of notable people with whom Reatha would interact. She didn't know it yet, but her future would teem with high-profile politicians, university presidents, CEOs, civil rights leaders, and philanthropy icons.

Returning to Atlanta each September was bittersweet. While she was away from Georgia, Reatha missed her family, her classmates, and her chemistry classes, but she distinctly did *not* miss the South's overt brand of racism. Though the North was not without issues—1950s New York certainly had its share of slumlords, decrepit predominantly black schools, and bigots—it provided a glimpse into what life could be like for a young woman of color. It showed Reatha that black and white people could coexist on the same stretch of land, share many of the same public spaces, ride in the same subway cars, and work in the same areas.

As the train crept toward Georgia, the weight of the South's prejudice would grow heavier by the mile. Fortunately, Clark College, and many parts of Atlanta, were oases in a land whose river of compassion and empathy sometimes ran dry. On campus, Reatha found comfort and camaraderie with her classmates—determined young people who shared similar goals and aspirations. In her school, she felt safe and inspired. For the first time in her life, she could focus on her studies and walk through life without constant, gnawing fear.

Within the parameters of the Clark College campus, Reatha's ever-present fear lifted. Her shoulders lightened. She had never known what a heavy burden it was until it diminished. Back in rural South Georgia, fear was pervasive, thick. It's hard to capture, Reatha says. Hard to explain. How do you describe this kind of terror to someone who has never felt afraid in their own home? How do you paint a picture of constant uncertainty, persistent trepidation that you (or your father, uncle, friend) might be picked up, beaten, or locked away without reason? How do you convey the fear of being targeted? Of being *hunted*?

With its close-knit community of color and a campus that provided a buffer from the outside world, Clark College gave Reatha, and all its students, a gift. It gave them the confidence, the freedom, to *just be*. To exist in the world without worrying about anything much beyond their next essay test.

Reatha was grateful for this haven, this safe space, but she never forgot about the struggles of her community. How could she, when her family still felt vulnerable and afraid? How could she, when the charged atmosphere of 1950s Georgia was reaching a tipping point and the *Brown v. Board* decision was still reverberating through the racially tense South like a plucked guitar string?

She did not turn her back on the struggles for equal rights. This was part of her reality as much as Bunsen burners and beakers. Though her focus centered on her studies, she eagerly attended on-campus lectures by activists such as Martin Luther King Sr., who would regularly speak at the Clark College chapel.

She paid attention and joined the civil rights movement in her own way: by advancing herself and her people through education. In 1950s America, this action alone was a threat to white-dominated systems. Armed with an education, Reatha could more easily chip away at the barriers that kept black people out of laboratories, corporate leadership, and the upper echelons of colleges and universities.

When Reatha returned to school in autumn 1955, she dug back into her studies with the gusto of a hungry football player at an all-you-can-eat buffet. In her chemistry classes, she continued to be a standout student and an eager learner. When she wasn't learning new concepts or performing laboratory experiments, she was *thinking* about chemistry. More than once she caught her thoughts drifting to the lab and her latest set of experiments.

"Both the subject matter and methodology were interesting and challenging," Reatha wrote of her chemistry classes. "The laboratory and lecture sessions were exciting, and my fellow students in chemistry were both serious students and fun to work with."[29] She had found her niche. Her path.

Multiple semesters, Reatha earned an A in every single class, which earned her recognition in the school's "A" Club. Each semester, only a handful of students (sometimes as few as four or five) pulled off this feat of excellence, which may be why Reatha and one other student were nominated as the "most studious representatives" of their class.[30]

Though school remained Reatha's top priority, she decided to become involved in several extracurricular clubs on campus. During her second year, she joined the Chemistry Club and became secretary of the Intercollegiate Mathematics Club. She also extended her reach into more social activities, including pledging for the Sigma chapter of the Delta Sigma Theta Sorority.

Founded at Howard University in 1913, the DST Sorority had a history of working to improve society through community service and socially minded programming. But for many sorority sisters, Reatha included, one of its central functions was to provide a social outlet and a gathering place for like-minded, energetic individuals.

During her first year, Reatha joined the Pyramid Club, which Delta hopefuls are expected to join as a precursor to their official initiation. During her yearlong probationary period, Reatha began to develop friendships with her fellow pledges and was overjoyed when the

---

29. Warren, *Black Women Scientists*.
30. Reynolds and Matthews, *The Panther*.

Deltas officially accepted her into their sorority during January of her second year.

Reatha's involvement with first the Pyramid Club and then the DST Sorority empowered her in a way her classes could not. She was surrounded by a band of motivated, friendly, and educated young women—friends who raised each other up and supported each other's dreams. The fortitude and joy Reatha gained from the Deltas is aptly reflected in the first few lines of the "Delta Hymn":

> *Delta, with glowing hearts we praise thee,*
> *For the strength thy love bestows,*
> *For the glowing grace of thy sisterhood*
> *And the power that from it flows.*[31]

With a full roster of classes and her on-campus job, much of Reatha's spare time was devoted to her sorority, even becoming the chapter's secretary during her third year. She might not have had as many store-bought outfits or elaborate hairdos as some of her sorority sisters, but her sincerity, easygoing personality, and unwavering optimism won over pretty much everyone she met. People took notice of this young woman. People liked her. The Clark football team, in fact, had such a high opinion of Reatha that they took it upon themselves to nominate her to the homecoming court.

When Reatha heard the news, she about fell over in her chair! This was an honor she had never asked for, never expected, and yet it raised her spirits and infused her with a confidence she hadn't dreamed possible. After her nomination, the school held a campus-wide election and selected Reatha ("lowly me," as Reatha says) as their homecoming queen—that year's "Miss Clark College." She was nearly on cloud nine ... nearly. The only problem was she didn't have the funds to buy a homecoming dress or participate in some of the functions, like the homecoming parade. It was an embarrassing predicament, and she confided her distress to her longtime confidante: her sister Mamie.

During her third year at Dillard University, Mamie had decided to join the campus's Army Nurse Corps. Joining the army was an act of selflessness. Ola Mae needed financial assistance, Reatha was having

---

31. Reynolds and Matthews, *The Panther*.

trouble paying for school, and Dot would soon start her first year at Fisk University in Tennessee. The Clark women needed additional income, and Mamie would be the one to provide it. She didn't hesitate for a moment. She was the eldest, and she had taken responsibility for the family's well-being ever since she had the lexis and literacy to deal with bill collectors and grocery store clerks.

Working as an army nurse, Mamie earned a nice government paycheck of $200 each month and would send most of the money straight home to her mother. It was how Ola Mae was able to continue to afford payments for her home on the "nice side" of Moultrie. It was how, after years of ignoring her growing lumps and bumps, she was able to afford surgery to remove twelve large tumors (all, thankfully, benign). And it was how Reatha was able to pay for her homecoming dress.

When Reatha revealed her anxieties about becoming a homecoming queen without the proper attire, Mamie immediately sent Reatha the money she needed to pick out fabric for a new dress. Clark College's secretary to the dean, Mary Ector, had already eagerly volunteered to do the sewing, and she set about putting together a gown fit for a queen.

When it was finished, the cream-colored dress fell elegantly from Reatha's frame, touched the floor, and flowed behind her in a long train. Before her coronation, Reatha smoothed her natural curls, donned a pair of bold dangling earrings, and draped a plush red robe around her shoulders. At age nineteen, she had become a poised, winsome young woman. She shared her father's oval face and apple cheeks; she shared her mother's round, bright brown eyes (not yet framed by glasses) and effortless grace. Looking in the mirror, she took a deep breath, straightened her shoulders, and proceeded to the campus auditorium, where her coronation would take place.

As she glided down the aisle, all eyes were drawn to her. This would be one of many moments in the spotlight, and Reatha handled the pressure with characteristic composure and aplomb. She accepted her tiara from President Brawley, said a few words, and officially became that year's Miss Clark.

To this day, Reatha remains humbled by and grateful for her sister's sacrifices. It wasn't just about the homecoming dress; it was about something larger. Mamie's decision to join the Army Nurse Corps and earn a decent income paved the way for Reatha to pursue her dreams of graduate school: Mamie gave the Clark family the added security they needed so Reatha would not have to worry about returning home after graduation to teach in a local school and funnel money to the family. That gift—the freedom to carve out her own destiny—was priceless. Without it, Reatha may never have contributed to a NASA-sponsored chemistry project or worked in leadership in both academia and corporate America. She may never have attended graduate school. She may never have met her husband and had their two boys.

Though Mamie would tell you she was just doing her duty, in Reatha's eyes, she was doing so much more than that. She was weaving possibilities from threads of generosity, sacrifice, and love.

★ ★ ★

Though school, work, and extracurricular activities captured much of Reatha's attention in the mid-1950s, she caught rumblings about a new war overseas—one not far from Korea, where her sister was stationed. Vietnam was a nation divided, with North Vietnam championing Communism, while South Vietnam favored Western politics. The tension erupted into a violent, decades-long conflict that would eventually entangle the United States—and some of Reatha's family members—in arguably the most confusing and divisive war of the twentieth century. In later years, the tension brought about by the war would come home to roost right on Reatha's doorstep, as she worked as the dean of York College in New York City. But that would be years down the line, and right now Reatha was too busy attending to schoolwork to pay much attention.

Besides, the conflict in Vietnam scarcely seemed to concern the United States in its early years. It was just another country on the other side of the world embroiled in a domestic conflict. Most Americans would pay little heed to it until the United States stepped up its involvement in the mid-1960s.

For Reatha, there were more pressing issues closer to home. All across the South, black people were facing an ugly and occasionally violent backlash to integration in schools and public areas. At the beginning of the 1957–58 school year, nine high school students attempted to cross the color barrier in Little Rock, Arkansas, and were met with shouting white students and armed men from the Arkansas National Guard who blocked the entryway doors. The federal government intervened, with President Dwight D. Eisenhower sending troops to Arkansas to escort the so-called Little Rock Nine into the school. These nine young people became a symbol of civil rights and the struggle to integrate classrooms.

Also in 1957, six prominent ministers formed the Triple L Movement (standing for Love, Law, and Liberation), which aimed to desegregate Atlanta's city buses. Advocating planned, peaceful resistance, the ministers deliberately sat in the white section of a city bus and were immediately arrested. With staunch anti-integrationist Marvin Griffin occupying the governor's chair (a man famous for saying he would keep Georgia's schools segregated "come hell or high water"[32]), the Triple L Movement was inevitably met with resistance and not-so-veiled threats. The movement proved successful, however, and two years later, a federal district court ruled in the ministers' favor, upending Atlanta's longstanding tradition of segregating its city buses.

Perhaps the most chilling of all threats in the mid-1950s was the reinvigoration of the Ku Klux Klan. After a period of relative inactivity, the Klan had come surging back after the Supreme Court ruled school segregation unconstitutional. It began an organized, massive resistance that involved unbridled and largely unpunished violence against the black community and vocal white anti-segregationists. With the aim of demonstrating its member solidarity and clout, the Klan staged large rallies, many of which took place at Stone Mountain, just fifteen miles outside of Atlanta. Stone Mountain was a potent symbol—not just because it was a massive, bald quartz dome bedecked with an enormous (at the time partially completed) bas-relief sculpture depicting three Confederate leaders on horseback—but because it was where William J. Simmons had revitalized the Klan's anemic following in 1915. Following in Simmons's footsteps, 1950s Klan leaders began holding annual rallies on Stone Mountain in which members would trek to the top by the thousands and participate in rituals, burn crosses, and whip up their fellow members in a frenzy of white power.

Twenty miles west, Clark College provided a sanctuary for Reatha and her fellow students. There, they could fret over exams instead of

---

32. Bird, David. "Marvin Griffin, 74, Former Governor."

their personal safety. They were free to hold their heads high, make eye contact, and educate themselves—all of which were perceived as threats in the eyes of the Klan. When they ventured into the city of Atlanta, the Clark students could easily stay within predominantly black neighborhoods to do their shopping. If, however, they wanted a larger selection or needed some specialty item, they might have to visit other, less friendly parts of the city. They would take a segregated bus to a segregated department store. If they were hungry, they might buy a sandwich at a segregated lunch counter, where they rarely lingered for long. They knew when they were not welcome.

The Rich's department store chain was among the segregated downtown shops that Reatha occasionally visited. A couple years after she left Atlanta, it would become the epicenter of the downtown Atlanta business boycotts. Starting in autumn 1960, protestors picketed outside Rich's, calling for desegregation and systemic change. It was during one of these rallies that a certain protestor was arrested for the first time for an act of civil disobedience: Dr. Martin Luther King Jr.

But those protests were still a few years away, and, for the time being, a tentative peace (or tolerance, at the very least) existed between black and white Atlanta. Besides, Reatha and the other students at Atlanta's HBCUs could step away from segregation and fear if they wanted to. They could return to their campuses and be among friends and allies.

Reatha was well aware of that privilege. She knew her family in South Georgia did not have safe spaces like the campuses of Clark, Morehouse, and Spelman Colleges to retreat into. They were immersed in a blatantly racist, sometimes violent corner of the country. Whenever Reatha returned home, that pervasive fear—the heavy thing that had curled up and lain dormant in her gut—reawakened and began to gnaw at her. Everywhere, the fear. She could feel it in the downturned eyes, the people who shivered when they had to venture outside at night. She felt it among her relatives and church friends as they whispered about someone disappearing and someone else getting clubbed.

But Reatha's homecoming was also a joyful time. She would gather with family over lovingly cooked meals and field all the questions they threw at her. Millions of questions. They asked about college life and classes. They wondered about Atlanta and its black business district. They had heard about her summers in New York and wanted to know about the Dann family, the subway systems, Central Park. Reatha answered their questions as gracefully as she could, but she could feel herself becoming somewhat of a pariah in her once comfortable community. A gap was widening between her and those who had never had a chance to pursue an education. She was studying in an acclaimed black school; they were laboring for a living.

Reatha could sense the gap, and she did her best to reach across it and show her family and community that they still mattered, that their lives were still meaningful to her. "Lift as you climb," she'd been taught, and she intended to lift her community with her.

Though connecting with others was tough, she never stopped trying. What made it even more challenging, however, was her decision to deviate from her expected path. She was supposed to return home with her degree in home economics. She was supposed to settle back into her hometown and teach at a grade school, or maybe even a high school. But chemistry? That was never part of the plan. And Reatha was certain her choice of major would never make sense to her practical family members.

But she had to tell them—or rather, she had to tell her mother, who would then relay the news to the rest of the family. She had to come clean about what she'd been up to these past three years. Reatha put off the conversation for as long as she could, but toward the end of her third year, something happened that compelled her to come forward: she was awarded a scholarship. A big one.

She was selected to receive a highly coveted Woodrow Wilson Fellowship.

Reatha's fellowship did not fall, with the serendipity of Newton's apple, into her lap. This prestigious prize was the result of long hours of study and fieldwork, split between the library and the lab. Reatha's studies absorbed her, spongelike, and she found within herself a bottomless reserve of energy and enthusiasm for chemistry and its related fields.

Clark College had placed a rigid ladder between its students and a chemistry degree, and Reatha was expected to climb it, rung by rung. She advanced from inorganic chemistry and trigonometry to qualitative and quantitative analysis, organic chemistry, differential calculus, and physical chemistry. Along the way, she studied harder than necessary and was often the last student in the laboratory. She didn't want to just *pass* her exams—she wanted to learn the material inside and out.

When she did take a break from her studies, Reatha plunged herself into her extracurriculars. During her third and fourth years, she stayed active in Mathematics Club and Chemistry Club, cochaired the Holmes Hall Senate, and became secretary of the Clark Student Government Association *and* secretary of the Delta Sigma Theta Sorority.

On top of her activities, she was inducted into two prestigious societies: the Beta Kappa Chi Scientific Honor Society and the Alpha Kappa Mu Honor Society. She also received several awards, including the Chemical Rubber Publishing Company Award, which recognized her achievements in the area of physics. Additionally, she was chosen for *Who's Who among Students in American Universities and Colleges*, a directory of high-achieving undergraduate students who were selected "based upon a combination of scholarship, participation in extra-curricular activities," and (rather vaguely) the "promise of future usefulness."[33]

The cherry on top of Reatha's third-year honors was her Woodrow Wilson Fellowship. Her other awards and scholarly activities were meaningful, of course, but none were accompanied by a monetary prize. The fellowship was tangible. It opened the doors to graduate school.

Of the hundreds of thousands of college students in the United States, less than a thousand were awarded a Woodrow Wilson Fellowship that year, which was bestowed upon students of exceptional academic achievement. Reatha was one of them.[34] The fellowship would cover her entire tuition for graduate school for a full two years. This was *big* news, and Reatha wanted to celebrate it with her mom.

She had to tell her. Soon.

Over Christmas break, Reatha returned to Moultrie, determined to break the news to her mother. Sitting inside the clapboard house, Reatha could feel her heart pit-a-patting in her chest as she fidgeted in her chair. Reatha's aunt Loretha was also in the room, and Reatha glanced at her out of the corner of her eye. Was this the right moment? Should she wait until she was alone with her mother? Would she *ever* be alone with her mother, given how many visitors Ola Mae entertained?

---

33. Norman and Johnson, *The Panther*.
34. Reatha's classmate Avon Kirkland also received a Woodrow Wilson Fellowship that year—a testament to the strength of Clark College's chemistry program.

She decided to plow ahead and spill her secret.

She told Ola Mae and Aunt Loretha everything—how she had switched her major to chemistry, her plans to attend grad school, her selection as a Woodrow Wilson Fellow. When she was done, she sat back and let her mom and aunt react, and react they did.

Aunt Loretha was convinced that Reatha's plans were a recipe for spinsterhood. Reatha should forget about all this schooling, Aunt Loretha declared, and find herself a husband. As she put it, "No one is going to want to marry a woman with more education than he has."

Ola Mae seconded Aunt Loretha's misgivings and urged Reatha to reconsider. But Reatha refused to back down. By this point, she was convinced of her path and self-assured in her capabilities. She knew her mother and aunt's resistance was only one of many obstacles she would face as a fledgling chemist, but she was determined to forge ahead anyway and blaze a new path as she went.

Her tenacity and dogged determination would help clear the way for other female chemists of color to come. Though Reatha is quick to credit her mentors and the black scientists and scholars before her for making her transition into graduate school possible, the fact is she did something extraordinary for a young black woman in 1958. She dared to continue her education. She dared to step into territory as frightening and foreign as the surface of the moon.

CHAPTER SEVEN

City of Wind and Fire

"Whatever you do, strive to do it so well that no man living and no man dead, and no man yet to be born can do it any better."

—Dr. Benjamin E. Mays

Buoyed by her Woodrow Wilson Fellowship and plans to attend graduate school the following fall, Reatha sailed through her final year. True to character, she did not neglect her studies and fall into a fourth-year slump. Instead, she forged ahead with fire under her shoes and eyes on the future.

Soon, she had to decide where she wanted to attend graduate school. Soon, she had to fill out applications and send them out, along with a few prayers.

Reatha's criteria were not nearly as scientific as her studies. If the university (a) had a renowned chemistry program and (b) was the alma mater of respected Clark College faculty, it made the list. Eventually, she narrowed her selection to the University of Chicago, the University of Minnesota, and Washington University in St. Louis.

Chicago came out on top, partially because Reatha had tremendous respect and admiration for several of its alumni. Her professor of physical chemistry, Dr. Henry McBay, was a UChicago graduate. He instructed students at both Clark and nearby Morehouse College and had a reputation for being tough, but she admired his depth of knowledge and self-assuredness in the laboratory. Clark College's chair of sociology, Dr. William Hale, was also a UChicago alumnus—an intelligent professor whom Reatha perceived to be the best of the best. Finally, Dr. Benjamin Mays, president of Morehouse College, had graduated from the University of Chicago. Dr. Mays was a well-respected educator, a powerful speaker, and a champion of the civil rights movement. He was also a Baptist minister, and years later, he would officiate Reatha's marriage ceremony.

Reatha admired these three highly accomplished alumni and thought, "I want to be like them." Never mind that they were all men. Never mind that female scientists were about as rare in the late 1950s as black scientists. Reatha did not let her gender deter her from her goals. She would follow in the footsteps of McBay, Hale, and Mays. She would do everything in her power to earn her doctorate.

And the University of Chicago waited, ready to welcome her into its folds.

Once Reatha had made her decision and was officially accepted at the University of Chicago, she was summoned to the bursar's office at Clark College. Puzzled, she walked into the office and stood in front of the bursar's desk. Without meeting her eyes or offering a word of explanation, he handed her an envelope.

Reatha left, disquieted by the bursar's embarrassment. Opening the envelope, she found a $300 check tucked inside (a tidy sum, in those days!). It was from the state of Georgia.

In 1958, Georgia's public graduate schools were still stubbornly segregated, and the check was a partial tuition reimbursement for Reatha to attend graduate school out of state. In the era of *Brown v. Board*, the check could easily be seen as a bribe: "Please," the check seemed to say, "go to graduate school somewhere else. We'll help you. But don't stir up trouble in Georgia."

Looking at her check—that piece of paper encouraging her to leave the state—Reatha understood the bursar's embarrassment.

★ ★ ★

In the spring of 1958, Reatha donned a black cap and ankle-length robe and made her way to Davage Auditorium. The auditorium was in the same building as the school's chapel, and Reatha felt a special affinity with the space—a sense of comfort and belonging. In the yawning mouth of Davage, Reatha sat among her classmates and listened to the lilting melodies of the Clark College Philharmonic choral group. Today, she would graduate with honors and a near-perfect GPA. She would walk onto the stage to receive her well-earned diploma. Little did she know that she would return to Clark College fifty years later to attend another graduation ceremony. Instead of as a new graduate, she would take the stage as the keynote speaker. The bright-eyed twenty-year-old would be replaced by the world-wise, accomplished seventy-year-old.

But today, she knew little about the future that lay before her. Today, the only thing that mattered was claiming that piece of paper and celebrating this milestone with her family.

When President Brawley read Reatha's name, her mother and sisters cheered, and they continued cheering as he listed her honors: summa cum laude, Beta Kappa Chi (national sciences and mathematics honorary society), Alpha Kappa Mu (national academic honorary society), Woodrow Wilson Fellowship recipient, Miss Clark College. . .

With each honor listed, the hearts of Ola Mae, Mamie, and Dot swelled and tears prickled at their eyes. Such pride they felt for their Reatha! Such joy!

Ola Mae had made the journey to Atlanta reluctantly, fretting (as was her way) that her clothing, hair, and lack of an education weren't *good enough*, weren't *right* for this kind of environment. Preparing to be met with snobbery and disdain, she was shocked when faculty, students, and support staff alike were warm and talkative, especially when they discovered she was the mother of their beloved Reatha.

A certain brand of shame followed every impoverished, undereducated black person from the rural South. They were in a different class than their educated, city-dwelling counterparts, and many people (including Reatha's future in-laws) regarded them as lesser than. It was this stigma that Ola Mae feared and was mercifully spared.

Reatha says, "My mother talked about her experience at Clark College for *years*. She could hardly believe the sophistication of the place and how she was treated with such respect and kindness by the faculty and staff."

After that day, Reatha didn't pause. She didn't rest. Soon after graduation, she boarded the now-familiar train heading north to Pawling,

New York. This would be her fourth and final summer working for the Dann family. After the summer of 1958, she would begin a new chapter of her life at the University of Chicago.

Before the day she set foot on campus, she had never before been to the Windy City, let alone the university. She walked around with eyes upturned to the towering stone buildings, absorbing the ornate archivolts and gables and pointed spires characteristic of the school's impressive gothic architecture. It had the air of an ancient place. A scholarly place.

This was where Edwin Hubble (an astronomer credited with finding some of the first evidence of the big bang), John T. Scopes (famous for the Scopes Trial on evolution), Harvey Fletcher (father of stereophonic sound), and Carl Sagan (astronomer and cofounder of the Planetary Society) had studied. This was the home of the famous Doomsday Clock, ticking down the "hours and minutes" until humanity's demise. This was where the first sustained nuclear chain reaction took place in 1942, leading to several advancements in nuclear science. This was the school that had churned out dozens of Nobel laureates, Pulitzer Prize winners, and Guggenheim Fellows.

This was the university that opened its doors to a budding young chemist.

When Reatha began studying at the distinguished University of Chicago, the school was only two years shy of celebrating its seventieth birthday, having been founded in 1890 with joint funding from the American Baptist Education Society and John D. Rockefeller (whose initial donation of $600,000 has been referred to as "spare change").[35] The campus inhabits its own private nook of Chicago, located seven miles south of the bustling downtown area and nestled between two gigantic parks. Bearing the names of former presidents, Washington and Jackson Parks are connected by the Midway Plaisance, which abuts the south side of the university's parameters. With the two sprawling parks and the Midway, the University of Chicago rests within walking distance of about a thousand acres of greenery.

As she had with Clark College, Reatha found a safe haven in the University of Chicago. Her professors and classmates hardly acknowledged her skin tone, and she was free to pursue her studies without

---

35. Grossman, "University of Chicago Opens."

feeling inferior. In fact, all the "mixing and mingling," as she puts it, was a bit of a shock. Students of different races and backgrounds socialized in the classroom or on the quad, sat alongside each other, befriended each other, and occasionally developed romances. The university wasn't completely free of biases—and Reatha notes that her chemistry program was predominantly white males—but compared to South Georgia, it might as well have been Oz's Emerald City.

Off campus, life was not nearly so harmonious. Nearby neighborhoods were sharply segregated, with much of the black community shuffled into decrepit housing projects. Slumlords overcharged black tenants and failed to keep up on even the most basic repairs. Over the prior few decades, a wave of southern black Americans and eastern Europeans had flocked to Chicago in what is now called the Great Migration, causing the two groups to fiercely compete for working-class occupations. With so much competition for wages—and banks often refusing to provide lines of credit to black customers—Chicago's black population struggled to gain a foothold in the city.

When she left the campus grounds, Reatha would notice racial disparities in the neighborhoods, on the buses, and in the downtown department stores. But she rarely left. Her world spun inside a tight sphere consisting of classes, lab work, and the occasional visit to Rockefeller Chapel. She ate her meals in the school's dining hall. She studied in Harper Library. She slept in Beecher Hall.

Though other students would complain about the cafeteria food or cramped dorms, Reatha never did. How could she complain about regular hot meals? How could she possibly find fault in her snug and secure living quarters, regularly scrubbed clean by campus custodians? These things still felt like luxuries, and just knowing she would have access to a nutritious meal and a warm bed was a comfort.

Today, Reatha wonders whether all the instability (coupled with constant, numbing fear) that defined her youth hampered her studies. What might she have achieved if she had not had to worry about having enough to eat and reliable electricity and consistent housing? How might she have excelled if she hadn't had to fret about police knocking at the door when the sun when down?

She did not take her university haven for granted. She used it as a launchpad to soar as high as her wings would take her.

Reatha began her graduate studies on a PhD track, which emphasized classroom studies during her first couple years followed by laboratory work that would form the basis of her dissertation. She took several general courses—all part of the university's rigorous recommended curriculum for incoming doctoral students—before settling on a specific area of study. Energy had always interested and intrigued Reatha, and she decided to center her studies on thermodynamics.

Thermodynamics lay at the intersection of chemistry and physics. This area of study had captured the attention of legendary scientists such as Galileo Galilei (though often associated with astronomy, he also invented the thermometer), Leonhard Euler, James Joule, Edward Guggenheim, and the great Albert Einstein. Reatha saw energy, and thermodynamics specifically, as an integral part of the future. This scientific field had everything to do with fossil fuels, space travel, energy efficiency, and transportation. It was an area with plenty of potential (excuse the pun), and Reatha was perceptive enough to see that.

With her sights set on thermodynamics, Reatha plunged into her studies. Although Clark College had been no picnic, the University of Chicago proved to be truly challenging. Reatha remembers her advisor, Dr. Kleppa, saying, "You may have been a top student at Clark—a big fish in a small pond—but here, you're among a lot of big fishes. Here, everyone was a valedictorian."

Undeterred, Reatha took her classes one at a time. She continued to excel in her studies, but her success was not always enough to distract her from some of the harsh realities in Chicago. She was no longer in the comforting arms of her Clark College community, and she sometimes felt like an outsider on campus. Even though people were nice enough, Reatha was sometimes lonely, sometimes isolated. On top of that, Chicago winters were a force she had never before faced. The biting wind, gusting snow, subzero temperatures—these were weather extremes that Reatha, accustomed to Georgia's heavy heat, had never come close to encountering.

Refusing to give in to the chill brought about by Chicago's winter and her feelings of seclusion, Reatha bought herself a set of long johns, steeled her nerves, and continued her work.

Amid classes, tests, and getting to know a new campus, a new climate, and a new set of classmates and professors, Reatha found solace in the campus's heart: Rockefeller Chapel.

To Reatha, Rockefeller Chapel was the campus gem. Embracing the university's gothic motif, the chapel was built in the fashion of medieval cathedrals, all towering stone walls and carved details. The tower jutting from one end of the colossal church reaches 207 feet high, and the interior ceiling of the main chapel soars eighty feet above worshippers' heads. Bedecked as it is with over one hundred sculptures, it's easy to imagine that the chapel is always attentive, always observing with its multitude of stone-carved eyes.

Stepping through the doors of Rockefeller Chapel was an experience Reatha will never forget. Never had she been inside such a magnificent structure, with its tree trunk–like pillars and archways and vaulted tile ceiling. Greater still were the chapel's frequent guest ministers, who would speak to the students and call them to action. Of the guest speakers, the most exciting, by far, was the Reverend Dr. Martin Luther King Jr.

Dr. King had spoken at the university in 1956, when he was only twenty-seven and just embarking on his journey of activism and nonviolent resistance. His return in October of 1959 was greeted with feverish anticipation. Word spread quickly of the upcoming sermon, and by the time the clock struck eleven on the morning of October 25, the chapel was packed wall to wall with students and faculty. Above the rustling of programs and buzzing voices, the grandiose organ played, belting dramatic hymns from a tangle of nearly *seven thousand* pipes.

When it was time to deliver his sermon, Dr. King strode toward the podium and a hush fell over the crowd. In the packed audience, Reatha watched, enthralled, hardly daring to believe that this larger-than-life figure—this living legend—was standing before her. When Dr. King started speaking, his voice rolled through the cavernous room, following the now-quick, now-relaxed rhythm of his cadence. That voice had the power to stir every thrumming pulse and drum up hope in even the most cynical heart. He spoke of optimism. Progress. He could see the civil rights movement moving forward, inching along toward justice, and he wanted to imbue every individual seated in the chapel that day with his confidence in the movement. "We are, in the South," he said, "moving from a negative peace, where Negroes accept a subordinate place in society, to a positive peace, where all people live in equality."[36]

It was a speech Reatha would never forget—a speech that lent credence to her dogged work in the laboratory and validated her efforts to climb as far as she could reach (and, as she was taught, lift others on her way up the mountain). It reminded her that she was part of this fight, too—the great collective movement toward justice and equality.

Uplifting, encouraging, and energizing, Dr. King's words carried Reatha not only through the rest of that Sunday but through the entire school year and beyond.

★ ★ ★

During those first semesters at UChicago, Reatha gobbled up her studies and prepared to move from primarily occupying the classroom to occupying the laboratory. She had applied for, and was awarded, a fellowship through the National Medical Association, which would pick up where the Woodrow Wilson Fellowship left off and cover the cost of her next two years of school. With the grant, a burden lifted from Reatha's shoulders. Though she worked several hours each week as a classroom teaching assistant, she scarcely had money enough to spare for an off-campus Chicago-style hot dog, let alone tuition. In fact, money was so tight that when the campus cafeteria closed on Sundays, Reatha would visit the International Center with a few of her friends to eat the free meals that were offered there each week.

With her National Medical Association fellowship money, Reatha forged ahead into her third year at the university. In a blink, the 1950s gave way to the '60s, and women began trading in their gingham and floral-print dresses for bold patterns and miniskirts. The Shirelles asked, "Will you still love me tomorrow?" while Hank Ballard and the Midnighters (and, later, Chubby Checker) urged the bouffant—and pompadour-wearing youth of the '50s to let their hair down and do "The Twist."

Behind the day's pop culture ran an undercurrent of uncertainty that reflected national sentiments. Sam Cooke's "Wonderful World" and "Chain Gang" spoke to the mishmash of optimism and residual fear

---

36. Allen and Drapa, "When King Made History."

felt by black communities as they marched into undoubtedly the most potent and volatile decade of the civil rights movement. In 1961, directors Robert Wise and Jerome Robbins presented *West Side Story*, a tale that embodies racial tensions (white vs. Puerto Rican) and blurred loyalties. Concurrently, *A Raisin in the Sun*—which tells the story of a black family attempting to improve their circumstances on Chicago's South Side—also moved from the Broadway stage to the big screen. The latter film featured much of its original Broadway cast, including acclaimed actors Sidney Poitier[37] and Ruby Dee.

Though Reatha had little time to indulge in movies and music (aside from church hymns and spirituals), she was by no means unaffected by the influence of popular culture. It permeated the national consciousness; it motivated and mirrored widespread change. To be black in this era was to be political, and Reatha was just as much a part of the movement as those who marched and protested. She propelled change by squeezing through the doors that civil rights activists had cracked open and proving she had a right to be inside.

She knew she was in the classroom, and in the laboratory, because of the giants who came before her and the changemakers who were pounding the pavement and whipping up the people. In February 1960, when Reatha was starting the spring semester of her second year of grad school, four black college students refused to leave the whites-only Woolworth's lunch counter in Greensboro, North Carolina. Though other activists had participated in nonviolent sit-ins (patiently occupying stools and seats at segregated dining establishments until they were arrested or otherwise forced to leave), these four struck a national chord. The sit-in movement escalated and was accompanied by kneel-ins in segregated churches, swim-ins at segregated beaches, and read-ins at segregated libraries.

Reatha picked up the newspaper with trepidation in those days, wondering what type of unrest was gripping the southern United States that day. Just as Ray Charles had "Georgia on [his] mind," Reatha kept her home state and the turmoil it was experiencing close to her thoughts. She read about the boycotts in downtown Atlanta, which included the Rich's department store chain. She caught snippets of news

---

37. In 1964, Sidney Poitier won an Academy Award for best actor in the film *Lilies of the Field*, becoming the first black actor to earn this achievement.

about violence toward the protesters—toward people of color and white allies—but suspected she wasn't getting the full story. Later, she would learn of white aggressors and police officers verbally abusing, striking, or pouring ketchup or sugar on the heads of protestors at the lunch counters. But the protestors were trained to keep a level head and not retaliate. At a student leadership conference in Raleigh, North Carolina, Ella Baker, executive director of the Southern Christian Leadership Conference (SCLC), reminded activists that the purpose of the protests was "bigger than a hamburger." She then quoted a Barber-Scotia College newsletter, saying, "We want the world to know that we no longer accept the inferior position of second-class citizenship. We are willing to go to jail, be ridiculed, spat upon, and even suffer physical violence to obtain First Class Citizenship."[38]

This student leadership conference, held three months after the so-called Greensboro Four staged their quiet protest, led to the formation of the Student Nonviolent Coordinating Committee (SNCC). This group of energetic young changemakers was led by famous activists like John Lewis, who would go on to be a powerful force in the US House of Representatives for more than thirty years.

The energy and influence of the nation's youth were apparent. Young men and women who shared the same tenacity and stick-to-itiveness as Reatha were leading the charge to topple old institutions, harmful legislation, and racist attitudes.

★ ★ ★

With the civil rights movement ramping up and digging in for a long and arduous fight, Reatha did her best to focus on her personal mission to obtain her PhD. She burned with ambition and the urgency to not only obtain her degree but also prove that she was still a big fish in this highly competitive pond.

Reatha dedicated herself to her work in the chemistry lab. By now, she had narrowed her focus and began studying metallurgy in the University of Chicago's Institute for the Study of Metals (renamed the James Franck Institute in 1967). Fascinated by the properties of metals, the transfer of energy, and the creation of metallic compounds, Reatha

---

38. Baker, "Bigger than a Hamburger."

was naturally drawn to this branch of chemistry. She began exploring the realm of gallium and zinc, gold and aluminum, lithium and lead—elements that are lumped together in the periodic table but whose properties vary as much as a schnauzer and a Great Dane.

As she progressed in her studies and completed her requisite classes, she shifted her time and focus to working in the calorimetry lab under the wing of her advisor, Dr. Ole J. Kleppa. Dr. Kleppa was a mild-mannered, cream-complexioned scientist, sharp as a shard of glass and fiercely dedicated to his work. In his youth, he had actively resisted Nazi occupation during World War II and was eventually forced to flee his home country of Norway. An activist at heart, he empathized with the civil rights movement and understood the dangers the protestors were facing.

Dr. Kleppa lived and breathed chemistry (publishing some 350 scientific papers during his career) and was passionate about mentoring his students to do the same. It wasn't long before he grew to respect Reatha and her capabilities as a scientist. Her nimble mind, her attention to detail, and her problem-solving abilities earned her a place among his top students. He trusted her, and she refused to let him down. She showed up to the calorimetry lab on time, paid meticulous attention to her work, and only left when her tasks were completed to her scrupulous satisfaction.

Another of Reatha's mentors was research chemist Myrtle Bachelder, a supervisor in the analytical chemistry lab. In the male-dominated world of chemistry, having the chance to work alongside a female chemist was a rare opportunity. What's more, Bachelder already had a notable career in the sciences, having joined the Women's Army Corps in 1942 and worked on the famous Manhattan Project to test the purity of uranium for the world's first atom bomb. (She did not realize the implications of her work until after the bomb was dropped on Hiroshima, Japan.)

At the University of Chicago, Bachelder worked in metal analysis and would, eventually, study rocks harvested from the moon's surface (an assignment directly linked to Reatha's future work with NASA). For Reatha, Myrtle Bachelder was more than a mentor; she was an inspiration, a guiding light who illuminated possibilities for female scientists.

By the time Reatha entered the UChicago laboratories, women had already endured a long history of discrimination and exclusion in the sciences. The lab was thought to be a man's domain, and women were often shunted to the side or shut out completely. Though many of the prestigious scientific academies in Europe were founded in the seventeenth century—1660 for the Royal Society of London, 1666 for the Parisian Académie royale des sciences, 1700 for the Akademie der Wissenschaften in Berlin—women were forbidden from joining any of them until centuries later when physicist and mathematician Yvonne Choquet-Bruhat was admitted to the Parisian Académie in 1979.[39] Even acclaimed scientist and two-time Nobel Prize winner Marie Curie was denied admission to the Académie des sciences due to her sex.

Among the events that increased women's presence in the laboratory were World War I and World War II. During the war years, the demand for chemists, in particular, surged, and companies were forced to start recruiting and hiring women to address the dearth. But even when they were able to muscle their way into the laboratory, women were often forced to take the poorest-paying jobs, given little or no credit for their achievements or discoveries, and thrust into an often hostile and misogynistic environment. And many were promptly fired once the wars ended and they were no longer needed.

Discrimination against female scientists persisted into the 1950s and beyond, with the widespread belief that men were better equipped to be scientists and women were meant to stay at home and tend to their families. The women who dared to go against societal norms were labeled "poor parents, bad spouses, and unstable human beings."[40]

In the mid-1950s, when Reatha was just thinking about continuing her education in grad school, only 290 women across the United States were pursuing science-oriented doctoral degrees (compared with 4,500 men).[41] The situation began to slightly improve in the '60s, however, with the United States recruiting an increasing number of scientists—women and people of color included—to help defeat the Soviet Union in the space race. In 1957, Soviet scientists (including several women) had launched Sputnik, the first artificial satellite to orbit Earth, and pressure

---

39. Schiebinger, "Women in Science."
40. Rossiter, *Women Scientists in America*, vol. 2.
41. Rossiter, *Women Scientists in America*, vol. 2.

was mounting for the United States to outperform its Communist nemesis. Though science labs were still often less than welcoming for women, the number of female doctoral students began to tick upward. Reatha contributed to that trend and helped carve a path for other women to follow.

Still, most female scientists of the 1950s and '60s would become educators. Only a sliver would put their skills to work in the lab.[42] But Reatha didn't care a fig about statistics. She had made it this far, hadn't she? She had earned a place in a respected graduate school, despite widespread discrimination against both her race and her gender. She had persisted with her dream, even though she had precisely *zero* black female scientist role models. She hadn't heard of Marie M. Daly, who earned a doctorate in chemistry in 1947 (the first black woman to do so) and went on to make important contributions in the medical field. Or Alice Augusta Ball, who developed a widely used treatment for leprosy in the 1910s, when she was only in her early twenties. Or Sinah Estelle Kelley, a chemist who had contributed to the mass production of penicillin during World War II.

And any black male scientists Reatha had discovered were often treated more like footnotes than contributors. Even several decades later, as Wini Warren points out in her book *Black Women Scientists in the United States*, "These individuals still remain largely invisible in mainstream narratives, after a mere drop of their names."[43]

But even though Reatha did not have a black female scientist to take her under her wing at the University of Chicago, she did have Myrtle Bachelder. In the male-dominated lab, her presence helped. Reatha would never forget the importance of her mentorship, and, years later, she would provide the same kind of guidance and inspiration to countless young people. It was crucial, Reatha knew, for the younger generation to see people who looked like them in positions of power and prestige.

---

42. Even when women did find work in a laboratory, they were appallingly underpaid. In 1970, male chemists earned an average salary of $15,600, while women earned $10,500—70 percent of the salary of their male counterparts (Rossiter, *Women Scientists in America*, vol. 2).
43. Warren, *Black Women Scientists*.

★ ★ ★

In the metallurgy lab at the University of Chicago, Myrtle Bachelder was instrumental in helping Dr. Kleppa and the graduate students design myriad experiment apparatuses. She would carefully consider the research objectives and the elements or compounds undergoing testing and aid each student in picking out the proper materials for building their test apparatus. When working with extreme temperatures or reactive (and occasionally explosive) materials, selecting the proper components is critical.

Calorimetry, by its very nature, is a dangerous branch of chemistry. It involves measuring the heat released or absorbed by a substance when its properties are changed. Heat might be produced during a chemical reaction or physical modification, and calorimetry experiments can involve extreme temperatures or even explosions. Measuring heat release, loss, and/or transfer is a tricky business involving sophisticated equipment and carefully constructed flow systems. While working at UChicago, Dr. Kleppa made significant contributions to the field of calorimetry, including inventing the Kleppa calorimeter, used to measure minuscule amounts of heat during the formation of a new substance at high temperatures.

Many inventions in the lab, as Reatha discovered, were brought about by necessity. If you needed a particular device or tool for an experiment and didn't have it, she says, "you simply invented it."

While working in calorimetry, Reatha also learned just how finicky experiments could be. To properly measure heat, she had to build flow systems that catered to the materials being tested—flow systems on which she could run precise and accurate experiments. (Both precision *and* accuracy are necessary. As Reatha points out, "You can be precise over and over again, but you could be precisely *wrong*.") She had to take many factors into account when designing experiment apparatuses, from temperature control to gas control to corrosiveness of materials. The experiment had to also be controlled and repeatable, enough so that a perfect stranger could walk into the lab, follow a set of instructions, and duplicate the results.

With such high expectations (from both Dr. Kleppa and herself), it was not unusual for Reatha to spend eight or ten hours in the calorimetry lab, surrounded by sterile white walls and cabinets filled with some of the most sophisticated chemistry equipment of the day. She grew comfortable there, alongside her advisor and lab partners. These ambitious young scientists became some of her closest friends. In fact, it was through the chemistry department that she met her best college friend, a Hungarian immigrant named Susan Meschel.

Like Dr. Kleppa, Susan had sought refuge in the United States during a time of unrest and upheaval in her home country: her family had fled Hungary during the 1956 nationwide revolt against the Soviet regime. What had started as a peaceful, student-organized protest devolved into widespread violence as Soviet troops began assaulting and killing protesters. As the clash between the government and its people became increasingly bloody, citizens began to flee the country in a mass exodus. Susan's family members were Hungarian Jews and felt the strictures of the anti-religion Communist Hungarian government more sharply than most. In desperation, they crossed the ocean, relocated to Chicago, and did their best to find gainful employment in a place where they barely spoke the language.

Reatha and Susan bonded almost immediately. Though they came from seemingly disparate backgrounds, they shared a common history: Both had grown up in places that were, at times, hostile and dangerous. Both had to keep their heads low and not stir up trouble if they wanted to survive. Both understood what it was like to know instability and hunger.

Susan once confided in Reatha, "The one thing I wanted to do when I came to America was stand on the street corner and say 'I hate the government' without fear of being arrested or worse."

During long days in the fluorescent-lit, white-walled lab (where you hardly knew whether the sun was shining or the snow was falling), it was nice to be in the company of a friend. Of course, Reatha and Susan didn't have much free time to chat. Work was work, and when you're running experiments at temperatures of 450 degrees centigrade[44] and beyond, the consequences of letting your attention slip can be deadly.

Reatha respected the calorimetry lab chemicals and did her utmost to treat them with caution and concentration. She wore protective clothing, handled chemical compounds with extreme care, and always

---

44. 842 degrees Fahrenheit

donned eye protection. When a student reporter requested a photograph of her to publish in the on-campus newspaper, Reatha was flattered, but she was also dismayed by his staging. The photographer wanted her face in full view, and the goggles would have to come off. Though the picture is impressive—with Reatha adjusting a valve on a towering, labyrinthian flow system brimming with metal piping, coiled tubes, and air locks—she was, and still is, bothered by her unprotected eyes. Today, when Reatha shows the photograph to young people, she asks, "Can you spot what I'm doing wrong in the picture?"

To her delight, there are always one or two bright young people who can point out her safety gaffe.

Reatha's first major project involved measuring the heat of silver nitrate mixtures. Silver nitrate is a chemist's sweetheart, with its relative stability, low cost, and ability to dissolve into numerous solvents. Given its nickname of "lunar caustic" (assigned to the metal by ancient alchemists who associated silver with the moon), Reatha's subject matter was perhaps prophetic of her future contributions to the 1969 moon landing.

Along with Dr. Kleppa and fellow research chemist L. S. Hersh, Reatha combined silver nitrate with nitrates of lithium, sodium, potassium, and rubidium and measured the mixtures' enthalpies. (Simply put, enthalpy is a measure of a system's internal energy, plus the product of pressure and volume.) Through this work, Reatha and her lab partners discovered consistent calorimetric properties that could be translated into an equation and used to predict the heat of other similar mixtures.

Though many people would struggle to grasp even the basic concept of this work, let alone interpret the study's resulting representation of mixing enthalpies (expressed as $\Delta H_M \cong -X(1-X)[140\delta^2 - 24(\delta - 0.01)]$ kcal/mole), Reatha approached her lab work with confidence and familiarity. She lived in a world where terms like *interionic distances* and *binary alkali nitrates* were as familiar as *paper* or *pencil*.

The bulk of the work (as was the case with future calorimetric projects) involved building a flow system in which experiments could be conducted and contained, then used time and time again to reliably produce precise, accurate results. When working with heat that makes a bonfire look chilly, it's crucial to set up equipment that won't melt, explode, corrode, or weaken.

Even though Reatha and her lab partners took every possible precaution to maintain safety in the laboratory, accidents did occasionally happen. Reatha still bears the scars from one of them.

On the day of the explosion, she was working on a flow calorimetry experiment involving sulfuric acid. This clear liquid is strongly acidic and highly corrosive, and it has a wide variety of uses in chemical and industrial applications. It is a potent chemical, and even a small amount can cause severe skin burns. Reatha calls it "viscous and vicious."

Her experiment involved mixing gases with sulfuric acid at a high temperature, which prompted an explosion. Typically, the explosion would be controlled and contained within the experiment apparatus, but not today. "You shouldn't premix those chemicals before you ignite them," Reatha says, "and that's what happened. They weren't 'under the hood,' and an explosion resulted." The flow system burst apart, and sulfuric acid splattered against Reatha's right hand and arm, instantly burning the skin.

The pain cut through her, savage and red hot.

She cried out, clutched at her singed hand, and rushed to the wash station to rinse off the noxious chemical. However, it soon became apparent that she needed medical attention beyond the wash station. She was whisked away to Billings Hospital, where she was treated and kept overnight. When the gauze came off, her smooth, bark-brown skin was marred by angry red lesions and blisters.

Her boyfriend at the time, Judge King, visited her in the hospital, took one look at her hand, and looked about ready to pass out on the floor. "It looks a mess," he said.

After the accident, Reatha might have taken a break. She might have spent some time in her dormitory, healing and feeling sorry for herself. But she didn't. In her words: "I was a big girl and just kept going. Besides, I was fortunate. My goggles were on, and the chemical spray didn't hit my eyes."

Reatha continued her work in the lab, setting up chemical reactions (and facilitating the occasional controlled explosion) and meticulously recording the results. Her experiments still emphasized silver nitrate, and eventually she compiled enough data to publish her first scientific paper.

Reatha, Dr. Kleppa, and L. S. Hersh described their experiments and findings on silver nitrate mixtures in a paper called "Studies of Fused

Salts. III. Heats of Mixing in Silver Nitrate-Alkali Nitrate Mixtures." It was picked up and published by the *Journal of Chemical Physics* in 1961, with "Clarke, R. B." listed as one of the coauthors. The article marked a milestone in Reatha's life: her first published scientific paper.

Over the next few years, Reatha would contribute to two more publications that came out of the University of Chicago's calorimetry lab: "Heats of Formation of the Solid Solution of Zinc, Gallium and Germanium in Copper" and "A Thermochemical Study of Some Selected Laves Phases." With each experiment, her methods and her writing style grew more sophisticated. She became even more comfortable in the lab (with so many more available resources and much more advanced equipment than Clark College's laboratories) and working alongside her fellow chemists. She grew confident in her abilities and began to view herself as a chemist. A researcher. A *contributor*.

This early work on combining metals and measuring the reactions' heat was a stepping-stone toward Reatha's work at the National Bureau of Standards. Working in the University of Chicago's lab, she wasn't quite sure where her path would lead. Conducting government research, perhaps. Or working in the fossil fuel industry. The future, she believed, would take care of itself. The most important thing at the moment was building her flow systems, conducting her experiments, and achieving the precise and accurate results for which she always strove.

★ ★ ★

Reatha's lab work at the University of Chicago primarily spanned from 1960 until 1963. These were volatile years in the civil rights movement, and, as Reatha likes to say, "As protestors were setting fires in the streets, I was setting fires in the lab."

When it became clear that many southern states would stubbornly ignore newly passed integration laws, the fed-up members of civil rights groups such as CORE and SNCC began to take action. One of their integration strategies included stationing black activists in the traditional "whites only" areas at Greyhound and Trailways bus stations while their white counterparts sat in the traditional "colored" sections. When the bus rolled up, the group of black and white activists would again subvert the traditional seating expectations, with whites shuffling to the back and blacks seating themselves toward the front of the bus. These Freedom Rides officially began on May 4, 1961, when Reatha was well into her third year at the University of Chicago, with thirteen intrepid activists leading the initiative (including the indefatigable John Lewis). She read about the groups' actions with interest as they passed through South Carolina, Louisiana, Alabama, and her home state of Georgia. They were threatened by angry mobs, beaten with metal pipes, and even attacked with a bomb, but the Freedom Riders persisted. In the fall of that year, under guidance from the Kennedy administration, the Interstate Commerce Commission (ICC) officially banned segregated travel for all interstate transit.

That fall, in November of 1961, Georgia was once again at the center of civil rights protests. In Albany, only forty miles north of Moultrie, where Reatha's mother and some of her extended family were still living, the Albany Movement began.

Later, Dr. King would describe the Albany Movement as one of his greatest failures, but when it began, it was an initiative buoyed by hope and the will to change the unyielding status quo. Black activist groups from around the city, including SNCC and the NAACP, joined together to challenge racial segregation practices and discrimination in Albany. Protestors held jail-ins, sit-ins, and boycotts. They formed a biracial committee to strategize their next steps to end desegregation. As the movement grew, hundreds of protesters were thrown in jail, and the nation began paying attention to this midsized city in South Georgia. To support the movement and hearten those who had been jailed, Martin Luther King Jr. and the SCLC decided to get involved.

King's involvement, however, led to a leadership clash. While Albany-based groups generally preferred a long-term approach that took into account all voices involved in the movement, King's approach was quicker and more authoritative. The two groups pressed forward anyway, with King leading the charge.

Just one day after his arrival in the city, King was arrested during a peaceful protest. While he sat in jail, Albany officials made an agreement with Albany Movement leaders: get Dr. King out of the city and they would desegregate public transit *and* release all incarcerated protesters on bail. It was an offer too good to pass up.

It was also an offer the city failed to uphold.

Despite activists' efforts and King's continued involvement (and two more arrests), Albany remained stubbornly segregated for several more years. The city was a microcosm of the white-controlled South and a testament to the staunch racism Reatha and her family had experienced and would continue to experience in their homeland.

★ ★ ★

Reatha the scientist, Reatha the academic, the stalwart student, the trailblazer, the symbol of progress was, at the end of the day, a human being. She valued family, friendship, and church. She thought it would be nice to find a husband someday and start a family of her own. Even though this thought didn't occupy her every waking hour (far from it!), the impulse was deeply ingrained in her psyche. She was, after all, descended from generations of family-first caregivers and part of a tightly knit group of relatives (it was not unusual for several dozen Wattses or Clarks to show up for their respective family reunions or funerals).

So, when she fell in love, she didn't fight it. Her feelings were not at odds with her career path; rather, they complemented it. Love, like her intimate knowledge of calorimetry, grew gradually.

It started with a basketball game.

Reatha's friend and classmate Finley Campbell was a Morehouse alumnus, and when he heard his alma mater would be playing Fisk University at Englewood High School, he invited Reatha and their mutual friend Ulysene Gibson (a Fisk grad) to attend the game with him. The young women agreed, and Finley took no small amount of pleasure in escorting the two women to the game.

On a chilly autumn night in 1960, the trio made their way to Englewood High School, just two miles southwest of the university, and walked into the raucous gym. The rivalry between the two schools electrified the crowd and sent a pulse of excitement through Reatha, even though she didn't have a personal stake in the game. The friends were picking their way through the wooden bleachers when a young man called out Finley's name. He was tall and slim, with short-cropped hair and friendly, deep-brown eyes.

Finley's mouth dropped. "Judge? Judge King, is that you?"

"Great to see you!" Judge called. "Come on over and take a seat."

The group of four arranged themselves in the bleachers, and Finley introduced the young man to Reatha and Ulysene. He was a fellow Morehouse graduate who went by Judge, short for his rather impressive name, Napoleon Judge King Jr. During the game, Judge and Finley yakked away, reminiscing about their years at Morehouse and catching up. Though Judge only spoke with Reatha in snatches, she was struck by the young man's bright smile and witty sense of humor. He hailed from the South, as she did, and his Birmingham accent felt warm and comfortable.

But Reatha tempered her expectations. Judge seemed much more engrossed with his old friend than with her. So it caught her by surprise when he called on her and asked her to be his date for a casual get-together. Perhaps her presence—all brains and beauty—had made him a little shy at the basketball game. Perhaps he was a tad intimidated by this young graduate student who carried herself with such poise. Whatever the case, after they got to know each other, Judge was rarely shy again.

A week or so later, while they were driving together to their first outing, Judge opened up and Reatha began to understand the many folds and textures of his sweet, outgoing personality. As it turned out, the couple had ample time to get to know each other during that first car ride: they were headed to a house party in Gary, Indiana, over twenty miles southeast of the University of Chicago. During the ride, Reatha learned that Judge had followed his sister Gwen to Chicago after earning his undergraduate degree in chemistry from Morehouse College. She learned that he had struggled to find work at first, settling for a job at the Chicago post office (a role just as common for black Chicagoans in those days as the popular occupation of railroad porter). Finally, he landed a position at Englewood Junior High teaching middle schoolers math and science. To earn a little extra income, Judge also drove a cab, which had the added bonus of familiarizing him with the Windy City's grid system. Though Reatha remembers little of the house party in Gary, she recalls her conversation with Judge clearly, chugging along Interstate 90 in Judge's crimson sedan as they swapped stories, laughed, and caught a glimpse of each other's souls. As with so many life events, the journey was more important than the destination.

With that initial date (if *date* is the right word for their first outing), the seeds of a relationship were planted, and the pair began a yearlong courtship that would blossom into over fifty years of marriage, two sons, and three grandchildren. The early days of their relationship, however, were not always rose gardens and sunshine.

When their relationship was just beginning to take root, Judge's parents, Napoleon Judge and Lafronza Bonner King, made sure to voice their disapproval of Reatha. She was a low-birth *country girl* and an unsophisticated Baptist—a country religion, according to Congregationalists like the Kings (never mind that their son had attended a Baptist college). Her parents were uneducated and poor; she was descended from common fieldworkers. They, on the other hand, were refined professionals from Birmingham, Alabama. They were educators with college degrees. They had savings accounts.

And they were not about to let their only son marry someone beneath his station, no matter if she was doing her damnedest to climb society's rungs through higher education.

It was a classic narrative, a plot we've seen in so many fairy tales and romantic comedies: the prince and the pauper, the comfortable class and the ambitious ladder climbers. Never mind that Judge's four sisters all liked Reatha and approved of the match. Never mind that Reatha was midway through her PhD studies. Fortunately, as the fairy tales and rom-coms so often go, Judge's parents eventually softened and, despite their initial knee-jerk reactions, came to like and appreciate their daughter-in-law. That softening, however, did not occur in earnest until three years *after* the couple's marriage, after the birth of Judge and Reatha's first son. Before then—up to and beyond their wedding—Mr. and Mrs. King made their disapproval abundantly clear.

Similarly, a different set of King parents had also tried to talk their son out of his choice of a partner a few years earlier. Coretta Scott, in their opinion, was too low class to date their son, Martin Luther King Jr. The King family had connections to all the best families in Atlanta, and, by God, any of *those* daughters would be a better match for their son.

Like Martin Luther King Jr., Judge stubbornly ignored his parents' haranguing and dated the woman he loved anyway.

On December 16, 1961, two years before Reatha earned her PhD, they were married. The ceremony was performed by none other than Dr. Benjamin Elijah Mays, president of Morehouse College, civil rights activist, one of Martin Luther King Jr.'s many mentors, and one of Reatha's inspirations for attending the University of Chicago. Like Clark College's

President Brawley, Dr. Mays was a minister as well as a college president. He was a distinguished academic, graduating with Phi Beta Kappa honors from Bates College in Maine and later obtaining his PhD from the University of Chicago. When Judge and Reatha asked him to officiate their wedding, he readily agreed, eager to marry one of Morehouse's own to a promising young scholar. Perhaps, he thought, she would teach in the Morehouse chemistry department once she obtained her degree.

Benjamin Mays was none too subtle about his motives. After marrying Judge and Reatha, he hounded Reatha for years, requesting that she apply for a position at the college. Often working with limited budgets, historically black colleges and universities have long struggled to find and retain science professors with PhDs, who can usually find higher-paying positions outside of academia. Reatha was a prize, and Mays meant to claim her. Though flattered (and reluctant to say no to such an important public figure), Reatha would stand her ground and continue to turn down Mays's requests. Her heart was set on working in the laboratory, not the classroom, and little could sway her from her goal.

Reatha and Judge's wedding was held at Morehouse's Danforth Chapel. The modest red brick building stands at the edge of a long green lawn and is hemmed in by shrubs and leafy trees. Set apart from the rest of the school, the little chapel has the air of a friendly cottage, beckoning students to come in, shed their schoolbooks and worries, and rest awhile. Today, it stands in stark contrast to the school's 2,500-person-capacity Martin Luther King Jr. International Chapel, with its towering ceilings and six-thousand-pipe organ. Danforth was never built to be showy; it was constructed as just one of a couple dozen chapels through the Danforth Chapel Program, created by businessman and philanthropist William H. Danforth.

Reatha and Judge didn't need their wedding to be showy, either. They simply needed God's seal on their relationship. They only wanted to say their vows, surrounded by family and their dearest friends.

When the day dawned, Reatha put on the knee-length (as was the fashion), modestly flared gown she had purchased from Marshall Field's—one of the few times she ventured into Chicago's Michigan Avenue shopping district. She arranged a tiara with a short veil around her updo and donned a pair of white gloves and practical pumps. Judge had also taken the time to look his best for his wedding day. He stepped up to the altar wearing a bow tie and a corsage pinned on the satin lapel of his black tuxedo, his tightly curled hair and mustache neatly trimmed.

When Reatha walked down the aisle, clutching a bouquet of delicate white flowers, she felt an outpouring of love and affection from fifty of the couple's closest friends and relatives—many of the important people in their lives. Dr. Mays, dapper in his pinstriped trousers and suit with long coattails, delivered an eloquent sermon and pronounced them man and wife. Reatha's family—once so fearful that her *over*education would hamper her ability to find a husband—rejoiced. The evening was spent at Paschal's restaurant, celebrating the couple's commitment to one another with plates of melt-in-your-mouth fried chicken, cake, and hours of dancing.

That day, Reatha Belle Clarke would drop her surname's superfluous *e*, take her husband's family name, and become Reatha Clark King. With the transformation came little change, at first. She returned to the University of Chicago to finish her studies while Judge worked toward his master's degree in organic chemistry at Atlanta University,[45] where he had started a few months prior. They spent the first couple years of their marriage as a "commuting couple," as Reatha calls it, flitting between Atlanta and Chicago whenever they had a few days to spare.

Though it would have been easy to drop out of school and share the same roof as her husband in Atlanta, Reatha never entertained that option. She was committed to obtaining her doctorate, and tying the knot did little to impede her laser-like focus. Judge supported her decision. He knew from the early days of their relationship that Reatha was determined to earn her degree, and he wouldn't dream of standing in her way. In a notoriously sexist era, Judge dared to acknowledge the importance of Reatha's education and future career. He dared to build their relationship on equality and respect. Reatha's skeptical mother and Aunt Loretha needn't have worried.

---

45. In 1988, Atlanta University merged with Clark College to become Clark Atlanta University.

CHAPTER EIGHT

The Nation's Beating Heart

"Change does not roll in on the wheels of inevitability, but comes through continuous struggle."

—Martin Luther King Jr.

In the thick of her studies, Reatha did not have the time or the means for frivolities such as a honeymoon. The handful of days she took off for her wedding had already pushed the envelope, and she knew her lab team needed her. As much as she wanted to linger in the South, soaking in the camaraderie and love that flowed from her family and new husband, she knew it wasn't possible. The laboratory beckoned.

She returned to the frigid North just as Chicago was gearing up for Christmas. Strings of multicolored lights and garlands bedecked bustling State Street and Michigan Avenue. In front of Marshall Field's department store, crowds gathered and children stood on tiptoe to catch glimpses of the retailer's elaborate window displays, all glitter and garnish with singing porcelain dolls, chugging trains, jaunty holiday music, and lifelike robotic figures moving through cozy Christmas backdrops. Across the city, children and adults alike donned ice skates and glided across frozen ponds or local skating rinks that dotted their neighborhoods.

Though the days were short and chilly, Reatha found comfort in the city's collective cheer and found warmth in the university's calorimetry lab.

THE NATION'S BEATING HEART

Back in the laboratory, back under the guidance of Dr. Ole Kleppa, Reatha pressed on. Much of her work during her last couple of years centered around three magnesium compounds: $MgCu_2$ (cubic), $MgZn_2$, and MgNi2 (hexagonal). These three compounds form their own area of study called laves phases—intermetallic phases that have a specific composition (AB_2 stoichiometry) and are known for their efficient electrical conductivity. Reatha's experimentation mostly involved the heat of formation of selected laves phases.

Though this work may seem complex or even utterly opaque to the average person, Reatha was not intimidated or befuddled. Chemistry had an order to it. There were rules, and all she had to do was learn them. In a world that often was unfair and illogical, chemistry was a comfort.

Reatha's work with the laves phases culminated in her PhD dissertation, titled "Contributions to the Thermochemistry of the Laves Phases." The paper represented hundreds of hours in the laboratory and countless experiments. When it came time for Reatha to defend her dissertation to a committee, she was prepared. She fielded every question with the aplomb of someone who not only knew their area of study but *lived* it.

Having now studied calorimetry for several years and coauthored three papers, Reatha became a (literally) hot commodity for science-oriented companies that were seeking new chemists. These early years of the 1960s were a golden era in science and the public's interest in it. The nation was alit with space travel fever, captivated by President John F. Kennedy's 1961 announcement that the United States would attempt to put a man on the moon by the decade's end. Widespread interest in all things outer space prompted a flood of funding to the National Aeronautics and Space Administration (NASA) and the many affiliated organizations that supported it. In the mid-1960s, NASA's funding reached its zenith, garnering well over 4 percent of the entire federal budget.[46]

And the public loved it. The pervasive obsession with space travel was reflected in the movies, TV shows, and books of the era. This was the decade when *Star Trek*, *Lost in Space*, and *Astro Boy* made their TV debuts. On the big screen, blockbuster movies like *Planet of the Apes* and

---

46. "NASA Budgets."

2001: A Space Odyssey premiered to packed audiences. On the literature scene, science fiction books streamed off the presses. Classics such as Ursula K. Le Guin's *The Left Hand of Darkness*, Frank Herbert's *Dune*, Madeleine L'Engle's *A Wrinkle in Time*, and Kurt Vonnegut's *Slaughterhouse-Five* all made their way onto household bookshelves and into the sci-fi canon.

From a practical standpoint, all the excitement about the cosmos meant more job opportunities for scientists. Demand for research scientists was on the rise, and the Bureau of Labor Statistics for the National Science Foundation projected the addition of more than a million scientists and engineers to the workforce by the end of the decade.[47] Reatha would be entering the job market at an opportune moment—a time when the nation's shortage of qualified scientists was forcing employers to look beyond their usual candidate pool of light-skinned men.

During the first semester of Reatha's final year of school, recruiters were already taking an interest in the promising young chemist. Among her better prospects were IBM, located in Endicott, New York; the US Naval Research Laboratory in the Washington, DC, area; and the National Bureau of Standards, also based in Washington, DC. Though these employers were finally broadening their horizons and beginning to hire more female scientists than in years past, intrinsic bias was woven into their systems and mentalities. Case in point: when IBM's recruiter interviewed Reatha, he casually asked her, "If you get married, will you have a baby?"

The question was far from shocking in that era, but Reatha remembers how small it made her feel. In that moment, all her education, credentials, and long hours in the lab evaporated; her qualifications boiled down to her gender.

Though Reatha answered the interviewer's insulting question satisfactorily (with restrained politeness) and IBM ended up extending her a job offer, she refused. She decided to select the company whose work excited and interested her the most: the National Bureau of Standards (NBS), which would be renamed the National Institute of Standards and Technology (NIST) in 1988. Created in 1901 by the federal government, the NBS was the government's first physical science research lab. It was founded at a time when the nation sorely needed an impartial authority

---

47. "Scientific Manpower, 1962."

to oversee quality control of commercial goods and provide universal standards. Even the volume of a US gallon was not standardized at the time. Additionally, as the agency itself explains, "the growing electrical industry needed measuring instruments and was often involved in litigation because of the lack of standards. American instruments had to be sent abroad for calibration."[48]

From its practical roots, the organization grew and developed. It tested the durability of materials for the railroad industry, helped improve early aircraft, fine-tuned dental equipment, conducted research on effectively harnessing electricity, and operated the nation's first atomic clock. As the organization rocketed into the space age, it began contracting with NASA to develop and test fuel systems, research the effects of extreme temperatures on different materials, and more.

Reatha would have the opportunity to work among the nation's top scientists, conducting research, designing carefully calibrated experiments, and taking measurements. The NBS was known for its precise work, rigorous standards, and unbiased approach to science. It was where companies and entire industries turned when they needed impartial, clean results. It was, in short, a workplace designed for scientists as meticulous and adept as Reatha Clark King.

Another factor that played into Reatha's decision to apply to the NBS, and later accept the agency's offer, was Judge. Her husband had earned his master's degree from Atlanta University and was now pursuing his doctoral degree in organic chemistry at Howard University in Washington, DC, under the tutelage of his research advisor, Dr. Lloyd Ferguson. If Reatha accepted a position with the NBS, she would, for the first time, have a chance to live in the same city and under the same roof as her husband.[49]

Reatha started work at the National Bureau of Standards over three months before she officially graduated, which speaks to the organization's urgency in hiring her. While she was settling into her new home in DC, she kept in touch with the University of Chicago and tied up all the

---

48. National Institute of Standards and Technology, "The Founding: Overview."
49. Reatha's decision to work for the NBS in Washington, DC, also marked the end of Dr. Benjamin Mays's quest to recruit her to work at Morehouse College. It was important, he decided, for Judge and Reatha to live together in the same city, and he would not attempt to pull them apart.

loose ends that needed securing before she could graduate that spring and formally become *Dr.* Reatha Clark King. The UChicago faculty were not only supportive of her decision to join the National Bureau of Standards but overjoyed. When Reatha announced her acceptance at the NBS, there was much hullaballoo and encouragement. Dr. Kleppa, Myrtle Bachelder, and all of Reatha's other professors and mentors were ecstatic that one of their most promising students had been recognized for her talents.

Amid the praise and good cheer, however, Reatha caught the slightest whisper of worry. How would she—the first African American female chemist in the history of the National Bureau of Standards—fare in the professional world? Outside the University of Chicago's safe harbor, would she face storms of discrimination and bias?

Though the organization had never before employed a black female chemist, the NBS had a long history of hiring both women and people of color. Female chemist Marilyn Jacox, for instance, was unable to find a teaching position after applying to an astounding *seventy-five* universities; her doctorate from Cornell University did not seem to matter. Her colleague Anneke Sengers recalls, "When Marilyn and I arrived at the NBS . . . there were virtually no tenured women scientists at major research universities and black scientists were simply not hired."[50] But the NBS was more inclusive than much of academia and hired Jacox one year before hiring Reatha.

The NBS was not flawless, however, and women and minority scientists were often subjected to the same kind of discrimination and doubt they received in the scientific community at large. For instance, in 1939, Ruby Worner, an assistant chemist at the NBS, discussed the intrinsic bias at the agency in a paper entitled "Opportunities for Women Chemists in Washington." In it, she reported government agencies' failure to promote women or pay them as much as their male colleagues for equivalent work. She lamented the many difficulties women encountered when seeking promotions, saying, "It is much easier for women to enter the service in a higher classification than to advance from a lower grade to a higher one"—though few women reached the higher levels either way.[51]

---

50. Hovis, "Alumna's Bequest."
51. Rossiter, *Women Scientists in America*, vol. 1.

THE NATION'S BEATING HEART

That said, both the scientific community and society in general were changing and growing, becoming (inch by painful inch) more equitable. And the NBS was growing and changing in tandem. Reatha's direct supervisor, Dr. George Armstrong, was known for his open-mindedness and progressive thinking. He cared little about skin color and quite a lot about results.

In the spring of 1963, Reatha accepted her diploma from the University of Chicago and turned her full attention to her new life at the National Bureau of Standards. She and Judge settled into a one-room apartment in the Columbia Heights neighborhood of Washington, DC, north of the city center and only a mile away from Howard University. Reatha's commute to the NBS headquarters was also short—only a few miles to the northwest—but it felt as though she were traversing between different worlds.

Prestigious northwest Washington, DC, was defined by old money, grand architecture, and tidy landscaping. Compared to Columbia Heights, filled with plain apartment buildings, laundromats, and corner stores, it might as well have been the moon.

The NBS sat on a sprawling seventy-acre lot atop a hill, surrounded by lush greenery. Scattered among the leafy trees, nearly ninety buildings made up the complex. Before the first red brick buildings were erected in the early twentieth century, strict rules were put in place regarding their construction:

> "The laboratory had to be well outside the city proper, somewhere completely free from vibration, traffic disturbances, and the electrical interference caused by streetcar lines. It had to be solidly built, using twice the construction materials of an ordinary office building, heating and plumbing lines that were twice as complicated as an average building's, and four or five times the usual amount of wiring. . . . Ancillary buildings would also be needed for engines, pumps, heavy machinery, and the fabrication of sensitive scientific instruments."[52]

A handful of miles from the NBS's handsome neoclassical revival buildings and sophisticated equipment, Reatha and Judge settled into

---
52. DeFerrari, "Lost Hilltop Home."

their new apartment. It was a basic, one-bedroom setup, but the young couple didn't need much. They were simply grateful to find housing—*any* housing. Certain neighborhoods in 1960s Washington, DC, strictly prohibited black residents (doctoral degrees or not), and those that *did* open their doors to the black community quickly became overcrowded. The city tended to underfund and neglect these cramped neighborhoods, failing to accommodate even the most basic needs. In 1960, more than 12 percent of black homes in the city lacked running water; more than 16 percent lacked electricity.[53]

But where Reatha and Judge lived was not so grim. Located on Fourteenth Street and Park Road, their apartment rested in the center of a bustling black commercial district. Shops of all persuasions lined the road, churches rang out with praise songs and sermons, and the community stood on solid footing—despite prevalent redlining practices that denied many of the residents loans or mortgage insurance—until its fate took a sudden and calamitous turn in 1968 (a story for a later chapter).

In those early years, with Judge attending grad school and Reatha starting her first postcollege job, the couple didn't have much money to spare. Luxuries, such as dining out, going to the movies, or shopping for clothing that wasn't strictly needed, were rare. But Reatha was accustomed to getting by on less. She capped their weekly grocery budget at twelve dollars, rarely shopped for pleasure, and took satisfaction in Judge's company rather than shelling out money for entertainment. Before her wedding, Reatha had been counseled by Benjamin Mays's wife, Sadie Gray Mays, on making a marriage successful through frugality. Judge used to tease Reatha mercilessly about this lecture. "That's why you're so stingy," he would say with a laugh.

But being careful with money had been a part of Reatha's life for as long as she could remember. It wasn't about being stingy; it was about survival. Coming from a background of poverty and uncertainty, frugality was a habit that was difficult to shake.

★ ★ ★

Reatha officially began her work at the National Bureau of Standards on January 1, 1963. Stationed in the organization's Heat Division, she

---

53. Zickuhr,"Discriminatory Housing Practices."

would continue to run experiments that centered on calorimetry. Her days were long—often ten or twelve hours—and her work was held to the same scrupulous high standards as that of every other chemist at the NBS.

Working as they were for an independent government agency, NBS chemists were expected to conduct their work through a meticulous and neutral lens, which, sadly, was not always the standard for scientists who received private backing. To help achieve accurate and precise results, NBS scientists were furnished with the most sophisticated and advanced equipment of the day. In studying chemistry, Reatha had moved from Moultrie High School's humble laboratory (really, a classroom) to Clark College's more robust but underfunded lab to the University of Chicago's well-stocked and modern setup. Now, she had finally landed the holy grail of laboratories: a lab that enjoyed the same level of sophistication and funding as Chicago, coupled with work that regularly involved real-life stakes and constant innovation.

Reatha recalls one incident in particular that illustrates the NBS's impact on very real issues for private enterprises. She was asked to run a test for an anonymous company for reasons that would only become clear to her later. At this point, she had been working with the agency for two years, and her supervisor, Dr. Armstrong, fully trusted her to conduct independent tests for its clients. This particular test, Dr. Armstrong told her, was quite urgent, and he asked whether she could stay late to complete it.

Though she was seven months pregnant at the time and exhausted, Reatha agreed. She sensed the gravity behind Dr. Armstrong's request and knew he would not ask her to stay late unless the need were truly pressing. She listened carefully as he described the test she needed to run and gave her instructions to call a "Mr. Jack" once she had completed her work.

"It doesn't matter the hour," Dr. Armstrong said. "Just call him."

Reatha threw her full concentration into her assignment. She set up and ran the test, then ran it again to ensure the results matched. By the time she finished all her measurements and calculations, it was two o'clock in the morning, and she had been working alone in the lab for several long hours. Bone-tired and bleary-eyed, she picked up the phone and dialed the number she'd been given. A man answered on the first ring.

"Mr. Jack?" Reatha said.

"Yes, that's me."

"I have the results from the National Bureau of Standards tests."

The man's anxiety was palpable. It prickled through the phone line as Reatha relayed the numbers her tests had yielded. On the other end of the line, Mr. Jack exhaled a sigh of relief.

"Thank God Almighty," he said. "Thank God."

The next morning, Dr. Armstrong asked about Mr. Jack's reaction to her test results.

"He sounded . . . relieved," Reatha said.

Dr. Armstrong nodded and explained that Mr. Jack's company was embroiled in a lawsuit with a submarine company, with the submarine company laying blame on Mr. Jack for a malfunction. Reatha's test was actually a retesting, meant to either confirm or refute another set of results. Apparently, the results were confirmed, and Mr. Jack's company would be absolved of blame. To guarantee the neutrality of her work, it was crucial that Reatha did not know any of this context before running her test.

This instance was one of many in which George Armstrong trusted Reatha with the very reputation of the NBS laboratory. From her early days at the NBS, Reatha proved her proficiency in the lab, her dedication, and her keen grasp of even the most complicated scientific concepts. It didn't take long before Dr. Armstrong trusted her to conduct her work with relative autonomy. He knew she had a scientist's brain and the stalwart commitment of someone who has something to prove. And, as the first black female chemist hired by the NBS, Reatha really *did* have something to prove. Her success or failure could impact the organization's inclination to hire more scientists who looked like her. It was a heavy weight to carry on her shoulders, but Reatha tried not to think about it. She threw herself into her work and focused on her day-to-day tasks of conducting experiments, measuring outcomes, and solving problems with innovation and intelligence.

Though her lab could feel isolated at times, Reatha was part of a larger ecosystem—a web of black professionals who were doing exactly what civil rights activists had intended for them to do: disrupting traditionally white industries and occupations by squeezing through the door and proving that they belonged.

In April 1963, only four months after Reatha began her work at the National Bureau of Standards, her husband's hometown grabbed the nation's attention. Dr. Martin Luther King Jr. was arrested in Birmingham—one of the most segregated and brutally racist cities in the United States—while nonviolently protesting racial segregation and discrimination. Behind bars, in a cell no bigger than a modest-sized closet, he penned his famous "Letter from a Birmingham Jail," which urged continued action in the streets, as opposed to waiting for decisions from courts of law.

The letter was a direct response to a newspaper article written by a group of Birmingham clergymen, who criticized King and his proactive brand of protest. King refuted the clergymen's call to fight battles of injustice solely in the courts, saying that too many promises had been broken and too many laws ignored. He talked about nonviolent direct action as a way to garner attention and force action—a tactic that seeks to "dramatize the issue that it can no longer be ignored." King went on to say, "It is unfortunate that demonstrations are taking place in Birmingham, but it is even more unfortunate that the city's white power structure left the Negro community with no alternative."[54]

One of Dr. King's most famous and enduring quotes emerged from this letter. In responding to the clergymen labeling him an outside agitator, he said, "Injustice anywhere is a threat to justice everywhere."[55]

In the meantime, the Birmingham protests persisted, with young people filling the ranks. In what became known as the Children's Crusade, hundreds of kids, ranging from first graders to college students, marched downtown with the intention of meeting with Mayor Albert Boutwell. They had been trained in nonviolent resistance tactics, and leaders of the Birmingham campaign hoped they would be effective in swaying public opinion. It was a controversial move, especially when, on the second day of student protests, the infamous commissioner of public safety, Eugene "Bull" Connor, had the young protesters blasted with high-powered fire hoses and attacked by police dogs. The hoses

---

54. King, "Letter from a Birmingham Jail."
55. King, "Letter from a Birmingham Jail."

were powerful enough to rip shirts from bodies and send full-grown adults, let alone children, flying through the air from their force.

The brutality of Birmingham's reaction to the nonviolent protesters proved to be a tipping point in the civil rights movement. Confronted with pictures of German shepherds baring their teeth and kids pinned against walls by the force of the hoses, the public could no longer ignore Birmingham's violent defense of segregation. Politicians, other leaders, and news journalists across the country expressed their disgust and outrage, demanding government intervention and anti-segregation legislation. Pressure was put on Washington to make real, lasting change—pressure that would eventually lead to the Civil Rights Act of 1964.

Amid the chaos, the violence, the uncertainty in Birmingham, Judge's parents hunkered down, praying every night for an end to the chaos. They prayed for the safety of their daughters, their friends, their community. As older citizens of Birmingham, they supported the protests from the sidelines and cheered on the younger generations who were taking to the streets and demanding change. Judge's sisters were more active in the movement, throwing their voices and dollars behind the cause and organizing resistance actions through their churches.

With the nation awhirl with emotions, hard-line opinions, and fervor, Reatha had a sense that the ground was shifting—that old systems and traditions were ready to topple. As Sam Cooke wrote in his iconic song, "A change is gonna come." Reatha believed it. Despite massive resistance and backlash, she was confident that people of color would gain recognition and rights, that they would make progress in the fight against inequality. She kept up her ten—and twelve-hour days in the lab, but she paid attention. Stationed in the nation's capital, it was impossible not to.

At the end of a mild and cloudy August in 1963, Reatha learned about Martin Luther King Jr.'s plan to hold a March on Washington for Jobs and Freedom. This would be the largest civil rights demonstration to happen during the 1960s, and one of the top fifteen largest marches to the present date—a massive rally of anti-segregation civil rights activists of all backgrounds and skin tones. The planned march thrilled Reatha, but she didn't dare ask for time off. She had been raised to show up, roll up her sleeves, and get to work . . . no matter the circumstances. On

August 28, 1963, Reatha arrived at the lab, ready to put in another long day of work.

However, Reatha's supervisor sensed she did not want to be there. Dr. Armstrong approached her and said, "Reatha, if you want to go downtown, you're excused to go."

It was an act of humanity she would remember for a long time. A mountain of work waited for her in the calorimetry lab, but Dr. Armstrong knew what the March on Washington meant for her and the civil rights movement. And he knew Reatha should be there.

So, Reatha went.

Or, at least, she tried to go. At midday in downtown Washington, DC, over 250,000 people had already marched from the Washington Monument down the highly symbolic Independence and Constitution Avenues and were now bunched together in a mass of humanity that stretched from the Lincoln Memorial down the National Mall and beyond the Washington Monument (over a mile away). The temperature never crept above the low eighties, but with so many people shoulder to shoulder, it was difficult to keep cool. Pictures from the march show protesters bunched together under slivers of shade, wearing brimmed hats, and even dipping their toes in the Reflecting Pool.

Reatha did her best to join the throng, but try as she might, she couldn't get anywhere near it. She remained on the outskirts of the march that day, but her heart was squarely in its center.

The now-famous March on Washington program began at two o'clock that day, with acclaimed contralto Marian Anderson stepping up to the podium—chic and poised with her patterned scoop-neck dress, wide-brimmed hat, and white gloves—to sing the traditional African American spiritual "He's Got the Whole World in His Hands." Her rich vibrato rolled through the crowd, stirring up emotions and tears.

When she finished, the crowd poured forth a thunderstorm of applause and cheers. The electric energy of the day was tangible, and it continued as speaker after speaker took the podium. The legion of protesters watched and listened as some of the foremost civil rights leaders of the day—John Lewis, Roy Wilkins, A. Philip Randolph, Bayard Rustin—stepped forward and delivered their remarks. Toward the end of the program, Reverend Dr. Martin Luther King Jr. took the stage and delivered his famous and oft-quoted speech "I Have a Dream."

Part of the speech was improvised, with King speaking straight from his heart.

The March on Washington caught the nation's attention. It energized people on both sides of the civil rights fight and forced Washington politicians to act—it was nearly impossible to remain neutral. Though President John F. Kennedy had been leery of the march because he was afraid it would devolve into chaos (which it didn't), he ended up reluctantly supporting it. In the aftermath, he stated, "One cannot help but be impressed with the deep fervor and the quiet dignity that characterizes the thousands who have gathered in the Nation's Capital from across the country to demonstrate their faith and confidence in our democratic form of government. . . . This Nation can properly be proud of the demonstration that has occurred here today."[56]

Then, three months after the March on Washington, the president was assassinated in Dallas, Texas, as he rolled through the city in a motorcade. He died within a half hour, with his wife, Jacqueline Kennedy, by his side.

The news shocked and horrified the nation and rocked the black community. Again, Dr. George Armstrong encouraged Reatha to take the rest of the day off. Again, Reatha did, and she joined the nation in mourning the president.

Despite his flaws and inconsistent allyship, President Kennedy was an important figure in the civil rights movement, and activists wondered what would happen to his Civil Rights Act, which had been languishing in Congress since June of that year. Fortunately, newly appointed president Lyndon B. Johnson took up the mantle, and the bill passed, despite a sixty-day filibuster by its opponents.

All the momentous events of 1963—the Birmingham protests, the March on Washington, JFK's assassination—surrounded Reatha like billowing fog, but she refused to lose focus. Letting her work fall by the wayside would be a disservice not only to herself but to any young black women who had their sights set on the sciences. It was her responsibility as a trailblazer to whack away as many barriers as she could—to clear a path for the next generation of scientists who looked like her.

So, she carried on.

---

56. Kennedy, "Civil Rights."

She carried on for the civil rights activists who had fought so hard for her freedom and opportunities.

She carried on for her family and mentors, who had raised her up and believed in her potential.

She carried on for the deceased president, who had promoted space travel and would shape the very nature of Reatha's work at the NBS.

At the time of JFK's passing, Reatha did not know how closely entwined her work would become with the late president's ambitions. In only a few months, she would become the lead scientist on a major project for NASA.

This was work that would keep Reatha up at night, excited about its potential and anxious about the consequences of one miscalculation, one slipup. This was work that would turn her attention to the heavens as she pondered its implications.

The sharecropper's daughter was destined to soar well beyond the fields of South Georgia. She was headed for the moon.

CHAPTER NINE

To the Moon

"Never be limited by other people's limited imaginations."

—Dr. Mae Jemison

In her early days at the NBS, Reatha dedicated much of her time to studying and conducting experiments with aluminum carbide (Al4C3). A carbide is a type of chemical compound that involves the combination of carbon with another element, in this case aluminum. Aluminum carbide is a refractory material with a hardness roughly equivalent to topaz (an 8 on the Mohs hardness scale of 1 to 10). Working with this compound, Reatha used a technique with an attention-grabbing name: bomb calorimetry.

Though Reatha was working during the Cold War years—an era governed by widespread fear of nuclear warfare, "duck and cover" school drills, and the construction of private underground bunkers—bomb calorimetry had nothing to do with the types of bombs the public feared. However, for the scientist working in close proximity to a bomb calorimeter, the dangers were no less real. This type of calorimetry is used to measure the heat of combustion when a reaction takes place within a bomb calorimeter—a thick-walled vessel that is an integral part of the experiment's apparatus. In Reatha's experimentation, gases would flow in through the top of the bomb calorimeter, where a carefully measured sample of aluminum carbide was waiting in a pure oxygen atmosphere. The gases were ignited, a contained explosion would take place (the "bomb" part of bomb calorimetry), and Reatha would observe and record the properties of the explosion and its aftermath.

The results were surprising. The aluminum carbide would transform from a crystalline solid to a powder. No laboratory had ever produced these results, so Reatha and Dr. Armstrong were intrigued by the reaction and felt compelled to publish a paper on their findings. They were unsure of the real-life application of the resulting yellowish powder, but, as Reatha says, "In chemistry, you publish your results because your work might help someone else along the line."

While studying aluminum carbide, Reatha published two papers in as many years: "Heat of Combustion and Heat of Formation of Aluminum Carbide" and "The Heat of Formation of Aluminum Carbide." These publications solidified Reatha's standing as an expert in her field, and they also gained her additional respect and autonomy from George Armstrong. He began entrusting her to speak publicly about the lab's findings at national chemistry conferences (one held by the American Chemical Society and another a calorimetry conference), representing the entire Heat Division of the NBS.

Standing at a podium in front of an ocean of white men, Reatha could have easily wilted and let her nerves get the better of her. But, as was her way, she rose to the occasion. "I wasn't nervous," she says, "because I knew much more than they did about my research. I was rigorous in my experimentation. I had tested every facet of a flame, diffusion processes, corrosive tendencies. I knew there wasn't a single question they could throw at me that I couldn't answer."

To this day, Reatha is grateful for Dr. Armstrong's trust. He could have leaned over her shoulder every step of the way. He could have assigned all the difficult or prestigious tasks to white male colleagues. He could have kept her tucked away in the lab while someone else represented their work at conferences. But he didn't. Dr. Armstrong's absolute faith in Reatha led him to appoint her as lead scientist of a major project involving the principles of oxygen difluoride, backed by none other than the space-travel-obsessed public's most beloved federal agency: NASA.

Reatha's role as lead scientist on the NBS's NASA project would eventually earn her an outstanding performance rating from the US Department of Commerce. It was this role that would, decades later, secure her place in CIBA-GEIGY Corporation's Exceptional Black

Scientists project. It was her three years of relentless lab work that would give her the opportunity to make history by helping send a crewed rocket to the moon.

The National Aeronautics and Space Administration was determined to send astronauts to the lunar surface by the end of the decade. With this goal in mind, it mobilized professionals from every industry and background—tens of thousands of contractors, in addition to in-house scientists and engineers—to contribute to the effort. Among them were the chemists at the NBS.

NASA was coy about the purpose of NBS's research assignment. Reatha and her team were instructed to study the properties of oxygen difluoride (and, later, chlorine trifluoride) through a lens of calorimetry, but they were not told why. Like many of the other experiments and tests the NBS ran, these studies would be conducted with carefully enforced neutrality. If the scientists were not attached to the results, how could they bring bias into their work?

Reatha did not dwell on NASA's intentions, but she *did* grasp the nature of her assignment. She knew oxygen difluoride was an important substance in aerospace propellants (the fuel that makes rocket ships take off), and she knew NASA had its sights set on the moon. It wasn't difficult to put the pieces together. With NASA determined to land astronauts on the lunar surface before the Soviets, Reatha could sense the gravity of her assignment. As she puts it, "It's the kind of work you pray over."

There was certainly reason to pray. By the time Reatha became lead scientist of her division's NASA assignment in 1964, a number of disasters and near disasters had occurred in both the United States' and the Soviet Union's space programs. Satellites and rockets had crashed, astronauts and support staff had perished or sustained major injuries, fires had erupted. Rocket ship failures were common, with faulty propulsion systems, failing ignitions, malfunctioning hydraulics, or vehicles simply breaking apart at the launch. Miscalculations were just as common, leading to wonky trajectories or missed targets.

Missions in both the US and Soviet space programs, with powerful names like Vanguard, Sputnik, and Pioneer, sometimes succeeded, sometimes failed spectacularly. But as the years ticked by and scientists and engineers fine-tuned their calculations and constructions, they began to succeed more often. In 1959, the Soviet Union successfully landed its Luna spacecraft on the surface of the moon. One year later, it sent two dogs and a few dozen rodents into orbit and safely returned them to Earth's surface. In 1961, the United States sent a trained chimpanzee named Ham into space, successfully communicated with him, and returned him safely to Earth after a nearly seventeen-minute flight.

Despite the improvements in the US and Soviet space programs, the likelihood of mishap was still high and the perils great. But the two powers barreled forward, each determined to claim the ultimate space exploration milestone: landing an astronaut on the moon.

Reatha understood the stakes. And she understood how risky space exploration was, with its myriad components and players. But, with a prayer on her lips and a beaker in her hand, she plunged into her new assignment. Already accustomed to the rigor and meticulousness that defined the NBS, she treated the NASA appointment with the same care and precision as any other project. Her first subject of study was oxygen difluoride.

Reatha describes oxygen difluoride (OF2) as "one of the most toxic and challenging combustible materials you can ever work with." Taking the form of either a gas or an amber-colored liquid, it is indeed a particularly wicked compound. As a gas, it is poisonous and can cause shortness of breath, a buildup of fluid in the lungs, or pulmonary bleeding. It is highly corrosive and can provoke severe skin irritation or even "frostbite" if it comes into contact with the skin. After exposure to OF2, a person might experience negative side effects for months or even years. The myriad health risks associated with OF2 have earned the compound a place on OSHA's hazardous substances list.

Not to mention oxygen difluoride is explosive. Highly explosive.

Water—that life-giving compound we associate with fighting fires—is just one of the substances that can cause oxygen difluoride to erupt in a violent explosion. Other elements and compounds that might react with OF2 and generate an explosion include alumina, aluminum chloride, antimony pentachloride, boron, carbon monoxide, charcoal, diborane, hydrogen, hydrogen sulfide, lithium, metal halides (in general), methane, nitrogen oxide, nitrosyl fluoride, potassium, red phosphorus, sodium, silica, sulfur tetrafluoride, tungsten ... the list goes on.[57] Even exposure to air can set off OF2.

---

57. National Center for Biotechnology Information, "Oxygen Difluoride."

It is so volatile because it is an oxidizing agent. Oxidizing agents readily accept other elements' and compounds' electrons, which can destabilize them and potentially cause them to explode. Interestingly, OF2 itself does not burn. It will, however, readily support or catalyze the combustion of other substances.

This, Reatha understood, was why NASA was so interested in it. With a propensity to catalyze violent explosions, OF2 was the perfect propellant.

Given the momentous task of studying the twitchy and potentially volatile OF2, Reatha took her time designing a flow system to contain and assess this volatile compound. Her first task was to measure the temperature at which OF2 is formed. It is no easy task to capture the temperature of something during a process that takes place within a fraction of a second. Not to mention that the OF2 was forming within a highly specialized enclosed vessel—a vessel that could explode if the OF2 were exposed to oxygen, water vapors, or any number of other substances. This was no matter of sticking an oven thermometer in and calling it a day.

Reatha was just digging into the project—designing and setting up her equipment, determining the steps she and her team would take to measure the heat of formation—when life took an unexpected turn. She discovered she was pregnant.

Overjoyed as she was, Reatha was also a bundle of nerves. She would have to sit down with Dr. Armstrong and tell him the news—tell him that she would need to take some time away from her all-consuming NASA project.

Hands quaking, heart pattering in her rib cage, she pulled him aside and made her announcement. "There's something I need to tell you," she said. "I'm expecting."

As it turns out, Reatha needn't have worried. Dr. Armstrong congratulated her and, with a warm smile on his lips, said, "Reatha, this will be your best invention yet."

★ ★ ★

Reatha paused her involvement in the NASA project to start the equally exciting adventure of motherhood. She continued working in the lab nearly until her baby's due date, and only took six weeks off as she attempted to learn to perform the decidedly unscientific and highly variable task of mothering an infant.

On March 2, 1965, Napoleon Judge III was born in Freedmen's Hospital (now known as Howard University Hospital) on the south side of the Howard University campus. He was a cheerful, healthy eight-pound baby, and Reatha and Judge began to develop a bond with this little life that was stronger than any chemical compound concocted in a lab. This bond was unbreakable; this bond was for life.

Jay, as Reatha and Judge called their son, was baptized at the Plymouth Congregational Church, where they attended services every Sunday. With Reatha's demanding work schedule and Judge's rigorous doctoral work, church was a welcome reprieve. It was a pillar of their lives; whenever they moved to a new city or state, they joined a church as soon as they were able. Few places offered the same kind of community and support. At church, they were among friends.

Upon learning that their son and daughter-in-law had given their first son the family name, Judge's parents softened toward Reatha. Her stalwart hard work and PhD hadn't quite done the trick—their hearts only truly opened after she agreed to honor the King family through the simple act of passing along a family name. Perhaps Judge's "country girl" was a suitable addition to the family after all.

In Reatha's own family, her mother was especially thrilled. Already a grandmother to Mamie's eldest child, Stephanie, born in 1962, and Dot's daughter, Cyndy, born in 1961, she had fretted about her middle daughter. Reatha had always been . . . unconventional. She lived and worked in a sphere Ola Mae could never really understand. But *motherhood*, that she understood. To her, nothing—not putting a man on the moon, not earning advanced degrees—was more important and valuable than family. In time, Reatha came to agree.

Two months after Jay's birth, Mamie would give birth to her second daughter, whom she named Terri. Again, Ola Mae and the Clark sisters celebrated. Their children were a blessing, unparalleled to anything else on earth.

Reatha's father was just as thrilled to receive the news about his brand-new grandchildren. However, still living and working in central Florida, he did not have a chance to see Jay, his first grandson, until he was almost three years old. Reatha will never forget this particular trip back to the Deep South. She and Judge had decided to take Willie B. to a nice restaurant in a hotel in Orlando (150 miles north of Belle Glade). They made reservations, picked up Reatha's father, and drove to the restaurant with three-year-old Jay in tow. During the trip, Willie chattered away and played with his grandson, whose resemblance to his grandpa—with the same oval face, bright brown eyes, and warm skin tone—was uncanny.

When the family arrived in Orlando and rolled up to the restaurant, Willie grew quiet. When they exited the vehicle and neared the restaurant doors, he halted and shook his head. Reatha could see fear creasing his face and freezing his legs.

"I can't go in there," he said. "This establishment doesn't allow Negros."

"Yes, it does, Daddy," Reatha said, gently guiding him through the door. "Come on—let's sit down."

Though the restaurant had integrated several years earlier, Willie was not comforted or convinced they were welcome. The era of Jim Crow was not so long ago, and he knew what happened to black folks who dared to cross into "whites only" territory.

In the end, Reatha and Judge convinced Willie to pass through the restaurant doors and sit at one of the linen-covered tables, but the older man's fears never truly abated. It was a sharp reminder that, even though black Americans had more rights in the late '60s than they had a couple decades earlier, systemic racism was embedded in the collective consciousness of the nation—and it still is.

★ ★ ★

The mid to late 1960s were a boiling point for the civil rights movement. The Senate had passed the Civil Rights Act, but many parts of the country were still set in their old, discriminatory ways. The same year little Jay King was born, activists took to the streets in Selma, Alabama, to fight for black voting rights through a series of nonviolent marches. Though the Fifteenth Amendment had granted black men the right to vote in 1870 and the Nineteenth Amendment had granted all women the right to vote in 1920, these rights were often not realized in practice.

Especially in the southern United States, polling places established a system of discriminatory obstacles to keep black voters from casting their ballots. Voters might be charged a poll tax (poor white voters were often exempt, while poor black voters rarely were) or asked to pass a literacy test.

The tests were timed and intentionally convoluted, and one incorrect answer would result in a failure. In Reatha's home state of Georgia, questions might include "If the Governor of Georgia dies, who exercises the executive power, and if both the Governor and the person who succeeds him die, who exercises the executive power?" or "What does the Constitution of Georgia provide regarding the suspension of the writ of Habeas Corpus?"[58]

In Louisiana, literacy tests were even more abstract, with a series of commands such as "Draw a triangle with a blackened circle that overlaps only its left corner," "Spell backwards, forwards," or "Print the word vote upside down, but in the correct order."[59]

Black voters were frustrated and tired of these prohibitive voting measures. They decided to act.

In Selma, one voting rights demonstration would become forever immortalized as "Bloody Sunday." On March 7, 1965, a group of several hundred protestors led by John Lewis and other SNCC organizers began marching in Selma with the intention of walking all the way to Montgomery to confront Governor George Wallace about voting restrictions, in addition to condemning the recent murder of civil rights protester Jimmie Lee Jackson. They didn't get far.

On the Edmund Pettus Bridge, stretching southward from Selma over the Alabama River, the protesters were met with militaristic resistance. Armed state troopers, accompanied by a contingent of white males (citizens who had conveniently been newly deputized that morning), attacked the protestors, beating them with nightsticks, trampling them with horses, and dousing them with tear gas. They injured dozens, and the event whipped the nation into a fury.

Fortunately, the protesters' sacrifices were not in vain. Five months later, Congress passed the Voting Rights Act, which prohibited literacy tests and authorized widespread federal oversight of voting practices.

---

58. "1958 Citizenship Test."
59. "State of Louisiana Literacy Test."

Though the Voting Rights Act did not entirely solve voter discrimination, it was an important step on the road to equality.

Some black activists, however, viewed federal legislation as an ineffective and inadequate way to secure equal rights. They saw, time and again, how it was trampled underfoot by staunch racists who would rather break the law than change their ways. The only way to incite real change, they believed, was to fight for it.

The Black Power movement emerged from this "fight for your rights" mentality, with activist Stokely Carmichael at its helm. The movement promoted racial pride, taking an active stance against racial oppression and severing ties with white America by becoming as self-sufficient as possible. Unlike the nonviolent protests arranged by SNCC and other activist groups, the Black Power movement did not shy away from violence as a means to an end.

Another group that diverged from passive resistance ideologies was the Black Panther Party, founded in 1966. Originally created to patrol neighborhoods and protect residents from malicious cops, the Black Panthers evolved into a political group with its own set of philosophies and tenets. Stokely Carmichael was also involved with the Black Panthers' efforts and played an active leadership role in the group.

Though Reatha preferred Martin Luther King Jr.'s or Roy Wilkins's brand of nonviolent resistance, she did not discount what the Black Power movement was trying to accomplish. She understood their frustration and their desire to be heard. To be respected. Even though she did not always agree with their tactics, she knew they had a place in the larger civil rights movement. They lit a fire under many who, up until then, had been complacent or too downtrodden to act.

★ ★ ★

Once again, civil rights activists set fires in the streets, and once again, Reatha matched their fires with her own in the chemistry lab.

Over the course of three years, she studied fluorine compounds for NASA and reported her findings every quarter. Her experiments yielded insights into the properties of these volatile substances and demonstrated how one could control them. One piece of equipment Reatha invented during her experimentation—a cooling coil that would help reduce the temperature of dangerously hot liquids—was of particular interest to NASA. The agency could use such a coil to temper the fluorine compounds in its fuel system, which, unabated, could reach catastrophically high temperatures and cause an explosion.

Reatha's work also resulted in three published papers: one on the heat of formation of oxygen difluoride and two on fluorine flame calorimetry (one of which focused on the heat of formation of chlorine trifluoride).

Engrossed as she was in her work, it was only after Reatha's multiyear testing concluded and the Apollo 11 rocket launched that she would reflect on how her project had contributed to the moon mission. Oxygen difluoride—along with similar compounds, such as hydrogen–fluorine, oxygen difluoride–hydrocarbon, and FLOX (mixtures of fluorine and oxygen)—has important propulsion properties. In other words, it has the potential to explode with such force that it can send a rocket weighing several million pounds[60] into space. Such a propellant could be a crucial component in the rocket's fuel system.

A 1965 report authored by the National Aeronautics and Space Council (a committee that fielded space policy matters) and delivered to Congress by President Johnson, describes efforts to study liquid propulsion systems—research with which Reatha was directly involved:

> "To cope with the high reactivity of fluorine and oxygen difluoride, effort was directed to developing adequate design criteria. Also, since the high combustion temperature produced by oxygen difluoride and diborane (about 8000°F) cannot be contained by current flight weight combustion chambers and nozzles, research on high temperature components was continued for a practical design approach which would permit further investigation of oxygen difluoride and diborane and similar high energy propellant combinations."[61]

In other words, the challenges associated with using oxygen difluoride were many, but scientists such as Reatha were working to mitigate

---

60. Apollo 11's Saturn V rocket weighed 6.2 million pounds, the equivalent of about four hundred elephants (NASA, "Rocket Park: Saturn V").
61. Johnson, "United States Aeronautics and Space Activities."

the potentially deadly effects of these volatile chemical compounds so they might be safely used in rocket ships. Reatha's aforementioned coiled tube, which helped cool high-temperature combustible liquid propellants and prevent explosions, was among the innovations that ultimately led to a successful, safe Apollo 11 mission.

Reatha's invention is a fitting metaphor for the role she would play in her later career. Whether working in academia, in community and philanthropic organizations, or on corporate boards, she has always been known for keeping a cool head and being a peacemaker. With her even-keeled, logic-based approach and her ability to build bridges between people with widely differing opinions, she has mediated many a volatile situation.

In the NBS lab, thankfully, volatility was reserved for chemicals, not people. This was a place governed by calculations and rationale. You set up your experiments. You ran them and took measurements. You recorded your findings. There was no place for guesswork or subjectivity.

For three years, working day in, day out in the calorimetry lab, Reatha focused on the tasks in front of her, barely sparing a thought for how they might fit into NASA's larger picture. Others, however, highlighted the value of her contributions. After she published her findings on oxygen difluoride, the US Department of Commerce awarded Reatha an Outstanding Performance Rating. The honor was accompanied by a $200 monetary prize, but one of the most valuable pieces of the award was the words of her supervisor, Dr. Armstrong.

In his justification statement to the Department of Commerce, Dr. Armstrong lauded Reatha's contributions to her area of study and described her investigation as "remarkable in its field for its completeness, and for the thoroughness with which all aspects of the problem were investigated. It showed an exceptionally good balance between the need to trace unknown factors affecting the accuracy of the experiments, and the need to obtain reasonably accurate data without delay." He went on to say that her work had "been characterized by attention to detail, careful planning, industrious prosecution of the experimental work, and a refusal to be daunted by the numerous problems that needed to be solved."[62] In other words, even though Dr. Reatha Clark King had been handed a momentous assignment with a tight timeline, she had

---

62. Armstrong et al., "Justification for Performance Rating."

risen to the occasion and worked quickly, accurately, and with precision. She deserved every accolade bestowed upon her.

Though Dr. Armstrong's statement brims with praise for his lead scientist and her accomplishments, Reatha is quick to point out the final sentence: "She has acted as a judge representing the American Chemical Society in a local high school science fair."[63] This line is meaningful to Reatha because it shows that Dr. Armstrong respected her not only as an accomplished scientist but as a human being and a contributing member of the community. He remembered how she volunteered to help at a local science fair *and* he thought it was representative enough of her personality to reveal this detail to the Department of Commerce. Reatha was pleased that he did.

Though she was not destined to stay at the NBS through the 1969 Apollo 11 launch, she followed the mission religiously, counting the days until Buzz Aldrin, Michael Collins, and Neil Armstrong would fly to the moon inside a vessel she had helped to propel.

On July 16, 1969, Reatha was terrified. What if something went wrong? What if, despite her careful calculations, an explosion ripped apart the craft and the astronauts lost their lives?

With clenched teeth and shaking hands, she watched on a little black-and-white television as the Saturn V rocket thrust the Apollo 11 spacecraft from its launchpad. They were off—the voyage to the moon had begun. Though seeing the launch gave her some measure of relief, Reatha's nerves were not truly steadied until the astronauts set foot on the lunar surface and Neil Armstrong delivered his famous line: "That's one small step for man, one giant leap for mankind."[64]

"It was pure joy," Reatha recalls. "I said, 'Oh thank you, God.'"

A year and four months earlier, Reatha had experienced another type of pure joy of a more personal nature. On March 8, 1968, she gave birth to her second son: Scott Clark King. He was a healthy baby who quickly developed a tenacious streak. In time, he would grow to resemble his father, with the same high cheekbones, russet complexion, oval face, and bright smile.

---

63. Armstrong et al., "Justification for Performance Rating."
64. Armstrong maintained that he was misquoted and that he actually said, "That's one small step for *a* man . . ." (Levs, "Neil Armstrong's 'Small Step for Man'").

When baby Scott made his appearance, Reatha had completed her NASA contract and was still working for the NBS, but she knew change was in the wind. Judge was wrapping up his doctoral work at Howard University and was in the midst of interviewing for jobs, including a promising teaching position at a New York City college. A move was inevitable. But before they worried themselves with house hunting and boxing up their belongings, they decided to pause for a moment to enjoy their brand-new baby boy. They decided to take their first major family vacation, to Disneyland.

Little Scott was only four weeks old, and Jay had just turned three, when the King family boarded an airplane bound for Los Angeles. Holding her little baby in her arms, with her husband and eldest son beside her, Reatha could not imagine being much happier than this.

Then, tragedy struck.

While still in the air, the pilot turned on the airplane's intercom and announced, voice quavering, that Dr. Martin Luther King Jr. had been shot.

The news hit Reatha straight in the gut. All the joy she had felt a moment earlier washed away; she grew nauseous and terrified and was on the verge of tears. The rest of the flight was long and tense. Reatha and Judge comforted each other and put on brave faces for their sons. Maybe he would pull through, they thought. Maybe the bullet wasn't fatal.

When the plane pulled into LAX airport, however, the pilot came on the intercom again and flipped away their remaining sliver of hope. "I am sorry to report," the pilot said, "that Dr. King is dead."

Though their vacation was ruined, it was perhaps for the best that Reatha and Judge were grieving thousands of miles away from the nation's capital. Violence and looting broke out, and their apartment on Fourteenth and Park was located at the epicenter of the destruction. Looters broke shop windows, stole merchandise, and set fires. The damage was so severe that the area never truly recovered. Today, the Columbia Heights neighborhood, though still diverse, has experienced waves of gentrification—expensive housing has pushed out longtime residents, and revitalization projects have attracted a new set of higher-income residents. The neighborhood is a faint echo of what Reatha knew in the 1960s.

Dr. Martin Luther King Jr.'s assassination shook the nation and signaled that the fight for civil rights and equality was far from over. People grieved in different ways, with some doubling down on Black Power ideals and pointing to Dr. King's murder as proof of the ineffectiveness of nonviolent tactics, while others committed to honoring Dr. King's legacy by continuing his nonviolent resistance. And there were those, of course, who were too shocked and heartbroken to know what to do or where to turn. Judge's mother fell into this category. Unsure of how to move past her horror and grief, Lafronza King packed a suitcase and headed to Washington, DC, where she slept on Judge and Reatha's couch for several weeks until the clouds lifted and she felt fortified enough to return to her life in Birmingham.

Amid the sadness and turmoil of 1968 (Robert Kennedy was assassinated just two months after Dr. King), life marched on for Reatha and Judge King. Judge accepted a professorship at Nassau Community College just outside New York City, the couple busied themselves with parenting their two young boys, and Reatha began wrapping up her work at the National Bureau of Standards in addition to exploring her career options in New York.

They didn't have much time to pause, to mourn. But, looking back, Reatha thinks about her role as a black professional in a predominantly white world and how it furthered and supported the work of the civil rights movement. No small amount of pressure rested on her shoulders as she showed up to work each morning, kept a level head and a sharp mind, and proved time and again to her white colleagues that she was qualified and capable. That she deserved her position. That she deserved a voice. All the while, she left a series of open doors in her wake—doors that women, black professionals, and, especially, black female professionals could pass through a tad more easily than she had.

During her hunt for a new job—a new career—in New York, Reatha was given the same advice time and again: consider looking into academia.

New York was packed with colleges and universities, nearly all of which had chemistry departments. And with the fairly flexible schedule of a professor, she could more easily tend to young Jay and Scott. Reatha was, of course, disappointed to leave her beloved laboratory and her distinguished career as a research chemist, but she took the advice she received to heart. She would consider academia.

★ ★ ★

July 16, 2019, marked the fiftieth anniversary of the US moon landing. Celebrations and news stories erupted across the nation, and suddenly people started remembering the name Reatha Clark King. She was interviewed by myriad news outlets and scientific organizations, including several video interviews for news stations based in Minnesota, which was by then her longtime home. The University of Chicago ran a multipage article about her background and contributions to the space race. The Adler Planetarium featured her in its online exhibition *Voices of Apollo* and hosted her as a guest of honor at its Moon Bash celebration.

Though over the course of her decades-long career, Reatha only worked at the NBS for five years and conducted research at the University of Chicago for another five, this part of her life captures the public's imagination and sends people's thoughts soaring beyond the clouds. Her era as a chemist blazed bright as a supernova before she moved on to other skies. What came next was not accompanied by the same glamour as NASA and the moon mission, but it was arguably just as important.

The next era in the saga of Dr. Reatha Clark King involved her quiet shift into academia and into a very different life of service. Instead of serving national interests in the lab, she would serve hundreds—*thousands*—of students, first in New York City, then in the Twin Cities of Minnesota. After helping three astronauts touch the surface of the moon, she would help a multitude of young people reach out and grasp their dreams. This legacy may have gone unnoticed by much of the nation, but for those whose lives she did touch—the many students and faculty whom she served—the depth of her impact was much more profound.

CHAPTER TEN

The City So Nice

"You may not control all the events that happen to you, but you can decide not to be reduced by them."

—Maya Angelou

When Reatha and her family migrated to Long Island in 1968, they found themselves in a place of transition and growth. The stretch of land east of downtown New York City was losing its innocence and gaining residents. In the 1950s, Nassau County, just east of NYC's parameters, was the fastest-growing county in the United States. In 1961, Suffolk County, elbowing against Nassau County's border and stretching to the eastern tip of Long Island, earned that title. With the influx of people came a variety of opinions, beliefs, and backgrounds. Construction boomed, and new retail stores, restaurants, places of worship, grade schools, and universities began popping up across the island. What had previously felt like the suburbs, or even the countryside, began to feel like an extension of the city (albeit much sleeker and more modern than the grand old brick buildings in the oldest parts of downtown New York). Potato farms morphed into ranch-style housing. Neighborhoods experienced population jumps of 200 or 300 percent in only a handful of years.[65]

In 1968, Long Island was already beginning to feel different from the 1964 Long Island that had hosted the New York World's Fair in Flushing Meadows, Queens. The World's Fair—teeming with fountains, halls of innovation, cheap trinkets, displays of cutting-edge technology,

---

65. Ruff, "Long Island in the 1960s."

and corporate sponsorship (Sinclair Oil's Dinoland! General Electric's Carousel of Progress! Ford's Magic Skyway!)—showed the world through a myopic, rosy lens. The emerging counterculture filled with "sex, drugs, and rock and roll" was nowhere to be found among the futuristic buildings and cheery, inoffensive music. The increasingly devastating war in Vietnam was stubbornly omitted from the convivial displays.

But by the time the decade tiptoed to its close, things were beginning to change on Long Island. Opposition to the war heightened, and the public was starting to vocalize its dissent. By December of 1968, 312 Long Island soldiers had perished in the war, making the conflict in Vietnam personal and close to home.

At the same time, the civil rights movement had reached a fever pitch, and Long Island residents (like Americans in many other parts of the country) were beginning to question longtime practices in home buying, banking, employment, and interracial friendships and marriages. Activists such as Lincoln Lynch kept civil rights issues at the forefront of Long Islanders' consciousness and claimed that there existed in the area "shameless evidence of undisguised discrimination."[66]

When Reatha, Judge, and their two young boys moved into their home in Hempstead, east of Queens on Long Island, the United States felt like a country far removed from the Coca-Cola–and–bubblegum Long Island of years past. The innocent façade had been replaced by an acute awareness of the Vietnam quagmire and social inequalities. In the upcoming election between Richard Nixon and Hubert Humphrey, the stakes seemed higher than ever.

Music and pop culture reflected the mood of the time, with James Brown declaring "I'm Black and I'm Proud," Bob Dylan singing that "The Times They Are a-Changin'," and Phil Ochs strumming his "Draft Dodger Rag." Otis Redding, meanwhile, took a more introspective approach to the turmoil with his "(Sittin' on) the Dock of the Bay."

Reatha and Judge, distracted by moving and wrangling two small children, sensed the tension of the era but would not face it directly until they started their new careers. In the meantime, they settled into their new neighborhood—a hamlet called Roosevelt, located about four miles south of Nassau Community College—and focused on Judge's new professorship and Reatha's job hunt. Reatha was the "trailing spouse"

---

66. Ruff, "Long Island in the 1960s."

this time, and she followed Judge to New York with the unquestioning faith that she would find gainful employment before long. As advised, she began setting her sights on academia.

Rumor had it the City University of New York (New York City's public university system, often shortened to CUNY) was always hiring. That might be a good place to start.

It wasn't long before Reatha's job hunt led her to York College. Founded only two years prior, York College was one of the newest members of the CUNY system, though, surprisingly, not the newest. Colleges were springing up like dandelions in ever-expanding New York, and CUNY alone established ten new colleges in just twelve years (from its official founding in 1961 to the establishment of the CUNY School of Medicine in 1973). Part of the rapid growth was spurred by the baby boomers' hunger for higher education, which required more and more schools to accommodate them. Additionally, colleges were opening their doors to an increasing number of women, racial and ethnic minorities, and lower-income students. The long-held domain of middle—and upper-class white men was diversifying more rapidly than ever. In 1960, the ratio of female to male students in four-year institutions was 37 percent. By 1976, that ratio had increased to 46 percent (a 24 percent increase). Colleges also increased their enrollment of black students from 13 percent in 1967 to nearly 23 percent in 1976.[67]

It was in this atmosphere of increased growth and inclusion that York College was born. In 1967, the college officially opened its doors— doors to classrooms it was renting from the Oakland Jewish Center in Bayside, Queens. During its inaugural year, fifty instructors taught a first-year class of 371 students in subjects ranging from calculus to English. After its first year, the college shifted about a mile to the north and began sharing real estate with Queensborough Community College (QCC). Hugged by a horseshoe of green, the college sat at the northeastern edge of Queens, where Little Neck Bay trickles into Alley Pond Park's 655-acre expanse of green grass and walking paths. Queensborough itself had only been established nine years prior and had joined the CUNY system in 1965.

While Queensborough offered two-year associate's degrees, York was designed for students on the four-year bachelor's degree track. With

---

67. Karen, "Politics of Class."

rapid-fire growth reminiscent of a particularly fertile rabbit colony, the school began acquiring faculty to teach its expanding course offerings. Almost everything at York was in short supply in those early days—funds, faculty, classrooms—but what the school really needed in those early years was science and math professors.

Dr. Lewis J. Bodi, Dean of York College's science division, was quick to accept Reatha's application and bring her in for an interview. Dr. Bodi, like Reatha's college advisor Dr. Kleppa, was a first-generation Norwegian man with a pleasant demeanor and an appetite for all things academic. Like Kleppa, Bodi cared more about Reatha's qualifications than her gender or race. He was impressed by her University of Chicago doctorate and the acclaimed research she had conducted at the prestigious National Bureau of Standards. With experienced scientists in short supply (a perennial issue in academia), Dr. Bodi jumped at the chance to usher her in for an interview.

During the interview, Reatha discussed her background and credentials with the quiet confidence and ease of someone well qualified for the job. She knew her way around the physical sciences—that much was clear—and it did not take Lewis Bodi long to determine she was capable, competent, and well suited to teach at York College. As the interview wound down, however, Reatha felt compelled to add one piece of unsolicited information. "By the way," she said, "I have a six-month-old baby at home."

Later, Dr. Bodi would jibe Reatha for her confession: "That wasn't the smartest thing to say, you know. But you were so open, and I was already determined to hire you."

And hire her he did. Dr. Bodi knew talent when he saw it, and he decided that Reatha, six-month-old child and all, was a risk worth taking.[68] She would begin her academic career as an associate professor, teaching three different chemistry classes to York's newest batch of students.

Once again employed, Reatha sat down with Judge to determine how to shape their lives in New York. As two busy parents with two

---

68. Many employers during this era considered female hires a "risk." As a paper published in the *Michigan Journal of Gender & Law* states, "Women's biological capacity to become pregnant has been the basis for the belief that women are unfit for employment in the public sphere" (Molnar, "'Has the Millennium Yet Dawned?'").

young children, it was clear they could not tackle all their responsibilities on their own. They found a reliable babysitter in Hempstead who was willing to watch the children while they taught at their respective colleges. The young professors would take turns dropping off the boys and picking them up, splitting their duties in a manner that reflected their egalitarian partnership.

One of the few times Reatha felt the weight of parenthood rest squarely on her shoulders was during Judge's flying days. From the moment he embarked on his first plane ride in his early twenties, Judge fell in love with the open skies. While still attending Howard University, he had begun taking flying lessons with the goal of obtaining his pilot's license. In New York, the lessons continued out of Roosevelt Field, and he became fixated on flying the requisite hours to obtain his license. While Judge soared around the northeastern United States, Reatha remained grounded, tethered to household and childcare duties. She did not, however, begrudge Judge his aviation passion. She knew how much he loved flying. She noticed the way his whole face lit up when he talked about airfoils and altimeters, tarmacs and transponders.

But she couldn't resist jabbing him every now and then about his aviation obsession. She called it his *hobby*—a term she knew he despised. It wasn't a hobby, he insisted. It was much more than that.

Judge's mother never understood her son's fixation on flying, and, frankly, it terrified her. She was vocal about her stance, but that did not stop her intrepid son. Once, after the King family had flown to Birmingham through particularly dense fog (they were "socked in," as aviators of that era used to say), Lafronza King approached her daughter-in-law and pointed to the nearby plane. "Reatha, how much can I give you to tear that thing up?!"

Judge's father, however, loved that his son was a budding aviator. For him, it was a source of pride and a bragging point. It was news worth spreading around his social circles and family. *Our Judge is a* pilot. *Can you imagine?*

Reatha's mother shared Napoleon King Sr.'s enthusiasm. Whenever Judge would fly down to Moultrie with Reatha and the boys, the plane became the talk of the town, with locals bunching around it to get a better look. Ola Mae reveled in the attention and took pride in her son-in-law's affluent hobby.

While Judge took to the skies, Reatha spread her wings within her newly launched career. In the classroom, she proved to be an empathetic instructor, paying close attention to her students' struggles and triumphs, but she also believed in assigning rigorous coursework and expected her students to rise to the occasion. Beginning as an associate professor, Reatha climbed her way through the system, becoming a full-fledged chemistry professor before stepping into the role of associate dean for the Division of Natural Sciences and Mathematics in 1970. After serving in that position for four years, she was selected to be the school's associate dean for academic affairs, a position she held from 1974 to 1977. Her precipitous assent through the ranks was unsurprising to anyone who knew her. Reatha never did anything halfway. She was eager to learn anything and everything about effective teaching and, later, effective leadership. The straight-A valedictorian from Moultrie High had become the thirtysomething pedagogue at York College.

When she began her role as an associate professor, the college leadership handed Reatha a textbook and the rough outline of a curriculum, and she did the rest. She went to education conferences and picked up teaching strategies. She studied the practices of fellow professors. She paid close attention to her students and responded to their needs. Though the learning curve was steep, Reatha was willing to put in the legwork. This was a different beast from the neat and tidy world of the NBS, she realized, and she was determined to figure out how to tame it.

But, as those in academia can attest, working as a professor is rarely as simple as showing up and teaching the material. Schools grow and change; leadership comes and goes. And, far too often, the faculty becomes embroiled in controversy.

Reatha glided into the CUNY educational system—a public college system whose constituent institutions date back to the mid-1800s—during an era of volatility and rapid growth. Demonstrations abounded against the Vietnam War, against institutionalized racism, and for the expansion of public policies that would level the playing field in colleges and workplaces. New York, with its tapestry of races, ethnicities, genders, and incomes, attempted to include a wider variety of students in its public college system through citywide initiatives and programs. Though some NYC colleges already boasted free tuition in the 1950s, CUNY decided to make free tuition a standard practice, starting in the 1964–65 school year. A year later, the city agreed to adopt an open admission plan (although it was not scheduled to be enforced until 1975), which would ensure that every graduate from a New York City high school could attend any CUNY college of their choosing, regardless of grades, achievements, or test scores.[69]

The open admission policy was a source of controversy. Some believed it would set a low academic bar for CUNY schools, while proponents of the plan argued that it would remove unfair systemic barriers that had made college enrollment difficult for minority students since the very founding of the first US colleges and universities. At York College, the official president, Dumont Kenny (former Queensborough Community College president), opposed the idea of open admissions. However, the school's *acting* president, David Newton, was a vocal proponent of the policy, saying that York College would "not be an ivory tower."[70] As one might imagine, this was a confusing time for the college, with a string of acting presidents (all with differing opinions and approaches) holding temporary power while Dumont Kenny governed from afar.

Despite resistance, the open admission policy passed. However, the rollout, to take place nearly a decade after the policy passed, was not coming quickly enough for the thousands of students who wanted access to higher education *now*. In 1969, widespread protests by mainly black and Puerto Rican activists put pressure on the government to adopt the policy much sooner. With support from Mayor John Lindsay, CUNY administrators sided with the protestors and decided to officially implement the open admission policy for its 1970–71 school year.[71]

Almost overnight, the student population exploded.

Enrollment in CUNY colleges nearly doubled over the next three years, skyrocketing from 19,959 in 1969 to 38,256 in 1972. Among those students, the number of black and Puerto Rican students nearly tripled (enrollment increased for black students from 16,529 to 44,031 and for Puerto Rican students from 4,723 to 13,563).[72] It was truly a momentous time for chronically underserved populations.

---

69. "Creation of CUNY."
70. Parmet, *Town and Gown*.
71. Schmidt et al., "History of Open Admissions."
72. Parmet, *Town and Gown*.

The York College student body ballooned from fewer than 400 in its 1967 class to over 2,000 students in 1970.[73] With York pupils elbowing for space among the 8,900 students of Queensborough Community College, classrooms became even more cramped, and communal spaces were pushed past capacity toward their bursting points. After York College had shared campus space with QCC for three years, it became clear that the younger school would soon have to leave the nest.

The decision to move York College to a permanent home had been made a couple years earlier, but now—with the average space per student reduced from 65 square feet in 1969 to just 48 square feet in 1970[74]—the situation felt desperate. Those who lived in the Queensborough neighborhood began complaining about congestion in the streets and students commandeering every inch of parking space. The cafeteria, designed to accommodate three hundred students, was now serving two *thousand*. York College even went as far as renting part of an old supermarket (and, later, a renovated former Montgomery Ward department store, a YMCA, a Roman Catholic church, and various other buildings in Jamaica, Queens) to accommodate the burgeoning student body. Innovative as these solutions were, they were all temporary fixes to satisfy the ever-growing student populace and its immediate need for more space.

Change was inevitable. But the school's transformation was no smooth and practiced caterpillar-to-butterfly tale. The battle to secure a site for the school was long, clamorous, and political. It was Reatha's first true test as a mediator and leader.

---

73. Parmet, *Town and Gown*.
74. Parmet, *Town and Gown*.

CHAPTER ELEVEN

Moving On Up

"You don't make progress by standing on the sidelines, whimpering and complaining. You make progress by implementing ideas."

—SHIRLEY CHISHOLM

In 1968, Reatha did not have a crystal ball. She couldn't have known how much tumult and anxiety and angst would blossom among York College's faculty members and students over the next few years. She couldn't have known she would be appointed to a leadership position and expected to wrangle her outspoken coworkers as they name-called and griped their way through faculty meetings. She couldn't have known the extent to which the protest culture and unrest sparked by the Vietnam War would spill over into the CUNY campus system and permeate both student and faculty psyches.

In 1968, she was too busy settling into her New York life, raising two little boys, and learning how to effectively run a classroom.

But two years blazed by. Jay celebrated his fifth birthday, Scott his second. Judge earned his pilot's license and was appointed assistant to the president at Nassau College, in addition to continuing to teach chemistry. The family sold their first New York home in the Roosevelt neighborhood and moved into a lovely house in Freeport, Long Island, with a big yard for the boys and a little garden for Judge.

Outside the relative harmony of the King household, the nation—and the world—looked downright chaotic. Though many Americans were already doubting the legitimacy of and approach to the Vietnam War, 1968 marked an important turning point in public sentiment. Major events such as the Tet Offensive, which began on January 31, and the My Lai Massacre, which took place on March 16, threw the brutality of war into stark relief. News reporters began expressing their distaste and doubts about the war, with respected journalist Walter Cronkite declaring that the United States was "mired in stalemate." A year later, *Life* magazine would take a none-too-subtle stance against the war by publishing the names and photographs of the 242 young soldiers who had died during a "routine week" in Vietnam.[75]

Before his tragic assassination, Dr. Martin Luther King Jr. had also weighed in on the war in Vietnam. In April 1967, he spoke at the Riverside Church in New York, calling for the "madness" to cease and saying, "I speak as an American to the leaders of my own nation. The great initiative in this war is ours. The initiative to stop it must be ours."[76]

Tensions among the public bled over into college campuses. Students were among the country's more active protestors and began forming antiwar groups such as the Students for a Democratic Society, attacking ROTC buildings, and burning draft cards. At City College (part of the CUNY system), nearly 150 students were arrested in November 1968 while protesting the draft. It was the largest mass arrest in the school's history. At Queens College (also part of CUNY), thirty-eight students were arrested on April 1, 1969, during a peaceful protest. They were shuffled off to jail on Rikers Island and locked away for fifteen days.[77]

Protests and student activism reached a boiling point on May 4, 1970, when the Ohio National Guard opened fire on unarmed students at Kent State University. Three days prior, some of the peaceful protests near the campus had turned violent, with both students and nonstudents setting fire to buildings, breaking windows, and looting. What started as a protest against the United States dropping bombs on Cambodia, a neutral country in the Vietnam War, had escalated into a riot.

On May 3, about one thousand National Guard soldiers were deployed to Kent State's campus. Some protesters treated the Guard's presence with hostility, taunting the soldiers and throwing rocks at

---

75. "Vietnam: One Week's Dead."
76. Zinn, *The People Speak.*
77. Asaro, "Campus Unrest Part I."

them. The soldiers reacted with disproportionate force and began breaking up crowds of protesters with tear gas and bayonets. On May 4, at a noontime rally, soldiers fired more tear gas before opening fire on the protesters with live ammunition. They killed four and wounded nine.

The shots reverberated around the nation and rang the loudest on college campuses. In New York, nearly a thousand protesters gathered in the downtown financial district on May 8 to hold an antiwar rally and memorial march for the murdered Kent State students. When they reached Federal Hall, the protesters were rushed by a mob of prowar construction workers and sympathizers who, through their labor union leadership, had orchestrated the attack. Police officers stood by as the construction workers beat the antiwar protesters with their hard hats, struck them with clubs, and kicked them with steel-toe boots. Seventy people were injured, many requiring hospitalization. The incident became known as the Hard Hat Riot.

Six days later, on May 14, fifty students were arrested in an antiwar protest on the campus of the Borough of Manhattan Community College (another member of the CUNY system) after they occupied several of the college's buildings. Following the incident, the president of the college, Dr. Murray Block, resigned.[78]

Looking back at these events fifty years later, Reatha sees the parallels between 1970 and 2020. She feels a similar tension and outrage. She understands the public's comparable violent reaction to authority and militant policing. In her Minneapolis home in May 2020, Reatha watched as her city burned and chaos reigned. The context of the unrest was different, with the public reacting to a white police officer suffocating a black man, George Floyd, under his knee, but the emotions and public outcry were the same. Aggressive policing had cost lives. And the public was not going to stand idly by and take it.

As with the unrest of the late 1960s and early 1970s, Reatha approaches the 2020 protests from multiple angles. She is a person of color and an advocate for the black community, but she has also worked closely with the Minneapolis Police Department as a philanthropist and founder of the Hawthorne Huddle, a North Minneapolis initiative that brings all members of the community (including police officers) together to improve public safety and well-being.

---

78. "College Head Here Quits after Strife."

In 1970, Reatha understood and empathized with student protesters who spoke out against the Vietnam War, demanded lower tuition fees, and called for college admissions reform, but she was also distressed by the students' general distaste for authority and how that tended to bleed over into college classrooms. Tension among students, faculty, and school leadership became palpable, and it was difficult to keep attention and order in the classroom and on campus.

Reatha also understood and supported the widespread antiwar sentiments, but she was appalled and saddened by the treatment of veterans. She came from a family of soldiers. Some of her relatives were stationed in Southeast Asia, trekking through the humid jungles and carrying out their duties as they had been ordered to do. They did not deserve to be snubbed or spit on. They were but tiny cogs in the great, groaning war machine.

Many activists—students and faculty alike—took a staunch black-and-white view of the war: you were either for it or against it. There was no room for discussion. Since there was little room for shades of gray when it came to the Vietnam War, Reatha decided to pick her battles, so to speak. One of her battles involved a decision closer to home: where would York College build its permanent campus?

★ ★ ★

In 1970, after she had proven her mettle as a chemistry professor (moving from an associate professor to a full professor in just one year), Dr. Reatha Clark King was appointed associate dean for natural sciences and mathematics. The appointment made history: she was the CUNY school system's first dean who was both a woman and a person of color.

She had already left an indelible mark on the school, at the tender age of thirty-two, and she did so while raising two young boys. The school's acting president, David Newton, remarked upon Reatha's meteoric rise after her appointment. Newton said in a press release published by York College, "In a relatively short period of time, [Dr. King] has achieved a unique record of accomplishment, both as a scholar and a teacher ... I am confident the limitless devotion and enthusiasm she has displayed as a member of the faculty will be even more evident in a capacity of leadership."[79]

Congratulations flooded in from across the country, recognizing the milestone Reatha had achieved as CUNY's first-ever black female dean. Clark College's director of alumni affairs wrote, "The Clark College faculty and staff are elated to learn of your well-earned appointment. You left Clark and have achieved outstanding recognition and many achievements that make your alma mater, your friends, and your professors very, very proud..."[80]

Reatha's high school principal, George Parker, wrote, "This is simply to say, 'Congratulations and best wishes.' I wish you would accept an invitation to come to us as a consultant next spring..."[81]

Reatha had punched yet another hole through the glass ceiling, and she had done it just two years after starting her teaching career. She did not, however, have time to revel in her accomplishments. With her new appointment came greater visibility, the imperative to develop a deeper understanding of the school's math and science disciplines (she learned more about geology than she'd ever imagined she would!), and a certain obligation to take a stand on matters concerning the school. She stepped into the role during a tricky time in both the school's and the nation's history. In a landscape rife with tension and little appetite for authority or order, Reatha tried to be the adult in the room.

Never before had she been immersed in such chaos and disrespect. Never before had she had to cope with fires outside of the laboratory.

At meetings to discuss the fate of York College, faculty would interrupt, talk over, or make rude comments to each other. On more than one occasion, Reatha was called an Uncle Tom by her fellow black or liberal white faculty members who perceived her as siding with "the establishment" on certain issues. Though she could usually shake off the jabs that flew around the room, that one stung. Reatha never felt that she acquiesced to anyone—she was simply weighing the options with the careful analysis of a scientist and making the decision she deemed best for all parties.

---

79. Acker, "Professor Reatha C. King Appointed."
80. Tucker, letter to Reatha Clark King.
81. Parker, letter to Reatha Clark King.

This was New York, and the person who called you a cruel epithet today could move on tomorrow and pretend it never happened. Even so, the echoes of those painful insults rattled around in her brain long after they were said, enduring even to this day.

In time, Reatha grew accustomed to the disorder of faculty meetings, which were as different from the order and methodology of the NBS as a stormy sea from a goldfish tank. She also took comfort in the fact that the college's fate had already been decided two years earlier, whether the squawking faculty liked it or not.

She and several like-minded colleagues had worked tirelessly to convince CUNY's Board of Higher Education to build the new school in inner-city Jamaica, in the heart of Queens. The area was in desperate need of a revitalization—it had been deteriorating for years as its middle-class occupants slowly leaked into surrounding suburbs, leaving behind poorer residents and taking their purchasing power elsewhere. In the late 1960s, inner Jamaica lived in the (literal) shadow of the massive Brooklyn-Manhattan Transit (BMT) elevated railway, and, according to one account, "abandoned dogs roamed an urban landscape of deserted buildings and gutted automobiles."[82] It was, as a story in the *New York Times* describes, "a bleak expanse of weeds, parking lots, gas stations and a towering Brooklyn Union gas tank."[83]

But rather than abandon the area to descend into further decay, advocates—including religious leaders, community activists, and New York mayor John Lindsay in addition to Reatha and certain other members of the York College faculty—pushed hard for CUNY to build York's permanent home in inner Jamaica. The director of the Office of Jamaica Planning and Development, G. Andrew Maguire, called York College a "keystone of the redevelopment of the Jamaica area"[84] and presented a comprehensive vision of how the school could revitalize the neighborhood and spur additional growth and improvements. In May of 1968, CUNY's board agreed to designate inner Jamaica, Queens, as the college's new home.

Though CUNY's leadership made its stance clear in 1968, plenty of York College faculty resisted the decision and refused to back down for

---

82. Parmet, *Town and Gown*.
83. Hevesi, "Milton Bassin Dies at 88."
84. Parmet, *Town and Gown*.

several long, raucous years. Many faculty members (including President Kenny) complained that the selected area was dirty and unsafe—an "urban blight." They proposed that the campus be built, instead, on the old Fort Totten Golf Course, which was located on a spit of land in north Queens where Long Island Sound spilled into Little Neck Bay. It was hard to ignore that this area, labeled "safer" and "cleaner" by its proponents, was also situated within the folds of a predominantly white neighborhood.

Despite the backlash against CUNY's decision to build the York College campus in Jamaica, the Board of Higher Education would not back down. This college was slated to be an urban renewal project. How could the school achieve any meaningful impact if it were located on the outskirts of urban life? How could it help uplift the community if the only thing in need of revitalization was the occasionally limp grass at Fort Totten's rolling greens?

Urban renewal projects, by their very nature, are breeding grounds for controversy and conflict. At their core, they aim to clear out dilapidated areas and redevelop the land to make it attractive and economically viable. While that goal is not inherently problematic and *can* lead to positive changes, too often "urban renewal" is synonymous with "black displacement." From the 1950s to the 1970s, when urban renewal was in its heyday, communities of color were literally bulldozed in disproportionate numbers (about two-thirds of displaced people were minorities[85]) to make way for highways, retail stores, office buildings, and housing.

Sometimes, these urban renewal sites were redeveloped with luxury apartments or expensive shopping centers—housing and entertainment for those with money to spare. Sometimes, no housing was built in these sites at all, forcing residents to permanently move and, perhaps, live farther away from their places of employment. Each urban renewal project was different and brought forth its own unique set of complications and controversies.

The York College site was no different. It enjoyed the support of Jamaica community members and activists... and the dissent and mistrust of others. It would clean up a severely depressed area,

---

85. Small, "Wastelands of Urban Renewal."

dominated by an automobile junkyard and a tangle of BMT train lines ... but it would also displace several residents and small businesses.

Reatha, however, believed in the power of the school to bring about positive change, and she was not alone. In Jamaica, "seventeen organizations led by Dr. C. O. Simpkins, chairman of the Jamaica Community Corporation, came together to bring York College to the Greater Jamaica area."[86] They were advocating for the school from the inside out. They had a stake in their community and viewed the school as a way to make higher education more accessible to the area's residents. As Dr. Simpkins expressed, "We feel the time has come for our people to gain an education ... as long as it is in our own backyard."[87]

So, with the community of Jamaica and CUNY's leadership at her back, Reatha pressed forward, determined to give Jamaica the kind of renewal it desired—the kind that was sustainable and benefited the community as a whole. Years later, after York College's first permanent building (a science building!) opened on the brand-new Jamaica campus, the *New York Times* reached out to Reatha for an interview. When asked about the school's relationship with the surrounding community, she said, "The community has been responsive to our needs. This gives us a chance to reciprocate.... I am optimistic about the impact that York College will have on the city."[88]

Although it's difficult to measure the impact of the school on its surrounding community, there is no denying it has had a positive effect on local communities of color. Today, about 90 percent of York College students belong to a minority group. According to the college's website, "The majority of our students are female, live in Queens, attend full-time, are under the age of 23, and live in a household with an income of $30,000 or less. Approximately one-third are first-generation-to-college students."[89]

These students share a kinship with Reatha Clark King. She understands their path intimately and knows how difficult it can be to walk it. Having helped develop and grow York College—a place where underdog students can thrive—is a point of pride for Reatha. In a nation where

---

86. Parmet, *Town and Gown*.
87. Parmet, *Town and Gown*.
88. Schumach, "Dean Stresses York's Citywide Role."
89. York College, "York College at a Glance."

many opportunities are only afforded to those with college educations, she understands the value of a college that thrusts open its doors and says, "Welcome. Welcome, no matter who you are."

★ ★ ★

At the end of the day, Reatha was happy to escape the tumult and tantrums she regularly encountered on campus. She enjoyed her family's new home in Freeport, situated in a pleasant neighborhood just down the street from the Long Island Rail Road station and only a few miles from Warren Methodist Church, which they attended every Sunday. To the south sat a series of marinas and waterside parks, overlooking the spray of islands and channels in Great South Bay.

Scott King describes the neighborhood as "all-American," with kids of all nationalities and backgrounds running around, playing games, and riding bikes.[90] It was a good place to settle for a time, a welcoming place. Judge joined the school board; Reatha volunteered at their new church.

Every time the King family moved, they prioritized finding a church above almost everything else. As it had been in their childhoods, the church was the center of Judge and Reatha's life. The church: that sanctuary for praying, singing boldly, and swaying. That gathering place for friends, with their smiling faces and arms that hugged and reached to the skies in praise. That shelter from outside turmoil and ingrained bigotry.

The family attended a string of Christian churches until they finally landed on Warren Methodist. Little Scott had guided the decision, saying, "I want to go to Johnny's church." The church Scott's friend attended was as good as any. In the end, *Johnny's* church became *their* church. This was where the boys, dressed in their Sunday best, would receive their first communion. It was where Judge would become Scoutmaster for the kids' Boy Scout troop (and Reatha would contribute by providing her famous meatballs at potlucks). It was where the Kings would enjoy the company of their second family until they left New York City and began the hunt for a new church once more.

---

90. Scott King, interview.

Outside of church, Reatha and her family found solace and joy in each other. Though both she and Judge worked long hours and dedicated time, energy, and attention to their occupations, they were also committed to their two boys—boys who, day by day, were growing into young men. Both Jay and Scott proved to be excellent students and, like their parents, thrived in the classroom.

Bright boys with boundless energy, they seemed to have a natural talent for whatever they chose to pursue. Jay picked up the violin at the age of eight and became something of a prodigy, rising head and shoulders above his violinist peers. He was also part of the school chess club and, with a knack for strategic thinking, quickly became a nearly undefeated champion. Scott, who was quite young when the family lived on Long Island, was initially more interested in sports than music or chess. Eventually, however, he would develop an interest in the guitar, which would later prompt him to pursue a degree in performance from Berklee College in Boston.

Reatha and Judge expected much from their sons, and Jay and Scott rose to the occasion. But at the end of the day, they were still kids. They roughhoused and played raucous outdoor games with scads of neighborhood friends. They biked up and down their neighborhood streets, played in the family's big backyard, and splashed around in their neighbor's pool on hot summer days. When Reatha had to work on the weekend, she would sometimes take Jay and Scott with her to her trailer office or one of the many York College buildings. The boys remember having free rein of the school—running around, exploring, hiding—while Reatha chipped away at whichever project was occupying her precious weekend hours.

Jay describes his childhood in New York as being "happy, safe, and clean."[91] Tucked inside relatively affluent neighborhoods with loving parents to support their endeavors, the King boys thrived.

Despite a few troubling incidents, many of the King family's days in Freeport and, later, nearby Rockville Centre were good ones. They were healthy, they were happy, and they had all the money they needed to pay their mortgage and grocery bills. But Reatha never forgot where she came from—all the poverty, the backbreaking labor, and the way her mother would coax a meal out of a few soup bones or a handful of

---

91. N. Judge King III, interview.

flour, salt, and a smear of cooking fat. She regularly mailed checks to her mother in Moultrie (as she'd done since her college days) and spoke with her on the phone, but her father . . . that was a different matter.

In his adopted home of Belle Glade, Florida, Willie B. Clark was as difficult to pin down as a gust of wind. He did not have consistent access to a telephone, and, without the means to read or write letters, he did not regularly send or receive mail. Reatha would go for long stretches without hearing from or about her father—only learning the occasional piece of news from his sisters—and she often wondered how he was doing in rural middle-south Florida, a place about as different as possible from New York City.

During a particularly punishing blizzard in the winter of 1969, while the King family was busy shoveling mounds of fresh snow off their driveway, Reatha received a rare update about her father. He had passed away.

"A heart attack," a cousin from South Georgia reported on the telephone. "It was over quickly."

Reatha's breath hitched and she steadied herself on the kitchen counter. He was so young—just a shade past fifty—and she had assumed he had plenty of time left on God's green earth. She knew diabetes and cardiac issues ran in the family, but fifty years old? How could this be? He hadn't even met Scott, his youngest grandson. And now it was too late.

Too late to see him one last time.

Too late to tell him how much he meant to her, how she respected his ingenuity and uncanny natural talent.

Too late for a final embrace.

Too late to say goodbye.

Reatha's sister Mamie arranged for Willie B.'s body to be transported from Belle Glade to Pavo. Determined to attend her father's funeral, Reatha fought her way through the chaos of JFK Airport in the thick of the heavy blizzard. Despite delays and grounded planes, she hopscotched her way from New York to Atlanta, to Albany, to home. To Pavo.

There, in his humble southern town, Willie B. Clark was laid to rest near the minuscule church he loved so dearly: Mount Zion. This was where he had spent many of his happiest hours, and now he would have permanent respite under the slim pine trees and green grass of the church's cemetery. He no longer had to stoop to pick cotton or slash sugarcane stalks. He no longer had to repair machinery for his boss. He no longer had to struggle to get by—to simply live.

Willie B. Clark was free.

CHAPTER TWELVE

On the Right Side of the Tracks

"Don't sit down and wait for the opportunities to come. Get up and make them."

—Madam C. J. Walker

Decades after her sons had grown and she had left the bustle of New York City, Reatha sat down for a quiet lunch with her grandson. Over plates of sushi rolls, he met her eyes across the table and asked, "Grandma, what do you like to do for fun?"

Rarely in her life had Reatha tripped over a question, but she was caught off guard by that one. For her, life meant learning and growing. It meant throwing your full self into an assignment and not surfacing for air until you understood its every twist and tendency, until you completed the work that had to be done. There wasn't time for hobbies. Spare moments were few, and Reatha's main respite was her Sunday mornings at church.

At the lunch table, Reatha smiled at her grandson and told him the truth. "NJ," she said, "I like to learn. And to think. That's my definition of fun."

When Reatha worked to develop York College—and, later, Metropolitan State University—she was required to do a fair share of both learning and thinking. She approached her endeavors with the dedication of an Olympic athlete, picking up new skill sets and strategies along the way and refusing to "just slide by."

As she navigated the dicey waters of settling York College into its permanent location, she also performed her deanship duties *and* ran the physical sciences and mathematics department. She had never done any of this kind of work before, but, true to form, she was game to learn.

Running a department came with a whole new set of challenges that Reatha hadn't encountered in the classroom. In her role as associate dean, she was now responsible for major decisions as well as the fates and futures of the science and math faculty. One of her most challenging tasks was determining whether or not to approve the department's tenure recommendations. If she chose to deny a professor's tenure request, that professor was no longer permitted to teach at the school. This was a pass-fail situation; there was no such thing as granting partial tenure.

As always, Reatha approached the job through a scientific lens. She would study the requests and consider whether the professor in question was sufficiently engaged in their research, whether they had published enough academic papers, and whether they had received any complaints from students regarding their teaching. Although her decisions were never personal, tenure denials were often met with ferocious backlash. Since the faculty was unionized, professors had the right to appeal Reatha's decisions. However, none of the appeals went anywhere. Her rationale for dismissal was always grounded in evidence and sound reasoning, and, in the end, the professor was inevitably let go.

Reatha did not enjoy making these tough decisions. People's livelihoods were on the line. Many of the faculty were young, with young families. A dismissal from York College could be devastating for their careers and their revenue streams.

But she grew into the role and learned as she went along. She absorbed as much information as she could from academic conferences and other department heads, and she stretched herself to learn skills that some considered superfluous, such as computer programming.

Reatha threw herself into the rapidly changing realm of computers with admirable foresight. She attended an IBM continuing education seminar (the only woman and only person of color in a group of thirty) and learned about both the hardware and the software of modern-day computers. She refreshed her knowledge of Fortran, a computer programming language she had briefly studied while working at the NBS. Her interest in computers would carry over to her work, as she advocated for including computer classes in the curriculum at both York College and Metropolitan State University.

Although Reatha continued to pursue lifelong learning and was passionate about bringing innovations to the classroom, much of her time was occupied by the ongoing battle to build York College a permanent home. As the '70s wore on, those efforts continued to run into all manner of twists and snags.

★ ★ ★

At the beginning of Reatha's deanship, Dumont Kenny (who had vehemently opposed locating York College in Jamaica, Queens) stepped down as York College's president, leaving a vacancy that would not be filled for almost a year. In his letter of resignation, Kenny stated that he found himself "disappointed in the rate of development of York College."[92] Perhaps the *rate* of development was slower than he would have liked, but it was no secret that the *direction* of development was his true hang-up.

Fortunately, the next president supported CUNY's decision to build the new campus in Jamaica. Milton G. Bassin, then president of New York City Community College, was elected by New York City's Board of Higher Education to lead York College on June 21, 1971. With Bassin in the driver's seat, plans to break ground on the new campus forged ahead.

During Mr. Bassin's two-decade-long presidency, $200 million was poured into York College's construction. It was a venture that limped along at a snail's pace, with many delays and hiccups. While the new campus project was still struggling to find its footing, the college remained split, with some classrooms and disciplines lingering on Queensborough's campus and others located throughout the surrounding Bayside and Jamaica neighborhoods, including the old five-story Montgomery Ward building (nicknamed Monkey Ward by some students and described in the student newspaper as being full of plaster, pink insulation, pillars in the middle of classrooms, and bare telephone cables and having an acute shortage of restrooms, which caused permanent lines to stretch

---

92. "Dumont Kenny Resigns."

down the hallways).[93] To move between the disparate buildings of the split campus, students relied on a shuttle bus or their own vehicles, and they struggled to find parking on the overcrowded streets. During these trying, uncertain early years of the school, both students and staff had to have a good deal of patience and flexibility as they studied and taught in crowded conditions and makeshift classrooms.

Construction on York's new campus began in December of 1971, just south of the Long Island Rail Road tracks. These strands of steel track bunched together and splintered apart as they cut their way, scar-like, through the belly of Queens. Archer Avenue and Jamaica Avenue lay north of the campus, parallel to the Long Island Rail Road tracks, and South Road (later Tuskegee Airmen Way) framed the south end of campus. If a person wandered too far west, they would bump into Van Wyck Expressway. Too far east, they'd land in Bricktown, named for its brick-clad row houses. This was a true urban area—the apartment buildings, shops, and pavement scarcely interrupted by a park or even a stretch of green. The fate of Ashmead Park, just east of York College, represents the extent of Jamaica's urbanization. The park began as a sprawling green space in the late nineteenth century, filled with flower gardens and a playground large enough to accommodate four hundred children. But the burgeoning population overtook the land, squeezing and pinching it until it was reduced to a mere 0.27-acre triangle of weeds surrounded by concrete.[94]

The first academic building slated for construction on the new campus was (much to Reatha's delight) the natural sciences building. However, the process wasn't nearly as simple as putting up the walls. The school ran into all manner of setbacks and turns as the financial crisis of the early '70s ramped up and New York City's government tightened its belt. Governor Nelson A. Rockefeller, alarmed by the state's $770 million budget gap in 1971, suggested ending free tuition for all city-operated colleges. He also announced his intention to close ten New York City colleges and slash the budgets of the others. In December of 1971, just as York College was preparing to build its first permanent structure, the school's $62.5 million master plan for the campus was denied.

---

93. Impellezerri, "At Last!"
94. Kadinsky, "York College-Ashmead Park, Jamaica."

Construction halted. The area was temporarily abandoned, leaving behind torn-up land, demolished buildings, and a community that had been uprooted and disturbed to make way for the new school.

Governor Rockefeller's actions twisted at Reatha's emotions. She had fought tooth and nail to bring York College into the Jamaica community, and now the hard-won construction project lacked the funds to proceed. The very survival of York College was called into question, but Reatha and her colleagues were prepared to continue their crusade for a permanent home for the school. They had already invested too much heart and soul in securing York's new campus to let it sink into the tar pits of bureaucracy.

Rockefeller's proposal to close schools and cut public education funding did not sit well with many New Yorkers. Activists organized in droves, vocalizing their distaste for the governor's money-saving tactics. There were other ways to reduce the budget gap, they argued, than slashing funding to vital institutions, such as CUNY colleges. Among the dissenters, York president Milton Bassin was one of the most vocal. He (and many others) saw Governor Rockefeller's actions as racially motivated and declared, "The door to college had been opened to poor blacks and Puerto Ricans. Now we're being forced to close the door."[95]

With pressure mounting to save CUNY schools and continue York College's construction, Governor Rockefeller eventually acquiesced. During the spring legislative session of 1972, the city's school budget was only minimally cut and free tuition was preserved. In August of the same year, after "months of 'Save York' fighting, begging, [and] organizing from Queens to Albany and back,"[96] the governor approved a revised version of York College's master plan. He cut the originally proposed square footage by 15 percent and eliminated plans for a dormitory and parking structure, but at least the temporarily stalled plan was sputtering to a start once more.

Construction resumed on the school's science building, and a new architecture firm was hired to draw up plans for the remaining buildings and campus facilities. However, the complications and snags continued. The campus site was tricky for traffic flow, and plans were made to add a new subway route, in addition to widening some streets

---

95. Parmet, *Town and Gown*.
96. "Master Plan Ok'd."

and straightening others. Although the plot of land encompassed fifty acres, the campus had to zigzag around cemeteries, a large gas tank, and several permanent institutions.[97] The cemeteries proved to be especially problematic.

Three cemeteries rested within the planned campus's perimeter: Prospect Cemetery, St. Monica's Cemetery, and the First Methodist Church of Jamaica Cemetery. By the early 1970s, these sanctuaries for the dead were largely neglected and seldom used, but their significance and symbolism remained. Of the three cemeteries, Prospect, founded in 1668, has the longest and most distinguished history. It counts among its residents Revolutionary War soldiers and members of Queens's founding families. Though York College had no intention of plowing over burial plots, it did have to figure out what to do about them. For a while, there was talk of moving the remains to a different plot of land, but that would have been expensive and impractical. In the end, the school preserved the cemeteries and built around them. They became green lakes in a concrete desert.

As the efforts to build the York College campus bumped along in fits and starts, Reatha divided her attention among myriad duties. Permanent campus or not, she had students to attend to and faculty to guide, and she wasn't about to let them fall through the cracks. This was an exciting time for the college, despite its lack of a permanent home. The faculty members were busy designing and growing their curriculum, attempting to distinguish York College from the other, more established CUNY schools.

Reatha took an active role in shaping the school's academic program. Many faculty members were transplants from other CUNY schools, especially Brooklyn College, and they brought with them preconceived ideas of how a school should operate and what it should offer. For most, that meant perpetuating a traditional curriculum filled with classic liberal arts courses. However, Reatha and other faculty members saw the flaws in this approach. The students of York College were not necessarily traditional students. They might not find a philosophy or English literature or world history course particularly useful.

That's not to say Reatha believed these types of courses were without merit; they simply did not necessarily appeal to many of York's students,

---

97. Zylber, "Campus to be Completed: 197?"

many of whom were first-generation college-goers and were specifically seeking practical courses that emphasized job training. Instead of filling the students' academic plates with theoretical knowledge, Reatha and other faculty (including President Bassin) pushed for the inclusion of utilitarian courses and majors that were relevant to the student body. These offerings would expand on the practical courses the school had already established, such as prelaw and social work focuses, and include fieldwork, business classes, and urban studies.

Determined to get the ball rolling on major curriculum changes, President Bassin decided to hold the First Annual York College Faculty Conference on Curriculum in April of 1973. One of the conference's main presenters was Dr. Reatha Clark King, who closed the event by making a strong case for career education. She took her place behind the lectern at the front of the conference room, looked over the crowd of faculty and administrators, and launched into a long and (unsurprisingly) well-researched presentation on the merits of a career-oriented curriculum. During the presentation, she asserted that career majors are "functional and practical in that they show students a definite purpose for their studies." She went on to say that such majors make students "feel employable" because they learn to master practical, career-focused skills, and they also give students "more careers to choose from."[98]

At the end of her talk, she presented her colleagues with a meticulous master plan, which outlined how to incorporate career-focused programs into York's curriculum.

Though some faculty applauded Reatha's proposal and fully supported York's trajectory to becoming a more career-focused school, resistance was fierce. Some faculty claimed that York College's reputation would be sullied, since it would become, in their eyes, a "four-year community college." Even though York College students were eager to enroll in practical courses that would apply to their future careers, many faculty members viewed career-oriented programs as inferior to a traditional liberal arts education, and nothing could sway them from that stance.

In the end, York College maintained its liberal arts core but added several career-related majors, especially in the healthcare arena. In 1973, with Reatha leading the charge, the school initiated several

---

98. Parmet, *Town and Gown*, 87.

undergraduate programs in medical technology, occupational therapy, and environmental health—all pioneering programs at the time. These programs were made possible by a grant from the US Department of Health, Education, and Welfare and were considered to be pilot programs "of national importance."[99]

In addition to the curriculum changes, York College opened its doors to the Jamaica community by beginning to offer continuing education classes to local residents. The college was endeavoring to hold up its end of the bargain with the community of inner Jamaica. The residents had been promised urban renewal, and, by God, York College would do its best to deliver.

★ ★ ★

In 1974, Dr. Reatha Clark King was promoted once more. Her new role would be the associate dean of academic affairs, and she would join the prestigious ranks of the precious few women of color who held, or had ever held, such a distinguished position in academia. What made the appointment even more remarkable was that York College was not a historically black college. It had started as a predominantly white school with a majority-white faculty. Racial tensions were a source of constant stress and discussion, especially since York's student body was becoming increasingly diverse.

With Reatha's new position came another shift in responsibilities. As dean of the science and math department, she had managed the department's personnel and resources in addition to developing and implementing an impressive nine degree programs, including chemistry, biology, physics, and computer science and programming. Now, her role would encompass a broader scope of responsibilities. She would begin to examine the whole college curriculum and determine which programs were best serving students, which programs should be placed on the chopping block, and which programs might be introduced.

As associate dean for academic affairs, Reatha collaborated with the college's departments to develop and strengthen the school's thirty baccalaureate-level degree programs in the liberal arts disciplines and allied health professions. Each new program had to be evaluated before

---

99. "Pioneering in Health Services."

it could receive accreditation from the Middle States Association, and Reatha worked tirelessly to ensure that they all would.

As she strategized, budgeted, collaborated, and innovated, Reatha kept the school's students at the center of her focus. She was committed to serving a diverse populace and never wavered from that goal. Among the programs she implemented were the Community Professional Program (for older students whose work or community experience could earn them college credit), the Extended Day Program (night classes for students who had to work or tend to their families during the day), and the CUNY Baccalaureate Program (for ambitious students designing their own programs of study).

During her three years in this role, the York College campus remained split. In February 1974, the college's new science building opened its doors, but the other structures still only occupied space on blueprints and in collective imaginations. The campus was always meant to be constructed in phases, but the timeline lagged more than initially anticipated.

Reatha's office was crammed into a trailer, parked on borrowed space on Queensborough's campus. The shuttle bus doggedly continued its route, running between Queensborough College, the newly completed science building, and various other York College buildings spread across Bayside and Jamaica. Reatha was in charge of managing York's Queensborough site, which occasionally included struggles with the shuttle bus passengers.

Whether out of boredom or amusement, high school students would occasionally hop on the York College shuttle bus and ride it around. They were often loud and irreverent—an unwelcome headache for the already stressed bus drivers who had to navigate their boxy vehicles down narrow, crowded streets. When the bus drivers were frustrated enough with the high school students, they would call Reatha. "Dean King," they would say, "we have a problem."

With a million and a half items on her to-do list, Dean King had better things to do than deal with miscreant high school students. But deal she did. She would leave her trailer office, trudge across the campus (more often than not in cold drizzle or downpour), and step onto the shuttle bus. Most of the time, the high school students were white and the driver black. Even in the mid-1970s, the black bus drivers felt uncomfortable giving orders to white teenagers. But not Reatha.

She didn't believe in creating a scene, but she did believe in speaking with clarity and confidence. She would look at the mischief-making students and say plainly, "Could you please leave the bus?"

Inevitably, they would.

Reatha's work during her last three years at York College came in all shapes and forms. The shuttle bus incidents were minor footnotes compared to the overarching issues the college faced in the form of budget cuts, faculty headbutting, and struggles to retain funding for a permanent campus, but they took time and energy (both of which were in short supply).

Such a young school demanded attention, and Reatha gave it. She helped develop the relatively blank canvas of York College into a colorful, vibrant fixture in the New York City public school system. But working so close to the canvas, it was sometimes difficult to see the big picture. Years later, after Reatha had shifted into a different role in a different state, she was invited back to York College to give a presentation. When she strolled onto the completed campus, she overflowed with pride and felt her whole self brighten and lift, as if she had swallowed the sun. The campus, with its tree-lined sitting areas, numerous art installations, and myriad academic buildings, had the cohesive, stately presence of a well-established school. It had the distinct feeling of a neighborhood fixture.

And then there was the surrounding neighborhood. This particular pocket of Jamaica, Queens, underwent a transformation that was nothing short of remarkable. During the 1970s, the New York City government invested hundreds of millions of dollars in Queens, and the Jamaica neighborhood specifically. New businesses opened their doors, crime rates dropped, and major organizations (like the New York Telephone Company and the Social Security Administration) began putting down roots in Jamaica. The new Archer Avenue subway line improved transportation by connecting South Jamaica with York College and Jamaica Center. The hulking Brooklyn Union Gas tank, holding 10.5 million cubic feet of natural gas in its belly, was dismantled—a clear symbol of the "tidying up" that was going on.

Though Reatha witnessed some of these transformations during her years at the college, many others occurred years later. In fact, major construction on York College's permanent campus did not take place until 1980, with the approval of Governor Hugh Carey. The school's Academic Core Building was not completed until 1986 (nearly a decade after Reatha left New York) and its Performing Arts Center and Health and Physical Education Building did not open until 1990. After the opening of the Academic Core Building, the *New York Times* published an article about the school, saying:

> "After 20 years of growing pains, York College of the City University of New York, a symbol of upward mobility for working-class students and a cornerstone of the hopes for redevelopment of Jamaica, Queens, finally has a permanent, $100 million home.
>
> What began its life on the campus of Queensborough Community College, a two-year school, and later moved to a vacant Jamaica department store is today a thriving four-year liberal-arts school of 4,300 students, continuing the City University's traditional mission of bringing higher education to New York's poor."[100]

★ ★ ★

In the mid-'70s, Reatha and her family made their third and final move in New York. From Freeport, they shifted three miles due west to the neighborhood of Rockville Centre. Their new house was slightly larger, their yard bigger. Judge began growing flowers, and his carefully curated garden became a neighborhood showcase.

But their beautiful, modern colonial home in their quiet corner of Long Island was not always the refuge the Kings had hoped it would be. One sunny summer day, Judge took a break from digging around in his prized flower garden to step back and admire his work. It was mid-August, and the hyssops and purple coneflowers were in full bloom. The garden was the first thing any visitor to the Kings' house would see—an inviting splash of green fecundity—and Judge was immensely proud of

---

100. James, "York College in Queens."

it. He was standing in front of the house, hands on hips, when a police car crawled through the neighborhood.

The car rolled to a stop, and a patrolman hung his head out the window. "What are you doing in this neighborhood?" he sniped. "Show me your ID."

Outraged, humiliated, and too stubborn to comply, Judge refused.

The patrolman kept pestering. "Show me your ID. Now."

Again, Judge refused.

The commotion caught the attention of the Kings' neighbors. A circle began forming around the front yard and the police car. Neighbors began calling out, "Leave him alone, will you! He's not doing anything."

Still, the policeman persisted.

Reatha, who had been cooking dinner in the kitchen, heard the hubbub and came rushing outside. The patrolman didn't see her emerge from the house, and a neighbor pulled her aside and said, "Don't let on that you live here. It doesn't matter. That cop has no right to do this."

Eventually, one of Judge and Reatha's friends—a man named Dr. Martin, who lived down the street—barged into the gathering crowd and said, "For God's sake, the man owns the house! He lives here!"

When the officer discovered that this was, indeed, Judge and Reatha's house, he flushed pink and backed down. He muttered an apology and sped away, leaving in his wake a throng of angry neighbors, a thoroughly shaken Reatha, and an outraged and humiliated Judge. If their elegant home, their affluent neighborhood, and their own yard were not safe from police bias and scrutiny, what was? Where could their boys play, if not their front yard? Where could Judge garden in peace?

This was just one of many racially charged incidents in the lives of Reatha and Judge King. They had been badgered by police officers before (with one officer looking at Judge's driver's license and saying, "You're not related to that Martin Luther King fellow, are you?"), and they would be badgered in the future. In truth, the incident in front of their Rockville Centre home could have ended much worse than it did. To challenge a police officer as a person of color means gambling with your safety, and sometimes your life.

Two decades into the twenty-first century, brutal policing is as problematic and pervasive as it was in the 1970s. Each year, a disproportionate number of black men and women are assaulted or killed by police. Between 2015 and May 2021, nearly two and a half times as many black people were victims of fatal police shootings than white people.[101] During the course of their lifetimes, black men have a one in one thousand chance of being killed by a police officer—a touch under three times the rate of white men, despite making up a much smaller portion of the population.[102]

In the past decade, news headlines have overflowed with the names of black victims of overly aggressive policing. In 2012, Trayvon Martin was shot and killed while walking home from a 7-Eleven after purchasing a bag of Skittles and a can of Arizona watermelon fruit juice cocktail. In 2019, Atatiana Jefferson was gunned down while playing video games with her nephew. In 2020, Breonna Taylor was murdered by police in her home.

In the mid-1970s, Judge avoided a similar fate. He wasn't killed, but he was assaulted while gardening. He was made to feel unsafe on his own plot of land. After that heart-twisting, anger-bubbling day, Reatha and Judge pressed on, but they never forgot.

This kind of blatant discrimination permeated neighborhoods and workplaces, including public universities and colleges. As Reatha fought for academic programs that would serve the needs of York College's diverse array of students, Judge fought his own battles for equality. At Nassau College, he joined forces with two other black associate professors to unveil the barefaced biases they regularly encountered in the school, particularly from the personnel and budget committee—which, they claimed, continually blocked their promotion to full professors. Rather, promotions were regularly awarded to less qualified white colleagues by the all-white personnel board. "We have been ignored and excluded in practically all phases of the department," Judge King said in a *Newsday* article. "We are caught in a vacuum with nowhere to go."[103]

Though the college leadership was quick to write off the men's accusations as stemming from "personality clashes" and poor job performance rather than bias, Judge and his colleagues held firm. In a letter of grievances to the college's board of trustees, they outlined several examples of racial discrimination in the chemistry department, including "no

---

101. Statista, "Rate of Fatal Police Shootings."
102. Edwards et al., "Risk of Being Killed."
103. Alexander, "3 Blacks Accuse."

black has ever been recommended for promotion by the departmental committee" and "no black was ever elected to any committee position in the department."[104]

Though Judge King would end up leaving Nassau College before witnessing much real progress toward racial equity, he started a dialogue and forced the school to confront some uncomfortable truths regarding imbedded biases. Today, Nassau College looks a lot different than it did when Judge was a faculty member. Its faculty is much more diverse, and its current president is a person of color. It's difficult to measure how effective the efforts of Judge and his colleagues were in creating change, but one thing is certain: it takes a persistent chorus of voices to topple Jericho-stubborn walls.

★ ★ ★

Over the next three years, Reatha pressed on with her work as associate dean of academic affairs. She continued to mold the college's nontraditional curriculum. She served on a number of committees, including the Advisory Committee to the York College Center for Urban and Community Affairs and the college's Committee on Afro-American and Hispanic Studies. She continued to coordinate between the college's departments and introduce innovative program ideas that were relevant to York College's students.

When she wasn't working on York College matters, Reatha was often in Queens and surrounding communities, speaking at high schools and elementary schools about higher education opportunities. Others took notice of her consistent involvement in community relations, and she was awarded the Builder of Brotherhood Award in 1976.

Though she enjoyed academia and the profound impact she could make on young lives, Reatha was not fond of the behind-the-scenes politics that sometimes occurred and the occasional tension between faculty members. She wondered, at times, whether she would be better suited to business than academia. She admired the efficiency and growth mentality of the corporate world, and she couldn't help but be impressed by the businesspeople with whom she interacted.

---

104. Alexander, "3 Blacks Accuse."

As associate dean of academic affairs, she sometimes met with businesspeople in her office—those selling textbooks or classroom materials—and was always taken with the way they carried themselves and their polished appearances ("Always so dressed up and dapper!"). Not only that, the decorum and articulateness of the salespeople reminded Reatha of the professionalism of the National Bureau of Standards and made her sorely miss that atmosphere, steeped in civility and class.

When she expressed her admiration of these sales professionals to Judge, he chided her, saying, "Reatha, you are so naïve. *Of course* those people are eloquent, well dressed, and polite. They're trying to *sell* you something!"

Unperturbed by Judge's teasing, Reatha couldn't stop thinking about this other world—the businesses that kept America's name relevant in global markets, that kept the nation chugging forward. This arena was completely foreign to her, and it captivated her inner scientist's curiosity. It was also practical, she reasoned, to develop a deeper understanding of business. Such knowledge could help her become a better dean by allowing her to view academia through a more enterprising lens.

After some deliberation, Reatha made up her mind: she would pursue a master of business administration degree.

The timing was right. Faculty who had worked at York College for seven years or more qualified for a sabbatical, and Reatha had crossed the seven-year mark a year earlier.

However, she worried about broaching the topic with President Bassin and the York College faculty. Obtaining her MBA was not, after all, a strictly academic pursuit. In many ways, it provided an exit from York College and from academia in general. But the college leadership supported her decision, and Reatha began exploring her options. Naturally, she started with the best program in the region: Harvard Business School.

Harvard piqued Reatha's interest because it offered a rigorous and highly acclaimed yearlong MBA program. She arranged to meet with a representative of the school and made the two-hundred-mile journey to Massachusetts by train.

After a long morning bumping along in a railroad car, Reatha found herself on the shady lawns of Harvard's campus. She made her way to the office of her Harvard Business School contact, where she was ushered into a plush chair and fell into conversation. Immediately, the representative took a liking to Reatha and was impressed by her background and credentials. However, as much as he wanted Reatha to enroll at Harvard, he understood how difficult her commute would be, especially with an eleven-year-old and an eight-year-old at home.

At one point, the rep paused and said, "You know, Reatha, you have a top business school right in your own backyard."

He was referring to Columbia Business School.

Up until that point, Reatha had not seriously considered Columbia, but now she began to see the logic in opting for a program closer to home. Besides, the Harvard rep was right: Columbia did have a top-notch business program, and a degree from this institution was nothing to sniff at.

The more she thought about it, the more Columbia Business School appealed to her. The Long Island Rail Road ran within walking distance of her house, and she could easily hop on a train and ride straight to the school's doorstep. Instead of covering a couple hundred miles (one way!) to reach Harvard, she would only have to travel thirty miles to downtown New York, just northwest of Central Park. For the working mother of two boys who were not quite old enough to care for themselves, the short commute would be a godsend.

After deciding on Columbia, Reatha began to figure out how to pay for the not-insubstantial tuition. She looked to the Rockefeller Foundation, which happened to sponsor a fellowship that was, as Reatha describes it, "made for me": it was designed to cover tuition for a black professor seeking their MBA degree. Reatha applied for, and was granted, the fellowship. It would cover her entire tuition.

In the fall of 1976, as the New York days began to grow shorter and chillier and York College students prepared to go back to their (still geographically scattered) classes, Reatha began her first business courses at Columbia Business School. Over the next school year and a quarter, she would immerse herself in her studies, working her way through a twenty-course curriculum. Ever the perfectionist, Reatha maintained a near-perfect grade point average, but, never one to brag, she describes her performance by saying, "I did pretty well."

Doing "pretty well" involved plenty of hard work and heart from Reatha and certain sacrifices by her family. This was no vacation, and she had to set aside time to study and attend classes. Judge supported her as she immersed herself in her courses and completed final papers and tests. Reatha had decided to emphasize finance and management of organizations, and she tackled her work with characteristic diligence, dedication, and top-of-her-class performance.

Though Reatha began her MBA work to open new doors and broaden her opportunities, she wasn't sure what she would do once she tossed her graduation cap in the air and claimed her diploma. As it turned out, Reatha's future was waiting in the wings, ready to snap her up and carry her into the next chapter of her life.

Toward the end of her coursework at Columbia, a fledgling university in the upper Midwest began searching for a new president to help it take root, grow, and define itself. The ideal candidate would have a background in developing a new college or university, a deep understanding of pedagogy and curriculum development, and experience working with a diverse population.

In short, this budding university was looking for Dr. Reatha Clark King.

CHAPTER THIRTEEN

The School without Walls

*"Just because it's a unique perspective,
doesn't mean it can't offer something universal."*

—Lynn Nottage

Reatha's life changed with a letter.

In spring 1977, she was busy with MBA classes and homework, essay tests and presentations. Her appetite for learning was only whetted by each new subject she explored—financial management, economic studies, business leadership, ethics. She sailed through each subject, aced her tests, and inched ever closer to earning her degree. If everything went as planned, she would have a diploma in hand by summer's end.

With life revolving around her studies, her family, and her commitments to church and community, Reatha didn't have the time or headspace to think about much else. She hardly noticed the release of the Eagles' enduring hit song "Hotel California" or the bouncing disco music by ABBA and the Bee Gees that flooded the airwaves. She scarcely took note of *Star Wars* making its big-screen debut or *Rocky* winning best picture at the Academy Awards, with Sylvester Stallone as lead actor. Nor did she care much about the garish styles of the late '70s, with their fringes, shiny nylon, bell-bottomed jeans, and boxy moon boots. Her hairstyle would loosen to a neatly trimmed natural afro, and she would don a pair of oversized glasses, but little else would change.

Style and pop culture sat at the bottom of Reatha's priority list. She kept her focus trained on her classes and marched forward. That coming fall, she planned to resume her deanship at York College, and she had plenty to do in the meantime. So, when she received a letter from the American Council on Education (ACE) asking her to consider a new position in a new state, Reatha was caught off guard. This was not part of her carefully crafted plan.

Her two closest connections on the American Council on Education (and the ones who had facilitated sending her the letter) were Emily Taylor and Donna Shavlik. Taylor was then the director of ACE's Office of Women in Higher Education, and Shavlik would later succeed her in that position. These two women were fierce advocates of diversity in higher education and were vocal in their admiration for the glass-ceiling-shattering dean. Reatha describes them as go-getter feminists—activists who were ardent and passionate about securing women's place in the upper echelons of the traditionally male-dominated leadership in colleges and universities.

Earlier that year, Taylor and Shavlik had cofounded the National Identification Program (today known as the ACE Women's Network) with the goal of placing more women in higher education leadership positions. In the 1970s, the vast majority of leadership positions in higher education were filled by men, and they were determined to change that. Since NIP was so new, the cofounders were eager to establish the validity of their program by coaxing a trusted female leader to apply for an open leadership position.

Reatha would become their Exhibit A.

The world of higher education is smaller than one might think, and Reatha had crossed paths with Emily Taylor and Donna Shavlik on more than one occasion. They would come to New York and hold seminars to prepare promising female educators for leadership positions in higher education, training them on everything from finance to ethics to the role of university trustees. For them, Reatha—with her distinguished background as a chemist, her role as associate dean of academic affairs, and her reputation as a changemaker and trailblazer—was a shining example of what women could become in higher education if they were only given half a chance.

Metropolitan State University, an institution that had opened its doors just six years prior, was seeking a new president, and Reatha, Taylor and Shavlik decided, was the precise candidate for the job.

Spread throughout various locations in Saint Paul and Minneapolis, Minnesota, with a student body that comprised mostly nontraditional students, the university was reminiscent of York College. From its very founding, Metropolitan State University (which had been called Minnesota Metropolitan State College until 1976 and was also known as Metro State or, rarely, MSU) embraced a radical new structure that eschewed traditional curricula, classrooms, tenured faculty, and even letter grades. With its first president, Dr. David E. Sweet, leading the charge, it had dared to explore a new way of learning—all for the sake of catering to a student body largely composed of older students who were often working full-time and tending to families.

President Sweet resigned from Metro State on January 20, 1977, to accept a presidential position at Rhode Island College. After his departure, the school had trouble finding its footing and was in dire need of strong leadership to shore up both its dicey finances and its reputation. When Emily Taylor and Donna Shavlik noticed the vacant presidential seat advertised in higher education journals, they sensed an opportunity to disrupt the academic-leadership boys' club with a female president, specifically Dr. Reatha Clark King.

Reatha read the letter from the American Council on Education. Read it again. ACE wanted to nominate her for the presidency position at Metropolitan State University. Would she be interested?

Thoughts spiraling in a dozen different directions, Reatha padded into the kitchen and sat down next to Judge—her confidant, her dearest friend. She showed him the letter and relayed what it contained. "What should I do?" she asked.

Judge did not hesitate for a moment. "You should go ahead and apply," he said.

"What if I get it?" Reatha asked.

"Well," Judge said with a shrug, "we'll just move."

In that moment, the piece of paper in Reatha's hand spoke of a remote possibility—the seed of an opportunity that might or might not take root. It was no secret that leadership in the higher education system in the United States skewed heavily male, with over 90 percent of institutions employing male presidents.[105]

---

105. Klotz, "Journey to the Top."

Even less common were female presidents of color. At the time, one could count the number of black female presidents of accredited colleges and universities on a single hand... and still have fingers left over. There was Mattie Cook of Malcolm-King: Harlem College Extension, who had helped found the school in 1968 on a shoestring budget and a dream (the first class consisted of thirteen students and attended for free). And there was Mable Parker McLean, president of the historically black Barber-Scotia College, who was selected as acting president in 1974 and then awarded a permanent position in 1975.[106]

But a black female president of a school that was *not* historically black? *That* was simply unheard of.

The night after she received the letter, Reatha retreated to her upstairs office and pondered her decision. If the impossible happened and she were awarded the position, she would step into a role with unprecedented responsibility. All eyes would be watching, and she would have to work hard (twice as hard as any president who fit "traditional" demographics) to prove her worth. Not to mention she would have to uproot the boys and Judge, separate them from the lives they had established in New York, and transplant them in the upper Midwest. In Minnesota.

Minnesota. Reatha knew little about the nation's thirty-second state. She had only visited Minnesota on one occasion—when she had accompanied Judge to a conference—and her main impression of the state was that the people were friendly and it was exceedingly clean. She recalled former New York City mayor John Lindsay joking about Minnesota after returning from a trip there, saying that he "didn't trust air he couldn't see."

Beyond her surface-level impressions of the state, Reatha only knew Minnesota by its reputation: this was the land of liberal vice presidents. Minnesota senator Hubert H. Humphrey had served as the nation's VP from 1965 to 1969 and was an influential liberal leader, a stalwart ally of the civil rights movement, a proponent of nuclear disarmament, and a supporter of socially minded legislation. Walter Mondale was a Minnesota senator from 1964 to 1976 before stepping into the role of vice president the same year Reatha was considering applying

---

106. Jackson and Harris, "African American Female College and University Presidents."

for the presidency at Metro State. Mondale was more of a centrist than Humphrey but still had predominantly liberal views. He is known for supporting the civil rights movement and advocating for gender equity—when he ran for president in 1984, his running mate was the first female vice presidential candidate, Geraldine A. Ferraro. Reatha admired both Humphrey and Mondale and assumed that their home state would reflect their values.

In the end, despite the upheaval her family might experience, she decided to apply for the position. In very little time, she received a positive reply: the Minnesota State College Board had reviewed her application and wished to invite her to a first-round interview in Saint Paul. She was going back to the land of clean air and noteworthy politicians.

Before her interview, Reatha did her homework. She began reading up on the university, its history, and its tenets. What she found fascinated her.

★ ★ ★

In the spring of 1971, Minnesota was woefully unprepared. That, at least, is what the Citizens League claimed in its forty-two-page report entitled "An Urban College: New Kinds of 'Students' on a New Kind of 'Campus.'"[107] The Citizens League drew several conclusions, including that the state did not have the infrastructure necessary to accommodate the inevitable influx of nontraditional students who were beginning to enroll in higher education programs.

The report was the result of months of research, committee meetings, and interviews. The thirty-member board, comprised of community members from all walks of life, from physicians to so-called housewives, had been assigned to "review the magnitude of the growing demands for the third and fourth year of college education for students in the Twin Cities metropolitan area, the adequacy of existing plans to handle this demand, and make recommendations on how to meet the demand."[108] In other words, politicians and academics concerned with Minnesota's higher education wanted to know whether the state was

---

107. Saeks et al., "An Urban College."
108. Saeks et al., "An Urban College."

adequately serving older students (it was not), and the Citizens League was tasked with organizing the investigation.

Founded in 1952 and still in existence today, the Citizens League is an independent, nonpartisan organization in Minnesota that specializes in conducting research and making evidence-based recommendations for government planning, education, parks, and more. In 1971, Minnesota (and the United States in general) was beginning to see signs of an anemic economy, accompanied by rising unemployment and runaway inflation. After two and a half decades of economic expansion after World War II, the nation was finally slipping toward a recession. Many believed that one of the ways to combat the new state of affairs was to expand education opportunities and put people to work in a new set of jobs.

Minnesota State System Chancellor Mitau proclaimed, "As we look ahead in the mid-1970s, there is a new reality which both education and this country must confront. While society is adjusting for the first time in history to what may become a decreasing standard of living, education must re-examine and rediscover its role in such a society." He went on to assert that "higher education has a significant but unfulfilled role to play in solving the problems of society."[109]

The time was ripe for an educational revolution.

The Citizens League underscored the need for an overhaul of the state's higher education system by calling for unconventional solutions to the problems it had identified (the main one being the state's need to accommodate an increasing number of students—especially older, nontraditional students—who wished to participate in higher education). It boldly declared that traditional education patterns would not be sufficient and that new approaches were necessary.

A new type of school was needed, and the Citizens League had myriad ideas for developing such an institution. Its recommendations included offering classes on nights and weekends for those students who worked full-time or had families, providing career-oriented programs, centering its faculty on teaching instead of research, and using existing buildings instead of establishing a new campus. "We must strike from our minds," the report reads, "our common conceptions of a college

---

109. Mitau et al., *1973–75 Biennial Report*.

campus, such as tree-lined walkways, student unions, lecture halls, football games, fraternity houses, and the like."[110]

The Citizens League also underscored the urgency of the matter. Change needed to happen, and it needed to happen *now*. In the 1971 legislative session.

Fortunately, Minnesota legislators were listening. The Minnesota State College Board was listening. The news media were listening.

Though the idea of creating a nontraditional school aimed toward older students was met with its fair share of skeptics, a dedicated cadre of supporters began to form, enthusiastically backing the Citizens League's recommendations. Among them were Minnesota State College System Chancellor G. Theodore Mitau, Vice Chancellor Dr. David Sweet, and several Minnesota state representatives and senators.

Every supporter in the state legislature was white and male. This fact alone is not unusual—politics and academia were dominated by light-skinned men in 1971—but what *is* unusual is the outcome of their efforts: a state-run institution that would become the most racially diverse university in the state of Minnesota.[111]

The hidden story behind the enthusiasm and support for a new kind of higher education program involves women. Though the public-facing politicians and academic leaders who supported the program were male, they were often influenced by the women in their lives— the wives, mothers, sisters, and daughters who could potentially benefit from a nontraditional program. For instance, Mitau's wife, Charlotte Mitau-Price, was a homemaker who had never had the opportunity to go to college. As their son explained years later, "I believe that my father had my mother in mind as he developed the concept of a college without walls. My mother was a very accomplished person ... she had great political and leadership skills, but not her degree. [She] was exactly the type of student that my father envisioned for this new college."[112]

On a societal level, a new push for equal treatment and representation was stemming from the women's liberation movement (WLM). More and more women were declaring themselves feminists and challenging the patriarchal status quo, and their collective voice was becoming

---

110. Saeks et al., "An Urban College."
111. Johnson and Kolmar, "10 Most Diverse Colleges."
112. Lofquist, *Metropolitan State University Buzz*.

difficult to ignore. In 1970 in Minnesota, feminists had highlighted the fiftieth anniversary of the passage of the Nineteenth Amendment (granting women the right to vote) by holding protests and workshops and adorning Minneapolis's iconic Foshay Tower with an enormous banner reading "Women Unite!" That same year, the "gentlemen only" Minneapolis Club opened its doors to women for the first time.

The movement was gaining momentum and visibility, and that undoubtedly influenced the politicians who were deciding whether or not to support a school that would be well suited to working mothers and women who had put their educations on hold. As is often the case, some politicians embraced the WLM and supported its efforts, while others resisted.

Though the Citizens League and its allies made compelling arguments for establishing a college for upper-level nontraditional students, it was easy to dismiss the idea as too idealistic, too "out there," and too lax in its proposed structure. It was, in short, easy to oppose this unconventional school, and many did.

In April 1971, the Minnesota Legislature convened and began discussing HF No. 3137, which outlined the budget for an array of educational operations and activities, including the planning of "a Metropolitan State College Center."[113]

Tucked away in Section 3, Subdivision 2 of HF 3137 was the clause pertaining to Metropolitan State College. After the senate had hashed and rehashed the bill, the final wording read that funds would be allocated to the state college board for "planning and operating an educational program for a state college center." The center would not have a central campus but would acquire facilities "by gift or lease." The purpose of the new college would be to "serve primarily the needs of the graduates of the state junior colleges and the area vocational-technical schools. Such programs should also include curricula for retraining adults to meet the technological demands of the changing economy."[114]

Backing the initiative to plan and commence operations of a new, innovative state school was a group of politicians who stalwartly supported Chancellor Mitau and the Citizens League's recommendations: Representative Del Anderson, Senator Jack Davies, Representative

---

113. "Chapter No. 966—H.F. No. 3137."
114. Lofquist, *Metropolitan State University Buzz*.

George Humphrey, Senator William Kirchner, Representative Verne Long, US Commissioner of Education Sidney Marland, Representative Rolf Nelson, Representative Fred Norton, Senator John Olson, Representative Joe O'Neill, Representative Rod Searle, Representative Jim Swanson, and Representative Chuck Weaver.

This group of men, whose only real diversity was socioeconomic status and whether or not they wore glasses, became the founders of Minnesota Metropolitan State College along with Chancellor Mitau and Vice Chancellor Sweet.

Eventually, HF 3137 passed through the Minnesota legislature and $300,000 was allocated to plan the new school. It would join Minnesota's six other state colleges and the University of Minnesota.

The passage of HF 3137 was a small victory accompanied by a much larger test: Could the new college open its doors and begin serving students with only $300,000 (a paltry sum when it comes to establishing and operating a college) to support it? Or would the school become stuck in the planning phase, with no real means of making it operational?

Most traditional colleges and universities, even in 1971, would easily gobble up $300,000 by paying the salaries of a handful of faculty. Metro State would have to use this sum to pay its entire staff, purchase office supplies, develop its tenets and system of operation, pay rent for its administration offices and classrooms, recruit students, plan curriculum, and everything else in between. Fortunately, David Sweet, newly appointed as president, was up for the task.

Sweet was a bright man with a keen mind. Like Reatha, he had received a Woodrow Wilson Fellowship for his academic achievements. He also had a way with people. After securing his presidential position, he began calling potential donors and managed to secure a few major gifts from independent foundations—$213,000 from the Carnegie Foundation, $50,000 from the Hill Foundation, $40,000 from the Bush Foundation. In total, he scraped together $1.1 million, including the initial $300,000 allocation from the state legislature. Even that sum was on the lean side, and, as Metro State associate professor Monte Bute wrote, "A cautious and conventional administrator would hoard the meager funds, initiating a small pilot program only near the end of the second year. A more entrepreneurial executive would bet the bundle, operating a full-blown college within six months. Sweet was a riverboat gambler."[115]

In its recommendations, the Citizens League report suggested opening the doors of the new school in September 1973.[116] Sweet did it a year and a half earlier, in February 1972.

The months between the passage of HF 3137 and Minnesota Metropolitan State College serving its first students were frantic and jam-packed with activity. One of the initial faculty members, Bob Fox, put together a survey to track the hours of his fellow faculty and administrators. He recalled, "We were averaging about 100 hours per week in what we called 'Metro time.'"[117]

The new president was a man who did not require sleep, it seemed. David Sweet was a charismatic ball of energy, wholly consumed by his mission to establish a school unlike any other in the area, and to do it *now*. One of the first orders of business: establishing a central administration office.

The school's first offices were located in downtown Saint Paul in an old Northwestern Bank building. Sweet furnished the space with donated furniture—items he obtained from a friend whose family owned a large furniture outlet. With a few tables and chairs scattered throughout the offices, Sweet settled in and began personally conducting interviews to hire a skeleton staff, which included only five full-time faculty and a handful of administrators. The rest of the teaching staff was comprised of "community faculty." This eclectic group of community volunteers were tasked with teaching students practical skills and information, gleaned from the jobs they held and the work they performed. They were field experts, not teachers . . . and that was the whole point. Metro State advocated for the practical above the theoretical, the enthusiastic volunteer above the tenured professor.

From its first home in the old bank building, Metro State moved into a rather shabby, unfinished space above a Walgreens drug store, also in downtown Saint Paul, at the juncture of Wabasha and Seventh Streets. The office space reflected the general cobbled-together nature of

---

115. Bute, "Riverboat Gambler's Utopian Experiment."
116. The report also noted that $600,000 would be a reasonable funding request from the state legislature.
117. Lofquist, *Metropolitan State University Buzz*.

the school in its early days. Bare lightbulbs hung from wires, and staff supplied their own floor lamps and office supplies. For a time, a hand-lettered cardboard sign adorned the front door, reading "Minnesota Metropolitan State College."

The dingy atmosphere of the place, however, belied the enthusiasm and optimistic spirits of the early administrators and faculty who worked there. The offices buzzed with energy as the Metro State team began sussing out the logistics of operating the school and developing the academic framework for its future students. As they worked, they kept the tenets of President Sweet's "prospectus" in mind:[118]

- We believe that you should have responsibility for, and authority over, your education.

- We believe that you should seek an urban-orientated education.

- We believe that you should direct your education toward the acquisition of competence rather than toward the accumulation of credits.

A self-directed, practical education was the desired outcome for Metro State's students, and the faculty had to figure out how to make that happen. What emerged was a program based on individualized education programs (IEPs). With the help of a faculty advisor, each student would write their own IEP, which would outline their ultimate goal and what they would need to do to get there. "Getting there" might include taking certain classes from a faculty or community faculty member, job shadowing, volunteerism or civic involvement, or independent research. Faculty would review the student's work and provide written feedback (there were no letter grades), and once the student completed all the assignments outlined in their IEP, they would graduate with a degree.

In essence, each student coauthored their own curriculum with a faculty member and could only graduate if each of their goals was completed to the faculty's satisfaction.

---

118. Bute, "Riverboat Gambler's Utopian Experiment."

Reatha's mother, Ola Mae Clark, with (left to right) Reatha (age 7), a childhood friend, and Reatha's sister Mamie (age 9), 1945

Reatha Belle Clark in her homecoming queen regalia at Clark College, 1958

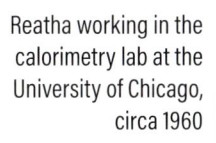

Reatha working in the calorimetry lab at the University of Chicago, circa 1960

Reatha Clark King and N. Judge King on their wedding day, December 16, 1961

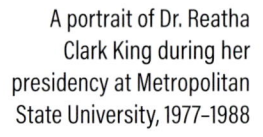

A portrait of Dr. Reatha Clark King during her presidency at Metropolitan State University, 1977–1988

The King family: Reatha, Jay, Judge, and Scott

Reatha Clark King with Metropolitan State University's founding president, Dr. David Sweet

Reatha Clark King with legendary tennis professional Billie Jean King

The King family: Jay, Judge, Reatha, and Scott

Reatha Clark King with former jurist and professional football player Alan Page

A portrait of Dr. Reatha Clark King

Reatha Clark King with businessman and philanthropist Wheelock Whitney at the gala to celebrate the Reatha Clark King Endowed Scholarship, 1987

Dr. Reatha Clark King receiving an honorary doctorate degree from Metropolitan State University, 1998

Reatha Clark King with Wilson G. Bradshaw, president of Metropolitan State University from 2000–2007

Reatha Clark King speaking at an elementary school in Moultrie, Georgia, after winning the Colquitt County Career Achievement Award, 2017

A portrait of Dr. Reatha Clark King, circa 2018

Reatha speaking at the funeral of her sister Dorothy "Dot" Clark Green, 2011

The King family: Scott, Jay, Reatha, and Judge, 2011

Reatha Clark King and Ginny Arthur, March 20, 2019

Judge and Reatha at an Exxon Mobil board meeting event in Scotland, 2003

It was a revolutionary approach (one that would ultimately be unsustainable as the college grew), and it would provide students with the kind of individualized attention rarely found in higher education.

One other major difference between traditional colleges and Metro State was its target demographic: adults who may have had previous college experience, those who had delayed pursuing a college degree (homemakers were a primary target), and those who found traditional colleges to be either unaccommodating or too expensive (the initial cost of tuition at Metro State was $650 for the duration of their enrollment, even if the student took classes for half a decade or more).

The school would be designed as an "upper-level college," serving only third—and fourth-year college students (or, more precisely, the *equivalent* of third—and fourth-years, since the college would not have designated class levels). Those who wished to attend could use a combination of past college courses and real-life work experience as credit. In the early 1970s, only eight other schools in the nation were designed to be "senior colleges," which skipped lower-level courses altogether. It was truly experimental and innovative—words that appealed to Dr. Reatha Clark King when she was considering whether the school's model would be a good fit for her.

In addition to developing the school's program, early Metro State staff members were tasked with finding spaces to hold classes. With little money to rent classroom space, the university called upon the community, once again, to step up and provide assistance. Churches, community centers, and other public spaces opened their doors and loaned their buildings to the "school without walls."

As college staff worked to transform the acorn of an idea into a fully leafed oak, the first set of students began to enroll. That first year, fifty intrepid students would become part of the Metro State experiment, attracted to its innovative and inclusive approach. Recruiter Mel Henderson pounded the pavement, touting the school's mission in churches and community organizations, at conferences, and pretty much anywhere he could find a platform and an interested audience.

With the school's year-round academic calendar, the target launch date of February 1, 1972, seemed as good as any. However, only a month before the opening, there were still many wrinkles to iron out. The staff worked tirelessly to get everything in order for the big day. As faculty advisor Judy Pendergrass described, "We would sit in a conference room above Walgreens Drug Store day after day, building from the ground up, testing ideas and kicking them around."[119] Ever the optimistic cheerleader, President Sweet would hold conferences with his team, during which he would remind them of the school's mission and vision. Sweet is often described as bouncing up and down on his toes and waving his arms as he spoke, so enthusiastic that his assistant would sometimes have to stand behind him and tug on his coattails to get him to stand still. A big fellow—well over six feet tall, with broad shoulders—he had a presence that could easily fill the room.

It was Sweet's drive and enthusiasm that made the February 1 start date a reality. With his dedicated team at his side, he and Minnesota Metropolitan State College ushered in their first set of students.

The nation watched, keenly interested in this new experimental model to emerge from the upper Midwest. The *New York Times* ran a half-page article about Metro State, describing it as a school with "no campus, no classes, no semesters, no classrooms, no grades, no required courses, no library, no student organizations, no tenured faculty, and no teen-age students."[120]

The *Cedar Rapids Gazette* in Iowa reported, rather disparagingly, "When you hear about 'the new college' you might be tempted to call it 'the no college.'" It went on to describe the hodgepodge of buildings the college would consider a campus, saying, "Classrooms and laboratories will include libraries, factories, museums, parks, schools, churches, business and government offices . . . any place there are people and an environment conducive to learning will be part of the campus."[121]

The *Washington Post* explored Metro State's target demographic, saying, "those which the upper division college is interested in serving are adults who have dropped out of other colleges, acquired the equivalent of the first two years of college through work or other experience, or transferred from the six metropolitan area junior colleges." The article then describes this group of individuals as mainly "housewives, service

---

119. Lofquist, *Metropolitan State University Buzz*.
120. Malcolm, "Minnesota College."
121. McCormack, "Minnesota's New College."

veterans, minority group members and working people who would like to further their education in general and job skills in particular."[122]

It was a grand experiment, a new approach in a tired, old system.

And the stakes were high. Sweet and company had to prove that this new school was viable—that the students would come, and the students would gain degree-worthy educations. Otherwise, the state legislature and private backers would not be keen to funnel more money into the school without walls.

Despite everything—Sweet's propensity for ambiguity, the shabby offices, the makeshift classrooms, the untrained army of community instructors—the experiment began to show promising results. After only one year, Metro State graduated its first twelve students, who spoke highly of the school and its flexible structure. Enrollment increased from fifty to over five hundred students and was expected to double again within the next two years. The number of community faculty members increased from only twenty-five at the onset to over three hundred in just one year. Recognizing the school's progress and potential, Governor Wendell R. Anderson authorized an additional $1 million budget for the school, while several private companies decided to gift the college additional grant money.

Metro State had momentum, and, most importantly, it had alumni. Yusef Mgeni, a 1974 graduate, described his classes as "valid and authentic" with "passionate and enthusiastic" instructors and advisors. Virginia McCain, another 1974 grad, said she felt "very free" and had the unprecedented opportunity to work with community professors who were "industry leaders or experts in their professions."[123] These student testimonials were (and would continue to be) the fuel that kept the grand Metro State experiment chugging along. They validated the school's mission and lent it credence.

The experiment was beginning to bear fruit, and the school was gaining supporters. However, these were early days, and no one was entirely certain of the sustainability of the school's model.

For one, Sweet was known for his high tolerance of ambiguity, which sometimes left his faculty and staff floundering or feeling unsupported. Some faculty were uneasy with the loose structure when it came

---

122. Brettingen, "Minnesota College."
123. Lofquist, *Metropolitan State University Buzz*.

to assessing credits and measuring student progress. Some missed the efficiency of hosting classes within a traditional classroom. Even a college without walls needs a foundation.

The school also continued to struggle financially. The lean budget made growth difficult. With more students came more needs, including new community spaces to occupy, new faculty to hire, and more paperwork to process (applications, credit transfers, progress reports, and on and on).

Aside from financial difficulties and problems stemming from its lack of structure, Metro State was faced with a more nebulous issue: its image complex. Traditional colleges and universities tended to view the school with skepticism at best, and with downright criticism or disdain at worst. People often mistrust what they don't understand, and that inclination was apparent when it came to Metro State. Faculty from other schools looked down on the new college, viewing it as substandard and as a school with no real place in higher education.

The Minnesota Metropolitan State College staff knew how they were viewed, and they became self-conscious of the school, despite its progress. Even when the college gained accreditation from the North Central Association in 1975—a huge moment for the school *and* a massive surprise for its critics—the feeling that Metro State was somehow inferior did not entirely dissipate.

Yet another issue the school grappled with was, surprisingly, attracting a racially diverse set of students. It had established a plan to attract female students, with President Sweet intentionally hiring female staff and faculty. He is quoted as saying, "To reach women you need women in key positions. To act as 'models' to furnish insights.... So I consciously set out to find women who would articulate the needs of women. If you don't have women in decision-making, their needs and aspirations don't get heeded."[124] True to his word, Sweet placed women in four of the seven high-level executive positions and three of the first five faculty positions. The school also published newspaper ads and articles geared toward women.[125]

However, the strategy was not so intentional for racial minorities, many of whom were first-generation college-goers and viewed enrolling

---

124. Bute, "Riverboat Gambler's Utopian Experiment."
125. Derickson, "MMSC."

at Metro State as a risk (would a diploma from this unconventional institution carry the same weight as a diploma from elsewhere?). Even though President Sweet was known to be personally open-minded and inclusive, he had trouble attracting the very people that might have benefited most from Metro State's low tuition and flexible structure.

When David Sweet left the presidency on January 20, 1977, to take on the role of president of Rhode Island College, he left a trail of issues in his wake. The school desperately needed a president with a strategic mind, strength of character, ambition, and the financial and fundraising know-how to pull together the threads of innovative ideas and patchwork of progress and stitch them into a respectable institution with a clear-cut strategy.

If Dr. Reatha Clark King became president, she would have her work cut out for her. But she was well suited and well equipped for this kind of challenge. She had experience developing and nurturing a new school, she knew how to handle controversy and external opposition, she wasn't afraid of innovative problem-solving, and she had recently developed a strong foundation in financial management through her MBA courses at Columbia. On top of all that, she believed in Metro State's mission and pioneering approach. This was the kind of school she could rally behind; this was the kind of school she could lead.

CHAPTER FOURTEEN

In the Land of Lakes

"Some people want it to happen, some wish it would happen, others make it happen."

—Michael Jordan

Reatha flew to the Twin Cities of Minneapolis–Saint Paul in the summer of 1977. Looking out the airplane window, she saw a land painted with leafy trees and lakes, neighborhood homes and meandering roads. Here, there was less congestion and thinner crowds than along the East Coast. Here, there was room to breathe.

Her first interview brought her to downtown Saint Paul, not far from the classical façade and towering cupola of the state capitol building. Before stepping into her interview with the Minnesota State College Board,[126] Reatha took a deep breath and steadied her nerves. She had done her homework and knew her stuff; now, she had to demonstrate that to the board.

Even though she was still wrapping up classes at Columbia University, she had spent hours researching and preparing for her interview. She knew that Metropolitan State University was a new school and, like York College years earlier, was struggling to build a solid reputation while carving out its own unique academic niche. The same battle that Reatha had fought at York was raging at Metro State: the advocates

---

126. Today, one board governs all Minnesota state colleges and universities. It is aptly called the Board of Trustees of the Minnesota State Colleges and Universities System.

of traditional liberal arts education tended to look down upon career studies and nontraditional curriculum, and the faculty members at Metro State were feeling self-conscious and under attack. On top of that, the university had run into some financial trouble the year before and had performed poorly in an audit (in which thirty citations were issued on the school's financial records).

Reatha knew she would have to address these topics during her interview. With her hands-on experience at York and her newly elevated business and financial acumen from Columbia University, she walked into her first interview armed with both practical knowledge and theoretical strategies.

She nailed it.

The Minnesota State College Board invited her back for a second interview and insisted that Judge accompany her. Moving halfway across the country was no light matter, and the board wanted to make sure the entire family would be on board with the decision, *if* they were to offer Reatha the position.

Reatha was one step closer to becoming a university president, but she tried to keep a level head. The position was not yet hers, and she still had to wade through a second interview. But she couldn't help the excitement that wrapped around her heart and brightened her smile. Besides, she had her community and her family behind her, rooting for her and cheering her on every step of the way. Even York College was supportive. Her supervisor, Lewis Bodi, applauded her decision to apply for the job and did not bemoan the fact that York College might lose one of its most dedicated and determined faculty members. He knew she was well qualified for the position and possessed all the attributes and intelligence necessary to make an outstanding university president.

Judge and Reatha packed their things and readied themselves for the trip to Minnesota. The boys had a vague idea of what was going on but didn't ask many questions. Their mother was interviewing somewhere. They would stay on Long Island while their parents were away (one with a friend, one at a summer camp). And life would continue as usual. They didn't even consider what would happen if their mother were awarded the job—moving away from their New York home was too remote an idea to entertain.

Reatha's second interview took place on the lower level of the state capitol building. To this day, whenever Reatha finds herself in the Minnesota State Capitol, she thinks about that interview. She was one of four finalists—the field whittled down to two men and two women. Each finalist interviewed with the board for a full hour and did their best to field questions about how, as president, they would lead the university and guide it toward a better future.

As if that weren't pressure enough, the interview was also open to the public. The state of Minnesota's so-called "sunshine laws" mandated that any interview for a high-level public position could not be performed behind closed doors. Because of that, representatives of local newspapers crowded into the room alongside members of the general public, including Judge King. Judge was formally escorted by one of the board's staffers to a seat from which he could peer down and watch the interview unfold. With a tendency to find humor in any situation, Judge found the whole charade rather amusing (even though he was well aware of what was at stake for Reatha).

At the front of the room, Reatha stood as tall as her five-foot-three frame would allow. She appeared every bit the professional in her neatly pressed business suit with its shoulder pads. Surrounded by politicians and members of the press, a less self-assured person might have buckled under the pressure, but Reatha exuded confidence and poise. She was prepared, and she knew it. Just as she had presented her findings on oxygen difluoride to a sea of white men at American Chemical Society conferences, so, too, did she make her case in front of the Minnesota State College Board.

The board comprised fifteen governor-appointed members and represented the state of Minnesota's collegiate system. In their hands rested the power to plan academic programs, control school budgets, establish admissions requirements . . . and decide whether Reatha was worthy of the president's chair. As the newest member of the state university system (which included Bemidji State, Minnesota State Mankato, Minnesota State Moorhead, St. Cloud State, Southwest Minnesota State, and Winona State in addition to the nationally renowned University of Minnesota), Metropolitan State University inevitably had a lot of growth and development in its future, and the new president needed to be up for the task.

Reatha answered the board's questions with her usual preparedness and aplomb. She pulled from her own experience as well as from information she had gleaned from her classes at Columbia University. The depth of her fiscal knowledge, in particular, gave Reatha an edge over the other applicants, who did not have the same kind of training in business finance. For a full hour, the board hurled questions at Reatha, and she fielded them like a professional baseball player, hitting each one out of the park.

After the interview, Judge greeted Reatha with a big smile. "You answered all those questions well," he said, beaming. "I didn't know you knew all *that*."

Reatha laughs when she recalls this moment, but she also looks at it as an unfortunate microcosm of the bias that existed during that era. Women's abilities were (and still are, in many cases) underestimated. Even someone as enlightened as Judge—a man who advocated for his wife and her career—could occasionally underestimate his spouse's capabilities. But Reatha knew he meant his statement as a compliment. Judge *was* impressed by her interview, as was (it turns out) the entire state board.

After all four candidates were interviewed, the board huddled and made its decision—that very afternoon. At this point, the Metro State presidential seat had been vacant for half a year, with an interim president filling the gap, and the school was in dire need of new leadership. A gambler might have bet on George Ayers winning the presidential seat. He was the current vice president at Metropolitan State, had been instrumental in the school's development, and possessed insider knowledge of the inner workings of the university that the other candidates did not have. But despite the odds tilting in his favor, the board passed over Ayers in favor of the capable, well-prepared young dean who had not only developed a college with a similar mission but was also equipped with an MBA.

In a five-to-four vote, they chose Dr. Reatha Clark King.

After the board made its announcement, preparations unfolded quickly. Reatha had little time to celebrate her new appointment with Judge, let alone digest the enormity of the decision. The board immediately pulled her into a meeting room to go over some logistics while a staff member took Judge on a drive to look at nearby neighborhoods. If they were moving to Minnesota, they might as well become acquainted with the desirable spots to live—the cities and neighborhoods that were safe, kid friendly, and within easy driving distance of the school's main offices. In an era when realtors would often shuffle their black clients into the same (often neglected) neighborhoods, it is noteworthy that the board did not participate in such shenanigans. From the onset, Reatha and Judge were afforded the respect they deserved, at least from the Minnesota State College Board.

On the flight back to New York, the couple mulled over the many changes and decisions they would have to make that summer. Reatha would resign from York College, the boys would transfer to new schools, Judge would determine how long he would stay on at Nassau Community College. Not to mention Reatha was set to receive her master's in business administration degree soon and would have to accept the diploma in absentia.

But Reatha was a master problem-solver, and she began tackling each challenge one at a time.

She and the boys would move to Minnesota almost immediately.

Judge would remain in New York and complete another school year in the chemistry department at Nassau College before moving inland and joining the family in Minnesota.

Reatha and the boys would live in temporary housing before moving into a more permanent residence in one of the northern suburbs of Saint Paul.

She would hit the ground running as the new president of Metropolitan State University.

In the summer of 1977, Reatha charged forward with her career, and Judge became the trailing spouse. This was a role reversal for them—she had left her prestigious job at the National Bureau of Standards to follow him to New York—and a subversion of societal expectations, but Judge did not complain. Theirs was a relationship of give and take, and Judge knew it was his turn to give. In an era when men were widely considered the breadwinners whose careers took priority over their wives', his amenability was radical. Perhaps his easygoing nature and respect for Reatha's career were the products of being the only boy among four sisters, or maybe they were attitudes he developed over time after witnessing the achievements and intellect of his partner. Regardless,

Judge became a hero among feminists and progressive thinkers. They praised and doted on him—attention, Reatha recalls with a smile, that he was more than happy to receive.

Though neither Reatha nor Judge knew much about their new midwestern home, they moved forward in the only way they knew how: with the confidence that if they worked hard enough and threw their hearts and souls into this new chapter of their lives, they would succeed.

In the summer of 1977, neither Reatha nor Judge knew just how much they *would* succeed. They hadn't the faintest notion of how much Reatha would accomplish for Metro State University. They didn't realize how many positive changes she would make, awards she would win, and lives she would touch. They didn't know that a distinguished career was waiting for Judge in 3M's engineering department, or that Reatha would eventually exit academia and step into a leadership role at a major Fortune 500 company in the Twin Cities.

In the summer of 1977, they were simply focused on packing their belongings in cardboard boxes, saying a few quick goodbyes, and thinking about the Land of Lakes in the central part of the United States that neither of them knew much about.

★ ★ ★

Minnesota. The Twin Cities.

The King boys knew precisely two facts about the Twin Cities of Minneapolis–Saint Paul:

1. This was the home of the Minnesota Vikings football team.

2. Winters were cold and snowy.

The only home Jay and Scott King had ever known was the East Coast, and, with Jay three years old and Scott only a baby when the family moved to New York, most of their memories and friends had been made in New York City. They loved their neighborhood, their schools, their church. Moving across the country, 1,500 miles from the nearest ocean, was a shock.

Though their young lives were in upheaval, they knew complaining about it wouldn't do a lick of good. The decision was made, and they would do their best to adapt to their new home in the middle of the country. With only a few days to gather their things and prepare for the move, the boys said a few hasty goodbyes and readied themselves to begin their next chapter.

Reatha and Judge piled their two boys, several boxes of belongings, and Kay, the family's cocker spaniel mix, into Reatha's Dodge Dart and began their journey west. They made haste, racing the clock as the first day of the school year ticked ever closer. When the family finally rolled into the Twin Cities, it was Labor Day evening, and the boys would have just enough time to squeeze in some sleep before starting school the next day.

That night, the King family slept within the beige walls of the Holiday Inn that would be the temporary home of Reatha and the boys for the next several months. The hotel perched on the edge of downtown Saint Paul, a stone's throw from the capitol building and a string of theaters and museums. Though their living space was cramped and the shag carpeting well worn, they knew it was a temporary arrangement. Soon, they would move into a nearby apartment building and Judge King would return to New York.

In the meantime, the King boys started school: Capitol View Junior High School for twelve-year-old Jay and North Heights Christian Academy for nine-year-old Scott. Both institutions were situated in the northern suburbs (Little Canada and Roseville, respectively), where the family hoped to find a permanent residence. For now, however, they would tolerate their close quarters and temporarily split family. They would begin to learn, little by little, about their new home in the Land of Lakes.

With over ten thousand lakes dotting the state and the Mighty Mississippi wending its way from Lake Itasca and through the Twin Cities of Minneapolis and Saint Paul, Minnesota is a state built around water. The state's first major flour and paper mills took advantage of river-generated hydropower, lumberjacks transported logs by floating them downstream, and power companies generated electricity from river flow. The name Minnesota is rooted in a Dakota phrase, *mni sota*, which means "sky-tinted waters."

Unfortunately, the settlers who streamed into Minnesota did more than borrow words from the area's first inhabitants. They staked their claims around the plentiful lakes and rivers, often heedless of the displacement and distress they imposed on the lives of Native peoples.

The newcomers settled down, and the cities sprang up. The rapidly expanding Twin Cities became home to multiple major Fortune 500 companies, including General Mills, Honeywell, Ecolab, and 3M; a wealth of colleges and universities; myriad parks and other public green spaces; and a burgeoning arts and culture scene with an abundance of museums, art galleries, music venues, and theaters.

Though winters were frigid, Reatha was warmly welcomed by her new university and by most Minnesotans she met. She describes the people as "approachable" and says that when she was new, near strangers wouldn't hesitate to "offer the name of a real estate agent or someone to service your car."[127]

Reatha and the boys settled in as best they could in their newly adopted home and began adjusting to their new lives in the upper Midwest. They were "brash little boys," Reatha says, and they fit in without too much of a struggle. Though living in a small apartment wasn't ideal, and all three felt rudderless at times, they busied themselves with work and school and looked forward to Judge's occasional visits.

Whenever Judge would visit from New York, he and Reatha would house hunt, mainly searching in the first-ring suburbs, within a few miles of downtown Saint Paul. Judge's informal tour of nearby Twin Cities neighborhoods had given the couple an idea of where they wanted to settle, and it wasn't long before they found and purchased a home in Maplewood, an oddly shaped suburb that wraps its way around the eastern and northern borders of Saint Paul like a right-angled *Tetris* block.

The Kings quickly fell in love with their house. After a grueling day of work, Reatha would roll up the long driveway, under a canopy of leafy ash trees and bristly pines, and feel the stress fall from her shoulders. The driveway ended in a loop, and the house sat facing it with a wide, welcoming façade. Similar to their house in Rockville Centre, the Kings' new home was a large, two-story building, with plenty of space for the family. Sunshine leaked through the rows of windows and washed the house in gentle light. A wood-burning fireplace sat in the family room, ready to provide warmth and comfort during long winter nights. The

---

127. "Checking In with Some Neighbors."

previous owners of the two-acre lot had raised horses, and the King family eventually used one of the old barns to house a workshop, where Judge would build an airplane from the ground up.

In the back of the house, the family had a patio and a stretch of lawn that led to the banks of funnel-shaped Keller Lake. In the summers, the Kings spent many an evening by the water, barbecuing and swatting at mosquitos (two major pastimes of Minnesotans!) while enjoying each other's company. Eventually, the family would sink even deeper into Minnesota life and purchase a motorboat, which they would take for periodic spins around Keller Lake or use for the occasional fishing outing. But Judge wasn't much of an angler and considered fishing a bit too dull for his taste, so the fishing gear mostly served as decoration, collecting dust in the family's garage. Why sit around, waiting for stubborn fish to nibble, when there were airplanes to build and skies to traverse?

The large house and funnel-shaped lake and fishing boat were part of the King family's future, but during the fall of 1977, the only shelter Reatha and the boys had was their cramped apartment, with no lawn or lake to speak of. During those first months, Reatha and her sons did their best in tight living quarters while Reatha settled into her new role as president of Metropolitan State University.

★ ★ ★

"Black Woman Named Head of Metropolitan State 'U.'"
"New Yorker 1st Woman to Lead State College."
"Black Woman to Head Metro State University."
"Dr. Reatha Clark King Heads Midwestern University."[128]

The media swiveled its collective head toward Reatha and began bombarding her with interview requests. At York College, she had periodically been at the center of public attention, but now the attention was persistent and widespread. Though she received accolades from a number of print and television news outlets across the country, the praise that mattered most came from her family and friends.

---

128. Headlines from the *Minneapolis Tribune*, St. Paul *Pioneer Press*, and the *Minneapolis Star* (all three from August 17, 1977) and *York College News* (October 10, 1977).

"My mother was so proud," Reatha recalls. Though Ola Mae wasn't a braggart, she would often talk to her friends and family members about her accomplished daughter. It was news that whipped through Reatha's family and spread through South Georgia.

In November of 1977, the *Moultrie Observer* ran an article entitled "First Black Woman: Moultrian Now Heads Minnesota University."[129] In it, the paper claimed Reatha as one of its own and touted her accomplishments as a valedictorian and research chemist. A shade over two decades earlier, the same newspaper had neglected to even acknowledge Reatha's high school graduation class. Though the American South was sometimes stubbornly slow to change, this article demonstrated that some ground had been gained in the march toward equality.

Forty years later, the region would go a step further, awarding Reatha Clark King with the Colquitt County Career Achievement Award. Given to distinguished graduates of the Colquitt County school system, the award recognized Reatha's remarkable accomplishments and contributions to scientific research, academia, and corporate leadership. In conjunction with receiving the award, Reatha would give several speeches in the area, including presentations to area high school and elementary students. In 1977, Reatha's appointment as university president of Metro State warranted only a few paragraphs on the second page of the *Moultrie Observer* (appearing after an article about the unseasonably cold weather and a column noting when city Christmas lights would appear for the holiday season), but her career achievement award in 2017 was considered front-page news, with several subsequent articles and photographs of Reatha after she delivered her series of talks. Inch by inch, her representation in the paper was improving.

As she began her presidency in 1977, Reatha felt an enormous pressure resting on her shoulders. Not only did she have a momentous task ahead of her—defining and developing the path of a fledgling university and improving its reputation—but she had to do it while under both a state and a national spotlight. She had to do it while feeling the very real pressure of representing both her race and her gender. Reatha later recalled:

---

129. "First Black Woman."

"We were always made aware that our experiences as 'the first black' and 'the first woman' were clearly not undertaken for our benefit alone, but they were for the benefit of our whole race, and especially for those who did not have the earlier opportunity. We represented the pride of older blacks, and we were the inspiration for younger blacks. . . . We had to succeed if the numbers of us in the positions would ever increase. Similarly, as a black woman, a lot was riding on my success in order to open up more opportunities for women."[130]

This was not a moment for timidity. Reatha had to move forward with bold strides and a level head. A lesser person would have crumbled beneath the weight of responsibility, but Dr. Reatha Clark King was a titan. She was determined to be a shining example of what young black women were capable of accomplishing. In a *Minneapolis Tribune* article, she declared, "I hope my functioning will be so effective that they can't avoid appointing another black or another female to similar positions."[131]

Fortunately, Metro State's faculty and administration were ready to assist Reatha in her goal of being the best of the best. They were excited to welcome her into the fold and confident that the state board had selected a capable president for their school. This was made clear on Reatha's very first day in the office, when she was warmly greeted and given "a bundle of advice" to help her ease into the presidency. Even George Ayers, whom Reatha had nudged out of the presidency during the interview process, remained in his post as vice president and continued to support her for a couple more years until he took a new position as president of Massasoit Community College in Brockton, Massachusetts.

The Metro State staff knew that President Sweet had been a visionary with big, sweeping ideas, but what the school needed at this point was a practical strategist—someone to come in, shore up the leaking levees, and wrangle the big ideas into a sustainable model. They hoped Dr. Reatha Clark King would be that strategist.

As the rest of academia still reeled from the appointment of a black female university president, Dr. Reatha Clark King got to work. She started creating a strategic plan to fulfill the main assignments she had

---
130. Harvey, *Grass Roots and Glass Ceilings*.
131. Biano, "Black Woman Named Head."

been given by the Minnesota State College Board: improve the image of Metropolitan State University, rescue it from financial difficulty, and develop its reputation as a quality academic institution.

She took the mission to heart but also refused to compromise Metro State's budding reputation as an innovative institution that welcomed nontraditional students with open arms. She understood the importance of such a school and knew it occupied a much-needed space in the community by catering to an underserved population of learners.

Reatha celebrated Metro State's model and fully supported its innovative path, but others were not so sure. She recalls that the faculty members were "self-conscious" and felt that their institution was lesser than other universities, such as the nearby University of Minnesota. They were constantly comparing themselves to other schools and fretting about their unconventional model.

And their worry was justified. Faculty from other schools *did* sometimes look down on Metro State, thinking it inferior to their traditional academic structures.

Granting college credit for work experience? Who ever heard of such a thing!

Holding classes at night, in all corners of Minneapolis and Saint Paul? That doesn't sound like a legitimate school to me!

Emphasizing career-oriented degrees instead of a solid liberal arts education? That denies students a well-rounded education and cheapens the definition of a university!

The naysayers buzzed about Metro State, and the staff began to believe them. Maybe they *were* inferior to other four-year schools. Maybe they *did* have a flawed program.

When Reatha discovered how very downtrodden and harassed the faculty felt, she made it one of her prerogatives to quash their trepidations and make them proud of their school. She had to convince them that, yes, they had been (and would continue) approaching higher education from a different angle, but that made them innovators, not inferiors. She believed in Metro State's emphasis on career preparedness and fully supported its flexible class schedules, which opened the door to nontraditional students. "I realized early in life," Reatha says, "that education is our best enabling resource, that technical skills are important, and that my stamina for championing educational opportunity for all people is inexhaustible."[132]

Metro's staff supported the school's mission, too, but they needed validation. As she began her role, Reatha vowed to provide that validation—to make everyone who worked at Metro State proud of their school. "I inherited an opportunity," she says. "An opportunity to build its reputation, an opportunity to create."

She began to plan.

Pulling from her MBA courses, Reatha developed a comprehensive strategic plan and presented it to the Minnesota State College Board. The plan included initiatives to increase funding, develop strategic relationships, and maintain the heart of Metro State's vision while building its reputation. Impressed by the thoroughness of her vision, the board gave her its resounding support. She would have free rein to implement her ideas however she saw fit.

Every day, Reatha went into her office with an agenda. Keeping her big-picture goals in mind, she would lay out her task list and get to work. Through careful strategic planning, community outreach, and calculated relationships with local businesses and other universities, she would steer the university into an era of unprecedented growth and success.

During her first three years, the main focus of Reatha's attention was simply learning the myriad duties of a university president, laying the groundwork for successful fundraising, and gaining local and regional acceptance for Metro State. A large part of that responsibility involved, as she calls it, "friend-raising." If she wanted to make any progress, she would have to make connections with those in power—the politicians who could pass favorable legislation, the corporate leaders who could become financial backers, the academics who might become allies in the fight to build the school's reputation.

But, in a new city and a new state, Reatha did not know at first who held the power and the purse strings. Fortunately, Metro State University already had loyal allies who fully supported the school's mission and were invested in its future. Among these ardent supporters were a band of wealthy suburban women who had earned their diplomas from Metro after spending several years as homemakers. These women, in

---

132. Boston University, "Reatha Clark King."

addition to other well-connected allies, welcomed Reatha into their fold and began giving her the names of Minnesota's influencers.

You simply must *contact the CEOs of 3M and Honeywell. I can get you their phone numbers.*

Let me connect you with former governor Anderson. He's still influential around here.

Don't forget about Senator Jack Davies or Representative Rod Searle—they were instrumental in Metro State's founding, you know.

Among Reatha's first important contacts were Peter Gillette (executive VP of Northwestern National Bank), Wheelock Whitney (CEO of the investment firm Dain Bosworth, now RBC, Gordon Sprenger (CEO of Abbott Northwestern Hospital), and Minnesota governor Rudy Perpich. A handful of Metro alumni partnered with Governor Perpich to host a welcome reception for Reatha almost as soon as she arrived in the Twin Cities. At the governor's mansion, they rolled out the red carpet for the new Metro State president and let her know that she had Perpich's full backing.

These early supporters remained staunchly by Reatha and Metro State's side as the university grew and developed—a testament to Reatha's trusted, adept leadership. Peter Gillette commented in 1984, "Metro U's high quality programs... have served thousands of adults who might otherwise not have been able to finish college. I am particularly pleased to see how Metro U has been able to successfully serve this broad cross-section of our adult population."[133]

As her knowledge of the "who's who" in local politics and business grew, Reatha began reaching out and forming connections. Her method was simple: place a phone call, chat for a few minutes, and schedule an in-person meeting. When building her web of connections, Reatha leaned on the lessons she had learned from her 1971 Dale Carnegie course, which centered on the concepts in Carnegie's famous book *How to Win Friends and Influence People*. She made it clear that she wanted to start a dialogue with business and political leaders and learn about their interests and goals instead of begging them for financial backing.

Reatha's grandma Mamie had always said "Treat everybody right," and Reatha extended that lesson to her emerging connections. She was genuinely interested in other people and had a knack for identifying

---

133. Acosta, *Building a Legacy*.

others' abilities and motivations. In her "friend-raising," Reatha cast a wide net, mixing and mingling (as she puts it) with anyone and everyone. Though she enjoyed getting to know other leaders and go-getters in the Twin Cities, she always networked with a purpose. "You have to make friends *before* you might need them," Reatha says. "It's about learning to recognize others' talents before you need their help."

It wasn't long before Reatha became a known entity. Her efforts to connect with others, coupled with a good deal of media attention, helped build her reputation as a public figure. She also happened to be a memorable individual, given her gender and race. In the pale-faced, testosterone-dominated throng of community leaders, she stood apart from the crowd. Though the Twin Cities is now relatively diverse (with the largest Somali population and second-largest Hmong population in the United States), in 1980, people of color constituted less than 6 percent of the population. Of that population, even fewer (*far* fewer) held high-level leadership positions. Being a pioneer was, at times, lonely and isolating. Reatha would sometimes feel like an outsider in a world constructed for people who did not look like her. However, ever the optimist, she has also spoken about "feeling at the same time greatly fulfilled by the challenge of the work and the tremendous intellectual stimulation."[134]

The King boys also noticed the lack of diversity in their neighborhood and in their schools. They had left their overtly multicultural New York City for a state that often seemed as white as its winters. The Kings' neighbors in Rockville Centre had been a rainbow of nationalities, with kids of all races and ethnicities playing together. In Minnesota, the neighbors didn't look like them, and the houses were cordoned off with fences. It was an adjustment for the young King boys, but they followed their mother's lead. "Mom didn't get into looks or skin color," Scott says. "It's all about 'What do you bring to the table?'"[135]

Despite the new state, new demographics, and new climate, the family adapted. Fortunately, Reatha says, Minnesota's reputation for being open-minded and welcoming held true most of the time. She was treated with the respect and dignity her doctorate degree and prestigious position deserved. There were moments, however, when people

---

134. Harvey, *Grass Roots and Glass Ceilings*.
135. Scott King, interview.

focused on Reatha's gender and skin tone rather than her merits. Rather than her *humanity*. During those trying moments, she had to do what she always did: keep a level head and focus on her work.

Reatha was too busy to dwell on those who doubted her capabilities. She was also too busy to pause and contemplate her place under the public microscope. She had work to do.

Her first year as university president was, in her words, a "trust-building year." Relationships took time, Reatha knew. They had to be planted and nurtured. And she had to demonstrate her capabilities as a leader and tactician to all interested parties—Metro State's faculty, other university presidents, politicians, and corporate and community leaders.

After just one year, however, she had begun to develop a reputation as a tireless worker, a planner, and a fiscally responsible university head. She knew that every move she made would be scrutinized, so she carefully tracked her expenditures—every luncheon, every mile driven, every meeting over coffee. She made certain to keep private and public donations to Metro State separate and earmarked for different initiatives (an expectation of the state legislature and Minnesota State College Board). Even Reatha's choice of vehicle was decidedly unflashy—a practical Ford sedan. (By contrast, President Sweet drove a cherry-red 1966 Volkswagen convertible.)

By the end of the 1977–78 school year, Metropolitan State University was on track for another year of growth, another year of advancement. Approximately 2,200 students were enrolled in the school—students ranging from age twenty-one to seventy-five whom Reatha called "the most fabulous students I've seen anyplace."[136] An astonishing 90 percent of students held a job, most of them full-time. Reatha tirelessly advocated for these students, determined to "convince legislators and the taxpayers about the value of [Metro State's] concept as a higher-education resource to the citizens of the state of Minnesota."[137] She would continue to keep a tight ship at the university, supported by a foundation of strategic planning and fiscal responsibility.

Metro's faculty, along with many other public figures (both local and national), were beginning to trust Reatha at the helm of this

---

136. Alnes, "Metropolitan State University."
137. Alnes, "Metropolitan State University."

unconventional, innovative university. Though she hadn't been given much guidance, she was already steering the ship, moving it decidedly forward. Reatha was proving to be a capable, driven leader with endless potential. Though many business leaders, politicians, and other university faculty still had reservations about Metro State itself, they were beginning to warm to its leader. And that, Reatha knew, was a start.

CHAPTER FIFTEEN

Building Bridges

"One important key to success is self-confidence. An important key to self-confidence is preparation."

—Arthur Ashe

While she was busy adapting to her new role, forging valuable connections, and becoming the champion Metro State so sorely needed, Reatha never forgot the three other pillars in her life: her family, her faith, and her community. She had spent her first year in Minnesota as a single mom while Judge wrapped up his final year at Nassau Community College. This position would have been difficult for anyone to handle, let alone someone who had just stepped into a prominent public role and was expected to improve a university's reputation and amplify its fundraising. But Reatha made the boys a priority, right alongside faculty performance reviews and placing phone calls to potentially valuable connections.

Keen to support her budding musician, Reatha arranged for Jay to continue his violin lessons in Minnesota. He would take private lessons at MacPhail Center for the Performing Arts and play with the Greater Twin Cities Youth Symphonies for six years. Scott would develop an interest in music later in life when, at age sixteen, he decided to pick up the guitar. He proved to be a talented musician, and his passion for the guitar would eventually propel him into music school.

In addition to music, both boys were also involved in sports. Jay played football, basketball, and baseball, while Scott would play high school football, run track, and become involved in BMX bike racing. In true King family fashion, both excelled at their respective extracurricular activities. Scott says, "I was an achiever in sports... I was very goal oriented like my mom."[138]

At an early age, Scott proved to be a talented artist, and Reatha remembers him eagerly showing her his latest creations. This propensity for the visual arts continued into his teenage and adult years, eventually leading to a career in photography.

Reatha's boys were her pride and joy. Every evening, she made sure dinner was ready and waiting and took the time to ask the boys about their day, their schoolwork, their music lessons. She would slip off her pumps, hang her suit coat in the closet, and morph, Mister Rogers–like, into the role of Mom.

Growing up, Jay and Scott had only the vaguest notion of what their mom did all day. To them, she was the loving mother, the concerned parent, the person who made sure they did their homework and mowed the lawn. Occasionally, they would catch a glimpse of her other world—they would don suit coats and attend this gala or that award ceremony—but most of the time, she was simply Mom.

In the spring of 1978, Judge King completed his tenth year as a chemistry professor at Nassau Community College and began preparing to move to Minnesota. Part of the preparations involved looking for a new job. With his background in chemistry, Judge's skills were in demand, both within and outside of academia, and it wasn't long before he was approached with an opportunity.

The man who presented that opportunity was named Charles "Chuck" Poe. Chuck worked with the Metropolitan Economic Development Association in Minneapolis and made it his mission to help people of color establish their own businesses. He worked tirelessly to provide the funding and management advice needed for aspiring business owners to realize their dreams. Through his work, he had connected with people from all over the Twin Cities, in every position and every industry. It was these myriad connections that proved valuable to Judge.

Chuck had read about Reatha's appointment and began thinking about the other half of the King duo. When he discovered Judge King was a scientist, his wheels started to turn, and he began thinking of

---

138. Scott King, email to author, August 26, 2020.

potential roles Judge could fill in any number of major companies in the area. Finally, he called Reatha and asked, rather bluntly, "What is your husband going to do in the Twin Cities?"

When Reatha said she wasn't sure, Chuck decided that was his cue to step in. He knew some people at 3M, and he was sure he could land Judge an interview.

The opportunity excited and intrigued Judge. Up to this point, his professional career had been spent entirely in academia, and he was itching to try something new. Besides, 3M was a respected Fortune 500 company with deep roots in Minnesota.

Judge interviewed and was hired as a research chemist. Over the next decade at 3M, he would work on a variety of projects, including cutting-edge studies of wind and solar sequestration. He would also find fellow aviation enthusiasts and amateur pilots in the 3M Aviation Club. It was through this friend group that he learned about the annual Experimental Aircraft Association (EAA) air show in Oshkosh, Wisconsin.

Then called the EAA Annual Convention and Fly-In (now AirVenture Oshkosh), this air show attracts a multitude of novice aviators, airplane builders and restorers, and aviation enthusiasts every year. What started as a modest event in 1953 grew by leaps and bounds in the 1970s and '80s and today attracts hundreds of thousands of visitors each year. After he attended his first Oshkosh air show, Judge was hooked. He was in his element, talking shop with fellow enthusiasts, watching aerobatics demonstrations, attending presentations, and enjoying the fair-like atmosphere of the EAA convention.

Most summers, Judge and the rest of the 3M Aviation Club would take a Greyhound to the event while Reatha and the boys drove to meet him there. Reatha says of the club, "It was a lot of fun and a lot of lies!" The members would swap stories (or tall tales) as they perused the grounds or settled in for the night at the campground. It was always a memorable event, with thousands of unique airplanes on display and attendees from across the globe.

On a few occasions, Judge decided to eschew the Greyhound and fly his own plane to the air show. He would display the plane proudly (wearing a T-shirt with a matching blue and red stripe) and talk to anyone who was interested in his plane.

Through aviation, Judge found not only his passion but also his peers. He made several close friends through the club and the Oshkosh event—friends from across the country, including other black pilots. Friends who understood that aviation was more than a hobby; it was a way of life.

Within their first year in Minnesota, life was beginning to come together for the newly uprooted King family. Reatha had established herself as a competent and dedicated president, the boys had already made a new set of friends, and Judge was about to begin a new career at a well-respected company. But the Kings' life picture could not be complete without a church to call home.

The church where they eventually landed was Pilgrim Baptist, in the Summit-University neighborhood, west of downtown Saint Paul. This inviting brick building, built in 1928, would become their second home for well over a decade.

Pilgrim Baptist Church is steeped in history. Founded by a group of formerly enslaved people who traveled up the Mississippi River and landed at Fort Snelling in 1863, it became Minnesota's oldest predominantly black Baptist church.[139] Within its walls, Reatha and her family could pour forth their hearts and untether themselves from the cares of the week. There, they made some of their dearest friends. There, Reatha made a concerted effort to encourage the church's youth and mentor students who showed academic promise.[140]

Finding their new church in Minnesota made the King family feel whole.

★ ★ ★

Reatha's first couple years as president of Metropolitan State University were indicative of the years to come. In addition to getting to know and understand the school *and* gaining the trust of faculty and admin, she spent many an hour at galas, award ceremonies, networking events, and social gatherings, using each event as an opportunity to bend the ear of potential allies and supporters. She had learned how to dress for success (the title of a popular book written in the 1970s that Reatha had studied

---

139. Pilgrim Baptist Church, "Our Story."
140. Groat, "Metro State President King."

and internalized), and she became a master at mingling and striking up productive conversations. Her quiet charisma was contagious, and people began describing her as a careful listener, honest and straightforward, and someone who never looks down on people, even though her intelligence was "so far above where you are."[141]

Reatha knew that her friend-raising efforts—all those polite conversations over chicken cordon bleu and crumb cake—would lead to *fund*raising, and that was one of the critical areas in which Metro State sorely needed improvement. President Sweet had established the framework of a school foundation, but it was abandoned and remained inactive for eight years, until 1980.[142] The foundation needed a guiding hand to start its engines once more and prioritize strategic fundraising efforts. Reatha's job was to make the foundation *functional*. It was time to raise some meaningful money so the school could not only continue to function but thrive.

In 1980, Reatha hired Terry Crowley as the first director of development for Metropolitan State University. He would spearhead the fundraising efforts through the Metro State Foundation and help Reatha "reorient" the foundation. Up to that point, the foundation's board of trustees had not been expected to fundraise at all; under President Sweet, it had primarily served as an advisory committee. Now, board members would have to learn a different set of skills and take on new responsibilities.

Reatha later said, "Early on, we needed to do role-clarification work with the trustees, so they would better understand their role and responsibility for fundraising... I worked with Fran [Naftalin, current president of the Metro State Foundation Trustees,] to recruit additional trustees, re-shape the role and responsibilities of the trustees more toward fundraising, and to develop that body into being a great resource for support of the University."[143]

In helping Terry Crowley reinvigorate and reorient the foundation, Reatha made certain to emphasize relationships. In reflecting on her

---

141. Various testimonials from Ken Frazier, chairman and CEO, Merck.; Bonnie Hill, cofounder, Icon Blue, director, Banc of California; and Kenneth Daly, former president and CEO, NACD ("Corporate Governance Hall of Fame").

142. Acosta, *Building a Legacy*.

143. Acosta, *Building a Legacy*.

tutelage, Crowley said she taught him "the importance of relationships. Not to simply send in the proposals but that it was important to develop relationships with our funders."[144] This philosophy helped Reatha become one of the most successful presidents in the school's history in terms of fundraising. She was strategic, visible, and unafraid to pound the pavement and do some of the fundraising work herself, instead of relying only on her team. Even though a faculty or staff member would often write the first draft of a grant request, Reatha would always review them and send them from "the president's desk." She believed in personal accountability and thought it important to play an active role in fundraising. She was also a talented grant writer, and taught others how to effectively put together a grant request. Eileen Deitcher, hired as a grant writer in 1981, reflected that she could "hear Reatha's voice" while writing grants.[145]

The school perpetually needed funds and new donors. Reatha understood the importance of private backers, and as a proponent of private enterprises, she wasn't afraid to ask local businesses for their support. In fact, part of the school's early fundraising strategy was to orient its fundraising toward major corporations, since it didn't have the budget to focus on smaller individual donors, and courting corporations would likely yield more "bang for the buck."

One of Reatha's very first missions was to gain the backing of a nearby corporate giant, a company with which she happened to have a quite personal connection: 3M. Founded in Two Harbors, Minnesota, in 1902, the Minnesota Mining and Manufacturing Company specialized in sandpaper and other abrasives at first. Over the decades, it expanded to include products as diverse as color copiers, Post-it Notes, thermal insulation for clothing, and traffic signs. In 1977, the year Reatha and the boys moved to Minnesota, the company celebrated its seventy-fifth birthday with eight thousand employees spread across the globe. At its headquarters, by now in Maplewood, the company employed thousands of workers and was a major presence in the area.

In years past, 3M's leadership team had largely ignored Metro State University, considering it a school not worthy of being taken seriously. Determined to change their minds, Reatha—ever the tireless

---

144. Acosta, *Building a Legacy*.
145. Acosta, *Building a Legacy*.

optimist—began connecting with those in the company's upper echelons. Slowly, she chipped away at past biases and impressions. One of her arguments was simple: Several 3M employees attended Metro State, taking advantage of the school's night classes to further their education. Wouldn't it make sense to financially support the school that had provided so many employees with new skill sets and expertise?

It was this, perhaps more than anything, that won over the 3M Foundation. After 3M's leadership understood how Metro State's offerings aligned with the desire of many of its employees to further their education, the corporate giant became one of Metro State's most consistent and generous donors.

In addition to gaining support from 3M, Reatha and her fundraising team succeeded in winning the support of several other major corporate foundations by the end of the decade. Honeywell, Ecolab, the Ford Motor Company, Securian, Norwest Bank (now Wells Fargo), and Xcel Energy were just a few of the major Twin Cities–area corporations to give to the school without walls. Slowly, local organizations were warming to the unconventional university in their backyard.

★ ★ ★

It wasn't long before the leaders of local enterprises began to view Reatha as a "friend of business." Not every leader in academia was affable with or accepting of corporations or the business community at large. But Reatha fully embraced business and understood how corporations could become valuable partners with academic institutions.

In this post–Vietnam War era, "pro-business" was not necessarily a popular stance; since many people viewed businesses as greedy, money-driven machines that profited off war, anti-business protests were widespread in the United States during the 1960s and well into the '70s. Historian Benjamin C. Waterhouse writes of the anti-business sentiments of the time: "Protesters viewed the business corporation as an integral part of the 'establishment.'" They saw corporations as entities that "[snuffed out] dissent, promoted imperialism abroad and injustice at home, and stifled free expression. Never removed from the issues of war and social justice, business was at the heart of the tumult of the 1960s."[146]

Some of the anti-business protests during the Vietnam era erupted in Minnesota, with one notable protest taking place at Honeywell's headquarters in Minneapolis on April 28, 1970. Honeywell, which specializes in chemicals and machine technology, produced fragmentation bombs, napalm, land mines, and other weapons that were shipped overseas to Vietnam. Outraged by the company's role in the war, a throng of several thousand activists disrupted its annual shareholder meeting, conveying their dissent through shouted chants and handwritten signs.

Still leery of public opinion, businesses in the late 1970s could never be certain of who supported and who despised them. Reatha's consistent efforts to connect with local businesses, coupled with her MBA, assured the Twin Cities business community she was not actively against private enterprise.

Because of her pro-business stance, Reatha unwittingly positioned herself as a viable candidate to serve on local corporate boards. Not only that, she embodied a sorely underrepresented demographic in business leadership. In the late 1970s, corporate boards were composed almost exclusively of white men. Almost 90 percent of Fortune 100 boards did *not* include a single female board member in 1975, while 93 percent of Fortune 1000 boards in 1973 were completely devoid of people of color (although this was an improvement from the 1960s, when figures showed *zero* African American people sat on those corporate boards).[147]

In the late '70s, with the women's liberation movement in full swing, those demographics were beginning to (slowly) change. Corporate boards began to actively diversify their composition and seek board members who would represent a wider range of voices. Although it might be argued that the companies did this to enhance their public image and court potential customers from diverse backgrounds, at least the status quo was shifting, regardless of the reasons.

Reatha's first invitation to serve on a corporate board came in 1978 from H. B. Fuller Company, an international adhesives business with a long history. Founded in 1887—a full ninety years before Reatha arrived

---

146. Waterhouse, "The Personal, the Political and the Profitable."
147. Fairfax, "Some Reflections."

in Minnesota—the publicly held corporation is known for its innovation and ethics, two attributes Reatha has long valued.

In 1978, the company's CEO was Anthony "Tony" Andersen. His father, Elmer Andersen, was the former president and CEO of H. B. Fuller as well as the governor of Minnesota from 1961 to 1963. When former governor Andersen learned about Reatha's presidential appointment and her positive view of businesses and corporations, he knew she would make a powerful ally. Tony shared that view, and he also admired Reatha's background as a scientist and her MBA degree.

The phone call came in the fall of 1978, just one year after Reatha began her presidency. Tony Andersen had done his homework and picked through Reatha's background and experience with a fine-toothed comb. When he officially invited her to serve on the board, he was confident in her abilities and eager to usher her in as a board member.

Reatha not only was flattered by the invitation but also saw it as a unique opportunity to validate her leadership and business skills. Serving on a corporate board could also improve Metro State's image—it would be known as a school led by a capable businesswoman.

After gaining approval from Metro State's board of trustees, Reatha enthusiastically accepted the offer and officially claimed her seat on a corporate board—the first of many. Just a few months later, she would be asked to serve on the local board of directors for Norwest Bank (rebranded as Wells Fargo in 1998) and would shift over to the company's corporate board in 1986. After that, the invitations streamed in. Reatha began serving on the board of Minnesota Mutual Companies in 1984, Exxon Corporation (later ExxonMobil) in 1997, Department 56 (which would become Lenox Group) in 2002, and Allina Health System in 2011. Additionally, she has served on over *fifty* nonprofit, philanthropic, and education-oriented boards from the early 1980s to today. (See page 315 in the appendix for details.)

After a few decades, Reatha would become "boarded out," but while she sat on each board, she treated her work with the same kind of diligence and care she brought to her presidency. After she received the National Association of Corporate Directors' prestigious Corporate Governance Hall of Fame award, former Exxon CEO and secretary of state Rex Tillerson commended her, saying, "What I immediately recognized about Reatha was her work ethic. She came to every board committee meeting, every board meeting, clearly fully prepared."[148]

When she started her board service at H. B. Fuller in 1978, Reatha had no idea how much she would learn and how far her influence would reach. Not only did she guide H. B. Fuller in its decisions to support underserved populations and diversity-centered causes (including directing the company to purchase from minority-owned businesses and recruit leaders from diverse backgrounds), but she also pried open the gate a little further to allow other women and people of color to get past the white male gatekeepers and secure their own spots at boardroom tables. She was willing to be outspoken, raise "touchy issues," and "take the lead in discussions of family, gender or race issues."[149]

During her twenty-five years on H. B. Fuller's board, the changes in corporate board demographics were noticeable. By 2003, at least one female representative sat on the board of every single Fortune 100 company, and by 2004, at least one person of color sat on the board of 76 percent of Fortune 1000 companies.[150]

Though this indicated progress, the work for equal representation in corporate America was (and still is) far from over. After serving on boards for two decades, Reatha had noticed this uptick in board members who were female and/or people of color but lamented the fact that they often seemed like "tokens." She told the *Star Tribune* in 1997 that once a board recruits its first female board member, it tends to lose "that eagerness, that sense of urgency to get the second woman and the third and the fourth and so on."[151]

In the same article, she says that her active participation in a given board prevented her from feeling like a "token." It wasn't enough to gain a seat at the boardroom table; she demanded a voice as well. Fortunately, most of her fellow board members welcomed and appreciated her views. She was famously overprepared and an excellent listener, and she asked tough questions that drove at the heart of *why* the board did things, not just *what* they did. Indeed, one of the characteristics Reatha attributes to her successful board service was courage. "Some people see board

---

148. "Corporate Governance Hall of Fame."
149. Merrill, "Veteran Reatha Clark King."
150. Fairfax, "Some Reflections."
151. Apgar, "Women Finding Place in Boardroom."

service as habitual work or routine work," she said, "but . . . it takes a bit of courage. That's one of the traits I brought to the table."[152]

★ ★ ★

Reatha's friend-raising was not limited to the business world. She understood that a community is made up of more than corporations—it includes schools, religious institutions, individuals (including alumni), and nonprofit organizations. It involves people from all backgrounds and occupations: politicians, academics, teachers, homemakers. It is multifaceted with myriad interests. And she was determined to familiarize herself with all facets, all interests. She attended events held by major nonprofit organizations, such as the United Way and any number of healthcare-oriented nonprofits in the Twin Cities. She gave presentations at local churches and became acquainted with many local ministers, priests, and pastors. She spoke at so many chambers of commerce and Rotary Club meetings that she lost track of how many ("Almost all of them in the state!" she says).

Propelled by her mission to connect with a diverse set of people, Reatha also endeavored to strategically network with one particularly important piece of the community: local legislators. As a state school, much of Metro State's funding came from public coffers—coffers that could be either closed or opened by legislators. Reatha had to prove that, yes, the school was worth supporting year after year, and, yes, taxpayers' money was being put to good use.

Part of her plan involved simply paying attention. She familiarized herself with the legislative schedule and knew when relevant bills or initiatives would be debated. Later in her presidency, Reatha would establish a Wednesday-morning "legislative huddle," in which Metro State fundraisers and staff would meet at 7:30 a.m. (Reatha would often arrive by 6:30) while the state legislature was in session to discuss strategies, review any relevant bills, and plan lobbying efforts. As Nancy McKillips, who began her work at Metro State in 1980 as the alumni relations director before becoming the director of the university's

---

152. Schneider and Schneider, "The Pioneer."

foundation, recalls, "Reatha would give us our walking orders for the week—who to call, what to say."[153]

Metro State's lobbying was intentional, directed. Reatha understood how important political connections were to the viability of the school, and she made sure the faculty and staff understood it, too. In the legislative chambers, funding for vital programs could be won or lost. The school's fate rested heavily in the hands of a handful of politicians. Thus, making strategic connections was a critical component of Reatha's long-term planning. By gradually building trust, she could convince the legislators to vote in Metro's favor.

It helped that several Metro State alumni went on to work in politics. Metro graduates have represented every district in Minnesota, leaving their footprints in the state's legislature. According to a 1987 news article, "Insiders say that when the political battles get tough, King calls on alumni for support, working from a list of graduates, their legislative districts and the names of legislators they should contact."[154] Metro State graduates, as Reatha attests, are one of the school's most valuable assets, and she never took them for granted.

Whenever the legislature was deciding on a relevant bill or discussing a higher education initiative, Reatha would attend the session. She says, "I learned that I had to be dressed to go to the legislature at all times." Wearing her well-pressed business suits, Reatha was a picture of professionalism. This, in addition to her preparedness, quickly earned her the respect of several legislators as well as local mayors and governors (and former governors).

> Former state senator and current chairman of Taylor Corporation Glen Taylor says, "I was fortunate to get to know Dr. King when I served as a Minnesota state senator and as a businessman. I found Reatha Clark King to be extremely intelligent and also genuinely thoughtful and caring when discussing the issues of the day. I valued her friendship."[155]
>
> Former representative Lyndon R. Carlson Sr. says, "During her presidency at Metropolitan State University, Dr. Reatha Clark

---

153. Nancy McKillips, interview.
154. Groat, "Metro State President King."
155. Glen Taylor, interview.

King was highly engaged in the Minnesota State Legislature. She was well respected as a strong speaker and a passionate advocate for higher education. I remember how well prepared and thoughtful she was whenever she testified before the legislature. When I think of Dr. King today, I recall her calm demeanor and keen mind—the mind of a true intellectual."[156]

It was clear Reatha was a passionate advocate for Metro State and her beloved community. She fought tirelessly and inspired others to do the same. But when asked about her contributions, she is quick to credit her support staff and faculty for helping her succeed. "All you need is willing hearts and willing hands," she says. "I was lucky enough to have both."

★ ★ ★

As a young girl in South Georgia, Reatha's world fit within a handful of miles. It was defined by familiar people and landmarks. Her feet knew every dusty gravel road, and she could find every important point in her life without difficulty: her family home; Mount Zion Church; the general store where Grandma Mamie bought flour, sugar, and cooking oil; the Normans' sun-beaten cotton and tobacco fields.

In that place and time, Reatha's dreams took her north: to Washington, DC, and Baltimore and New York City. These cities were within her grasp; they were places where her relatives had settled and carved out a living. Rarely did young Reatha think about the lands and oceans and cities outside the borders of the United States. These were places one read about in history books and novels. They were near fantasies—locales beyond the reach of her hardscrabble reality. Never did she imagine setting foot in India, Mexico, or Russia. Never did she dream of touring temples in Japan or viewing the Swiss Alps or strolling along canals in the Netherlands.

But these far-off places did become part of Reatha's reality. She would travel to five continents (all except Australia and Antarctica), delivering academic lectures, performing corporate board work, and involving herself in humanitarian service work. She would sip coffee in

---

156. Lyndon Carlson, interview.

France and eat olives in Morocco. She would meet people of all ages and backgrounds and learn one of her greatest life lessons: people are pretty much the same, no matter where you go. They care about their families, their careers, their futures. They have insecurities and fears. And, most importantly, the vast majority of people are loving and kind—spending most of their waking hours thinking about their tiny world in their tiny corner of this vast earth, much like Reatha did when she was a girl.

Though Reatha had been abroad once while working as a dean at York College (a 1970 NATO-sponsored trip to the Netherlands) and once for an H. B. Fuller board meeting (to Montreal, Canada), her international travel truly began in 1980 with encouragement from her colleagues Donna Shalala and Martha Church. Reatha knew these two intrepid, high-powered women through the American Council on Education and became close friends with both of them. In 1980, Donna was the president of Hunter College in New York City; she would go on to become the president of the University of Miami, serve in President Bill Clinton's cabinet, and become a US representative in Florida. Martha was the first female president of Hood College in Maryland. Known for her sense of adventure, she traveled to all seven continents and even went on a climbing expedition to Mount Everest.

These two women traveled frequently, delivering scholarly lectures to international students, and agreed that Reatha—with her wealth of experience, engaging public speaking style, and unique background—would also excel on the global stage. With visions of their friend and colleague on the international lecture circuit, they decided to nominate Reatha for a speaking role through the US Information Agency (USIA).

The USIA accepted their nomination, and Reatha embarked on a new adventure: traveling the world and delivering lectures as a USIA American Participant, or "AmPart."

Over the next eight years, Reatha participated in six education-focused international trips in nine countries. With each new tour, her horizons opened a little wider. She visited Cape Town and marveled at the mountains plummeting down to the blue ocean. She visited Austria and Germany, taking her youngest son, Scott, with her so he, too, could view the landscapes, ride on trains, and taste Bavarian cuisine. She even had a chance to tour the Soviet Union before its dissolution—an experience that exposed her to practical, blocky architecture, government-run shopping centers, and grocery stores that carried only one brand of soap or type of toothpaste. The Soviet secret police force, the infamous KGB, was active during this time, and Reatha and her travel companions had to tread lightly and maintain the proper respect and decorum.

Reatha approached her travels with the same eagerness with which she had explored new scientific subjects. She asked questions and she talked to people; in return, people took an interest in her. Her trips became an international exchange of information and ideas.

After she retired from academia, Reatha's international travels continued. She frequently traveled for corporate board work and ended up visiting twenty-eight countries and territories, from her first trip in 1983 (Mexico) to her final trip in 2007 (Gibraltar).

Most of Reatha's trips across the world were wholly positive, affirming experiences. She had engaging conversations with individuals and spoke to captivated audiences. (The USIA reported that "Dr. King's rapport with her audiences was excellent."[157]) However, she did encounter the occasional disheartening incident rooted in xenophobia, sexism, or racism. One of the most notable occurred close to home, during an H. B. Fuller board meeting in Montreal, Canada. After a long day of meetings, Reatha and her fellow board members boarded a shuttle bus at their hotel and rode to a high-end club for dinner. After an elaborate white-tablecloth dinner, the waitstaff ushered the board members out the back door of the restaurant, where their shuttle bus was waiting. Puzzled, one of the board members—a friend of Reatha's named Norbert Berg—asked why they were escorted out the back door and not the front door.

A staff member explained that it was because Reatha was with them. The club usually only catered to white men—no women or people of color allowed. The year was 1979. Clearly, segregation and racism hadn't evaporated after the civil rights movement.

When Norbert heard the staff's explanation, he about hit the roof. After spouting a string of expletives, he turned and apologized to Reatha. "The board would have never eaten here if we had known," he said.

Reatha nodded and steadied her jangled nerves. She was hurt and more than a little angry, but she contained her burbling emotions and

---

157. "Tanzania Evaluation."

comported herself with characteristic poise. The business trip moved on, and Reatha continued her work with the same focus and dedication.

But she never forgot the incident, and, more than forty years later, it still stings.

But the incident in Montreal was a rare smudge on a string of successful, stimulating international trips. In all corners of the world, Reatha connected with the people she met. Whether dining with a chargé d'affaires from Tanzania or riding in a bus with a Korean tour guide, Reatha made a point of building bridges. Perhaps due to her friendliness or her curiosity-driven tendency to ask questions, people would often open up to her and entrust her with private information. In Japan, a young tour guide shared his fears about his aging mother living alone ("I'm the eldest son, but mom doesn't want to live with me *or* any of my siblings!"). In Korea, a young woman told Reatha that she still lived with her parents—a fact that made her slightly embarrassed around Americans, who tend to fly the coop much earlier than Koreans.

"In the end," Reatha says, "people are much the same no matter where you go. They grumble about traffic jams, they care for their families, they worry about their jobs." This common humanity revealed itself during Reatha's travels and gave her a broader perspective on human life. Because of her myriad personal experiences with people across the globe, she will forever see the interconnectedness between humans—a web that knows no limits.

★ ★ ★

Reatha's efforts to connect with the community paid off. The school gained a few major financial backers, and Metropolitan State University began to work its way into the public consciousness. However, the university president was, for a time, better known than her school. Fundraisers would call potential donors and hear, time and again, "Oh, I know Metro State. That's Reatha Clark King's school, right?"

Reatha's name carried clout, but, for many people, the school itself was still shrouded in mystery. What was this place without a central campus or letter grades?[158] Who were these students, whose ages ranged

---
158. Under Reatha's presidency, students could choose between a written evaluation or a letter grade.

from early twenties to late seventies? What was a "community faculty member," and why on earth were they teaching most of the school's classes?

The public's befuddlement, however, was not clear to the Metro State team until Reatha decided to hire a fundraising firm from Chicago to conduct research and figure out how to improve the school's fundraising approach. That firm surveyed members of the community and confirmed two things: (1) people recognized Reatha's name, and (2) they knew very little about the school she represented.

To increase the public's understanding of Metro State and its offerings, the firm recommended some awareness building in the form of public outreach. Hold public events, it suggested, in which Metro representatives talk about the school and its structure in addition to fielding questions from the community.

Reatha and her team took the suggestions to heart.

What evolved was a series of breakfasts and lunches that centered on the theme "Lifelong Learning: Its Impact on You." At these meetings, attendees (several of them potential donors) would enjoy a complimentary meal and listen to presentations and testimonials from Metro State student speakers, alumni, and staff.

The first Lifelong Learning event took place in Wayzata, Minnesota, about twenty-five miles west of Saint Paul, and was sponsored by none other than one of Reatha's greatest champions: former governor Elmer Andersen. From the very beginning, the breakfasts and luncheons were a success. Attendance was strong, often with close to one hundred people present at any given event. The audience represented a large cross-section of the community: wealthy homemakers who were toying with the idea of going back to school, people thinking about a career change, business owners whose employees might benefit from continuing education, politicians and academics interested in the progress of their state's youngest university.

The Lifelong Learning events succeeded in helping the Twin Cities community understand the new, unorthodox school in its backyard. And the best ambassadors for the school were, undoubtedly, its students.

Though Reatha spent a good portion of her time on friend-raising and fundraising, her central focus was always Metro State's students and alumni. She called them "part of her beloved community" and understood that every action she took, every dollar she raised, was for them. And she wasn't alone. Metro State's faculty (both full-time and community) and its staff were wholly dedicated to their students. They knew that the school's growing number of attendees and alumni were its lifeblood—the reason for maintaining an unconventional structure, despite pressure to conform.

These students would become local politicians and changemakers. They would found nonprofits, produce films, write plays, teach, publish poetry and fiction, and earn numerous accolades and achievements. One even became vice president of Sierra Leone.

They were the voice of Metropolitan State University, and they were fierce advocates for the school and its mission. Vocalizing their support for the nontraditional curriculum and admissions system, they were quick to credit the school with giving them an unprecedented opportunity to reach higher, go farther.

These were students who came from a wide array of backgrounds and circumstances. Many were single parents, older students, people of color, or students from other marginalized backgrounds. Some started taking classes at Metro with the hope of reentering the workforce after a long hiatus. Others had not completed college and were seeking a second chance. At the Lifelong Learning events, their stories made an impact. Potential donors, community members, and politicians alike were drawn in by their sincerity and devotion to their school. The students' advocacy became one of the university's greatest assets.

★ ★ ★

In her early years at Metro State, Reatha Clark King proved to be adept and savvy, but she failed miserably in one department: delegation. She was the type of person who believed that if you wanted things done right, it was best to do them yourself, and because of this mindset, Reatha was busy. In fact, *busy* is an understatement—she was inundated with work. She would arrive at her desk around seven-thirty each morning, plan her day, and then bustle around making phone calls, hosting meetings, engaging in fundraising, and stamping out any number of little fires that sprang up during the day.

Reatha's colleagues recall her as busy and bright, managing a full schedule every day but never appearing haggard or worn down. Nancy McKillips, who worked closely with Reatha from 1980 on, would often ride with her to meetings and remembers her diligently poring over her notes in the car. Even if she only had fifteen minutes to spare, Reatha would use that time to review information about the person or organization with whom she was about to meet.

That was the kind of person Reatha was, and still is: energetic and prepared.

But even superheroes have sidekicks, and Reatha soon found herself in need of a personal assistant. The first person she hired was a woman who worked part-time (the slim budget could only stretch so far). This particular hire, however, quickly became problematic.

At first, she seemed to learn the ins and outs of her job and settle into her duties without much fuss. It wasn't long, however, before her true colors shone through her congenial façade. One day, Reatha had to attend to some crucial items related to Metro State's upcoming budget presentation to the state legislature and found herself flooded with work. When she asked her new assistant for, well, *assistance*, the woman flatly refused. "Do it yourself," she said.

A half dozen emotions swelled within Reatha. She was upset, shocked, angry, a little sad—but she didn't have time to be distracted. There was work to do and deadlines to meet, and she supposed she *would* have to do it herself. She kept a level head about her and delegated another task: she asked Metro State's director of personnel, Jan Anderson, to let the new assistant go.

Appalled by what had transpired, Jan assured Reatha she would take care of the situation. By the time Reatha returned from attending her committee hearing at the state capitol building, the impertinent assistant was no longer in the building and no longer part of Metro State University.

To this day, Reatha isn't certain whether the assistant refused to carry out her simple assignment because of Reatha's race or gender, but she *is* convinced that one of the two factors (or both) played a role in her impudence. The president of a university should command respect, especially if that president happens to be your direct superior, and

Reatha could not imagine the woman behaving the same way with a white, male superior.

She notes that opinion polls in the 1970s and '80s showed that "most employees preferred a male supervisor, and some actually resented and resisted reporting to women. Some people were blatant and said openly, 'I don't want no woman boss!'"[159] In Reatha's case, of course, she was fighting against a double bias, evidenced by the abysmal lack of both women and people of color in academic and corporate leadership positions.

The undercurrent of racism and sexism that flowed (and still flows) through the American psyche had reared its ugly head. It didn't matter that Minnesota was known for its progressivism and inclusion—racist and sexist attitudes could still lurk under the surface of those who appeared to embrace the state's attitude of "Minnesota nice."

---

159. Harvey, *Grass Roots and Glass Ceilings*.

CHAPTER SIXTEEN

Driving against Traffic

"If you stand on the shoulders of others,
you have a reciprocal responsibility to live your life so that
others may stand on your shoulders."

—Vernon Jordan

In the spring of 1981, right before Metro State's tenth birthday, Reatha sat in the Minnesota State Capitol building, listening to a legislative conference committee meeting. At her side were two of Metro State's directors, Marilyn Loen and Skip Menikheim. It was three o'clock in the morning, and the trio were bleary eyed and heavy headed, but they stayed awake, listening to the committee debate. This was too important to sleep through.

In those wee morning hours, the legislative committee was debating whether to grant more than a half million dollars to Metro State to establish a nursing program. For a school that prided itself on individualized education and student-defined majors, establishing a traditional nursing curriculum seemed to some like a major deviation from its unconventional norm.

Finally, the committee reached a decision: it would allot $525,000 to Metropolitan State University for its nursing program. Request granted.

Reatha and her colleagues cheered. This, they knew, was the start of a new, important chapter for their school.

In the months leading up to the legislative committee hearing, Reatha had been faced with the Sisyphean task of convincing the faculty, the state legislators, and her fellow academic leaders in the state university system that Metro State needed a nursing program. The faculty members, many of whom had been with the school since its inception or shortly thereafter, resisted the notion of introducing traditional curriculum. Reatha, however, perceived a need in the community for standardized programs, especially in science—and math-oriented areas. The most urgent need, she argued, was an accredited nursing program.

The local community was clamoring for additional nurses and had started recruiting scads of nurses from overseas to fill the gap. (Reatha says that Abbott Northwestern Hospital, for instance, was actively recruiting nurses from the Philippines.) Adding a nursing program to Metro State's offerings was a logical step—one that would help meet the growing demand for nurses and provide nontraditional students an accessible path for entering an in-demand field. But logic, as Reatha had long ago discovered, does not always prevail.

From the moment the idea surfaced and was made public, it was met with resistance. Opponents believed that the University of Minnesota, which already housed a highly acclaimed nursing program, would never allow Metro State to host its own program. Faculty would ask, "Will they *let* us do that?"

Reatha wanted to shout, "Who cares? We're our own school and we don't need permission to start our own programs!" But, with unflappable composure, she addressed the dissenters' concerns with an even temper and carefully constructed arguments. She knew that both the medical community and the public were desperate for more nursing programs, and she was determined to meet that need.

All the hubbub and resistance was for naught. Reatha, the master networker, had befriended the U of M's president, Dr. C. Peter Magrath, and she was confident he would support Metro State's nursing initiative. She was right. Magrath recognized that the area was suffering from a dearth of local nursing programs and saw Metro State's vision as *complementary* to that of the University of Minnesota, not *competitive*. With his blessing, Reatha forged on and began garnering the legislative and financial support she would need to fund a fully accredited program. She called upon the allies she had made over the past few years—the "friends in high places," as she calls them. Among these important supporters were Governor Al Quie, Abbott Northwestern Hospital CEO Gordon

Sprenger, and philanthropist and Metro alumna Beverly Grossman (who ended up gifting the school $30,000 for its nursing program).

After a good deal of planning, lobbying, and strategic meetings, in which Reatha laid out her case for establishing the program, the state legislature agreed to hold a hearing to decide whether or not to fund it. This was the hearing that dragged on until three in the morning. This was the hearing that ultimately granted the school's request.

Metro State would sail into its tenth year propelled by its newly established accredited nursing program and plans to expand its course offerings, including a women's studies program. Though some dissenting voices claimed that traditional curriculum would erode the school's very foundation, this fear was never realized. And these programs, which provided more options and career paths for Metro State's students—students who were often older, people of color, and/or first-generation college students—were applauded by national figures. Among these figures was Coretta Scott King, who showed her support for Metro State and, in particular, the newly established women's studies program by speaking at a Metro-sponsored event at Sabathani Community Center in Minneapolis. After they met, Reatha and Coretta Scott King became fast friends and would come to call each other "sister."

Today, as the school sails past its fiftieth year, many of the same values—focusing on underserved populations, catering to nontraditional students, emphasizing career-oriented degrees and field studies—are still very much intact. The nursing program has expanded into its own college, the College of Nursing and Health Sciences, and remains one of the vital areas of study at the school. Even today, forty years after it began, the College of Nursing remembers its roots by promoting "educational advancement through uniquely designed programs, community partnerships, scholarly activities, and academic excellence that are guided by the mission to prepare graduates to enhance the health of underserved and diverse populations."[160]

The beating heart of the school still thrums along.

★ ★ ★

---

160. Metropolitan State University, "College of Nursing."

On November 1, 1981, Metropolitan State University celebrated its tenth birthday. The day's activities included a pep rally, coffee and donuts, a pickup football game (faculty and staff versus students and alumni), and an open house in the Metro Square building's lobby (the administrative offices were right upstairs). In true early-'80s fashion, students and faculty members alike donned Metropolitan State University T-shirts over their turtlenecks and took to McMurray Field to play a friendly game of football. Since the school had neither the budget nor the inclination to sponsor collegiate sports teams, this was a rare treat for Metro State, and one that the faculty and students thoroughly enjoyed.

Like the school itself, the celebrations were not ostentatious or expensive. The budget was still too tight for much pomp and circumstance, but that scarcely mattered. The milestone Metro State had just crossed was nothing short of momentous. Ten years had passed—one whole decade—and the school was stronger than ever and showed no signs of slowing.

Reatha smiles when she recalls the anniversary. "At that point," she says, "we had the vote of confidence from the community. That's when you know you've arrived."

Those who had doubted or had actively spoken out against the school and its unconventional structure were forced to admit that *something* was going right. How else could Metro State continue to grow in both size and influence with each passing year?

In fact, many things were going right for the school without walls. Enrollment increased in the first ten years from an initial group of fifty students to well over two thousand; the school was accumulating a group of outspoken, dedicated alumni; and the Minnesota State Legislature continued to provide financial support. Local major corporations, nonprofits, and individual donors were backing Metro State with much-needed funds—a sign that the Twin Cities community was taking the school and its mission seriously.

For Reatha, this was a time of personal growth and skill development. She was growing more comfortable in her role, and her leadership was maturing with each crisis she overcame, each conflict she navigated. She had become well acquainted with delegation, speechwriting, and press conferences. She was gaining trust and clout in the community and the state of Minnesota in addition to her national and international recognition.

As Reatha gained respect and trust, so, too, did Metropolitan State University. One of the most important signs of the school's development and progress was its increased number of supporters and advocates in academia, both in Minnesota and across the nation. Among the school's (and Reatha's) most ardent and prestigious supporters were Harvard University president Derek Bok, Georgetown University president Timothy Healy, and University of Notre Dame president Father Ted Hesburgh. The heads of these nationally acclaimed universities, as well as other leaders, threw their support behind Reatha and Metro State, championing the school, its mission, and its structure.

Aside from persistent media coverage, Reatha garnered the attention and support of these nationally recognized figures through her participation in and contributions to the American Council on Education. ACE is a national nonprofit organization based in Washington, DC, that focuses on shaping and improving higher education through public policy initiatives and innovation. In it, Reatha saw an opportunity to make a profound impact on higher education on a national scale. In true Reatha Clark King fashion, she jumped into the heart of the organization and began serving on its board of directors alongside talented and ambitious academic leaders from across the country. She would serve on the board for about a decade and was its chair for four years. This position came with a good deal of power, and Reatha wielded it like a sword of justice.

Through ACE, Reatha fought for social justice and gender and racial equity. She recognized the systemic biases that existed toward women and people of color and made it a priority to face those biases head-on. This wasn't simply about shifting leadership demographics; this was about legitimizing women and people of color in their leadership roles. It was about equal respect, equal clout, and equal pay.

As chair of the board, Reatha was highly visible. Capitalizing on her place in the spotlight, she built strategic alliances, lobbied for legislative changes, and occasionally testified before Congress as a representative of the American Council on Education. The strategies, methodology, and work ethic she employed in Minnesota carried over to her work in the national arena.

★ ★ ★

Surprisingly, Reatha and Metro State earned the respect and attention of national higher education leaders more easily than that of local leaders. Perhaps the reluctance to fully accept the university stemmed from the fact that this wasn't just some pie-in-the-sky notion—this was a very real school, operating on state dollars. If it failed, the reputation of Minnesota's higher education system might suffer, and the state's residents would surely not take kindly to wasted tax dollars.

Some leaders in Minnesota's higher education system did, however, support Metro's mission, and they became more numerous and vociferous as the years ticked by. Metro State was proving that no, it wasn't going anywhere, and yes, it played a vital role in higher education.

Among the school's early local supporters was the University of Minnesota's president, C. Peter Magrath. He respected the school's model and considered it a much-needed offering in Minnesota's academic system. Other presidents of local universities (Augsburg University, the University of St. Thomas, Saint John's University, St. Catherine University, and more) also rallied behind Reatha and the Metro State's mission.

Two of Reatha's boldest supporters in her early presidential years were Carleton College and its president, Robert Edwards. Eager to start serving adult learners and other students who didn't fit the typical mold, Carleton College began designing an entire program exclusively for nontraditional students, mirroring the model created by Metro State. Edwards and the Carleton College board of trustees applauded Metro's vision and recognized Reatha's role in the school's sustained success. Because of their admiration and respect for her work, Carleton awarded her an honorary degree in 1982. This award is reserved for those who have "achieved eminence in their own profession or who have rendered distinguished service to society."[161] Reatha had accomplished both.

Reatha's honorary degree—the first of fourteen she would receive over her career—was a credit to both her institution and her. It affirmed her leadership abilities and helped solidify Metro State's standing in academia.

All the support Reatha and the university were gaining from the academic community was slowly chipping away at the faculty's

---

161. Carleton College, "Honorary Degrees."

self-consciousness. The school's allies bolstered the staff's collective confidence and validated Metro's structure and programs. In time, Metro State would become known for its academic leadership, fearless innovation, and dogged advocacy for underserved populations. It was not, as some had assumed, rudderless and underachieving. It was adeptly serving an ever-growing student body, and other schools were beginning to notice.

It did not take long, in fact, for other colleges and universities besides Carleton (both in Minnesota and across the country) to begin mimicking Metro State's approach. Reatha compares this gradual shift in perspective to the flow of traffic. It only takes one car driving against traffic to disrupt the accepted flow. If that disruption prompts other cars to turn around and drive the other way, you have the makings of a revolution. Once the majority of cars turn and go the other way, you have a "new normal."

In the early 1980s, Metro State was still one of only a handful of cars wending its way through the crush of the status quo. It was leading the way in a bold new world that dared to broaden its definition of *who* can be a student and *what* they are required to study.

Compelled by its innovative approach, and aware of the increasing demand for a flexible scholastic format that caters to older students, other university and college presidents began turning to Reatha for advice. They would approach her at a gala or fundraising event or call her on the phone, asking for guidance. After expressing their interest in starting a program for nontraditional students, they would ask questions that boiled down to "How did you do it?"

Reatha freely admits that she, alone, did not make Metro State. The school's founders, in addition to the dozens of dedicated faculty members, volunteer teachers, administrators, and students, made the school what it is. But she did steer the ship and help to bring about a new era of sophistication and strategy. She helped make an idyllic idea—and a loose model—tangible. She was, as Metro State professor emerita Bev Ferguson says, "the manager," complementing David Sweet, who was "the visionary." Reatha, as Ferguson puts it, "straightened out the university and put it on a more permanent course."[162]

---

162. Lofquist, *Metropolitan State University Buzz*.

The simple truth was that if the school were going to stay relevant and continue to grow, changes had to be made.

One of the major changes Reatha brought to Metro was the introduction of traditionally structured programs. Some degrees, she reasoned, required a more concrete path than what the individualized education programs typically offered. Especially in the sciences, mathematics, and healthcare-related areas of study, it made sense to follow a prescribed curriculum—one that logically built off the concepts learned in prior classes.

The introduction of traditionally structured programs was met with a good deal of resistance. The longtime faculty were especially reluctant to change and feared that offering predetermined curriculum would undermine the flexibility at the very core of their university. The system of IEPs was dear to their hearts, and they were not about to give it up without a fight.

Reatha understood the faculty members' concerns and agreed that the IEPs should stay. There was room for both approaches, she argued. Some students could follow a more traditional track, while others—those who sought flexibility and unconventional learning opportunities— could stick with the original system of cocreating an IEP with a faculty advisor. As she was introducing the new programs, Reatha navigated doubts and dissent with the adeptness and grace of a tightrope walker. She balanced the school's unconventional system with the traditional, the familiar approach with the new one, the reluctant faculty with those eager for change.

The addition of traditional curriculum was just one in a long line of changes that would occur over the years, and Reatha wasn't the only one to spearhead them. For instance, under the leadership of Dr. Susan Cole (president from 1993 to 1998), the school would begin to admit undergraduate students, add several traditional majors to its offerings, and hire several more permanent faculty members (which reduced the need for so many community teachers). Cole, who was more traditional in her approach than past Metro State presidents, also required professors to issue letter grades instead of written testimonials—they were no longer optional.

Toward the end of Reatha's tenure as president, the university would begin to construct its first official building—an administrative center dubbed Saint John's Hall, located in Saint Paul's Dayton's Bluff neighborhood. After that, walls would continue to go up until the school had its own central campus, in addition to the various spaces it rented across the Twin Cities.

Former Metro State president Sue K. Hammersmith (2008–2013) said of the university's changes that the school has "evolved and adapted to serve an ever-changing student population and region. But as much as this university has changed from its early days, some things never change. That spirit of innovation, focus on mission and determination to help learners achieve their individual education goals and potential remain at the core of Metropolitan State University."[163]

Reatha believed in that spirit of innovation and fought for it. Even though change was inevitable, she was determined to maintain its core principles and objectives. That meant keeping students at the center of her focus. She praises the students as some of the most brilliant people she has met. "Those who enrolled at Metro State were already diamonds," she says. "We just polished them up and made them shine."

Reatha saw reflections of her own community in the university's nontraditional students: her father, who never had the opportunity to attend school; her grandma Mamie, so bright, despite lacking a formal education; her sister Dot, who had dropped out of college. Metro State was a school for second chances, for people who had been shunned and blocked from higher education by the gatekeepers. Reatha never lost sight of that. And neither did the rest of her staff.

The students were the center of their focus when it came to introducing new curriculum and new programs.

They were central when it came to fundraising and alliance building.

They were central in every legislative hearing and committee meeting Reatha attended.

They were central from the day they enrolled at Metro State to the day they graduated.

Graduations were always special occasions at Metro, brimming with unabashed joy and hope for the future. Since many of the students were older and had spouses and/or children, the seats at graduation ceremonies would fill with those and other family members, who would

---

163. Lofquist, *Metropolitan State University Buzz*.

shout their encouragements and clap with the same enthusiasm as a crowd at a rock concert.

"Great work, Mom!"

"Go, Dad!"

"Hooray, Sam! Go get 'em!"

Reatha thinks of the students' graduation ceremonies as high points in her career. She would look across the packed-to-the-brim audience and her heart would flood with pride and pure elation. These were the school's cherished students—the core of Reatha's beloved Metro State community. They were the reason she worked as hard as she did, day in, day out.

For several years, the school held three graduation ceremonies each year. Since it did not have formal semesters during its early years, this format was as good as any.

Metro State graduations began as humble, almost casual, affairs. The students did not wear caps and gowns, the ceremonies took place in a small community space, and the graduates did not make a formal entrance but, rather, sat dispersed among the crowd. Though this type of bare-bones celebration was functional, it did not exactly reflect the immensity of the event. Many students were first-generation college graduates, and *all* students had worked hard and put in long hours (oftentimes late at night or on weekends) to earn their degrees.

Sheila Mohr, whom Reatha hired in 1985 as the commencement coordinator, began sending out surveys to alumni, asking for their input on graduation ceremonies. By and large, the graduates expressed a desire for a grander celebration to honor their achievements. The school listened.

After more than a decade of informality, the graduation ceremonies began to change. In 1987, the students began wearing caps and gowns, the school added a formal procession, and the day was marked with a good deal more ceremony. A luncheon to honor the graduating students at the top of their class was also initiated, during which tears and emotions flowed freely as the students told stories about their experience at Metro State. Some had taken classes for six or seven years before graduating—a class here, a class there. They squeezed courses and homework into the cracks of their busy lives.

Though some faculty opposed the changes (*Caps and gowns? Are we really going to conform to that pointless tradition?*), the students had the final word. They were planted squarely at the center of the school's focus, and even though much has changed at Metro over the years, the student-centric focus has not.

Another way Reatha and Metro State strove to serve the student body was by hiring and promoting faculty and staff that hailed from backgrounds, genders, and races similar to their students'. The school attracted a diverse set of well-qualified individuals due to its reputation for being fair and equitable. Women, for instance, were not hired simply to fill a demographic quota; they were hired due to merit and ability, and if they proved to be effective in their position, they were promoted.

★ ★ ★

The student graduations, the more equitable representation among faculty and staff—these were clear representations of Metro State's and Reatha's success. Reatha did her best to hang on to these positive reminders of the school's development when times got tough. And times did, indeed, get tough.

Reatha refers to the challenges she encountered as teachable moments. Every day, it seemed, some new fire would crop up that needed quelling. Reatha says, "When I left the office, there would be a bigger challenge on my desk when I returned."

One of the regular challenges she faced was making tough decisions about faculty tenure. As she had at York College, Reatha was in charge of reviewing faculty members who were up for tenure, and either granting or denying it. If tenure was denied, the faculty member was let go. People's livelihoods and futures rested in her hands.

Though it pained Reatha to let people go, she recalls steeling her nerves and facing the task with as much objectivity as she could muster— the objectivity of a trained scientist. That, coupled with her propensity for optimism, helped her dismiss faculty members as gently as possible. She remembers soothing one young, teary-eyed faculty member by saying, "Keep in mind, your entire life is ahead of you."

Dealing with the occasional faculty dismissal was a fairly typical challenge for any university president, but Reatha faced her share of unusual challenges as well. A particularly poignant one came in 1984, when she presented the state college board with a proposal for implementing a minority service program at Metro State. The program would aid in recruiting and supporting students of color, which Reatha viewed as an urgent and pressing need.

The request was met with crickets and complaints. Reatha's colleagues either remained tight-lipped or dismissed the initiative outright, saying it didn't belong in the annual budget. But Reatha knew it *did* belong and understood how such a program could benefit current and future students of color. Despite her arguments, her colleagues remained unmoved.

Sensing her endeavors with the university board were futile, Reatha instructed the Metro State Foundation to seek funding from private coffers. Their efforts proved successful, and a minority service program was founded, which Reatha has called "one of the finest services of its kind on any campus in Minnesota."[164]

In addition to race-related challenges, Reatha dealt with a threat of a different kind during her presidency: lawsuits. Every university, and, by extension, every university president, is in danger of being sued by *someone*. That's what happens when you lead a public-facing institution or company—you become an easy target for lawsuits.

Most lawsuits against Metro State were resolved quickly, with little fuss. Reatha, however, was the victim of "wrong place, wrong time" and was personally sued for an incident so bizarre that it instantly drummed up media attention: someone stole her car, struck a cyclist, and killed him.

In August of 1978, Reatha's car was parked in front of the Metro Square building in downtown Saint Paul when a man named Glenn Martin Woolf, under the influence of a cocktail of alcohol, marijuana, and PCP, stole it. In a strange and tragic series of events, Woolf picked up a hitchhiker and instructed him to take over the wheel. The pair then made their way to Prior Lake, a southwestern Twin Cities suburb, where the vehicle plowed into a cyclist and killed him. According to a *Minneapolis Tribune* report, Woolf pleaded guilty to two misdemeanors and served less than a year in jail.[165]

---

164. Harvey, *Grass Roots and Glass Ceilings*.
165. Smith, "Her Car Was Stolen."

The event left Reatha badly shaken and heartbroken for the victim and his family, but she managed to pick up the pieces and move on . . . for about a year. That's when the victim's family sued her, to the tune of $607,000.

The charge? Knowing the "criminal potential" of the neighborhood where Reatha had parked her car. It was a charge with legal precedence, determined by a 1978 Minnesota Supreme Court ruling that sided with an insurance company that did not want to pay damages to a claimant whose car had been stolen in a "bad neighborhood."

Reatha was shocked and outraged by the allegations. The Metro Square building was not in a bad neighborhood. Multicultural? Yes. High traffic? Of course. But *bad*? That was a personal insult. "They tried to prove that the area in which I work is a low-class neighborhood," Reatha said. "I object. I appreciate where I work."[166]

Saint Paul mayor George Latimer came to the defense of Reatha and the neighborhood—located in the heart of his city—in court testimony. Ultimately, Reatha won the lawsuit, but no one felt like celebrating. A man was still dead, and the criminal who had stolen her vehicle was walking around, scot-free.

---

166. Smith, "Her Car Was Stolen."

CHAPTER SEVENTEEN

To Grow a School

"Don't put a ceiling on yourself."

—Oprah Winfrey

During working hours, Reatha regularly met with high-powered politicians and corporate CEOs. She led a team of several hundred. She wore power suits and hosted power lunches. But at the end of the day, she fulfilled her most treasured role: wife and mother.

For a few blessed hours, she would set aside her endless to-do list, slip into casual clothing, and spend time with her family. This was the time for family dinners and catching up. This was the time for checking in with the boys about their schoolwork, their friends, Jay's violin lessons, and Scott's track-and-field practice.

In 1982, Judge was starting his fourth year at 3M, Jay was seventeen years old and would begin his fourth year at Kellogg High School in the fall, and Scott had celebrated his fourteenth birthday and would start his first year of high school.

The boys loved and looked up to both their parents and understood that each one played a distinct role. Reatha was the serious parent, the one who carefully separated her professional life from her family life. At home, she always made sure dinner was on the table and the family was seated around it. Her sons recall her as an incredible parent who ran a tight ship but who clearly cared about her family above all else.

Despite being such a revolutionary in society, Reatha was a traditionalist in the home. She was comfortable cooking dinner and cleaning the kitchen. She didn't mind driving her sons to their sports games and music lessons. When she slipped into her *mother* role, she didn't have to break new ground or strategize her every step. She only had to follow the playbook that had been passed down to her through generations of caring, attentive matriarchs. When so much of her life was spent trailblazing new paths under the scrutiny of the public eye, falling into her domestic role was oftentimes a comfort and a relief.

Judge King—the scientist, the aviator, the academic—underwent a similar "costume change" in the home. He cast aside his prestigious background and respect-commanding job title and simply became Dad. The King boys recall him as a nurturing and carefree parent. He had a wide, beaming smile; bright, bespectacled eyes that crinkled at the corners; and a contagious laugh. Like Reatha, he was driven and innovative, but he chose to direct much of that energy toward his aviation avocation. Sometimes the boys would accompany him in the family's outbuilding, where he built his own airplane from a set of blueprints he had purchased for $250. Though Jay and Scott would dip their toes in the aviation world, both boys taking flying lessons, neither was as enamored with it as their father.

But the boys' lack of interest did little to dampen Judge's enthusiasm. He tinkered with his homemade airplane until, after two years, he had completed a twin-engine Cessna 421 airplane that could seat ten people.

When Judge flew the plane to Alabama to show it off to his family, his mother, who had never approved of her son's risky hobby, appraised it with a cold gaze and a downturned mouth. "How much will you take for it?" she asked.

"Why do you ask?" Judge responded.

"So I can burn it up!" his mother declared. "If God wanted us to fly, he would have given us wings."

Judge took his mother's criticism in stride, as he had for years. He wasn't about to give up his cherished pastime—a pastime he was eager to discuss (and that many people found fascinating) at the many functions and fundraisers he and Reatha attended.

And there were *many* functions. During her presidency, Reatha was expected to attend an endless string of fundraising events, galas, and awards ceremonies. Judge was a good sport and would show up to these events armed with his quick wit, sense of humor, and distinct laugh. He carried those qualities with him wherever he went and, as a natural extrovert, could easily engage in conversation with just about anyone. At all those important events, surrounded by important people, Judge was in his element and enjoyed himself immensely. Reatha recalls her husband's buoyant spirit fondly.

"He would sing in the morning as he got ready for work. I was always quiet and contemplative as I started my day. I would sit on the bed and watch him get ready as he belted out songs. Sometimes, he would turn to me and say, 'What are you thinking about, country girl?'"

To Judge, Reatha was always his country girl, and he was her city boy. Under layers of sophistication and etiquette, degrees and certificates, the country girl still dwelled within Reatha. She was never truly separated from her roots, nor did she want to be.

In 2017, when Reatha returned to her hometown of Moultrie, Georgia, to speak at Moultrie Senior High School after receiving the Colquitt County Career Achievement Award, she talked about her roots and the humble clapboard church that served as her first schoolhouse. She discussed the sacrifices her family made for her sisters and her so she could gain an education and, eventually, take the Trailways bus out of town.

Reatha's humble beginnings colored her entire worldview and molded her into the driven, determined, and hardworking individual she became. Her beginnings made her value education above all else besides family and church. Her beginnings made her appreciate every dollar she earned and every luxury she could afford—the motorboat, the occasional trips to Disney World or the Oshkosh air show, the house with more than enough space for the four of them.

When Jay was in high school, he wanted to pick up a dishwashing job to earn some extra spending money. Reatha flatly refused. Her sons would not perform manual labor like she had all those years ago in the sun-scorched, sticky cotton fields. They would not scrub dishes. Schoolwork was the only work for Jay and Scott, as far as she was concerned, and if they needed extra money, she would give it to them.

This mentality, Jay says, is from growing up "po'." "Do you know what po' is?" he says. "Po' is when you're so poor, you can't afford the extra *o* and *r*."[167]

Reatha never forgot her background and never forgot the family who raised her. They continued to be each other's champions and supports. Whenever the Clark sisters had extra money, they would throw it in the communal kitty or send it straight to their mother. That was the way of things, and they did it without question.

Both of Reatha's sisters had settled on the East Coast—Mamie in Washington, DC, and Dot in Silver Spring, Maryland. Years earlier, Mamie had earned her doctorate from the University of Maryland and transitioned from the army to the classroom. She taught at Howard University and eventually became the chair of its family nurse practitioner program. In 1974, her pastor asked whether she was interested in starting a nursing program to provide basic care for members of the congregation; Mamie enthusiastically agreed and established the nurses unit for Nineteenth Street Baptist Church.[168] It became such a vital service for her community that Mamie would end up running it for forty-five successful years. Much like her sister Reatha, Mamie's days were filled to the brim. In 1970, she welcomed her youngest child into the family—a boy named Thomas Jr.—and proceeded to forge ahead with her nursing work while caring for her young family. In between motherhood duties, she continued teaching and running the nurses unit, advocated for health-related causes, and performed medical research, authoring or coauthoring sixteen publications. Mamie also made a concerted effort to keep in close contact with her mother and sisters.

Reatha's younger sister, Dot, also maintained an active lifestyle (in true Clark fashion). She worked for the National Academy of Sciences for twelve years before transitioning into real estate in 1978, shortly after Reatha moved to Minnesota to accept her presidency position. Dot kept active with volunteerism and was involved with the homeless shelter for women in Rockville, Maryland, as well as her church's "Benevolence Committee." For Dot, too, family formed the center of her life, and she reveled in her role as a mother (to her daughter, Cyndy) and a wife (to her husband, Jesse D. Green, whom she married in 1976).

---

167. N. Judge King III, interview.
168. Montague, "Thanks for Time Well Served."

Though they had long ago dispersed across the country, the Clark girls remained close and considered each other best friends and confidantes. Theirs was a relationship unbounded by years and miles—whenever they talked on the phone or paid each other a visit, it seemed as though no time had passed at all.

★ ★ ★

The year 1983 was shaping up to be a good one. This was the year that Reatha (who was still fascinated with space travel and science) had the opportunity to watch Sally Ride, the nation's first female astronaut, launch into space aboard the Space Shuttle *Challenger*. This was the year Dr. Martin Luther King Jr.'s birthday would become an official federal holiday (over the years, Reatha would be a featured speaker at numerous MLK Day events). This was the year Jay would graduate from high school and begin his studies at Brown University, while Scott started his second year at Kellogg High School.

Jay hadn't given much thought to where to attend college until the day Reatha sat him down with a pen and paper. He was closing in on his fourth year of high school, and Reatha thought it was time to get serious about his college plans.

"It was never a question of *if* I was going to college," Jay says. "Growing up, Scott and I were always told, 'You're going to school.' That was the expectation."[169] He just didn't know *where*.

Reatha was about to change that.

"Let's make a list of potential schools for you," she said. "Put Harvard on the list. That's a wonderful school, and I'm good friends with President Bok."

Jay wrote Harvard on the list.

"And Amherst," Reatha said. "That's an excellent liberal arts college. And Morehouse, of course. That's where your father earned his undergrad. And Howard, too. That's where your aunt Mamie went to school."

Jay added the schools to his list as Reatha continued.

"Then there's Brown University," she said. "It has wonderful academic programs, and I know President Swearer quite well. It might be an excellent fit for you."

---

169. King, N. Judge III, interview.

Reatha was right: Brown *was* an excellent fit for Jay. He would spend the next four years at Brown University, earning his bachelor of science degree in biochemistry and building friendships he still maintains to this day.

Three years later, when it was time for Scott to apply for college, Reatha took a different approach with her younger son. Scott remembers her walking into the living room while he was watching TV, sitting down, and saying, "Would you like to go to Morehouse College or Clark?"[170]

Scott didn't protest her selections or even consider another college. He chose to follow in his father's footsteps and attend Morehouse College. As one of the original historically black colleges in the United States, it was steeped in history and tradition. Scott figured he would do well there, and he was right. In fact, he was so taken with the city of Atlanta that he decided to put down roots and make the southern metropolis his home.

★ ★ ★

While Jay was piling his belongings into boxes and purchasing supplies for his dormitory at Brown, Metropolitan State University was tiptoeing into its twelfth year. In 1983, the school's classrooms dotted the Twin Cities, with over *one hundred* individual sites. Businesses with extra rooms, public venues, and other community and communal spaces willingly opened their doors to Metro. They knew the college was a reliable tenant—and they were beginning to understand the important role it fulfilled.

With a dozen years under its belt, Metro State was building up a solid reputation, a list of distinguished alumni, and a number of awards. Reatha and the staff were encouraged by the progress, but they knew there was room for improvement. Ever the forward thinker, Reatha advocated for computers in classrooms at a time when many schools thought they were cost prohibitive and unnecessary. She even paid the president of Dartmouth College a visit to study how the school had implemented computers and incorporated the COBOL programming language in the classroom.

---

170. Scott King, interview.

In addition to championing technology and innovation, Reatha was determined to implement several different master's programs so nontraditional students could access yet another educational tier. The first was the master of management and administration, initiated in 1983. The founding of this program was a milestone in Metro State's development, as it moved the school to an entirely new level and required new and different faculty members to teach the higher-level classes.

Establishing the school's first master's program took a good deal of lobbying on Reatha's part. Over the course of two years, she had placed phone calls to and met with the "powers that be" to convince them of the validity and necessity of such a program. She also—as she often did—reached out to alumni and asked them to call their local representatives. She worked tirelessly. For months. When the Minnesota State College Board finally granted permission for Metro State to implement its master's in administration program, Reatha breathed a sigh of relief. But she knew this was only the beginning of the battle. Not only would she have to ensure the successful implementation of the new program, but she was also determined to use the victory as a stepping-stone to initiate other master's degree programs at Metro.

Reatha believed that adding traditional and higher-level programs would encourage a more diverse set of students to enroll. This was one of her primary goals from the very start of her presidency. A 1977 *Minneapolis Tribune* article reported, "The major change in approach [President King] would like to make is to attract more minority students and students from such other 'underserved' populations."[171]

Even though Metro State had welcomed nontraditional students from the start, it was having trouble attracting minorities and underserved populations in general. Ken Zapp, a professor emeritus who worked under Reatha, discussed the recruiting troubles the school faced at the time:

"Here was the quandary: People who have not made it into society's mainstream, minorities in particular, were generally hesitant to join a system that was not mainstream. They wondered—'Is this university going to get me into the mainstream?' That was the challenge we faced. That led to the development of more traditional majors."[172]

---

171. Biano, "Black Woman Named Head."
172. Lofquist, *Metropolitan State University Buzz.*

However, adding traditional programs was little more than a nice notion until Kenneth Keller, who became the president of the University of Minnesota in 1985, announced that the U would shift its emphasis toward graduate programs and research, reducing the student body by about eight thousand undergraduate students.[173] The decision came with the expectation that other state schools would expand their undergraduate programs to accommodate more students. Metro State University was specifically identified as "an institution that could serve some of the students who now attend the University of Minnesota."[174]

Reatha responded with the voice of a forward-thinking strategist. "We welcome this opportunity to consider an expanded role for Metro U," she said. "I am confident that in carrying out different missions, our institutions can work together in a complementary and mutually supportive way."[175]

With the goal of expanding Metro's course offerings, Reatha sought $2.6 million from the college board as seed money to start seven new programs: accounting, arts and humanities, computer science, human services, journalism and communications, management, and marketing. The request, however, was only partially approved, and the school received only $650,000 of the $2.6 million it had wanted. Combined with nearly $200,000 from the state university system, this allotment was enough to initiate three new major programs, instead of seven.[176]

If Reatha was disappointed with the legislature's decision, she did not show it. "I live with the philosophy," she said, "that if you do a good job with what you have, there will always be an opportunity to go back [for additional funding]."[177]

With less than $1 million in its pocket, Metro State began to plan the launch of three new degree programs, slated to be added by 1989. Working with a lean budget was nothing new, and the school forged ahead fearlessly, ready to spin gold out of straw.

---

173. Janet Groat, "Funding Is Less than Sought."
174. "President King Welcomes Expanded Role."
175. "President King Welcomes Expanded Role."
176. Groat, "Funding Is Less than Sought."
177. Groat, "Funding Is Less than Sought."

CHAPTER EIGHTEEN

Foundational Shifts

*"It's hard work that makes things happen.
It's hard work that creates change."*

—Shonda Rhimes

The year 1986 started with a string of tragedies and proved to be an unrelenting, explosive year. On January 28, Reatha Clark King tuned in to the latest news from NASA: the Space Shuttle *Challenger* was launching from Cape Canaveral, Florida, with the goal of collecting data and observing Halley's Comet via two small satellites. However, *Challenger* failed immediately and spectacularly. The spacecraft broke apart less than a minute and a half after launch, claiming the lives of the seven crew members in its belly. Among them was the first civilian to venture into space, an elementary school teacher.

Reatha's heart plummeted with the spacecraft. She knew what it meant to contribute to such a major project—how many hands and brains had collaborated to build *Challenger* and prepare it for the launchpad. When she had contributed to the 1969 Apollo 11 mission, she could have easily witnessed a disaster rather than a success.

Though 1986 would also see the flawless launch of the Soviet Union's Mir space station, the *Challenger* disaster left a bitter taste in the public's mouth. NASA's space program would press on, but the hard lessons learned from the *Challenger* explosion (including overlooking questionable spacecraft components) would not soon be forgotten.

FOUNDATIONAL SHIFTS

The disaster was only one of a string of explosions heard round the world in 1986. On April 2, a bomb ripped apart a Boeing 727 aircraft while it was flying over Greece, instantly killing several passengers. In mid-April, the United States unleashed a series of bombs in an air strike against Libya, retaliating (in classic eye-for-an-eye mentality) against a bombing in a West Berlin dance club. The most significant and deadly explosion, however, was yet to come.

Toward the end of April 1986, a fireball erupted into the night sky above Ukraine's Chernobyl Nuclear Power Plant—the result of an unplanned, uncontrolled nuclear chain reaction that destroyed one of the power station's nuclear reactors. Though only two people died as the direct result of the explosion, the radiation that leaked from the station in the aftermath killed another thirty people within a few months and ultimately infected thousands more. (It is impossible to say how many people died as a result of their exposure to Chernobyl's radiation, but estimates range from the low thousands to the hundreds of thousands.) Further disaster—including the threat of another explosion caused by a buildup of steam—was averted in the following months, with the Soviet Union pouring money and manpower into containing the damaged reactor.

Two months later and five thousand miles from Chernobyl, Metropolitan State University had more to celebrate than to grieve. The only explosions that rocked the school were the concussive sounds of applause as distinguished speakers took the stage to celebrate its fifteenth anniversary. Special guests included alumni (guest speakers Stephanie "Assata" Brown and state representative Sandra Pappas); politicians (Minnesota house minority leader Fred Norton and several other legislators); activists (Metro's Hispanic liaison, Eduardo Gutierrez, and state executive director for affirmative action, Elsa Vega Perez); and several members of Metro's faculty and staff (including President King). As part of the festivities, the school honored its founding legislators, many of whom attended the celebratory luncheon.

The cherry on top of the celebration was an unexpected proclamation by Governor Perpich, delivered by Representative Norton: he officially declared the fourth week of June to be Metropolitan State University Week. The school, which had been greeted with such suspicion and contempt by some, was now fully accepted by the most prominent elected official in the state. The proclamation recognized Metro State's foresight and continued goal of providing quality education to nontraditional students in the Twin Cities. The point of the proclamation was to "encourage residents to take advantage of the opportunities for furthering their educational goals provided by this fine institution."[178]

Reatha's role in the school's widespread acceptance was undeniable. Over the past nine years, she had developed and nurtured the school through tireless friend-raising, strategic and innovation planning, and visionary thinking, all while remaining true to Metro State's core values and, above all, its students. There was nothing ephemeral about the school without walls. Its foundation had proven to be solid; it was here to stay.

★ ★ ★

At times, the growth and progress of Metropolitan State University felt akin to magic. With so many advancements, powerful allies in the business and political arenas, loyal alumni, and legislative victories, it was easy to see the successes and forget about the struggles.

But there were struggles, some of which affected Reatha personally and deeply. Not long after Metro State celebrated its fifteenth anniversary, she experienced a rare defeat: she was denied the chancellorship of the Minnesota State College Board.

Reatha was accustomed to going toe to toe with competitors and emerging victorious, but that would not be the case this time. In the summer of 1986, after learning of the board's need for a new chancellor, she decided to apply. The chancellor was the figurehead of the board and the highest-ranking official within the state's higher education system; with the board in charge of making system-wide decisions for state-run schools, the chancellorship came with a good deal of power and influence. It was a logical next step for Reatha, and she was confident she had the right qualities and capabilities to make an effective chancellor. Even though she was a favorite for the job, the board ended up choosing Robert L. Carothers, the president of Southwest Minnesota State University in Marshall, Minnesota. He had received six votes from the board, while Reatha secured just two.

---

178. Perpich, "Proclamation."

The decision was a difficult blow. Reatha tried not to dwell on it, but it gnawed at her occasionally and made her wonder whether the state college board truly had her back—whether its members truly believed in her qualifications and ability to lead.

This pronouncement, made on July 29, 1986, may have been a subconscious tipping point for Reatha. It may have planted the first seeds of discontentment that would eventually lead her away from academia and into the corporate world.

But Reatha does not attribute her decision to leave the Metro State presidency to this particular moment. The true catalysts, she says, were her commitment to lifelong learning, the desire to try a new role, and the potential to "create a whole lot of good for a whole lot of people."

And Reatha's exit from Metro was still another two years down the line. This was 1986, and she still had much to accomplish as president.

★ ★ ★

In the blink of an eye, the young university turned sweet sixteen. Of those years, ten of them had been spent under the transformative leadership of Dr. Reatha Clark King, and the university thought fit to acknowledge her contributions. A celebratory banquet was held on November 10, 1987, at a hotel in Saint Paul's riverfront district, where the Metro State faculty unveiled one of the most treasured gifts Reatha has ever received: a newly established scholarship fund in her name.

The first recipients of the Reatha Clark King Endowed Scholarship Fund were twelve individuals from a wide range of backgrounds—people of different genders, races, and ages. Several were parents who were juggling school with family life. Each received the scholarship based on financial need but also because of their strength of spirit and dedication to lifelong learning. Many were community volunteers and full-time employees. All were thrilled to be scholarship recipients.

One student, Gloria Haines, said, "I was wondering how I would be able to save money for tuition each quarter. I was determined to go on and get a four-year degree, and this will be a real big help."

Another, Sandra Holmes, said, "It would have been much more difficult to stay in school without the scholarship. . . . It lifts some of the burden of trying to make ends meet."

Yet another student, Marilyn Mendoza-Rita, called the scholarship her "proudest achievement."[179]

Recipient Kurt Zilley ('90), who now works with the Ramsey County public health department, said that receiving the Reatha Clark King scholarship helped him continue his studies at Metro State. "When I received the scholarship," he said, "my family was experiencing health and financial issues. I had considered quitting school. However, with the help of the scholarship, I decided to continue the program and make education a priority."[180]

The scholarship is still making a positive impact today and will continue to do so for years to come. As 2019 graduate Emily Blais said, "The Reatha Clark King scholarship was an exciting and stress relieving event during my last semester at Metropolitan State University. It made a huge difference."[181]

When she learned about the scholarship fund, Reatha couldn't help but get a little misty eyed. All her career—all her *life*—she had believed in helping others and giving back. "Lift as you climb," Grandma Mamie had said. This scholarship would allow Reatha to lift more than ever.

Years later, Metropolitan State University would help facilitate another scholarship under Reatha's name: the N. Judge and Reatha Clark King Family Endowed Scholarship. Both scholarships are designed to help low-income students, and they have granted thousands of dollars to dozens of promising scholars throughout the years. As many students have testified, they have helped make higher education affordable and realistic and also affirmed their decision to seek an advanced degree.

★ ★ ★

By 1987, Metropolitan State University had doubled in size since 1977, when Reatha had taken over the presidency. It now served about 4,300 students annually, provided a variety of both traditional and student-designed majors, and offered an accredited nursing program. Its presence stretched across Minneapolis and Saint Paul and into the

---

179. Metropolitan State University Foundation, "Reatha Clark King Endowed Scholarship Fund." 1988.
180. Kurt Zilley, "Testimonial," April 13, 2020.
181. Emily Blais, "Testimonial for RCK Scholarship," September 7, 2020.

suburbs, with classes sprinkled around the greater Twin Cities metro. Even its central administrative offices were split, with some staff based at the Metro Square building in downtown Saint Paul (where Reatha's office was located) and some at the Hennepin Center for the Arts in downtown Minneapolis. This hodgepodge of dispersed spaces had functioned well for a decade and a half, but it was becoming clear that the decentralized model no longer suited the university.

Metro State was growing and changing; it had a well-established fundraising foundation, and the number of permanent faculty members and administrative staff was increasing with each passing year. Not only that, but the Metro Square building management was planning to remodel the space, which would temporarily displace Reatha and her Saint Paul–based administrative team. The time was right for the university—now well into its teenage years—to establish a space of its own.

However, even with the conditions ripe for change, Reatha needed an extra push to begin considering a permanent home in which the school could centralize its operations. That push came from the east Saint Paul community—specifically, from a Saint Paul City Council member named Karl Neid.

Karl was a longtime resident of east Saint Paul and fervently devoted to his community. He knew Reatha well and had witnessed Metropolitan State University's overwhelmingly positive influence. He also knew the school's structure was evolving and that evolution would naturally include a new headquarters in a more permanent location. That location, he decided, would be the old Saint John's Hospital site.

Saint John's German Lutheran Hospital began its life as a twenty-five-bed facility in 1911. Perched on a hill overlooking the Mississippi River in the Dayton's Bluff neighborhood, it expanded in 1915 to accommodate forty more beds—just in time for the flu pandemic of 1918, during which hospital staff cared for approximately four hundred patients. In the 1950s, the hospital underwent two more major changes: it expanded to add another one hundred beds, and it created one of the first intensive care units in the nation. After its expansion, Saint John's Hospital became the area's largest employer, with 850 people on its medical staff. [182]

---

182. Trimble, "Centennial History."

Though it had solidified itself as a cornerstone of the Dayton's Bluff community, the hospital eventually shuttered its doors in 1987 due to a restructuring of the HealthEast Care System.[183] The building was abandoned and left to the elements. Weeds began to choke out its front lawn; rodents took up residence in its walls. To the area's longtime residents—many of whom had taken their first breaths inside the hospital's natal unit—this was a shame and an outrage. The hospital had been an important local fixture, and now it sat, slowly decaying, on a prime piece of property (9.2 acres) in a desirable location. Not only was the situation heartbreaking, but it was a waste of perfectly good real estate.

Furthermore, the surrounding neighborhood mirrored the old hospital—it was growing shabby and was in desperate need of a revitalization. Maybe, just maybe, fixing up the old hospital would resuscitate the once-vibrant blue-collar community.

Karl Neid became fixated on the old Saint John's Hospital site and began rallying fellow city council members, other politicians, and the community at large to support his cause. One key ally of the initiative was Saint Paul mayor George Latimer, who had been a close friend and champion of Reatha's for several years. Mayor Latimer, Councilman Neid, and a dedicated cadre of supporters began making their case to Reatha, attempting to sway her to select the site for Metro State's first permanent headquarters.

They placed phone calls, met with her one on one, and even invited her to a breakfast meeting (with nearly two hundred people in attendance), during which they laid out their arguments for selecting the Saint John's site. They wrote letters—not only to Reatha, but to their local representatives and the members of the Minnesota State College Board. At one point, Elizabeth Pegues, vice president of the college board, was receiving about three letters a day from people advocating for the site. Many claimed that if Metro State began holding classes on Saint Paul's East Side, they would enroll in an instant.

"The East Siders knew politics," Reatha says with a laugh. "It was a grassroots effort, and they lobbied to the point where no one could say no to them."

---

183. The HealthEast Care System was a nonprofit healthcare organization that would eventually include four hospitals, fourteen clinics, medical transportation, and outpatient services. It was active from 1986 to 2019 in Saint Paul.

The east Saint Paul community had presented Reatha with a solid case for its location, and she was nearly convinced to begin advocating for the Saint John's Hospital site.

Nearly.

First, she had to tour the proposed site for herself and see what all the fuss was about.

It was early morning, Reatha recalls, when she drove to the old hospital building with Susan Rydell, one of Metro State's founding faculty members. She parked her car on the street in front of the building's towering brick façade. Together, she and Susan climbed the walkway to the front door and stepped inside. "It looked as though the pigeons had just left," Reatha recalls. The building was dusty, neglected, and in need of a serious facelift, but she could see the potential in its tall ceilings and sturdy walls.

When Reatha and Susan climbed to the top of the building and peered out one of the smudgy windows, Reatha's breath hitched. It was beautiful. From their hillside perch, she could see the sleepy neighborhoods awakening, their lights dotting the landscape like so many fireflies. At the slope's nadir, velvety fog rolled across the Mississippi River, wending its way around the bridges and up the tree-lined riverbanks toward downtown Saint Paul. In those early-morning hours, the city was already stirring. Reatha could see the blink of headlights passing around and through the city. She could see the silhouettes of skyscrapers and museums and theaters as the first ribbons of sunlight gave the city shape.

The scene that sprawled before her was nothing short of spectacular—an exceptional setting for an exceptional school. She had driven by the old Saint John's Hospital hundreds of times, but it wasn't until this moment that she truly realized the site's potential.

The decision, however, was far from final.

Reatha would have to spend months lobbying politicians, making her case to the Minnesota State College Board, and convincing the Metro State staff that this was not only a good decision but also one that aligned with the school's missions and values.

Unsurprisingly, she caught a good deal of flak for advocating a permanent base of operations for Metro State. "I thought this was the university without walls," people would say. "Why do you need a building?"

But Reatha did not waver from her decision. She started whipping up support from members of the senate, starting with longtime allies such as Senators Gene Waldorf and Jerry Hughes (the latter of whom also served as the chair of the senate's education committee) and Representative Randy Kelly (later mayor of Saint Paul).

Then, she started in on the college board. And the dubious Metro State faculty.

In the meantime, other communities began taking an interest in the university's search for a spot to land its new headquarters. These communities began advocating for sites in other parts of the Twin Cities.

On the other side of the river, the city of Minneapolis (under the leadership of Mayor Donald Fraser) caught wind of what was going on and attempted to throw its hat in the ring. The city had identified a site in North Minneapolis—a ten-acre undeveloped plot of land north of Grant Park known as the Bethune site that would, in their estimation, make an excellent base of operations for Metro State. Plus, the neighborhood was racially diverse—more so than the east Saint Paul location—and also in need of a revitalization. The city was so determined to woo Metro State, in fact, that it offered to sell the Bethune site for one dollar, the equivalent of a couple 1980s candy bars.

Mirroring the efforts of Saint Paul, Minneapolis also initiated a grassroots campaign to win over Reatha, Metro State, and the state college board. As the Minneapolis *Star Tribune* reported, "About 150 civic leaders, activists and community groups in Minneapolis had written state officials recently endorsing the proposed location just north of Grant Park, near Plymouth Av."[184]

Concurrently, two other potential sites were identified: one in Saint Paul's Midway neighborhood and another in Minneapolis between Loring Park and the Basilica of Saint Mary. But these sites did not have the same kind of backing and community efforts behind them as the Saint John's and North Minneapolis locations.

Despite the city of Minneapolis's bold offer and community advocacy, it was late to the competition. Saint Paul already had momentum, and the East Side location was considered more attractive, since it

---

184. Groat, "State University Chief."

already had a paved parking lot and access to local restaurants and was in a "safer" area with a lower crime rate.[185] Still, it was tempting to accept Minneapolis's offer and purchase its proposed site for a dollar, rather than the estimated $1.3 million for Saint Paul's.

On December 11, 1987, Mayor Latimer said Saint Paul would not enter a bidding war with Minneapolis and called the whole thing "very tiresome."[186] Less than a month later, he changed his tune. The city of Saint Paul offered to purchase the Saint John's Hospital site and hand part of it over to the Minnesota State College Board, free of charge.

This decision was the straw that broke Minneapolis's bid. With less than three weeks before the board would review both cities' proposals, Minneapolis had lost its only leverage.

On Thursday, January 28, 1988, Reatha felt oddly at peace. She had rallied as much support as she could behind the Saint John's site, and now the decision rested in the hands of the state college board. There was nothing more she could do but sit back and wait for the decision.

Under the leadership of Chancellor Robert Carothers, the board reviewed the benefits and drawbacks of each proposed site and concluded that the Saint John's Hospital location was the superior property. Provided Metro State received the necessary funding from the state legislature, the school without walls would finally have a home base. And that home base would be on the scenic slopes of east Saint Paul.

Not long after the board's decision, the Minnesota State Legislature approved funding for the construction of Metropolitan State University's headquarters. The old hospital would undergo an extensive renovation to transform the maternity ward, operating theaters, and medical supply closets into administrative offices, classrooms, and a computer lab. An architecture team was hired to draw up plans, and a crew began prepping the space for its remodel. Setting down permanent roots for the college had seemed like a nebulous dream, a grand idea. But the dream was tiptoeing toward reality.

---

185. Some believed this claim to be racially motivated, since the proposed North Minneapolis site was located in a racially diverse neighborhood. The then president of the Minneapolis Urban League, Gleason Glover, said in a *Star Tribune* article, "In my opinion, the underlying cause of this is race. . . . I just think white folks don't want to come into a black community. It's as simple as that" (Groat, "East Side St. Paul Chosen").
186. Groat, "Minneapolis Joins Bidding."

In 1992, Saint John's Hall was completed—a testament to an era of major change and restructuring of the Metro State system. Though Reatha was no longer president when the new hall officially opened, she attended the ribbon-cutting ceremony and gazed upon the newly transformed building with tears pooling in her eyes. She knew how hard she had fought to convince dissenters that, yes, Metro State needed and deserved a central headquarters. She knew how fervently she had advocated for this hillside site, and how many hours she had spent in endless meetings and negotiations.

Securing the Saint John's Hospital site was a capstone in Reatha's career. It represented the culmination of her long hours, endless meetings, tireless fundraising, and stalwart devotion to her school and her beloved community.

This three-story tan brick building on a hill set a new standard for Metropolitan State University and, in a sense, gave the school permission to start putting up walls and establishing a central campus. Today, the Dayton's Bluff campus is home to eight buildings that include a state-of-the-art science center, a library and learning center, and a community garden and labyrinth. The campus library, which opened its doors in 2004, is open to the public and operates jointly with the Saint Paul Public Library. This type of collaborative setup is rare, and the Metro State library is one of just seven such joint-use libraries in the nation.

In addition to the central campus, Metro State still has a few branches across the Twin Cities—including in Saint Paul's Midway neighborhood, downtown Minneapolis, and the northwestern suburb of Brooklyn Park—in addition to several teaching locations in shared spaces. Though the school has become more centralized over the years, it still opens its arms wide and welcomes students of all ages, backgrounds, races, and genders. Today, its students range in age from sixteen to seventy-four years old, 50 percent are students of color, 59 percent are female, and a full 57 percent are first-generation college students.[187] Though Metro State can no longer be called the school without walls, it has clearly not walled itself off from nontraditional and diverse students.

★ ★ ★

---

187. Metropolitan State University, "Key Facts at a Glance."

While Reatha was ensnared in the bidding war for Metro State's new headquarters, James P. Shannon was preparing to retire. Reatha scarcely noticed. What did a vacant vice presidency position at General Mills have to do with her?

Everything, as it turned out.

H. Brewster "Bruce" Atwater Jr., the CEO and chairman of the board at General Mills, knew Reatha and had followed her career and successes over the past several years. He knew about her dedication to philanthropy and her commitment to assisting underserved populations. Since the vice president of General Mills was expected to run the company's charitable giving foundation, the role seemed custom-made for Reatha.

But would Reatha be receptive?

Before General Mills came calling, Reatha had already been thinking about her next steps. She had headed the university for eleven years (to date, this is still the longest stretch of any Metro State president) and was beginning to feel like a cooped-up bird that sorely needed to stretch its wings. Her steady presence had given the school continuity and leadership when it was still fragile and uncertain of its sustained future, but Reatha was confident it could soar without her now. Too many intelligent, capable people filled its ranks for it to fail.

What's more, it is not uncommon for university presidents to hold their positions for ten years or less. It's a stressful and demanding role, and ten years seems to be the limit for many presidents before they become burnt out. Besides, a shift in leadership can be beneficial for a school—a new leader can offer a fresh perspective and can start their position without any preconceived notions or old grudges from the board or legislators. In short, change is a healthy and natural part of school development.

Despite some job fatigue (and despite some of her closest colleagues and mentors asking, "Haven't you been there long enough?"), Reatha had not truly considered leaving Metro State until she had space and time to reflect. She found that space and time six thousand miles away, in Kyoto, Japan.

Reatha traveled to Kyoto as part of a lecture tour, during which she spoke to groups of young professionals in Israel, the Philippines, and Japan on the topic "What Was Martin Luther King's Legacy in

America?" This was her third and final international lecture tour, and she was enjoying herself immensely. Her presentations had been well received, she had met dozens of fascinating individuals, and she had toured several interesting historical and cultural sites. It was a business trip, yes, but it also served as a much-needed change of scenery.

In Kyoto, Reatha awoke early one morning to ready herself for a temple tour. She recalls sitting on the edge of her bed in a modest hotel room and swinging her legs as she sank into deep reflection. Amid a tangle of thoughts, a question floated through her mind: "Have I been at Metro State long enough?" She dwelled on that question a few minutes before tucking it into the corner of her mind and joining the morning's tour.

That quiet moment in Japan marked a turning point for Reatha. Something within her opened to the possibility of life and work beyond Metropolitan State University.

Even with her new receptiveness to change, however, Reatha was unsure of her next steps. She loved Metro State and the community that had grown around her, and she knew she could never leave her beloved community for any old job. It would have to be, in her words, "special."

The vice presidency at General Mills *would* be special. This role would allow Reatha to oversee the company's charitable giving foundation, which had distributed $6.9 million in 1988[188] to a variety of local, national, and international causes. She would have an opportunity to make a positive difference in people's lives that extended beyond the classroom.

But in the scorching heat of the summer of 1988 (which saw forty-four days at or above ninety degrees Fahrenheit—a record that still stands in the Twin Cities), Reatha remained focused and dedicated to her university. She had to write her year-end achievement report and submit it to the state college board. She had to plan the upcoming school year and review the school's budget. Leaving her current position was far from the top of her to-do list.

And yet, it would rocket its way to the top.

And she would ultimately decide to leave.

By the time Reatha left Metro State in the fall of 1988, a lot had changed. Enrollment had increased from 1,600 in 1977 to over 5,000

---

188. Brandt, "Metro 'U' Head Lead Firm's Charity."

in 1988. Traditional programs had been added to the school's offerings, including the accredited nursing program. Courses had been brought to the suburbs. The master of management and administration program was five years strong. Plans were underway for the school's first computer science program.

And on a slope overlooking the Mississippi River, a construction crew would soon break ground for the school's first permanent headquarters and, eventually, a campus.

Zooming out, it was plain to see that positive changes were being implemented in the state's academic system as well. Schools such as Concordia University and St. Catherine University, both in Saint Paul, saw the merit of flexible, career-oriented programs like the ones Metro State had implemented and began developing similar programs of their own geared toward nontraditional students.

What was more, the state's system was diversifying. When Reatha had first begun her presidency, no women of color served on the Minnesota State College Board. During her eleven years of service, three black women were appointed to serve on the board: Nellie Stone Johnson, Liz Pegues, and Mary Thornton Phillips.

On the national scene, academia was also diversifying, though at a slower pace than Reatha would have liked. In 1986, *Ebony* magazine ran a feature called "Black Women College Presidents," which profiled the fourteen black women presidents of accredited US colleges and universities. At the time, nearly three thousand universities and colleges in the United States were accredited, meaning that black women held not even 0.5 percent of presidential seats. Regardless, it was an improvement (if one can fathom it!) from 1977, when Reatha began her presidency.

But Reatha did not have the time or inclination to dwell on her legacy. It wouldn't be long after her transformative trip to Kyoto that her life would take a sharp turn. Soon, she would have to learn a new role, adapt to a new company, and blaze new trails. She would have to continue her pursuit of lifelong learning with gusto.

And this particular learning curve would be a steep one.

CHAPTER NINETEEN

Little Flour Mill on the River

"Knowing what must be done does away with fear."

—Rosa Parks

In the sweltering summer of 1988, Bruce Atwater didn't have time to pause and rest in the shade. The General Mills CEO knew his trusted vice president and General Mills Foundation head, Jim Shannon, would be leaving soon, and it was up to Bruce (along with the General Mills board of directors) to fill the sizable shoes he would leave behind. He hired a search firm to comb the Twin Cities and beyond and put together a list of viable candidates for the position. The candidates would have to be the right combination of idealistic and practical, with charisma, strong leadership skills, and the financial prowess to run a multimillion-dollar foundation. They would also need the heart of a philanthropist.

The search firm worked quickly, put together a list of candidates, and presented it to Mr. Atwater and the board. After reviewing the list, the General Mills board of directors recommended Mr. Atwater start with the candidate who sparked the most excitement: Dr. Reatha Clark King.

As Reatha would soon learn, the internal mechanisms of General Mills turn and click into place with rapid-fire speed. Once Bruce Atwater had his top candidate, he wasted no time in calling her.

On the morning of Bruce's phone call, Reatha was sitting in her office, staring at a blank piece of paper poking out of her typewriter. She had to write her year-end achievement report for the Minnesota State

College Board, but she was having trouble concentrating. Usually, she enjoyed touting Metro State's achievements and typing up these reports, but this year was different. Her enthusiasm had waned, and the task felt more like a chore than a joy.

At eleven o'clock, Reatha was jolted from her listlessness. Bruce Atwater was on the line, wondering whether she had a minute to talk.

Why, Reatha wondered, would the CEO of General Mills be calling? Perhaps the corporation was planning to offer additional financial support to Metro State, since the school was endeavoring to build new headquarters.

Bruce, not one to waste time, didn't keep Reatha guessing for long. He told her about General Mills' search for a candidate to replace Jim Shannon. He said her name had risen to the top of the list.

"What do you think?" Bruce asked. "Would you be willing to discuss the position in more depth?"

Reatha was stunned.

Though she had always been pro-business (and knew her MBA degree would be useful if she ever decided to transition into the corporate arena), she had never imagined she would have the opportunity to become part of a major corporation's leadership team.

But the timing was right, and she was feeling particularly restless that day, so Bruce's phone call felt as fortuitous as a pot of gold at the end of the Lucky Charms rainbow.

"Yes," said Reatha, recovering from her shock. "I would like to meet."

"How about this afternoon?" Bruce said. "I could be at your office by one o'clock."

Still reeling, Reatha agreed. She hung up the phone, took one look at the state of her office, and began tidying up. Like a whirlwind, she swept through the room, shuffling papers into drawers and stacking books. She rushed downstairs and purchased a couple of bottles of water and a box of cookies from the first-floor convenience store. By the time Bruce Atwater arrived, the cookies were plated, the water displayed, and her office cleared of detritus.

Bruce didn't bother with the cookies; he sat down and got straight to the point. He trusted and respected Reatha, he knew she was well connected in the local business community, and he hoped she would consider interviewing for General Mills' open vice presidency position.

He then handed her a folder of information about General Mills and pointed to the company's statement of values, which included diversity, innovation, leadership, and five other core tenets. "I've observed your work in this community," he said, "and your values seem to align with ours."

Reatha was impressed by GM's value statement and the CEO's apparent belief in it. But still, she hesitated. Bruce had barged, bull-like, into her china shop, and she needed time to process his offer.

"I'd like to tell the board of directors your decision soon," Bruce said. "Let me know as soon as possible if you're interested in an interview."

Reatha knew, given the CEO's personality, that Bruce Atwater was not the type of person who liked to be kept waiting. She resolved to make her decision by the next week—Monday, if she could.

It was a Friday.

Never mind that Reatha had to fly to Kansas that weekend to deliver a commencement speech at Wichita State University. Never mind that she had a major report to write for the state college board.

That evening, she told Judge and the boys (who were home from college) about the open position and the CEO's personal request that she come in for an interview. Judge and Scott responded with some hesitancy, pointing out how much Reatha loved Metro State and excelled in her presidential role. They weren't *unsupportive*—just skeptical that Reatha would thrive in a corporate setting. Jay, on the other hand, was pure enthusiasm. "Mom, you should pursue that job!" he said.

In the end, Jay provided the nudge Reatha needed. On Monday, she called Bruce and (with the state college board's blessing) agreed to an interview.

Reatha had pressed the launch button, and her career would soon begin rocketing in an entirely new direction. There would be no returning to a familiar home base.

She started to prepare for her interview by researching the corporation that was courting her. She knew General Mills had been a staple of the Twin Cities' corporate community for several decades, but she had not explored its history and the full extent of its operations and offerings until now.

General Mills, Reatha discovered, was born in 1866, when Cadwallader Washburn, an intrepid abolitionist from Maine, opened a flour mill along the Mississippi River. Originally called Minneapolis Milling Company, it competed with the Pillsbury Flour Mills Company, which set up shop across the river. The main attraction of the site was the formidable Saint Anthony Falls, which plunges seventy-six feet as the river streams past downtown Minneapolis. When Washburn beheld the falls for the first time, he saw the potential in the roaring river and was determined to channel it to power his mill.

After numerous partnerships and trade deals, victories and challenges (most notably the 1878 explosion that leveled the mill and claimed fourteen lives), Washburn's mill (then part of the Washburn-Crosby Company) merged with twenty-eight other milling companies around the country in 1928. Within months, the new milling giant rebranded as General Mills and became a publicly traded company on the New York Stock Exchange.

In the sixty years between General Mills' founding and Reatha's interview offer, the company became a titan in the food industry. It powered through the Great Depression, multiple major wars, and economic highs and lows by adjusting to the needs of the people and recalibrating its offerings. During the Great Depression, for instance, General Mills endeavored to develop a cereal rich in vitamin D. This led to the creation of Kix, its first puffed cereal (followed soon after by Cheerios). During World War II, the company switched gears entirely and began contributing to the war effort. It produced dehydrated foods for the military, manufactured artillery and sandbags, and even developed the jitterbug torpedo, which could alter its course midstream to strike an enemy target.

By 1988, General Mills had long abandoned its wartime products but continued to dabble in a diverse set of offerings. From toys (Play-Doh, Monopoly) to restaurant chains (Red Lobster, Olive Garden) to retail brands (Eddie Bauer, Lacoste), it stretched into many different industries that had little to nothing to do with flour and food. It did, however, stay firmly tethered to its food production branch. Grocery store aisles teemed with General Mills biscuits and cake mixes, cereals and frozen seafood, yogurt and Hamburger Helper. It made dozens of acquisitions and partnerships. It stretched throughout the United States and abroad. Though the company would eventually shift its focus back to strictly packaged foods, GM was still quite diverse and wide reaching in 1988.

Reatha studied General Mills' history and considered the company she might be joining—this sprawling, multimillion-dollar international corporation, which had little in common with Metro State's lean budget and personalized feel. Or York College's affiliation with grassroots civic engagement. Or the National Bureau of Standards' highly specialized laboratory work. Aside from her board service, she rarely immersed herself in the realm of private enterprise and profits, of catering to shareholders and rapid expansion.

But despite the myriad differences between her past work and the role at General Mills, Reatha saw the commonalities between government work, academia, and the private sector. She knew General Mills had a history of conducting pioneering research and promoting innovation. She knew that, despite its size and its drive for profits, the company began from humble roots and endeavored to give back to its community through charitable giving. This giving was facilitated by the General Mills Foundation, which she would run if the company decided to offer her the job.

She started to feel comfortable with the idea of working for the international giant that grew from a single flour mill on the Mighty Mississippi.

★ ★ ★

On a sticky summer day, Reatha hopped in her Ford Escort and made the twenty-mile drive across the Twin Cities from her home in Maplewood to General Mills' headquarters in Golden Valley, just west of Minneapolis. Turning into GM's entryway, she made her way to guest parking, past a well-groomed expanse of green lawns, purple and mauve petunias, and copses of leafy deciduous trees. A collection of glass-faced buildings bunched together, overlooking a wide, glossy pond. She couldn't help but notice how the manicured General Mills campus offered a sharp contrast to Metropolitan State, with its collection of classrooms and offices scattered across the Twin Cities in mismatched rented spaces.

This campus was planned. Precise. And it befit the capital and power behind the company's façade.

Impressed, and a tad intimidated, Reatha strode inside, walking with the poise and confidence her parents had taught her. She was well prepared, as was her modus operandi, and she knew it.

General Mills' interview process mirrored Reatha's meeting with Mr. Atwater. It was brief, candid, and to the point. First, she met with the board of directors for an hour-long interview. Then, she met separately with Bruce Atwater, Cliff Whitehill (who would become her supervisor), Mark Willis (GM's executive vice president), and a couple other board members for a private meeting and question and answer session. During this second meeting, Reatha's hesitations bubbled to the surface. She was interested in the job and knew it was an unprecedented opportunity, but she needed to make sure she was the right person for the position (and that the position was right for her).

Echoing the company's candidness, Reatha asked, "Do you think, at age fifty, I'm too old to learn this new role?"

Bruce waved off her question. "Not at all," he said. "My dad is eighty years old and he's still sharp as a tack."

The meeting continued, but Reatha's hesitations were not entirely assuaged. She found herself (to her horror) voicing another deep-seated reservation.

"I've been wondering," Reatha said, "whether or not it makes sense for me to continue working in an office setting or to go back to work as a chemist in the lab."

This time, Mark Willis spoke up. "Reatha," he said, "if it's a lab you're looking for, we have one of the finest in the world right here."

If Reatha became General Mills' vice president, she would not, of course, be working in the company laboratory, but she *would* be associated with it. And that proximity alone appealed to her. She would be part of a team of world-class scientists and innovators. This was the company that (in conjunction with the University of Minnesota) had invented the "black box" recording device for airplanes. This was the business whose electronics division had developed *Alvin*, the compact deep-diving submarine that was able to reach the ruins of the *Titanic* and capture the very first images of the wreckage.

In the end, Reatha's questions ran dry. In place of hesitation, she began feeling excited about the path that lay in front of her sensible pumps. It was a new kind of challenge, teeming with possibilities and the potential to continue following Grandma Mamie's adage: "Lift as you climb." From the heights of a vice presidency at a major corporation, Reatha could uplift thousands.

After a marathon day of interviewing, the General Mills executives made their decision. They wanted to hire Reatha for the vacant vice president position; they wanted her to lead the company's foundation. "We are prepared to offer you the position today," they announced.

Reatha was ready for their ask. She took a deep breath, feeling as though she were poised on the brink of a diving board, about to plunge into unfamiliar waters. She released her breath, steadied her nerves, and made the leap. She would accept General Mills' offer. Tentatively.

First, she said, she would have to speak with the state college board chancellor, Robert Carothers. Gaining the chancellor's permission was protocol, and Reatha wanted to make sure she exited academia gracefully, without burning bridges on her way out.

Fortunately, Carothers and the rest of the state college board were thrilled for her. In a *Star Tribune* article, Carothers applauded Reatha's "visionary leadership" and acknowledged her role in molding Metro State into a school that passionately and effectively served a diverse set of students.[189]

Reatha also announced her decision to the faculty and staff at Metropolitan State University. Though she was sorry to leave her treasured community, she knew the new position would offer her, as she put it, "an opportunity for creativity, a chance to work with stimulating people, and a chance to continue her community involvement."[190]

Though the Metro State staff members were sorry to see her go and deeply aware of their loss, they, too, gave their blessing. They knew the time was right for Reatha to undertake new, exciting endeavors, and they were grateful for the time they had spent alongside her. As Joyce LeClaire, a Metro instructor and director of the career/life planning

---

189. Brandt, "Metro 'U' Head Lead Firm's Charity."
190. Brandt, "Metro 'U' Head Lead Firm's Charity."

project, put it, "I worked with Reatha Clark King for a long, long time. She was a great mentor, a wonderful mentor to women especially."[191]

Former Metro State administrator John Mohr agreed. He reflected on his years working with President King: "[Reatha Clark King] was instrumental in opening doors and getting Metro on the map in a big way. We were working on solidifying the dream that the Metro pioneers had."[192]

After twenty years, Reatha exited academia and began readying herself for the next chapter in her life's story. Leaving Metropolitan State University was bittersweet. She loved working within a community of dedicated faculty and administrators, hearing the soul-affirming testimonials of Metro alumni, and fighting fiercely to carve out a better future for her school. But she was also excited for a change—an opportunity to turn her feet in a new direction and start blazing yet another trail.

★ ★ ★

In November of 1988, as Dr. Reatha Clark King stood on the precipice of another major life change, she felt compelled to take a step back and reflect on her journey—her first fifty years. The young girl in worn overalls and ratty shoes, picking cotton for six dollars a day, was a faint echo of the accomplished woman she had become. The scholar with a PhD and an MBA. The laboratory chemist. The college dean and university president. The vice president of a major corporation. But that little girl still clung, fiercely, to the core of Reatha's soul. She still sang in church every Sunday. She still remembered her aunties and uncles, her parents and sisters, her countless cousins. She still maintained her appetite for knowledge and unquenchable curiosity.

In 1988, Reatha lived nearly fifteen hundred miles from Pavo, Georgia, where her younger self attended school at Mount Zion and ate paper-bag lunches next to the cotton fields. In 1988, she lived eleven hundred miles from Washington, DC, where any errors in her work could cause serious damage or cost lives. In 1988, she lived twelve hundred miles from Long Island, New York, where she started her

---

191. Lofquist, *Metropolitan State University Buzz*.
192. Lofquist, *Metropolitan State University Buzz*.

deanship and worked tirelessly to serve a diverse student population and establish a permanent campus in Jamaica, Queens.

Somehow, the Earth had made eleven full revolutions around the sun while she and her family lived, worked, attended school, and supported one another in their adopted state of Minnesota.

Somehow, Jay had already graduated from Brown University and was now enrolled in medical school at the University of Minnesota.

Somehow, Scott was beginning his third year at Morehouse College and would graduate with a degree in mathematics in 1991.

Somehow, Judge King had completed his tenth year at 3M and was preparing for a transition of his own: establishing his own aviation company.

In 1988, Judge had been an integral part of Reatha's journey for over a quarter of a century. He had cemented himself as a pillar of her life—her most beloved and trusted companion—and proven time and again that he would support her in any decision she made. He would move across the country for her. He would cheer her on as she transitioned into her new role at General Mills. And, in return, Reatha would offer him her encouragement and love as he blazed trails of his own, including making aviation more accessible to a wider, more diverse set of people.

By now, it was abundantly clear that aviation was more than a passing fancy for Judge. He had built a ten-passenger airplane from the ground up. He had attended numerous air shows and logged thousands of hours of flight time. He was a longtime member of the Negro Airmen International (NAI), an aviation organization founded in 1967 by a Tuskegee Airman named Edward A. Gibbs.

NAI's primary focus was promoting and encouraging black aviators through educational programs and community outreach. In 1988, while Reatha was transitioning into her new role at GM, Judge gained the honor of becoming NAI's national president, a position he would hold until 1994.

Concurrently with his new appointment as NAI's president, Judge started his own aviation company, the American Air Center, based in Blaine, Minnesota. The center housed several airplanes and was a home base for pilots (including King) to teach lessons to budding aviators. Adopting the mission of NAI as its own, it actively promoted aviation in minority communities and eventually became a popular destination for school field trips.

To cap off an already eventful year, Judge was featured in the December 1988 issue of *Ebony* magazine, which showcased several black aviators. The article, entitled "Have Plane, Will Travel,"[193] depicts Judge at NAI's annual Tuskegee air show, speaking into a walkie-talkie as he strides away from his hand-built Cessna airplane.

With Judge starting his own business and Reatha heading the foundation of a major corporation, the King duo was closing out the 1980s as a powerhouse couple.

---

193. Narine, "Have Plane, Will Travel."

CHAPTER TWENTY

Philanthropy in the Emerald City

*"Where there is love and inspiration,
I don't think you can go wrong."*

—Ella Fitzgerald

Reatha officially began her position with General Mills on November 10, 1988. Just two days earlier, incumbent Republican vice president George H. W. Bush had defeated the Democratic candidate, Massachusetts governor Michael Dukakis, by a wide margin. Minnesota kept up its characteristic blue streak and was one of only ten states that had favored Dukakis. President-Elect Bush had campaigned on a platform that centered on the economy, in particular the continuation of President Reagan's policies, which advocated for small government, reduced taxes, and a reduction in federally funded public services. With fewer government-backed services, private philanthropy became more important than ever.

Despite the nation's preoccupation with the presidential election, Reatha's new role did not go unnoticed. The hubbub around her appointment was nearly as frenzied as when she had become president of Metro State. News rippled through business communities on both the local and national fronts. The *Chronicle of Philanthropy* announced her appointment immediately and applauded General Mills' decision. Feminists and black activists alike celebrated the appointment, vocalizing their hope that Reatha's vice presidency would usher in a new era of diversity in corporate leadership.

And, of course, the news media had a field day with Reatha's new assignment. As both a minority *and* a woman, she was a unicorn in corporate America—as Reatha puts it, a "double whammy."

A few years later, she appeared in an *Ebony* magazine profile on black executives, subtitled "How I Broke through the Glass Ceiling," which discussed the difficulties facing people of color who wished to climb the corporate ladder. The author didn't mince words: "Racism and sexism are still formidable barriers to advancement for any Black executive." In the article, Reatha emphasizes hard work and lifelong learning (two of her key tenets) as tools to overcome barriers. She told the magazine, "Just because you're out of school doesn't mean that learning should stop. People who realize this tend to do better than others."[194]

By now, Reatha was accustomed to being in the public spotlight. She fearlessly took center stage, rolled up her sleeves, and got to work.

Her predecessor, Jim Shannon, was not leaving her directionless. He handed her the equivalent of a map and a compass on his way out, and Reatha could choose to either follow his path or veer off in a new direction. Eventually, she would veer, but during her early days at GM, she was grateful for the guidance.

Jim had a stellar reputation among other corporate leaders—a reputation that stretched across the nation. A former bishop in the Catholic Church, he was known for being honest and industrious. He was highly respected and took it upon himself to mentor up-and-coming philanthropists.

The moment he learned that Reatha would replace him as vice president, he hopped on the phone and began placing calls. He called his close acquaintances at the Council on Foundations. He called nonprofit leaders who regularly partnered with the General Mills Foundation. He called other heads of major foundations with whom Reatha would likely work. By the time he was through, nearly all interested parties knew Reatha Clark King's name, if they hadn't already.

Jim's efforts allowed him to seamlessly pass the torch to Reatha—she began her role already familiar with many of the "who's whos" of corporate philanthropy. She also had a direct line to the Council on Foundations, Grantmakers for Effective Organizations, and the

---

194. Lyons, "Corporate Executives Tell."

American Council on Education, and would eventually sit on the board of directors of both the Council on Foundations and ACE.

Though Jim Shannon was well loved and respected by General Mills, he represented the old guard, the traditional ways of doing things. Reatha was tasked with "freshening up" the GM Foundation (innovation was, after all, one of the company's core values) and approaching charitable giving through her own unique methods and points of view. Soon, she would prove to be an innovative and insightful philanthropic leader (and she would certainly *freshen up* GM's charitable giving program), but first she had to do precisely what she had done at Metro State: learn the ropes and gain the trust of her colleagues and staff.

What became immediately apparent to Reatha was that good bookkeeping and even better communication were core components of the foundation's success. A separate entity from General Mills Inc., the General Mills Foundation had to track its own finances and was responsible for its own set of employees. The foundation was, however, a sister organization and was expected to work in tandem with its product—and profit-oriented sibling. Because of this sisterhood, Reatha was granted two different job titles: vice president of General Mills Inc. and president and executive director of the General Mills Foundation.

As had been her practice at Metropolitan State, Reatha made a conscious effort to keep all financial practices and decisions aboveboard and transparent. She worked diligently to make sure the foundation was compliant with financial regulations and admits she became "somewhat obsessed with the Internal Revenue Service and not violating tax code." In time, however, she came to realize that the foundation did not serve regulators. Rather, regulators served the foundation so that GM could become "better stewards of resources and do a good job in serving individuals and communities."[195]

As Reatha familiarized herself with her role, she also set about gaining the trust of her staff, comprising twenty or so full-time workers. In addition to the core staff, who handled finances and day-to-day operations, the foundation also counted several hundred volunteers among its ranks in all corners of the country.

When she was just settling in, Reatha was acutely aware of her status as an outsider—someone who had swooped in from outside the

---

195. King, "Accountability in Philanthropy."

company and snatched up a coveted role—and she knew that didn't sit well with everybody. Two General Mills "insiders" had also been in the running for the vice presidency, and she knew she would have to extend an olive branch to these individuals to help them trust and accept her leadership. One of the insiders passed over for the VP position was David Nasby, an associate director of the foundation. Reatha would be his direct supervisor.

Fortunately, David Nasby was a gracious individual, and he and Reatha ended up working well together. Their talents complemented one another, and David proved to be an adept liaison to the communities of Toledo, Ohio; Buffalo, New York; and Great Falls, Montana, where General Mills had established some of its plants—and, as a result, conducted a portion of its philanthropy work. Reatha, on the other hand, was a natural fit for conducting philanthropy work and research within the Twin Cities area. Over the past eleven years, she had sunk her roots into this place and stretched her branches to all corners of the community. She also became a valuable representative of GM in Washington, DC, where she had carved out a name for herself through her leadership and tireless advocacy for Metropolitan State University.

Reatha's other niche was financial. She enjoyed the logic of numbers and equations, just as she had during school and at the National Bureau of Standards. Her solid grasp of bookkeeping—a perennial task at Metro State—positioned her as the go-to person in the General Mills Foundation for any financial issues that cropped up. Her financial acumen also allowed her to work with competence and efficiency with both corporate auditors and General Mills' legal department.

During her first year at GM, as Reatha gained the respect of David and other members of the leadership team, she felt the urgency to connect with and earn the trust of two other parties: the rest of the foundation's staff and nonprofit leaders in the Twin Cities.

Reatha's continued friend-raising efforts stemmed from the genuine desire to make meaningful connections with others. Some of those connections might prove valuable to her work at GM, but others might not. And she was fine with that. At her core, Reatha has a deep, abiding love of humanity, and any new bridge she can build between herself and another person is valuable in itself. That's why she immediately formed a friendship with Sy Johnson, the head of building and groundskeeping at General Mills Foundation.

Though Sy was far from the upper echelons of GM, Reatha did not allow job titles to cordon her off from others. She was immediately drawn to his friendliness ("He was the first person to greet me in my new office," she says), his poise (as a former military officer), and his candidness. Reatha also befriended George Logan, a security officer at GM's campus, on her first day in the office. ("He had an impressive presence," Reatha says. "A presence that says, 'You'd better not step out of line!'") These two men—both black, both considered support staff at General Mills—became unlikely role models for Reatha. She could see the strength and wisdom each man possessed and was reminded of her father.

While she forged connections within the foundation, Reatha also turned her attention outward. She was aware that several nonprofit leaders in the community were not always happy with how the General Mills Foundation distributed its dollars, and she was determined to dig down to the root of their discontent. How could GM better serve the community? How could the foundation reach a wider swath of organizations? And which organizations needed its aid most?

Reatha set about gathering information and input. She soon discovered that many nonprofit organizations believed General Mills favored larger arts organizations while passing over smaller ones. They also noticed that General Mills tended to fund *project* grants rather than *operating support* grants for smaller organizations. While the support for project grants was necessary and appreciated, many organizations simply needed funding for their day-to-day operations.

Another piece of insight Reatha gathered from her research had to do with accessibility. Many smaller nonprofits, especially those operated by and focused on communities of color, were simply unaware of the grants available to them. This lack of awareness stemmed, at least in part, from the simple fact that the people who ran these nonprofits were not directly connected to executives of large foundations. They didn't necessarily play golf with grantmakers on weekends. They didn't regularly hobnob with corporate directors at charity benefits. In these pre-internet days, it wasn't always easy for small nonprofits to know which grants were available, open, and relevant.

A snapshot of the grant-issuing status quo was beginning to develop for Reatha. She saw that grant giving was heavily skewed toward major arts organizations, skipping over smaller organizations and nonprofits with other objectives. There was a need to issue a larger number of operating support grants so nonprofits could meet their daily needs (providing funding for copy machines, desk chairs, and monthly electrical bills is far less sexy than providing funding for an art mural project or a blood drive, but that was precisely the kind of funding many nonprofits sorely needed). Lastly, there was a problem with accessibility.

To solve this set of issues, Reatha decided, the General Mills Foundation would have to be both transparent and communicative with nonprofits of all stripes and sizes. Rather than take the reins and steer, Reatha began involving the local community in the problem-solving, starting with a request for proposals.

Reatha and David Nasby started a strategic effort to connect and communicate with nonprofit organizations, focusing on those operated by people of color. In which areas did these nonprofits need the most support? How would a General Mills grant help them reach their objectives? How much money was needed to make a significant impact?

Reatha kept an open line of communication with these nonprofit organizations. She built trust by, as she puts it, "letting those communities know they could be frank with us." She allowed herself—the face of the General Mills Foundation—to be vulnerable and took full responsibility for the foundation's actions and occasional shortcomings. To Reatha, "the buck stops here" wasn't just a quaint notion; it was her reality.

In return, nonprofits began answering her call for grant proposals and communicating their needs. A dialogue began—one that would lead General Mills to not only increase its charitable giving but also expand its outreach to communities of color and smaller nonprofits. Organizations that had never before received a dime from the General Mills Foundation began applying for grants. Small community nonprofits became emboldened to request funding for specific projects *or* daily operations. In the subsequent years, dozens of local and national organizations benefited from General Mills Foundation dollars.

In 1992, the foundation distributed $592,000 in grant money to Native American organizations across the country. Reatha said in a newspaper article that the fact this population suffered from "massive neglect"[196] led the foundation to specifically request grant proposals from Native peoples.

In 1988, North Minneapolis benefited from a $350,000 grant from General Mills to establish a public school academy, which would serve a diverse population of elementary school students.

In 1990, the foundation gave Penumbra Theatre in Saint Paul, a community theater that features actors, directors, and playwrights of color, an $86,500 grant for its general operations (the first of many the company would receive). According to Reatha, the largest grant the organization had received up to that point was $6,000.

Though the General Mills Foundation continued to issue grants to larger nonprofits and well-established arts organizations (the Walker Art Center, the Guthrie Theater, the United Way, the American Red Cross), a new precedent had been set. No longer would it overlook an organization because it was small, with a minimal operating budget. No longer would it fail to acknowledge the important contributions of minority-run nonprofits.

By immersing herself in the community and asking for input from local nonprofits, Reatha learned the vital importance of fostering an open line of communication and truly listening when the community spoke. "An important lesson learned by our foundation," she says, "is that *how* we serve communities is just as important as the grants we make to help them."[197] It is the responsibility of philanthropic organizations, Reatha believes, to be held accountable to the needs of the people they serve. It means, as she said in a 2001 speech, "putting forth the effort to understand the pain and fears of our communities, and then using the lessons learned from the community to change and improve."[198]

★ ★ ★

While Reatha was executive director, the General Mills Foundation focused on four main areas: arts and culture, education, youth and family services, and health and nutrition. The foundation's annual

---

196. Franklin, "General Mills Grants."
197. King, "Accountability in Philanthropy."
198. King, "Accountability in Philanthropy."

giving steadily increased under her leadership, going from $6.9 million in 1988 to nearly $19 million by the time Reatha retired in 2002.[199] As the charitable giving expanded, Reatha's team kept busy reviewing and screening grant applications and awarding grants to select applicants.

In addition to its grant work, the foundation provided another important service: it partnered with organizations to provide disaster relief when calamity struck. The Los Angeles riots in 1992, the Oklahoma City bombing in 1995, the dozens of black churches burned to the ground in the mid-1990s, the terrorist attacks on the Twin Towers and the Pentagon in 2001—these tragedies received an immediate response from the General Mills Foundation. Reatha recalls the company issuing a statement about the September 11th attacks just hours after the event; the foundation leaped to action to provide financial support to the emergency responders in New York City (while General Mills Inc. donated food products). The pace at which General Mills took action never ceased to amaze her.

But the disaster that hit closest to home for Reatha was the wave of attacks on predominantly black churches. In only eighteen months, spanning from 1995 to 1996, thirty black churches were set aflame in the southern United States. Churches in states such as Mississippi, Louisiana, Georgia, Tennessee, Alabama, and the Carolinas were burned to the ground, leaving little doubt as to the racist motives behind the attacks.

With each new incineration, Reatha's heart grew heavier. These churches were supposed to be safe havens—places to celebrate and sing, places to foster community and cast aside the week's troubles. Instead, the simple act of attending a Sunday service was beginning to feel like a risk. Which church was next on the list? When would the next arsonist strike?

The General Mills Foundation staff, some of whom attended predominantly black churches themselves, were also badly shaken by the string of attacks. Reatha recalls one woman calling her and asking, "What are we going to do about this? What do these corporate values mean, anyhow?"

To Reatha, GM's corporate values meant a great deal.

---

199. Merrill, "King Retiring from Foundation."

One of the values in GM's list of eight was "a bias toward action." Embodying that principle, Reatha acted. Under her guidance, the General Mills Foundation partnered with the National Council of Churches to rebuild the burned churches and provide communities with a measure of relief. It wrote about this important partnership in the company bulletin, which was always placed in a rack by the main entrance. Reatha recalls this particular bulletin flying off the shelf. "General Mills employees were proud of the foundation's work," Reatha says. "They cared."

The generous spirit of the General Mills Foundation was not an outlier in the Twin Cities. This was, and still is, an area known for its philanthropy and culture of giving. Consistently, Minnesotans are among the most generous Americans in terms of both financial gifts and volunteerism. In 2019, the state was deemed the most altruistic in the nation based off an evaluation of nineteen different traits,[200] but this spirit of giving is not a recent phenomenon. Minnesota has been declared the most generous state on several occasions over past decades. And that inclination to give trickles over into the private sector as well.

In 1946, the Dayton brothers—heirs of the Dayton-Hudson Corporation, which operated, among other ventures, the chain of Dayton's (later Marshall Field's) department stores—implemented a policy of donating 5 percent of their pretax earnings to charity. They were vocal about this policy, with one brother, Kenneth Dayton, declaring, "I say it's immoral for a company to take profits out of the community—without putting something else back in!"[201]

Partnering with the Daytons and adopting their giving philosophy, the Minneapolis Chamber of Commerce created the Five Percent Club,[202] which began with a group of Minneapolis corporations pledging, like the Daytons, to donate 5 percent of their pretax earnings to charitable causes. When the club was initiated, corporations were not often known for their philanthropy. The Commission on Private Philanthropy and Public Needs found that, in 1974, only 6 percent of corporations gave more than $500 to charitable causes annually. That number skyrocketed

---

200. Smith, "Minnesota Is Again No. 1."
201. Grimm, *Notable American Philanthropists*.
202. Today, the Five Percent Club is called the Minnesota Keystone Program and comprises over two hundred members.

in the 1980s, with corporate giving increasing by 52 percent between 1955 and 1989, and continues to increase to the present day. Today, it is almost expected that corporations will donate at least a portion of their profits. In a survey conducted by America's Charities, a full 71 percent of respondents agreed with the statement "It is imperative or very important to work where culture is supportive of giving and volunteering."[203]

In 1977, when corporate giving was far from the norm, John D. Rockefeller III applauded Minnesota's Five Percent Club in a speech, saying, "I heard so much about the city of Minneapolis—about its chamber of commerce, about the public spirit of its business community, about your remarkable Five Percent Club—that I feel a bit like Dorothy in the Land of Oz. I had to come to the Emerald City myself to see if it really exists."[204]

Though Rockefeller gave his speech decades ago, the "Emerald City" metaphor is still relevant to the Twin Cities. The *New York Times* ran an article in 2007 titled "Emerald City of Giving Does Exist," which touts the altruism of this particular part of the country. It declares, "Ask anybody in the world of corporate philanthropy and they'll tell you: Minneapolis-St. Paul is like no place else, a bastion of giving in an age when most companies are cutting back."[205]

Reatha Clark King agrees. "There's something special about the Twin Cities," she says. "The people are quite philanthropy minded."

It was fortunate, then, that she could conduct her philanthropy-oriented work in a community so receptive to charitable giving. With dozens of incredible nonprofits right in her backyard, the most difficult part of her job was screening organizations and deciding which ones would receive a General Mills grant. "People think giving away money is easy," Reatha says, "but, in truth, it is incredibly difficult. I consider my work with General Mills the hardest job I ever loved."

★ ★ ★

In 1988, Reatha was already a public figure, but her new position attracted even more attention and accolades. She had proven to be both

---

203. America's Charities, "Facts & Statistics on Workplace Giving."
204. Clotfelter and Ehrlich, *Philanthropy and the Nonprofit Sector.*
205. Nocera, "Emerald City of Giving Does Exist."

nimble and multitalented as she switched roles and began to excel in corporate philanthropy. And people noticed. As president of Metropolitan State University, she had already received numerous awards, given countless presentations and guest lectures, begun serving on three corporate boards, and received two honorary degrees, but when she became vice president of General Mills, those awards and responsibilities increased. Looking over her lists of professional memberships, volunteer commitments, international activities, keynote presentations, and various awards and recognition, one wonders whether she ever had time to sleep.

The year Reatha began working for General Mills, she added three more honorary doctorate degrees to her collection: one from Alverno College in Milwaukee, Wisconsin; one from Seattle University; and one from Rhode Island College in Providence (where former Metro State president and founder David Sweet became president in 1977). The next year, she would receive an honorary degree from her undergraduate alma mater, which was now called Clark Atlanta University, in addition to one from Marymount Manhattan College in New York City. The year after that, she would receive yet another from William Mitchell College of Law in Saint Paul. Over the coming years, Dr. Reatha Clark King would continue to attract honorary doctorates like metal shavings to a magnet. By 2001, she had fourteen to her name (see the appendix on page 311), including one from her very own Metropolitan State University.

The year 1988 not only marked the beginning of a deluge of honorary degrees but also ushered in an era of awards and recognition three decades long (and counting). Up to this point, Reatha had already received numerous prestigious awards, including the Distinguished Alumnus Award from Clark College (1983), the Drum Major for Justice Award from the Southern Christian Leadership Conference (1986), and the Educational Excellence Award from the Association of Black Women in Higher Education in New York City (1986). She had been featured in articles published in nationally distributed magazines and academic and scientific journals. She had appeared in television interviews and delivered keynote addresses across the United States and the globe. But that was just the beginning.

Reatha's honors and accolades accelerated in the late '80s and have not slowed since. In 1988, she received the Minnesota Public Administrator of the Year Award as well as a professional achievement award from the University of Chicago alumni association. The same year, *Mpls. St.Paul Magazine* declared Reatha the Twin Citian of the Year, an honor that had been bestowed upon a long line of exceptional Twin Citians, including activists, educators, newscasters, and entrepreneurs.

She would go on to receive awards and recognition from groups as diverse as the NAACP, the Boy Scouts of America, the League of Women Voters, the National Center for Black Philanthropy, the National Association of Corporate Directors, the Twin Cities–based International Leadership Institute, and many more local and national organizations. In 1999, the *Star Tribune* named her one of the hundred most influential Minnesotans of the twentieth century.

Among her awards, Reatha also received commendations from notable public figures, including a personal letter from Fred Rogers (of *Mister Rogers' Neighborhood* fame), who was an admirer of hers, and prestigious appointments from two presidents and a governor.[206]

For a list of Reatha's major awards and honors, please refer to the appendix on page 312.

From these myriad activities, achievements, and honors, Reatha could wallpaper every nook in her home with plaques and certificates. She has boxes brimming with award letters, newspaper clippings, and trophies. She has a collection of miniature flags, each one representing a country where she has given a guest lecture, participated in corporate board work, or performed humanitarian work. She has several posters from the Exceptional Black Scientists project—an initiative by Ciba-Geigy, a chemical company known for manufacturing dyes and resins. One poster depicts Reatha in both a lab coat and business attire, with beakers and a laboratory apparatus in the background. The series was accompanied by an Exceptional Black Scientist Award, which was bestowed upon Reatha in 1984.

---

206. From 1991 to 1993, Reatha was vice chair of the US Commission on National and Community Service under President George H. W. Bush; from 1994 to 1997, she served as vice chair for the US Corporation for National and Community Service under President Bill Clinton; and in 1998, she served on Minnesota governor Jesse Ventura's advisory team.

Each piece of paper and framed photograph and wooden plaque in Reatha's collection of achievements represents more than a passing flash of fame and recognition. They represent the sum of her staggering achievements and sterling work ethic. They speak not only of past achievements but of trails blazed and barriers obliterated. They are important, not necessarily because of what Reatha has accomplished for *herself* (although that alone is impressive), but because of the example she has set for young people of color, young women, and young people from low-income families who have been told, directly or indirectly, that they cannot do something due to their background or identity.

Reatha's award collecting was always a footnote to her actual work. With the same commitment and zest she poured into her work in academia and science, Reatha devoted herself to corporate philanthropy and board directorship. She took her positions seriously and made a conscious effort to press forward with fresh initiatives and improvements. When her former General Mills colleagues talk about Reatha, they inevitably bring up her industriousness, her sense of purpose, and her tendency to always show up prepared.

As Stephen Sanger, former CEO of General Mills, commented, Reatha "raised the General Mills Foundation to new heights."[207]

---

207. Merrill, "King Retiring from Foundation."

CHAPTER TWENTY-ONE

Reaching Wide

"A life is not important except in the impact it has on other lives."

—Jackie Robinson

One year, almost to the day, after Reatha began her new role at General Mills, the Berlin Wall was torn to the ground and the city's two sides reunited after twenty-eight long years of separation. Though an ocean and a continent away, Berlin's renewed unity was a fitting metaphor for Reatha's work at General Mills.

It was up to her to reconcile the wealth and power of General Mills with the poverty and vulnerability of the communities and nonprofits its foundation supported. She was an ambassador between races, genders, and income levels. She had lived on both sides of the tracks and knew how to navigate very different spaces. With the fluidity of a river, she could cut through varying terrain and create dialogues with disparate groups of people without breaking a sweat. She could attend a peace rally in an underserved corner of North Minneapolis in the morning and hobnob with nationally recognized politicians at a Philadelphia presidential summit in the afternoon (which is precisely what she did in April of 1997).

That was the core of Reatha's success: her willingness to engage people of all backgrounds and beliefs and have productive conversations. Instead of thrusting her views on others, she learned to listen, ask good questions, and find a common place from which they could work as a team to enact positive change. Even when she served on ExxonMobil's corporate board—a board composed mostly of white men whose viewpoints sometimes skewed far from her own—her fellow board members received her warmly and applauded her for her probing questions and willingness to engage in meaningful dialogues.

Ken Frazier, a fellow ExxonMobil board member who is now chairman and CEO of Merck, has said that Reatha was "a careful listener who was always thinking about how we could bring this collective judgment and wisdom to bear for the benefit of the company."[208] He also happened to be a personal mentee of Reatha's. As a young black man who had just begun serving on ExxonMobil's corporate board of directors, Ken looked to her for guidance, and she willingly took him under her wing. She had navigated this occasionally fraught turf for several years now, and she knew the decorum. She understood how to get things done and, most importantly, how to have a voice in the boardroom.

Reatha has spoken about crossing into racially homogenous spaces and plucking up her nerve to feel comfortable in her own skin. Her attitude is that "race is a beautiful thing," and she was able to "have greater respect for [her] fellow board members and feel the same way about their respective races."[209] She also made a concerted effort to contribute—to be a *participant*, not to be satisfied with merely gaining a seat at the table. Through her contributions, she hoped to demonstrate that she was an asset to the board and that other people who looked like her could be assets as well. "I was inspired," she has said, "by the thought that if I could continue participating, then number two [a second person of color] would eventually join me. If I dropped out, however, I knew that integration would not be sustained, and we would not get a second or third black or minority in the boardroom."[210]

This was Dr. Reatha Clark King. The trailblazer. The ambassador. The deep thinker and problem-solver.

She used her bridge-building tendencies to bring together disparate communities, organizations, and people and create positive change. Her contributions—both through the General Mills Foundation and through her personal charitable and volunteer work—are too numerous

---

208. "Corporate Governance Hall of Fame."
209. King, "Accountability in Philanthropy."
210. King, "Accountability in Philanthropy."

to list, but she is particularly proud of a few achievements, one of which is facilitating the creation of the Hawthorne Huddle.

★ ★ ★

The 1990s swept into Minnesota, full of promise and prosperity. In 1991, the Minnesota Twins clinched the World Series championship, nudging out the Atlanta Braves. In 1992, the Mall of America—then the largest mall in the United States, complete with the Camp Snoopy indoor theme park—opened to a crowd of more than 150,000 people and began accommodating tens of millions of visitors each year. In the presidential election that same year, the state's favored candidate, Bill Clinton, was elected by a wide margin.

Despite a string of global and national tragedies during the decade—the Gulf War in the Middle East, the Oklahoma City bombing, the devastating genocide of the Tutsi people in Rwanda, the deadly shooting at Columbine High School—this was also a decade for progress and hope. In 1990, antiapartheid leader Nelson Mandela was released from prison after being held for twenty-seven years for revolutionary activities. Four years later, he was elected president of South Africa in the very first multiracial election in the country. On the American national front, this was the decade of the Million Man March, held in October of 1995 to combat harmful racial stereotypes of black men. Judge King attended the event alongside about four hundred thousand other demonstrators in the nation's capital.

The early '90s also witnessed the first black female astronaut to travel to outer space. Dr. Mae Jemison, who had a background in both medicine and engineering, joined NASA in 1987 when she was just thirty years old. In 1992, NASA sent her on a mission to outer space, where she spent eight days aboard the *Endeavour* Space Shuttle running scientific experiments. The mission was successful, and Jemison and the rest of the *Endeavour*'s crew returned safely to Earth.

In Minneapolis, however, the 1990s were not just ball games and Camp Snoopy. A disturbing trend of violence and criminal activities began to overtake the city, and drug offenses started to rise. North Minneapolis was especially fraught with violence and experienced a rash of drive-by shootings, robberies, and gang brutality. The idyllic image of the Twin Cities—with its array of art galleries and theaters, Fortune 500 companies, and acclaimed colleges and universities—became badly tarnished. So troubled was Minneapolis in the mid-'90s that it began receiving national attention... and not the good kind. Dubbing it "Murderapolis," news reporters across the country began to wonder what was happening to the City of Lakes.

A 1996 *New York Times* article commented that the city's tranquil image had been "shattered by violence, with gang turf wars and drive-by shootings on streets where children play games of kick-the-can."[211] The article noted that the per capita crime rate in Minneapolis had surged past New York's, with 27.1 murders per hundred thousand people in 1995, compared to New York's rate of 16 per hundred thousand. In other words, Minneapolis's murder rate was nearly 70 percent higher.

Just as disturbing was the rise in homicides. In 1995, ninety-seven murders were recorded in Minneapolis, a figure 50 percent higher than in each of the past four years. In 1996, the death toll was nearly as high, with eighty-eight violent deaths recorded in the city.

The media, politicians, and community activists reacted with a frenzy of finger-pointing. The mayor blamed the influx of new residents in the Twin Cities, calling them "liabilities." The police spoke of an increased number of drug dealers and the prevalence of crack cocaine. The Minneapolis Foundation's president, Emmett Carson, claimed that impoverished populations were being scapegoated, declaring, "Much of this violence has been drive-by shootings, and that doesn't sound to me like welfare mothers."[212] Carson did, however, point to the widening income gap as a likely source of the problem.

Though community leaders bickered about the source of Minneapolis's troubles, they could all agree on one thing: there *was* a problem. And something needed to be done.

The communities affected by violence were especially motivated to put an end to the chaos and uncertainty—to reclaim their neighborhoods. Churches began creating violence prevention programs, communities formed neighborhood watches, counselors began taking on patients with drug addictions or who had experienced emotional trauma from the spike in violence.

---

211. Johnson, "Nice City's Nasty Distinction."
212. Johnson, "Nice City's Nasty Distinction."

During those troubling years, Reatha did not stand outside North Minneapolis, observing its issues like a naturalist with a pair of binoculars. Rather, she visited distressed areas, talked to residents, got to know community leaders and activists. She showed up for events, both as an attendee and as a guest speaker. She came to understand the grim situation from the inside out.

Reatha will be the first to admit that she wasn't always this connected with North Minneapolis. There was a time when she thought of her trips to this area as just another "to-do" on her jam-packed checklist. She would make an appearance, say a few words, and return to her comfortable office at General Mills or her cozy home in Maplewood. Her attitude shifted, however, after she attended a peace rally in April 1997.

It was a pleasant spring day when Reatha arrived in North Minneapolis. The peace rally was already underway, with people bunched together around tables, listening to music, holding signs, eating, chatting. She glanced at her watch.

She would attend the rally for a couple hours, but she could not stay long. She had a plane to catch that afternoon—a plane that would whisk her away to Philadelphia, Pennsylvania, where she would attend the Presidents' Summit for America's Future. Current president Bill Clinton would be there, and so would almost every living former president and their spouse. It was a prestigious event—even making the guest list was an honor—and Reatha was very much looking forward to it.

She made her way across the park to where the peace rally was underway and began to mingle with the crowd. Reatha knew only a few attendees, including the friend who had invited her, but she had no trouble engaging in conversation. People immediately recognized her. She was a community role model, an inspiration. One person after another approached her that morning, expressing their gratitude for her presence at the rally. "We are so glad you showed up," they said. "We know how busy you are."

Reatha was touched by the North Minneapolis residents' genuine appreciation and respect, and she admired their commitment to their community. They were not about to give up on their neighborhood, their home. As she listened to speeches and pep talks, Reatha was overcome with optimism and hope. When a young girl stood up and declared, "I came here because I want to raise peace in my community to a new high!" Reatha's eyes started to prickle and teardrops began rolling down her cheeks.

After delivering a short speech and saying a few goodbyes, Reatha made her way to the airport. Sitting on the plane, listening to the quiet hum of the engines as it flew east, she reflected on the rally—on the genuine, beating heart of it—and grew less and less excited about the Presidents' Summit.

That event, she knew, was a universe away from the peace rally's Sharpie-decorated cardboard protest signs, the nails-tough mothers, the children with grass-stained knees and sunshine-bright smiles. The people in North Minneapolis didn't need white linen tablecloths and decadent centerpieces. They didn't need floor-length gowns and bite-sized hors d'oeuvres. All they needed was the spirit of their movement, their tenacity to forge ahead and make change.

Guilt washed over Reatha, and she had the distinct feeling that she was not serving this population as well as she could. She was *squeezing them into* her busy schedule; she was dropping by when it was convenient. In the quiet cabin of the airplane, Reatha made a decision: she would begin to intentionally set aside time and resources to share with the people of North Minneapolis. She would remember her roots and not abandon the people who lived in impoverished and potentially dangerous conditions—conditions Reatha had known all too well as a young girl. Thinking back on that moment, Reatha later said, "Regardless of how far we advance in our careers in life, and how often we travel from country to country doing our successful work, let us never forget 'the road back to the homes that launched us to the high and mighty summits.'"[213]

Placing North Minneapolis at the center of her attention, Reatha began to work with a renewed sense of purpose. She knew better than to swoop into neighborhoods and begin solving people's problems for them. Instead, she put together a think tank composed of insiders—those in the community who had a direct stake in the area's well-being. "All minds were at the table," she says. Several groups of people—community leaders, ministers, judges, activists, police officers, parents, philanthropists—collaborated on designing a program to reduce crime and empower the community. It was a true grassroots effort.

---

213. King, "Accountability in Philanthropy."

After conducting research, gathering community input, and mulling over a series of proposals, the group landed on an idea: a monthly community forum dubbed the Hawthorne Huddle.

Hawthorne was one of the communities in North Minneapolis hardest hit by the rash of violent crimes. Its namesake event would take place on the first Thursday of every month at a local community center and would include any members of the community who wished to attend. With representatives from local businesses, police officers, teachers, ministers, and elected officials, they would discuss local issues (everything from litter to gang violence), potential solutions, and future objectives. The agenda was fluid and always left room for conversation, questions, and brainstorming.

The idea behind the Hawthorne Huddle was to pool both the resources and the brainpower of very different people from very different backgrounds. Just as a wicker basket grows stronger with each intersecting fiber, so, too, does the efficacy of diverse public forums like the Hawthorne Huddle. With enough threads woven together, such forums can carry a community.

Though the concept was powerful, what made it even more effective was the resources behind it. General Mills funneled $360,000 into Hawthorne neighborhood programs, including the Huddle, during its first two years. The funds would support community enrichment activities organized by the Huddle. Not only could the community dream up potential solutions, but it now had the capital to *act*. Additionally, powerful allies backed the Hawthorne Huddle, including the mayor of Minneapolis, Sharon Sayles Belton, and the governor of Minnesota, Arne Carlson. Other corporations also supported the initiative, including Fortune 100 company Honeywell. This was a true unification of powers. "Philanthropists brought trust and skills to the table," Reatha says, "but CEOs brought their power, voice, and influence." To make sure the Hawthorne Huddle would float instead of sink, the program needed the twin engines of trust and power.

All these alliances—the politicians, the corporate support, the community backing—were not accidental. Reatha and the other founders of the Hawthorne Huddle were intentional in their actions. Reatha prioritized "forming and fostering enduring relationships"[214] so

---

214. O'Keefe, "Hawthorne Huddle Celebrates 20 Years."

any initiatives or changes would be sustainable instead of fleeting. She understood the importance of community involvement and collaboration in making the most out of any funding provided. As she told *North News* in 2017, "Grant-making can be a short-term solution. That's the easiest thing to do. The problem solving is the hardest part. That comes from conversation and follow-up."[215]

Those conversations and follow-ups were directly tied to the community. From the very beginning, the Hawthorne Huddle was built on input from local residents, and that was and continues to be the source of its success and sustainability. Years later, Reatha put together a research paper for the Hubert H. Humphrey Institute of Public Affairs based on both her personal experience in philanthropy and dozens of interviews she conducted with philanthropy-oriented public figures. In it, she says, "Citizens are close to the ground. They are most affected by the changes they and others seek to make in communities. They know how best to sustain them. My experiences show that engaging, encouraging, and tapping citizen power are excellent techniques for sustaining community progress."[216]

With *citizen power* fueling it, the Hawthorne Huddle revved its engines and jetted into the last few years of the 1990s, determined to revitalize and reclaim Minneapolis's Northside. Every month, come downpour or snowstorm, community members piled into the Hawthorne Huddle morning meeting. First a handful, then a couple dozen, then fifty people on a regular basis.

Well-known public figures would often show up and participate, including superintendents, mayors, governors, and even former US vice president Walter Mondale and US attorney general Janet Reno. Reatha estimates that when Reno was the guest of honor, nearly three hundred people showed up to hear her speak. They bunched together in Farview Park as she stood up and addressed the enthusiastic crowd. Reno's presence helped validate and encourage the area's residents, although they

---

215. O'Keefe, "Hawthorne Huddle Celebrates 20 Years."
216. King, *Philanthropy and Public Policy*.

already understood the power of the Hawthorne Huddle. It's just that the nation was starting to take notice.[217]

Hawthorne residents saw their neighborhood transform within just two years of the Huddle's initiation. Neighbors began noticing quieter nights. Fewer robberies. "I just don't hear the gunfire," a local clergyman named Reverend Gregory Tolaas reported. "I think there is a feeling that gets into the air. . . . There is the message that people in the neighborhood care about the neighborhood."[218]

As other neighborhoods began to emulate Hawthorne's model, homicides and other violent crimes in Minneapolis began to decline. In just two years, annual narcotics-related warrants dropped from 108 to 51, vandalism incidents were nearly cut in half, and burglaries decreased from 240 incidents to 181 incidents.[219] In subsequent years, the murder rate dropped significantly, and tangible improvements were made to the Northside neighborhoods: improved housing, a greater investment in public services, the addition of a new elementary school (Nellie Stone Johnson Community School, built in 2001). Although many factors undoubtedly contributed to the decline in violent crimes—including community watch groups and better psychological care for those with neurological disorders—the Hawthorne Huddle deserves at least some of the credit.

In fact, the United States experienced a wave of new community-focused nonprofit organizations in the 1990s, and as the number of nonprofits grew, crime dropped. Significantly. A study published in *American Sociological Review* examined the relationship between crime and the number of humanitarian-focused nonprofits in 264 American cities and found that over twenty years, "every 10 additional organizations focusing on crime and community life in a city with 100,000 residents leads to a 9 percent reduction in the murder rate, a 6 percent reduction in the violent crime rate, and a 4 percent reduction in the property crime rate."[220]

---

217. Even prestigious Harvard Business School took notice, with two researchers authoring a case study on the runaway success of the Hawthorne Huddle (Barrett and McCarthy, "General Mills and the Hawthorne Huddle").
218. Rachel E. Stassen-Berger, "Foundation, Neighbors Huddle Together."
219. National Institute of Justice, "Excellence in Problem-Oriented Policing."
220. Sharkey, Torrats-Espinosa, and Takyar, "Community and the Crime Decline: The Casual Effect of Local Nonprofits on Violent Crime."

The trend is too consistent and substantial to be a coincidence. Community-centric nonprofits make a marked positive impact on the people and neighborhoods they serve.

But Reatha didn't need a study to know this was the case. She could see the changes sprouting from each seed the Hawthorne Huddle's initiatives planted. She knew from personal testimonials and local residents' consistent participation that this nonprofit was instrumental in uplifting, empowering, and uniting the community. That it enabled positive change and enacted intentional measures for deterring crime and promoting public enrichment.

The community agreed. In 2017, twenty years after the Hawthorne Huddle was initiated, a special anniversary Huddle was held to honor its founders and early leaders, including Reatha. Today, the Hawthorne Huddle is still a pillar of North Minneapolis and is supported not only by local residents but by several Twin Cities businesses and nonprofits, including, of course, General Mills.[221]

★ ★ ★

The Hawthorne Huddle was far from the only successful, impactful, and potentially life-altering program that Reatha Clark King either initiated or supported financially through General Mills Foundation grants. Her contributions were numerous, her reach wide. The stories and circumstances behind each General Mills–supported program could easily fill their own volume, but the following sections showcase a few of the highlights in the areas of education, equality, and the arts.

Education

Few people understand the value of education as Reatha does. For her, education was a prize—a passport to a better life and greater opportunities. It was the way to access news and other critical information. It meant upward mobility and a chance to make something of yourself (and make a decent living while doing it).

---

221. Support from General Mills is directed to the Youth Coordinating Board, which handles the funds for the Hawthorne Huddle (O'Keefe, "Hawthorne Huddle Celebrates 20 Years").

Reatha's passion for education extended to her work at the General Mills Foundation. Throughout her fourteen years as the foundation's executive director, she rallied behind several educational programs, including the A Chance to Learn project, Minneapolis Public School Academy, and a faculty diversity training program at Columbia Business School (which the foundation initiated with a $300,000 grant). A Chance to Learn was one of the earliest educational programs Reatha supported as foundation head, with the GM Foundation allotting $150,000 to the program in 1989 to be distributed over the course of three years. She believed the initiative to be of critical importance since it focused on providing thoroughly researched alternative methods of learning to young elementary schoolchildren who struggled to keep pace with their peers. These learning methods included physiological activities to improve hand-eye coordination and fine motor skills in addition to more traditional instruction. After only a year, Reatha was pleased to see A Chance to Learn already achieving success: as the *Star Tribune* reported, "About 125 students [moved] from the bottom 12 percent of readers among Minneapolis public school first-graders to the top 20 percent in just eight months."[222] These same students' reading pace improved dramatically, with the children reading, on average, five times faster than their peers.

One of the other educational programs the General Mills Foundation supported, dubbed Unlimited Possibilities, was inspired by one of Reatha's many classroom visits. On an ordinary afternoon in 1993, she paid a visit to an alternative school located on the Minneapolis Northside. It was designed for students who were struggling—young people who had not adapted well to traditional classroom settings in public school. Reatha enjoyed speaking with and mentoring students, and she made an effort to talk with the young people individually or in small-group settings whenever possible. At this school, one of the teachers encouraged her to sit down and talk with one student in particular—a young woman who had demonstrated a knack for writing.

Reatha approached the student and asked her about her current writing projects. The student, it seemed, was fixated on *pain*. That was her topic of choice—the subject that floated to the surface time and again in her writing.

---

222. Duchschere, "Hands-On Program."

Considering this, Reatha asked the student, "Why pain? Why not possibilities?"

From the acorn of an idea, an initiative took root: Unlimited Possibilities. The program paired General Mills with six different Minneapolis-based nonprofits that operated eight alternative secondary schools. Over two years, the General Mills Foundation would grant the organizations $1.4 million to improve their schools' programs, purchase much-needed educational resources, and hire a coordinator to represent and unify all six nonprofits and their respective schools. About six hundred students would be served, many of whom lived in impoverished conditions or with single parents. Some were gang members or teen parents. These were the second-chance kids who were in danger of falling through the cracks and perpetuating a cycle of violence or poverty.

But Reatha believed in them. She had witnessed too many "miracle" success stories *not* to believe. She hadn't been so different from those kids when she was young—living in a single-parent household for a time, just scraping by with her mother's domestic work and whatever she and her sisters managed to bring in. The only difference between Reatha and these students was the encouragement she had received from her family, her church, her community. She knew the power of a few empowering words, a supportive parent or teacher. She knew Unlimited Possibilities, in conjunction with the alternative schools, had the potential to change lives.

As one young woman from one of the alternative schools attested, "People [in the school] love you for who you are."

Equality

When Reatha began her sleuthing work, seeking to identify areas of need within the community, she found that nonprofit organizations that focused on people of color (or that were owned or operated by people of color) often did not receive the support they needed. She aimed to change that.

Organizations and institutions run by white people had, in general, enjoyed a massive head start in the United States. Philanthropic organizations and foundations had been—and still are—largely run by white folks, who had, wittingly or not, funneled their dollars into white-established and white-operated nonprofit organizations and foundations. In 1996, in the heyday of Reatha's philanthropy work for General Mills, precisely *zero* nonprofits that were founded and operated by people of color made the list of the top one hundred largest nonprofits in Minnesota; according to a *Star Tribune* article, they received "less than 6 percent of foundation and corporate giving."[223] Though times and attitudes were changing, it wasn't easy to close the gap and make up for that initial head start. But Reatha was determined to try.

During her tenure at General Mills, the foundation issued grants and supported organizations such as City Arts (multicultural art forms for inner-city youth), the American Indian Opportunities Industrialization Center (which focuses on job training for Native American individuals), the Metropolitan Economic Development Association (which helps kick-start minority-owned businesses in addition to offering ongoing support[224]), and Mercado Central (a collaboration of small Latinx-owned and Latinx-operated businesses).

Learning about and supporting these nonprofits energized and excited Reatha. She saw the possibilities in each one—the chance to make a significant difference in countless lives. Though each program offered vital and impactful services, some resonated more deeply with her than others. One, called LEAD (short for LEADership, Education and Development), provided business training and mentoring for underserved youth. With the goal of empowering minority high school students and introducing them to business concepts, the program included four weeks of summer classes and mentoring at renowned business schools, including the University of Minnesota's Carlson School of Management. The culmination of the program typically involved a presentation by the students to representatives from a corporation, such as General Mills—a marketing pitch for a fictitious product the students had invented.

Reatha understood the importance of career preparation and fully supported LEAD and its mission. While working at both York College and Metropolitan State University, she had spent decades defending

---

223. Franklin, "Honing Skills."
224. In 1995, General Mills pledged to double its annual contributions to MEDA in addition to doubling its purchase orders from minority suppliers within the next two years (Inskip, "Twenty-Five Years").

the validity of career-preparation programs and understood their efficacy and impact. And she knew mentorships worked. Study after study had demonstrated that young people with mentors were more likely to graduate, committed fewer crimes, and were more likely to find steady employment than their peers. In her own life, Reatha had benefited from the guiding hands of mentors.

Growing up, Ms. Frazier, her family, and her church community encouraged her to get an education—to "make something of herself." At Clark College, Professor Simpson and Dr. Spriggs saw the promise she brought to the classroom and opened her eyes to the possibility of a career in chemistry. During the summers between her undergrad classes, the Dann family instilled a confidence in Reatha she had never before known. They showed her she was an equal—someone who could thrive in and adapt to any setting, someone whose voice mattered. At the University of Chicago, Reatha had her advisor, Dr. Ole Kleppa, and chemistry lab supervisor, Myrtle Bachelder (one of the first female research chemists she had met). At the National Bureau of Standards, she had Dr. Armstrong. At York College, she had Dr. Bodi.

And the list went on.

Mentors were powerful. Business and career training provided practical skills and confidence. Reatha knew that combining mentorship with career training would benefit the young people in LEAD, and she was proud to sponsor the program through General Mills. Today, LEAD's impact is apparent. Its website boasts that 100 percent of program graduates complete high school, and nearly 100 percent are accepted into a college or university *and* complete their collegiate-level studies.[225]

With Reatha steering its giving, the General Mills Foundation continued to support programs that facilitated or advocated for equality or aided underserved communities. From supporting the African American Heritage Foundation in Cedar Rapids to funding a nonprofit magazine for people of color[226] to granting over half a million dollars to Native American organizations in a single year (1992), Reatha

---

225. LEADership, Education and Development, home page.
226. The magazine was called *Colors* and was initiated in the early '90s by Four Colors Productions (Franklin, "Agency Gets $2 Million").

consciously directed the foundation toward organizations that had previously been underfunded or completely neglected.

However, she wanted her work to be sustainable. One way to do that, she reasoned, was to encourage more people of color to become involved in philanthropy and strategic fundraising. It was no secret that "minority-oriented nonprofits weren't getting the same amount of money as their white counterparts,"[227] and Reatha was determined to change that.

Through the General Mills Foundation, she issued a substantial grant to support a ten-course, eighteen-month-long program to train minority nonprofit leaders in strategic philanthropy and fundraising. The local Communities of Color Institute sponsored the initial program, which was held at the Indiana University Center on Philanthropy. The program was successful, with graduates singing its praises and the CCI expanding its operations.

But Reatha didn't stop there.

In addition to issuing grants for fundraising and philanthropy education, she also became active in the Association of Black Foundation Executives (ABFE). In 2001, she was invited to give ABFE's tenth annual James A. Joseph Lecture, an honor she didn't dream of passing up. James Joseph is a formidable and pioneering philanthropist and fundraiser, a former US ambassador, and a former minister with a rebellious streak. He also happens to be a close friend of Reatha's.

The circle of nationally recognized black philanthropists was quite small, and both James and Reatha had served on the Council on Foundations. James had also been mentored by Reatha's GM predecessor, Jim Shannon.

At the ABFE lecture, Reatha took the podium and spoke to a rapt audience about carving a path forward in black philanthropy. She spoke about topics with which she had grown intimately familiar: promoting accountability, advocating for diversity on corporate boards, combating racism, working to alleviate poverty, and centering philanthropic work on the needs of the community. "I believe that being fully accountable means putting forth the effort to understand the pain and fears of our

---

227. Franklin, "Honing Skills."

communities, and then using the lessons learned from the community to change and improve our Foundation," she said.[228]

It is difficult to measure the impact of Reatha's work to increase engagement and representation in minority-focused philanthropy, but notable changes have occurred since she took the stage at that ABFE conference. In 2011, the month of August became recognized worldwide as Black Philanthropy Month (BPM). With the founding of BPM, events have cropped up all across the country (and the world) in the month of August to encourage charitable giving. In addition, so-called "democratized" philanthropy has become popular, with groups of people pooling their resources for a cause rather than relying on a single wealthy donor or organization. Democratized philanthropy is exemplified by black giving circles in which individuals combine financial resources and/or raise money for specific causes.

No matter the method of giving, one thing is certain: black Americans are a consistently generous demographic. A report by the W. K. Kellogg Foundation found that black households give 25 percent more of their income to charity than white households, and "almost across the board, communities of color are intensifying their charitable giving."[229]

Reatha is proud of the uptick in black charitable giving, but ultimately unsurprised. "We're generous people," she says. "From a young age, black children are raised to give back and contribute to our community."

The Arts

The General Mills Foundation had a well-established history of supporting arts and culture long before Reatha took the driver's seat. Surrounded by a wealth of theaters, museums, art galleries, and concert venues in its Twin Cities headquarters, General Mills could scarcely avoid contributing to the arts. It was, and still is, deeply ingrained in the local culture, as central as potluck suppers and ice fishing. The iconic red cherry and spoon displayed in the Walker Art Center's sculpture garden, the wildly angled and curved façade of the Weisman Art Museum, the

---

228. King, "Accountability in Philanthropy."
229. *Cultures of Giving.*

impressive, castle-like bulk of the American Swedish Institute—these are symbols of a well-established and well-funded arts scene.

But Reatha knew there was more to Twin Cities arts and culture than the major players. The Saint Paul Chamber Orchestra, the Guthrie Theater, and the Minneapolis Institute of Art were not the only attractions in town. Certainly, those institutions were important, but they had already been buoyed by substantial funding and were floating comfortably at the top of the Twin Cities' arts and culture establishments. What about the smaller theater companies and artistic venues that were struggling to stay above water? What about the spaces with shoestring budgets that mainly ran off love and elbow grease?

Reatha turned her attention toward these smaller institutions and started shuffling some of General Mills' grant money toward their programs.

One of the first projects the foundation funded under her leadership was the Capri Theater. Nestled in the heart of North Minneapolis and owned and operated by Plymouth Christian Youth Center, the Capri has been a landmark and a cornerstone of the community since 1927. One of its top priorities is to create an inclusive environment and a safe space for people of all beliefs and backgrounds.

Today, the theater is thriving, but in 1988, it was in sore need of financial support. Recognizing this, the General Mills Foundation awarded it $300,000 over several years. It was the largest gift, by far, the company had ever received, and the first of many from General Mills. The newly renovated Capri Theater remains a pillar of the Northside community and a constructive outlet for both adults and youth.

Not long after the foundation awarded the grant to the Capri, another theater captured the attention of Reatha and her team: Penumbra Theatre. Located west of downtown Saint Paul in the Selby-Dale neighborhood, this company was founded in 1976 with the intention of providing a platform and a microphone for black actors and voices. It was, and still is, Minnesota's only professional black-operated theater. In fact, "over its 42 year history, Penumbra has employed more actors, choreographers, dancers, directors, and administrators of color than all other theaters in Minnesota combined."[230] It is also the largest black theater in the nation.

---

230. Beck, "Sarah Bellamy."

Reatha knew this was no ordinary theater. With its goal to promote black actors and playwrights (it has, for instance, hosted more plays by Pulitzer Prize–winning playwright August Wilson than any other theater in the world), it was not only treading new ground in the arts community but also uplifting and advancing people of color. A community is a multifaceted composition, and Reatha understood how a theater like Penumbra could empower young people who quite possibly had never seen people onstage who looked like them.

In 1990, General Mills issued a grant of $86,500 to Penumbra Theatre (the first of many), enabling the company to not only continue its work but grow, reach new audiences, and begin providing educational and outreach activities. Today, the theater has received numerous prestigious awards and is "one of only three professional African American theaters in the nation to offer a full season of performances."[231] Equity, opportunity, and eliminating racism remain at the center of its work.

Though General Mills has supported numerous arts—and culture-oriented organizations over the years—including the Children's Theatre Company, the Minnesota Opera, and the Saint Paul Chamber Orchestra—only once did Reatha have a direct hand in *founding* an arts program.

In 1991, acclaimed choral scholar and conductor Philip Brunelle approached her with an idea. He envisioned a program tied to Black History Month—a program that would celebrate black artists and engage the community. As a longtime conductor, Philip understood the transformative power of music. He was also appalled by the public's tendency to gloss over the contributions of black musicians, both past and present, even during Black History Month.

Philip Brunelle is a buoyant silver-haired and silver-bearded man with an energy reserve that rivals Reatha's. He's a Grammy winner and a recipient of the Weston H. Noble Lifetime Achievement Award and has conducted concerts on every continent except Antarctica. He once declared, "If I had my druthers—which I don't—I'd have a concert every day. . . . There's so much to explore!"[232] It was this boundless energy that led Philip to found the choral group VocalEssence (originally called the Plymouth Church Music Series) in 1969, nurturing it into one of the

---

231. Penumbra Theatre, "History."
232. Grumdahl, "Twin Cities' Song Leader."

most distinguished, award-winning choirs in the nation. Starting with 120 volunteers, the choir steadily grew over the years and branched into several distinct groups. Today, the ensembles perform for over twenty thousand people each year and have received more Chorus America awards than any other choral group in the United States.

But in 1991, Philip Brunelle knew his choral groups needed to reach a wider audience, especially young people, and promote a more diverse set of singers. He knew of Reatha and her reputation as a doer and a go-getter—someone you wanted in your corner.

Reatha listened to Philip explain his idea with rapt attention. The notion of creating a branch of VocalEssence for young people to celebrate black artists was intriguing, and she understood how the initiative could benefit students, teachers, artists of color, parents—entire communities.

After some consideration, Reatha green-lit the project through the General Mills Foundation, and the VocalEssence WITNESS program was born.

It began humbly, with Saint Paul's Central High School hosting one concert. The first year was a huge success, and Philip was determined to keep WITNESS's momentum going. He began bringing in guest artists and conductors; he developed a school program to reach kids in the classroom. The program began attracting both local and national attention. In 1994, James Earl Jones (famous for his booming voice and his role as Darth Vader in the Star Wars movies) participated in WITNESS, narrating a work called *Frederick's Fables*, which was commissioned especially for him. Reatha recalls the way his voice filled the room. "He captivated the audience," she says. "He had such a huge presence." Other special guests have taken the stage at WITNESS concerts over the years, including former poet laureate Rita Dove, jazz singer Bobby McFerrin, jazz pianist Dr. Billy Taylor, and cellist Anthony Elliott.

Now three decades old, WITNESS has evolved into a multifaceted program that encompasses a classroom component (with teaching artists hosting interactive workshops for students), public concerts, professional commercial recordings, and national and international choir tours. Every year, about fifty schools and six thousand students are involved in WITNESS—students of all backgrounds, cultures, and creeds.

Reatha has remained involved, serving on the VocalEssence board for several years and, later, supporting the program as a private citizen through volunteer work and financial donations. She still revels in watching the music's impact on young people—both the singers onstage and the kids sitting in the audience. For many of the school-age audience members, the WITNESS Young People's Concert is their first opportunity to sit inside a concert hall and watch a well-trained choral group sing their hearts out. "I sit in the balcony and watch and feel so proud," said Reatha in a 2019 VocalEssence profile. "Minneapolis is at its best on those Mondays, giving this special treat to our rainbow of young people."[233]

---

233. "Donor Spotlight: Reatha Clark King."

CHAPTER TWENTY-TWO

A Living Legacy

"Every great dream begins with a dreamer." —Harriet Tubman As Reatha was never one to sit still, her life outside the General Mills Foundation was about as busy as her life within it. Despite her high-powered job, her endless work commitments, her press conferences, and the millions she oversaw as director of the foundation, she never forgot about her family and her church. No matter how jam-packed her work calendar became, she didn't lose sight of what mattered most.

She continued to participate in Pilgrim Baptist Church (and, after moving in 1992, Fellowship Missionary Baptist Church), volunteering for several committees and mentoring some of the youth.

She played an active role in the lives of her sons and husband.

She spent most of her Sunday afternoons catching up with her mom, sisters, and other relatives on the phone.

Despite the honors, the news interviews, the awards banquets, Dr. Reatha Clark King was still mom, sister, daughter, friend, *country girl*. Her family and church were a lighthouse when seas grew stormy. They were her comfort and joy.

Between 1988 and 2002, when Reatha was the executive director of the General Mills Foundation, many of her frustrations and triumphs, her anguishes and celebrations, involved her family, not her career.

In December of 1991, her youngest son, Scott, graduated from Morehouse University with a degree in mathematics. In a little less than a year, however, Scott changed his trajectory. He had an enduring passion for music and the arts, and he decided to continue his education at a music-focused school. Though Reatha and Judge both hailed from science backgrounds, they supported their son's decision. Ultimately, they wanted their boys to be happy, and they were confident both of them could excel in any area they wanted to pursue. So, with his parents' blessings and his guitar tuned, Scott applied to Berklee College of Music in Boston and began studying performance in the fall of 1992.

Seven years later, Scott's path would take another turn. With the goal of pursuing a degree in the burgeoning field of information technology, he enrolled at American InterContinental University in Atlanta in the fall of 1999. Within a year, he earned a master of information technology degree and began working in IT.

Jay, the eldest King son, took a much more linear path than his brother. After graduating from Brown University, his focus remained firmly on medical school, where he planned to specialize in radiology. Jay's only real distraction from his studies was a young woman he had known since high school.

Kristin Leigh Negaard graduated one year after Jay from Kellogg High School. As high school students, the pair knew each other and shared some of the same interests (they both played violin in the youth symphony), but they never dated. That changed when Jay began attending the University of Minnesota's medical program. The high school pals reconnected and started to date.

Kristin graduated from the University of Minnesota with an undergraduate degree in international relations just as Jay was beginning medical school. Later, when Jay was working his way through his residency in radiology in Cincinnati, Kristin continued her education at the University of St. Thomas, a private university located in Saint Paul. While he was learning to use MRI machines and interpret x-rays, she was studying cross-cultural communication and international economics to obtain her MBA in international management.

Despite their busy academic schedules, the young couple continued to date. They were now a major part of each other's lives and began to envision a future together. Before the end of Jay's residency, they decided to wed.

On a chilly January day in 1996, Jay and Kristin floated down the aisle of Park Avenue United Methodist Church in Minneapolis and said their "I dos" among a throng of family members and friends. In just one year, the newlyweds moved to Tucson, Arizona, where Jay would begin working as a radiologist in a private practice. But first, they would welcome their oldest daughter, MacKensey Elyse King—Reatha and Judge's first grandchild—into the family in November 1996, just before Thanksgiving. Two years later, in February 1998, the little family grew once more with the addition of their second daughter, Kayla Clark King. A second daughter herself, Reatha was delighted by the bond of sisterhood her two little granddaughters would share. Four years later, in April 2002, Jay and Kris King's youngest child was born. This time, their baby was a boy, and they decided to honor him with the family name: Napoleon Judge King IV. As Reatha says, "When passing down family names, nicknames become important, and Jay and Kris decided to call their son NJ."

These sunny, joyful years—when Reatha was working for positive change through philanthropy and the King family was welcoming new members into its fold—were not without the occasional cloud. In autumn of 1999, Reatha's beloved mother, Ola Mae Clark, passed away.

Despite her daughters' entreaties for her to move north, Ola Mae had spent her days in Moultrie, in the heart of South Georgia. She lived in the same house she had purchased when Reatha was in high school, on the *nice* side of Moultrie, across town from Dirty Spoon. Ola Mae lived simply and continued to enjoy cooking and hosting any relative or friend who dropped by. Ever the devoted mother and grandmother, she would occasionally venture north to Washington, DC, or the Twin Cities, where she would visit her daughters and grandchildren. But the South was home. The South was where she kept her heart.

But the South—at least where Ola Mae lived—did not provide the kind of quality healthcare and nutrition education one might find elsewhere. Ola Mae enjoyed her salt, her red meats, her various oils and fats. Vegetables were boiled, fried, covered in breading, doused in butter. Toward the end of her life, Ola Mae began experiencing cardiovascular issues and chronic headaches. She began taking a headache powder, which Reatha suspects did more harm than good. In the end, a stroke claimed her life.

In late autumn of 1999, the Clark girls lost a mother; their relatives lost a friend and matriarch.

Mamie, Reatha, and Dot arranged their mother's funeral and convened in South Georgia to lay her to rest. She was buried in a plot near Mount Zion Baptist Church, in the same cemetery as her former husband, Willie B. Clark.

At her funeral, just as in life, Ola Mae was surrounded by flocks of friends and family members. Well known for her buoyant spirit, unwavering faith, and magnanimity, she never hesitated to provide a seat at her table or a roof for those who needed shelter. Ola Mae's legacy lives on through her generous heart and the many lives she touched.

★ ★ ★

Shortly after Reatha's mother passed away, the world whipped itself into a frothing, panic-stricken frenzy. The century—the *millennium*—was about to end, and the public was convinced that every computer across the world would crash, sending the globe into anarchy. During the months leading up to the year 2000 (dubbed Y2K), it became impossible to turn on the nightly news without hearing a doom-and-gloom take on what might happen when the clock struck midnight. Online clocks will revert back to the year 1900, they said. Discombobulated calendars will cause banks and nuclear power stations to fail. The stock market will crash. The lights will crackle-pop out, and darkness and anarchy will reign.

Across the globe, people prepared for the worst. They built bunkers, stockpiled food and bottled water, and withdrew all their money from savings accounts. The US government spent about $100 billion on preventive measures to stave off the pending devastation.

Reatha observed the panic with the skepticism of a scientist and the optimism of a believer. She wasn't certain what would happen when the world spun into the new millennium, but she *did* know that panic wouldn't solve a thing.

Like the rest of the world, Reatha watched as midnight arrived in the first major cities west of the international date line: Auckland, New Zealand; Sydney, Australia; Tokyo, Japan. Electricity kept humming; computers did not crash. The only chaos to erupt in those cities was celebratory shouting, popping champagne corks, and relieved applause. Overhead, fireworks burst through the skies in a riot of colors, illuminating the Auckland Ferry Terminal, raining down around the Sydney Opera House, and reflecting off Tokyo's glass skyscrapers. The world entered the new millennium with a bang; Reatha celebrated with it for a moment before stepping into the new year and returning to her work.

By this time, she had worked at General Mills for eleven years, and she was beginning to wonder whether the time was right for her to retire. She would stay active—she had her volunteerism, corporate board service, guest lectures, and more—but she would no longer hold a regular work schedule or carry the heavy responsibilities of her vice presidency.

But for Reatha, *retirement* would never be synonymous with *rest*. She had too many goals and too many perceived responsibilities for that. Young people still needed a mentor; society still teemed with injustices. The world still needed the vision, leadership, and bridge-building qualities of Dr. Reatha Clark King.

★ ★ ★

Seven months before Reatha celebrated her sixty-fourth birthday, all American eyes turned eastward as New York City and Washington, DC, fell under attack on September 11, 2001. The terrorist attacks shook the nation in a deep, resounding way—the effects stretched from coast to coast and reverberated across the world. Airports ramped up security. A newfound suspicion of Muslims swept the United States, occasionally resulting in violence against people or places of worship. Countries across the world hesitated to send their star athletes to the Winter Olympic Games in Salt Lake City, Utah, in February 2002, for fear of a similar terrorist attack. In response, the Salt Lake City organizing committee considered hosting the games without fans in the stadiums, only allowing viewers to watch the events through their televisions (the idea was eventually nixed, and the Olympics marched on as planned).

In his State of the Union address, President George W. Bush declared that the United States would actively resist "regimes" such as those of North Korea, Iran, and Iraq. He famously labeled these nations and their allies an "axis of evil" and declared that they sought weapons of mass destruction and posed a "grave and growing danger."[234] A year later, the Iraq War would begin, with President Bush initiating an attack

---

234. "Text of President Bush's 2002 State of the Union Address."

on Baghdad. During the nearly nine-year-long war, no weapons of mass destruction were found.

Much of Reatha's focus was wrapped up in the aftermath of the terrorist attacks—her work at the General Mills Foundation, the initiatives by her corporate and philanthropic boards, and her volunteerism were all driven by that event. She and the foundation promptly authorized a $100,000 donation to the American Red Cross to support rescue efforts and heal those affected by the destruction.

In the Twin Cities, Minnesota state officials, including Governor Jesse Ventura, began organizing a memorial service at the state capitol. When they began discussing who should emcee the event, one name rose to the top: Reatha Clark King.

Three years earlier, Reatha had served on the newly elected governor's advisory team, so it made sense for him to call upon her again. Governor Ventura had trusted her (along with eight other advisors) to help him fill state government positions and prepare a budget to present to the state legislature. She had provided logic-driven intelligence, financial aplomb, and a calm voice in a sometimes clamorous room.

When a member of Governor Ventura's cabinet called Reatha and invited her to host the memorial service, she did not hesitate for a moment. "Yes," she said. "I would be honored."

Less than a week later, Reatha donned a navy-blue skirt suit with elegant white piping and strode to the podium in front of a crowd of thirty-five thousand people. Behind her, a group of veterans stood at attention while a marching band blasted patriotic songs. The crowd stood elbow to elbow, lining the capitol lawn and spilling onto the sidewalks. Children from across the state had journeyed to the site in yellow buses, and they stood among the throng with hopeful little faces turned to Reatha. Despite differences in beliefs, politics, and demographics, everyone in the crowd gathered in solidarity to pay their respects to those who had died and unite under a banner of hope and healing. Reatha addressed them: "We've heard many stories this week about the victims, these heroes on the planes, and about their calls to their family members when they knew they were going to die. One of the common themes in these conversations was a message of 'I love you.' Today was our opportunity to say to the victims, 'We love you.'"[235]

---

235. Donovan, "Community Leader's Voice."

Reatha's calming presence helped soothe the raw emotions and frayed nerves of those gathered in front of the Minnesota State Capitol. Once again, she had been called upon to lead. And once again, she rose to the occasion.

★ ★ ★

Though it was difficult to think beyond the repercussions of September 11th, the American people, Reatha included, did their best to move on with business as usual. Sporting events continued, movies were made, songs recorded. In January of 2002, Janet Jackson and Lenny Kravitz won top honors at the twenty-ninth American Music Awards, while Michael Jackson was declared Artist of the Century. Two months later, Alicia Keys took home her first Grammy Awards—five of them. A month after that, Halle Berry made history by becoming the first black woman to win an Academy Award for Best Actress. The terrorist attacks were not about to slow down the artists of America, and they certainly would not prevent artists of color from making strides and creating art, despite the fog of fear and uncertainty that seemed to be choking the nation. They were, after all, accustomed to fear and uncertainty. For many artists of color, this was simply life as usual.

Reatha decided to step down as director of the General Mills Foundation in May of 2002. Though she was still brimming with energy and the desire to create change, she knew that GM encouraged its executives to retire at age sixty-five. With her sixty-fifth birthday less than a year away, she determined that now was the time to quietly retire.

May 2002 was mild and sunny in Minnesota. Reatha spent the bulk of her final month tying up loose ends and training her replacement, Chris Shea. Shea was a General Mills insider who had started her career with the company as a marketing assistant in 1977.

During Reatha's last fiscal year at General Mills, the foundation awarded $18.7 million to nonprofits across the country—a significant increase from the time when she had begun her role fourteen years earlier. What's more, it had redefined itself by stretching into underserved communities and amplifying its support for communities of color and minority-operated nonprofits. Reatha was leaving as an accomplished, highly praised changemaker with her head held high and her bridges intact.

On June 1, 2002, she officially retired. Donning an elegant white skirt-and-bejeweled-jacket set, she attended her retirement dinner at the Minneapolis Club with Judge by her side. With a crowd of colleagues and companions, General Mills said farewell with the usual pomp and circumstance afforded to a high-level executive. It presented Reatha with a framed "resolution," which lauds her work with at-risk members of the community, recognizes her national philanthropic leadership, praises her mentorship, and expresses appreciation for "her leadership, her wisdom, her unfailing grace, and her friendship."[236] Several important figures, including CEO Stephen Sanger and VP of corporate relations Austin Sullivan, addressed the crowd, touting her achievements and wishing her well. The people at General Mills knew they were losing a gem. Very few people on this earth possess the kind of intelligence, poise, foresight, curiosity, and kindness of Reatha Clark King. The company had benefited from her fourteen years of leadership, and her community activism and outreach had set a clear precedent for the foundation.

After the first of June, Reatha scarcely paused to enjoy her retirement. She still had work to do.

She continued to sit on the boards of five corporations and many more nonprofit organizations.

She kept her post as chairwoman of the General Mills Foundation's board of directors for another year.

She spoke at countless business breakfasts, philanthropy events, and community activism forums.

She joined the board of directors for the local chapter of the National Association of Corporate Directors and participated in the steering committee for Minnesota's Eliminating Health Disparities Initiative.

She agreed to join a search panel to find a new University of Minnesota president.

Reatha's first year of retirement would set the stage for subsequent years. She is not the type to sit on a beach all day or cruise across the country in an RV. She doesn't look down on those who do choose this

---

236. "Resolution."

retirement lifestyle, but it's simply not for her. She is happiest when she's busy—when she's learning something new or creating positive change.

Lifelong learning and changemaking are so tied to the core of Reatha Clark King that she would be rudderless without them.

★ ★ ★

After two years of retirement, during which she accumulated several more prestigious awards, Reatha jumped headlong into her next big project. She began writing a sponsored research paper on philanthropy and public policy.

In 2004, she was honored with the Louis W. Hill Jr. Fellowship in Philanthropy, sponsored by the Grotto Foundation and the Northwest Area Foundation. These two organizations were co-established by the eponymous Louis W. Hill Jr., grandson of the famous railroad tycoon and philanthropist James J. Hill. The enterprising James J. Hill's name is stamped across the United States—Hillsboro, North Dakota; Hill County, Montana; and Hillyard, Washington (now part of Spokane), were all named after him—but the true family legacy is tied to philanthropy, not town naming. For generations, the Hills have sponsored various artistic, political, social, and environmental initiatives. James J. Hill was a noted conservationist and served on a federal lands commission for former president Theodore Roosevelt. His grandson established numerous foundations and was an ardent supporter of Native American communities; arts and culture; health and wellness (including the Minnesota Society for the Prevention of Blindness and Preservation of Hearing, the Minnesota division of the American Cancer Society, and more); and several community improvement initiatives. He also served in the Minnesota House of Representatives from 1937 to 1951.

As a Louis W. Hill Jr. Fellow, Reatha would further the family's focus on charitable giving by spending a year researching and writing a paper on philanthropy at the Hubert H. Humphrey Institute of Public Affairs. The Humphrey Institute (now the Hubert H. Humphrey School of Public Affairs), which promotes altruistic leadership and strives to "connect its work with communities beyond University borders,"[237] would also benefit from her work. Accompanied by a couple of student

---

237. King, *Philanthropy and Public Policy*.

research assistants and two members of the Humphrey Institute's staff—faculty advisor Dr. Melissa Middleton Stone and program advisor Dr. Marsha A. Freeman—Reatha decided to focus her work on the intersection of philanthropic institutions and public policy, two areas with which she was intimately familiar.

Working on the paper, Reatha was in her element. Ever the dedicated scholar, she immersed herself into her work and began interviewing and researching—gathering information with the gusto of a true lifelong learner. Leaning on the connections she had established during her years at Metro State and General Mills, she interviewed philanthropically inclined individuals hailing from all industries and backgrounds: politicians, activists, foundation heads, corporate executives, the mayors of both Minneapolis and Saint Paul. All told, Reatha conducted an impressive fifty interviews over the course of eight months.

But Reatha knew that executives and politicians didn't have all the answers. In addition to interviewing these local figures, she also put together a twice-monthly think tank comprising faculty, students, and staff at the Humphrey Institute. This group would read about charitable giving, learn about philanthropists from history, and discuss modern-day topics related to philanthropy and nonprofit work. Reatha delighted in these meetings and especially enjoyed talking with the students. "Young people can teach us so much," she says. "We just have to be willing to listen."

Toward the end of Reatha's fellowship, she compiled her findings in a paper entitled *Philanthropy and Public Policy: Working Together to Make a Bigger Difference*. It explores the strengths of the philanthropic and public sectors, effective philanthropic partnerships, and the public issues that might benefit from intentional philanthropic-public collaborations. Among the paper's recommendations (which range from examining case studies to dismantling the status quo so new issues and circumstances can be addressed) is a piece of advice that stems directly from Reatha's experience: involve *the people*. Citizens matter. Their voices count. Without the involvement of the people whom charitable organizations are striving to support, it is difficult to effectively allocate dollars or start initiatives that will actually produce results. Bring the public sector to the table, Reatha advises. They have the power to turn good intentions into long-lasting results.

Reatha's fellowship concluded with the publication of her paper and a symposium at the University of Minnesota. She considers this research opportunity an important supplement to her philanthropic career. In 2004, very little scholarly research had been conducted on philanthropy compared to other fields (something still true today). "As a profession," Reatha says, "we have not developed the more traditional methods of research, as in chemistry." The Hill fellowship helped Reatha contribute to philanthropic scholarship and leave yet another mark in the field of philanthropy.

★ ★ ★

Reatha marched through the first decade of the new millennium with a full calendar and an optimistic spirit. Though technically retired, she kept active by serving on corporate boards, engaging with her local community and church, and picking up a handful of new awards (NACD's Director of the Year Award, the National Center for Black Philanthropy's Lifetime Achievement in Philanthropy Award, the *Twin Cities Business* Lifetime Achievement Award . . .). She continued her work as a philanthropist, a community leader, a mentor. She traveled to Hong Kong, Costa Rica, Scotland, Cambodia, Spain, and more on business trips.

In 2006, she was invited to join the Minnesota Sesquicentennial Commission—a diverse group of prominent Minnesotans tasked with organizing events and commemorations to celebrate the state's 150th anniversary, which would take place in 2008. Comprising a mix of Democrats and Republicans, politicians and businesspeople, community leaders and activists, it was "fractious at times, with a lot of competing ideas and egos," recalls Tane Danger, the commission's communications manager and fundraising coordinator. However, he says, "Everyone respected Reatha. We listened when she spoke. We were all inspired by her passion. Her thoughtfulness and calm got us through some raucous debates."[238]

One of Reatha's contributions as part of the Sesquicentennial Commission was to commission a special postage stamp to honor the state's birthday. Once the idea of designing a state stamp was introduced,

---

238. Tane Danger, interview.

FIND A TRAIL OR BLAZE ONE

Reatha took it upon herself to make it happen. Tane relays her no-fuss, proactive approach: "In classic Reatha fashion, she went to the downtown Minneapolis post office herself, waited in line with everybody else, and, when she got to the counter, asked the USPS worker behind the desk if they knew how a state could get an official postage stamp." After a series of discussions and paperwork, the commission was given the go-ahead to submit its design. The commemorative stamp, which depicts a winding Mississippi River at sunset, was "unveiled to great fanfare at the Minnesota State Capitol with dignitaries ranging from Vice President Walter Mondale to Representative Betty McCollum in attendance. And it all started with Reatha standing in line at the post office."[239]

A year after being asked to join the Sesquicentennial Commission, Reatha was granted another major honor. In 2007, the Women's Foundation of Minnesota established the Dr. Reatha Clark King Fellowship with the goal of training and supporting women of color in philanthropy and nonprofit leadership. Today, the George Family Foundation, founded by former Medtronic CEO Bill George and his wife, Penny, is a major supporter of the fellowship. Bill praises Reatha as an authentic leader who "reaches out and helps others as she quietly walks past barriers of racial and gender discrimination."[240]

When she wasn't traveling the world or accepting awards or initiating the design of a new postage stamp, Reatha's life revolved around her family. She loves being a grandmother. One of her greatest joys in life is talking with her grandkids one on one and learning about their hobbies, their joys, their fears, their ambitions. That attention resonated with her grandkids. "My grandma is one of the most caring individuals you will ever meet," N.J. says.[241] Kayla agrees: "Amazing as she may be, she has always been my grandma—the woman who always met us at the airport with balloons, never missed a birthday phone call, and showed myself and my siblings nothing but unconditional love."[242]

MacKensey echoes that sentiment. "My grandma Reatha is a remarkable woman, but she was always just 'grandma' to me," she says.

---

239. Danger, interview.
240. George, "Reatha Clark King."
241. N. Judge King IV, email to author, October 9, 2020.
242. Kayla King, email to author, October 15, 2020.

"She was the woman who took my sister and me to the hair salon every time we visited. She's the one in the family who always insisted on going to church. She is incredibly accomplished, but she is also loving, caring, and a great grandma."[243]

As MacKensey, Kayla, and N.J. grew and began reaching milestones—starting elementary school, learning to play the piano, beginning high school—Reatha would visit them in Tucson and cheer them on at recitals, choir concerts, and award ceremonies. They were active kids, just like Reatha's sons, and they played sports (dance for Kayla, basketball and cross-country running for NJ, and volleyball for all three) in addition to participating in student government and the Assistance League of Tucson, a volunteer and philanthropic organization.

Reatha's grandkids hearten her. Each one proved to be sharp as a tack and possess the same determination as their grandmother. But Reatha is quick to credit their intelligence to her father, Willie B. Clark. "They've inherited their great-grandfather's keen mind," she says. "My father was a brilliant man, despite his illiteracy, and I can see his ingenuity and smarts in my grandkids."

The King children have honored Willie's legacy by seeking the education their great-grandfather never had the opportunity to pursue. In 2019, MacKensey graduated from Princeton University with a BA in economics before traveling to Mongolia for a banking internship. Kayla continued her education at Syracuse University in New York, earning her BFA in musical theater. And in 2020, N.J. followed his sisters to the East Coast and started his first year at Boston University, with plans to major in business or finance.

All three grandchildren have been influenced by Reatha's shining example and, as N.J. says, her "unmatched work ethic."[244] Kayla says, "My grandmother was a huge inspiration to me in my pursuit of my education and life/career goals and dreams. Faced with adversity and discrimination, she accomplished beyond what was readily available to her. Much of my own drive and work ethic has come from my desire to uphold her legacy."[245]

---

243. MacKensey King, email to author, October 7, 2020.
244. N. Judge King IV, email.
245. Kayla King, email.

Reatha is proud beyond words of her grandchildren. In them, she sees the fruits of long-fought civil rights battles. In them, she sees hope for a brighter, more equitable future.

★ ★ ★

Though the 2010s were tumultuous years, they began on a distinct high. Barack Obama, America's first black president, was in the middle of his first term in office. Obama's two-term presidency broke barriers and crumbled walls. No longer was the presidency out of reach for people of color. No longer was the nation's most important office controlled by white men. As president, Barack Obama appointed the most diverse cabinet to date in terms of race and gender. Both of his Supreme Court appointees were women, with Justice Sonia Sotomayor becoming the first Hispanic and Latinx person to serve on the Supreme Court.

Electing a black man to the highest office in the nation did not, however, eliminate racism or hate crimes. Systemic bias still ran through America's veins.

Armed with cell phones and surveillance cameras, people began capturing footage of violence against black people, particularly at the hands of police officers. The discrimination that had always existed was now in the spotlight, staring people in the face through YouTube or Facebook or Twitter. Despite video evidence of wrongdoings, police officers were continually acquitted for their crimes (the officers who killed Eric Garner in 2014, Michael Brown in 2014, Freddie Gray in 2015, Philando Castile in 2017, and on and on). After unarmed teenager Trayvon Martin was murdered in 2013, the Black Lives Matter movement sprouted, with a mission to "eradicate white supremacy and build local power to intervene in violence inflicted on Black communities."[246]

Reatha responded to the string of injustices by continuing to advocate for people of color, equality, and equal opportunities. Whether sitting on a corporate board or speaking about philanthropy, she kept these issues top of mind. Though she was still energetic and passionate about creating positive change, she *was* inching toward her eightieth birthday. Perhaps it was time to slow down.

Just a little.

---
246. Black Lives Matter, "About."

Years earlier, in 1992, Reatha and Judge had *attempted* to slow down when they made the decision to move from their beloved home on Arcade Street and settle into a condominium across the river from downtown Minneapolis. They would be close to the thrum of city life and a stone's throw from a grocery store, a historic movie theater, and several quaint restaurants lining the brick walkways of the Saint Anthony Main district. The building hovered over the Mississippi, and the pair could easily stroll down to the riverside park or cross the iconic Stone Arch pedestrian bridge to reach downtown.

They no longer had to mow a two-acre lawn. They didn't have to shovel snow or maintain their furnace or worry about the plumbing. But despite easing their household responsibilities, the couple still managed to fill their days with work and volunteerism, charity events and award ceremonies. They settled into their new church—Fellowship Missionary Baptist Church in North Minneapolis—and became active congregants. "I think I've served on just about every committee," Reatha laughs. "I'd like to think it's because people trust me."

The second decade of the new millennium—despite the many joyful moments Reatha experienced through her church, her volunteerism, her family—would prove to be one of the most difficult decades of Reatha's life. One year into the 2010s, her younger sister, Dot, passed away.

Dorothy "Dot" Clark Green was seventy years old when she slipped from this world to the next. She had been experiencing some chronic health issues, but her passing shocked Reatha nonetheless. No one should have to say goodbye to a younger sibling. It defies the natural order of things.

Reatha remembers Dot as a creative soul. She was a talented artist and jewelry maker, and she had a way with words. Around the time Reatha was named Director of the Year by the National Association of Corporate Directors, Dot put together a tribute to her sister in the form of a poem. She wrote, "When God saw you coming as a 'Speck' out in eternity, He must have thought 'Seed of Greatness' . . . and I praise God for allowing me to watch his workmanship in you as He raised you from the humblest of beginnings to these great heights and blessings."[247]

The words latched themselves to Reatha's heart and held on tight. She framed her sister's tribute and still looks at it from time to time

---

247. Green, "Tribute Flowing."

when she wants to hear Dot's words flowing through her, to feel her sister's love from the place beyond.

On March 12, 2011, Reatha flew to Silver Spring, Maryland, to sit by her fading sister's bedside as she took her final breaths. Reatha says, "God's timing was impeccable." Within ten minutes of Reatha's arrival, Dot was gone. "She couldn't speak at the end," Reatha says, "but I could feel her love."

One week later, Dot was laid to rest. At her funeral, she was surrounded by flowers, photographs and memorabilia, and the people who loved her—reminders of the brilliance and cheer she had fostered throughout her life. After the service, Reatha approached Dot's daughter, her niece, and said, "Cyndy, I'm so sorry about your mom."

Cyndy replied, "She lived all the years she was promised."

That sentence stuck with Reatha. It reminded her that every day is a gift, and we should all use our valuable time on earth as best we can. We are only granted so many days, and we might as well wake up each morning with the intention of making the most of each precious hour.

A few years after her younger sister passed, the foundations of Reatha's life shook once more. Her beloved husband and companion, Judge King, was diagnosed with lung cancer.

The diagnosis came as a shock to the family. After experiencing persistent pain and shortness of breath, Judge was checked in to a Hennepin County hospital in Minneapolis. There, a doctor discovered cancer clotting Judge's lungs and informed him that it was too far along to cure. The cancer would eventually claim his life.

Reatha heard the news filtered through Jay. She remembers the flood of sorrow that washed through her, mingled with disbelief. How could this be? Her Judge. Her longtime companion and beloved friend. She hugged Jay and let her emotions flow out through her tears.

After a brave and unrelenting fight with his illness, Judge succumbed to the disease on May 26, 2014, less than two weeks after his seventy-eighth birthday. Before he passed, one of the nurses at Judge's care center called Reatha and told her he was having trouble breathing. She didn't expect him to last through the night. Without hesitation, Reatha packed a few things and spent the night on a floormat, curled next to her husband's side. By the time morning dawned, Judge had passed.

Though his body had betrayed him, Judge never lost his sense of humor or his smile. He remained a kind, bright soul until the very end.

Reatha and her family mourned the loss of their patriarch. He was Reatha's greatest friend and fiercest advocate. His belief in her was unwavering—so strong, he did not hesitate to move a thousand miles inland when she was appointed president of Metropolitan State University. Reatha said, "Judge would say that it is okay for a man to be a 'trailing' spouse, which was his stance when the family [moved] to Minnesota."[248]

Judge was a role model in the Twin Cities and beyond for many people, particularly black men. His belief in education, community volunteerism, and civic engagement and his altruistic spirit touched innumerable lives. He was involved in the Saint Paul Urban League, volunteered as an Amicus Big Brother (helping those who were formerly incarcerated transition to a life outside bars), sang in several church choirs, served on the Minnesota Board of Teaching, and was a member of Everybody Wins!, an offshoot of a national literacy and mentoring nonprofit organization.[249] Through his aviation company, the American Air Center, he introduced hundreds of young people to the exciting possibility of becoming an aviator, no matter their gender or the hue of their skin. Reatha said of Judge's generous spirit, "He has long been involved in civil rights, educational issues, child advocacy work, and providing philanthropic support for community needs, particularly youth development."[250]

Judge's passing was difficult for the entire family. The beloved father, husband, and friend exited their life like a shooting star, leaving a sparkling trail of memories in his wake. They would miss his broad smile, his easygoing attitude, his keen wit. They would miss the way his eyes lit up when he discussed aviation and his distinct laugh, which bubbled at the slightest provocation.

Reatha's eldest son, Jay, talks about his father's passing as a time when he truly realized the strength of his parents' bond. Theirs was a union built on a solid foundation of mutual love and respect. She revered him and he, in turn, honored and admired her.

---

248. Hobbes, "N. Judge King."
249. Hobbes, "N. Judge King."
250. Hobbes, "N. Judge King."

FIND A TRAIL OR BLAZE ONE

His country girl.

Her city boy.

Napoleon Judge King II was a man so well loved and cherished the family arranged for him to have two funerals—one in Minneapolis and one in his hometown of Birmingham, Alabama. At Fellowship Missionary Baptist Church in Minneapolis, friends and family members, fellow aviators and churchgoers, former coworkers and like-minded philanthropists crowded together, shoulder to shoulder. Congregants from Pilgrim Baptist Church—including the pastor, who would lead the service—joined their brethren on the other side of the river. On the altar at the front of the church, Judge's casket rested in a field of bright bouquets and cards. Together, the mourners raised their voices in prayer and song to celebrate the life of their cherished friend and community role model.

After the Minneapolis service, Reatha and Scott escorted Judge's body to Birmingham. Though heartbroken and still reeling from her loss, Reatha steadied her nerves and put on a brave face. When the plane touched down, she thought of Judge and his tendency to critique other pilots on their landings. "This one would have been a thumb's-up," she said later, in her speech to the Birmingham mourners. "Judge would have approved."

Surrounded by family, friends, and former classmates, Judge was honored with one final service at the First Congregational Christian Church, his family's longtime place of worship, before being put to rest in Elmwood Cemetery. Occasionally, Reatha flies down to Birmingham to visit Judge's resting place in the cemetery's well-manicured expanse. There, she prays, reflects, remembers. Judge is never far from her heart, but when she's kneeling at his grave, his presence envelops her and she feels the acute sting of loss.

One day, Reatha knows, she will see her city boy again. She will rest alongside him in their grass-covered plot. But not yet. She still has work to do and miles to go.

A LIVING LEGACY

Today

The next several years caught Reatha in their current and swept her into the second decade of the twenty-first century. Along the way, she picked up several more awards; spoke at numerous events connected to philanthropy, equality, leadership, and education; and celebrated the fiftieth anniversary of the Apollo moon landing with scads of interviews and a VIP invitation to the Adler Planetarium's commemorative party in Chicago.

In 2011, Reatha was honored with the Defender of Democracy award from the Martin Luther King Jr. National Memorial Project Foundation. Months later, a national memorial to Dr. King was completed in Washington, DC, overlooking a quiet crescent-moon-shaped bay of the Potomac River's Tidal Basin. Among the inscriptions, walkways, and rows of cherry trees at the Martin Luther King Jr. Memorial, an immense granite statue of Dr. King stands in bold defiance, with arms crossed and legs encased in rock, reminiscent of a giant emerging from a mountainside. The rough-cut stone backdrop is a reminder of an iconic line from Dr. King's "I Have a Dream" speech: "With this faith, we will be able to hew out of the mountain of despair a stone of hope."[251]

The memorial was dedicated on August 28, 2011, precisely forty-eight years after Dr. King's March on Washington for Jobs and Freedom. On that same day, Reatha—twenty-five and brimming with hope and inspiration—had left her laboratory at the National Bureau of Standards and attempted to make her way to the crowded Washington Mall. Earlier that year, Reatha had made history by becoming the first black female research chemist at the NBS.

Reatha's Defender of Democracy award meant a great deal to her. Though she would continue to receive major awards, this one was special. This one touched her very core. She would continue to immerse herself in the perpetual struggle for equality, including contributing to the annual State of Minnesota Martin Luther King Day celebration. At the 2019 celebration, which focused on women of color in STEM fields, Reatha was presented with the Governor's Civil Rights Legend Award. She shared the spotlight with keynote speaker Dr. Mae Jemison, the United States' first black female astronaut, and Katherine Coleman Johnson, who received an award for her contributions to NASA as a

---

251. National Park Service, "Building the Memorial."

research mathematician. Johnson's role at NASA is immortalized in the book turned popular movie *Hidden Figures*.

One year later, Reatha received another honor tied to Dr. King. At the thirtieth annual Dr. Martin Luther King Jr. Holiday Breakfast in Minneapolis, she was granted the Local Lifetime Legend award amid the cheers and enthusiastic applause of 2,400 attendees. Reatha looked around at the packed-to-the-brim audience and felt a twinge of pride. Not only had she received a prestigious award, she had helped *build* this very event. The annual MLK Holiday Breakfast had been a General Mills Foundation initiative thirty years prior, created as a way to inform corporate workers about diversity issues and celebrate the enduring legacy of Dr. King. Today, corporations reserve tables at the annual breakfast one year in advance, and the event is always well attended by important local figures. General Mills continues to host the celebration, and Reatha was chosen to chair the 2020 planning committee.

The 2020 MLK holiday breakfast crackled with energy and optimism. In between musical performances and poetry, speakers took the stage to celebrate diversity and address ongoing race issues. The event's keynote speaker was former US attorney general Eric Holder, who declared, "We must not look back toward a past that was comforting to too few and unjust to too many—that is not how you make America great."[252]

It may be a coincidence that Dr. Reatha Clark King shares her surname with the nation's most iconic civil rights activist and one of the greatest changemakers of all time, but her achievements have been anything but coincidental. Everything she has in this world—the degrees, the awards, the recognition for her myriad contributions—she earned through hard work and diligence. Reatha was not handed a silver spoon in her childhood. She was given a pair of overalls and told to get to work. She was not carried into college by her parents' connections or their dollars; she was carried there by the support and encouragement of her family and community, in addition to endless hours of hard work and study.

Reatha Clark King has not scaled *just* one mountain in her life; she's scaled many.

---

252. Rao and Bierschbach, "Thousands of Minnesotans Gather."

As a youth, she stared down the steep cliffs of illiteracy and poverty. With the twin weights of racial and gender discrimination tethered to her ankles, she lifted her feet anyway and walked boldly forward.

She defied the odds and became not just a scientist but a doctorate-wielding research chemist. She marched through the laboratory doors of the National Bureau of Standards, knowing none of her colleagues would look like her. Not yet. But maybe her shining example would change minds and open doors.

In New York City, Reatha began to ascend the mountain of academia, maintaining her scientist-minded inquisitiveness and a propensity for logic. In a sea of mostly white, mostly male colleagues, she managed to keep climbing and earned the spot as dean of academic affairs at York College. As the first black female dean employed by New York City, her path up the mountain helped clear the way for other women of color who would climb after her.

At Metropolitan State University, Reatha carved yet another path upward as she stepped into her presidency. This time, the nation was watching. But Reatha didn't pause, didn't collapse under scrutinizing eyes. She used her journey as a platform to enact widespread change in academia. She encouraged other colleges and universities to rethink their programs and open their doors a tad wider to nontraditional students. In the meantime, she joined dozens of committees, boards, and nonprofit organizations, aiming to bring about positive change. "Lift as you climb," Grandma Mamie had said. So, Reatha lifted. She spent any extra energy and strength on amplifying diversity, improving her community, enacting political change, and spreading messages of empowerment and hope.

She carried that spirit of service into her leadership at the General Mills Foundation. Unwilling to tread the same set of well-worn philanthropic trails laid out by her predecessors, Reatha blazed new ground in areas of education, equality, and the arts. She went into communities and listened, knowing that sustainable change needs to happen from the ground up. She reached out to minority-run nonprofits and said, "What do you need? How can I help?"

As Reatha climbed, she accumulated hundreds of awards, honors, and interviews, but she did not let their glitter distract her or slow her pace. Reatha appreciated the recognition (and the honors she received *did* mean something to her), but ultimately, her work took precedence over awards. And there was always more work to be done.

But in between the activism, the board meetings, the initiatives to enact change, Reatha wanted little more than the company of her family and the comfort of her church. She turned to these two pillars in the interstices of her demanding work. She leaned on them, as she had since her youth, for affirmation and strength.

The Chemist, Dean, President, Director, Philanthropist was more at ease when she was called Mom, Sister, Wife, Daughter, Friend.

Though she's fearlessly cut new trails and transformed countless lives, Reatha is still, at her core, the young woman from South Georgia. She's still the churchgoing, family-centered daughter of two hard-working parents whose opportunities were stifled by illiteracy. She's still the four-year-old in Mount Zion's makeshift schoolhouse, sitting with bright-eyed, rapt attention as Ms. Frazier scrawls the alphabet on a chalk tablet. She's still the young woman on the Trailways bus, defying expectations by pursuing an advanced education two hundred miles away from the cotton fields of Pavo.

These experiences are part of the sinew and marrow of Dr. Reatha Clark King. And she has used them to propel her journey over mountains and through uncharted territory. Because of her willingness to break down barriers and carve new paths, others may navigate life with a little more ease.

They may, perhaps, pick up where Reatha left off and cut the trail a few feet farther.

ACKNOWLEDGMENTS

It is impossible to thank every individual who contributed to this book or aided in my life's journey. You number as the stars, and I am grateful for your luminosity and steadfastness. I will, however, attempt to name a few.

Thank you to those who raised me and molded me into the person I became, especially my late mother, Ola Mae (Watts) Campbell; my late father, Willie B. Clark; and the numerous aunties and uncles who brought such raucous joy and stalwart support to my early years.

Abundant thanks to my two sisters: my older sister, Dr. Mamie C. Montague, who sacrificed so much for the Clark family, and my late younger sister, Dorothy "Dot" Clark Green, who could light up the room with her smile and humor.

Thanks are due to my early educators (prominent among them the incredible Ms. Frazier) and my college professors, advisors, and mentors at Clark College and the University of Chicago. Professor Booker T. Simpson and Dr. Alfred Spriggs dared to see the potential of a shy chemistry student from rural Georgia and placed their trust in her absolutely. Dr. Ole J. Kleppa and Myrtle Bachelder provided daily inspiration and guidance.

I am grateful to the Harvey Dann family for becoming my first bridge into an utterly foreign and bewildering world. I will never forget how they introduced me to some of the great luminaries of the time, including radio legend Edward R. Murrow and several prominent ministers from New York. The Dann family also made my undergraduate education possible by employing me each summer and paying me a generous wage. I was even able to set some of that money aside for my mother, which was a blessing I shall never forget.

Thank you to the skilled scientists at the National Bureau of Standards, including my supervisor, Dr. George Armstrong, for their absolute faith in me and for entrusting me with highly sensitive (often explosive!) work.

My sincerest thanks to the professors and staff at York College and the CUNY system, including Dr. Lewis J. Bodi. Together, we sowed the seeds of a truly special institution.

Of course, my deepest gratitude goes out to Metropolitan State University. From the very start of my relationship with this extraordinary and singular school, I felt welcomed and appreciated. There are too many of you to thank individually, but please know you made an enormous difference in my life while I navigated the often tricky terrain of the presidency. You are among the most inventive and big-hearted people I have ever met.

Thank you to my incredible and talented students at both York College and Metro State. You always were diamonds; we only provided a bit of polish.

I must also, of course, thank the innumerable legislators, governors, mayors, and other political figures in both Minnesota and the greater United States who helped Metro State with meaningful legislation and initiatives. Your steadfast faith in our school was clear, and I thank you for that.

Thank you to my team at General Mills, especially President Bruce Atwater (who rooted for me from the start), Jim Shannon (who helped pave my way), and David Nasby (who was a kind and capable counterpart).

I am grateful to the many talented and ambitious individuals who served alongside me on various corporate boards. I knew I was more than a seat at your tables; I was a meaningful contributor with a voice that counted.

So many thoughtful and creative individuals assisted in the creation of this book. Thank you to the current president of Metropolitan State University, Virginia "Ginny" Arthur, for her enthusiasm and support of my biography project. Thank you to Rita Dibble, who guided this project with capable, loving hands, and to the team at Metropolitan State University, for their diligent work on this project. Thanks are also due, of course, to Kate Leibfried, who spent hundreds of hours diligently interviewing me, researching, and writing the pages of this book. I am both pleased and amazed that my life's story could fill so many pages!

ACKNOWLEDGMENTS

Many thanks to Madeleine Vasaly, who reviewed these pages with the keen eye of a seasoned editor.

Lastly, I want to thank my family, who are the absolute center of my world. My late husband, N. Judge King, was my best friend, my constant cheerleader, and the love of my life. He always knew how to make his "country girl" smile. My sons, Napoleon Judge "Jay" King III and Scott King, are kind, accomplished men who never forget their mother. They are a daily blessing. My grandchildren, MacKensey, Kayla, and N.J., are incredible individuals, bursting with potential. I am certain that nothing is out of their reach; they only have to follow the family tradition of working hard, moving forward with intention and focus, and picking themselves up whenever the world knocks them down.

APPENDIX

Table One: Honorary Doctorate Degrees

Year	School	Location
1982	Carleton College	Northfield, MN
1985	SUNY Empire State College	Various locations, NY
1988	Alverno College	Milwaukee, WI
1988	Rhode Island College	Providence, RI
1988	Seattle University	Seattle, WA
1989	Clark Atlanta University	Atlanta, GA
1989	Marymount Manhattan College	New York, NY
1990	William Mitchell College of Law	Saint Paul, MN
1993	Monmouth University	West Long Branch, NJ
1993	Nazareth College	Rochester, NY
1993	Smith College	Northampton, MA
1995	South Carolina State University	Orangeburg, SC
1998	Metropolitan State University	Minneapolis-St. Paul, MN
2001	Bennett College	Greensboro, NC

Table Two: Awards and Recognition

Year	Award
1958-60	Woodrow Wilson Fellowship
1960-61	National Medical Fellowship
1968	Meritorious Publication Award, National Bureau of Standards
1976	Builder of Brotherhood Award, National Conference of Christians and Jews, Queens-Long Island Chapter, NY
1976-77	Rockefeller Foundation Fellowship for Higher Education Administration
1979	Leader Award in Education, Minneapolis YWCA
1979	Merit Award for Consumer Rights and Advocacy in Education, Minneapolis-St. Paul Alumnae Chapter, Delta Sigma Theta Sorority
1983	Distinguished Alumnus Award, Clark College, Atlanta, GA
1983	Paul Harris Fellow recognition, Saint Paul Rotary Club
1984	Communication and Leadership Award, Toastmasters International, , Twin Cities
1984	Exceptional Black Scientist Award, Ciba-Geigy Corporation
1984	Leader Award in Education, St. Paul YWCA
1985	Minds in Motion Award, Science Skills Center, Brooklyn, NY
1985	Spurgeon Leadership Award for Community Service, Boy Scouts of America, Indianhead Council
1986	Drum Major for Justice Award, Southern Christian Leadership Conference, Atlanta
1986	Educational Excellence Award, National Association of Black Women in Higher Education, New York City
1987	Reatha Clark King Scholarship Fund, 10th Anniversary Recognition of Presidency, Metropolitan State University
1988	Minnesota Public Administrator of the Year Award
1988	Professional Achievement Award, University of Chicago Alumni Association
1988	Twin Citian of the Year Award, *Mpls.St.Paul*
1993	Sisterhood Award for Distinguished Humanitarian Service, National Conference of Christians and Jews, MN-Dakota Region

APPENDIX

Year	Award
1994	Minneapolis NAACP Community Service Award in Education
1995	Woman of Distinction Award, St. Croix Valley Girl Scouts, Saint Paul, MN
1996	International Adult and Continuing Education Hall of Fame
1996	Directors' Choice Award for Leadership as Outstanding Corporate Director, National Women's Economic Alliance Foundation
1997	Community Builder Award, Boy Scouts of America, Indianhead Council
1999	100 Most Influential Minnesotans of the Century, *Star Tribune*
2000	Civic Leader Award, League of Women Voters
2000	Legacy Award for Community Service, Saint Paul Foundation
2000	Minneapolis 2000 Award for Civic Leadership
2001	2001 Odyssey Award, Big Brothers and Big Sisters, Minneapolis Chapter
2001	National Black College Alumni Hall of Fame
2002	Community Service Award, Phyllis Wheatley Community Center
2002	Community Leadership Award, Hennepin County Office of the County Attorney
2003	Humanitarian Award, Minneapolis Community and Technical College
2003	Special Distinction Award, General Mills Sales Division
2003	The Cookie Cart Learning Center Community Service Award
2003	The Pioneer Award, WomenVenture, Minneapolis
2004	Louis J. Hill Jr. Fellowship in Philanthropy, Hubert H. HumphreyInstitute, University of Minnesota
2004	Director of the Year, National Association of Corporate Directors (NACD)
2005	Inducted into the Junior Achievement Business Hall of Fame
2005	Lifetime Achievement in Philanthropy Award (corecipient), National Center for Black Philanthropy
2009	Meritorious Service Award, Association of Occupational Therapy Board

Year	Award
2010	Winds of Change Award, Multicultural Forum, , Minneapolis
2010	Alvaro L. Martins Heritage Award, Executive Leadership Council (DC)
2010	Outstanding Corporate Director—Lifetime Achievement Award, *Twin Cities Business*
2011	Defender of Democracy Award, Washington, DC, Martin Luther King Jr. National Memorial Project Foundation
2011	NACD Board Leadership Fellow
2011	Award of Distinction, University of Minnesota Board of Regents
2012	Pathways to Excellence Award, Clark Atlanta University Alumni Association
2012	Community Leadership Award, The National Urban Technology Center, New York, NY
2012	Inducted into Minnesota Science and Technology Hall of Fame, Minnesota High Technology Association and the Science Museum of Minnesota
2013	International Citizen Award, Twin Cities International Leadership Institute
2013	Mother of Change Recognition, the Mastery School, Minneapolis, MN
2014	Trailblazer Award, Minneapolis Urban League
2016	Lifetime Achievement Award, TRUTH Preparatory Academy, St. Paul, MN
2019	Governor's Civil Rights Legend Award
2020	Wall of Fame, Minnesota African American Heritage Museum
2020	Local Lifetime Legend Award, Thirtieth Annual MLK Holiday Breakfast, Minneapolis, MN
2020	Mary Lee Dayton Catalyst for Change Award

APPENDIX

Table 3: Former Corporate Board Memberships

Years of Service	Board
3	Allina Health System
13	ExxonMobil Corporation
25	H. B. Fuller Company
8	Lenox Group
20	Minnesota Mutual Companies
28	Wells Fargo & Company

International Activities

- **The Netherlands**, NATO Advanced Study Institute, 1970
- **India**, Education Mission with US College and University Presidents, 1980
- **Mexico**, Corporate Board Work, 1983
- **Brazil**, International Higher Education Conference, 1983
- **India, Bangladesh, Tanzania**, USIA Lecture Tours, 1983
- **USSR**, USIA Lecture Tour, 1984
- **Canada**, International Higher Education Conference, 1983
- **Germany, Austria, France**, Corporate Board Work, 1984
- **The Dominican Republic**, Corporate Board Work, 1985
- **Japan, Israel, Philippines**, USIA Lecture Tours, 1988
- **Japan, Taiwan, Hong Kong, China**, Corporate Board Work, 1991
- **England, the Netherlands, Germany**, Corporate Board Work, 1994
- **Canada**, Corporate Work for General Mills, 1995

- **Malaysia, Singapore**, Corporate Board Work, 1997
- **Spain, Italy, Switzerland, Germany,** Corporate Board Work, 1997
- **Italy,** Corporate Board Work, 1999
- **Singapore, China,** Corporate Board Work, 2001, 2009
- **Costa Rica,** Corporate Board Work, 2002
- **South Korea, Hong Kong, China,** Corporate Board Work, 2003
- **Scotland,** Corporate Board Work, 2003
- **South Africa,** 2003
- **Japan, Vietnam, Thailand, Cambodia,** Corporate Board and Humanitarian Service Work, 2005
- **France, Spain,** Corporate Board Work, 2007
- **Gibraltar,** Corporate Board Work, 2007
- **Morocco,** International Trachoma Initiative Delegation

Past Board Memberships with Philanthropic and Civic Organizations

- American Red Cross
- Association of Occupational Therapy Foundation
- Clark Atlanta University
- Congressional Black Caucus Foundation
- Council on Foundations
- Eisenhower Exchange Fellowships
- Greater Minneapolis Chamber of Commerce

APPENDIX

- Guthrie Theater
- International Trachoma Initiative
- Hispanics in Philanthropy
- Indianhead Boy Scouts Council
- Ministers and Missionaries Benefit Board, American Baptist Churches
- Minneapolis United Way
- Minnesota Council on Foundations, Former Board Chair
- Minnesota Orchestral Association
- Minnesota Medical Foundation, University of Minnesota
- National Conference of Christians and Jews, Minnesota-Dakota Region
- Sabathani Community Center
- Saint Paul Chamber of Commerce
- Saint Paul Foundation
- United Way of the St. Paul Area, Former Board Chair
- Thurgood Marshall Scholarship Fund
- VocalEssence

Past Board and Task Force Memberships in Higher Education

- Advisory Council of Presidents of the Association of Governing Boards, Member
- American Association for Higher Education, Chair of the Board

- American Association of State Colleges and Universities, Task Force on Innovations and Alternatives, Chair
- American Council on Education (ACE), Chair of the Board
- American Council on Education (ACE), Member, Business Higher Education Forum
- Baptist Theological Union, Vice Chair of the Board
- Carleton College, Board Member
- Carleton College, Task Force on South African Issues, Chair
- Carnegie Foundation for the Advancement of Teaching, Board Member
- Contributions Council, the Conference Board, Member
- Educational Testing Service, Vice Chair of the Board of Directors
- Commissioner of the North Central Association Commission on Institutions of Higher Education, Executive Board Member
- William Mitchell College of Law, Board Member
- University of Chicago, Board Member

Past Services with Government Commissions and Task Forces

- Governor's Commission on Women's History (1985–1988)
- Minnesota Martin Luther King, Jr. Holiday Commission (1985–1988)
- Governor's Commission on Education for Economic Growth (1984)

APPENDIX

- Governor's Search Committee for the Chair of the Metropolitan Council (1985)

- Task Force on St. Paul Public Libraries (1982–1983)

- Governor's Judicial Selection Committee (1982)

- Minnesota Legislature Regents Candidate Advisory Council (1988-1994)

- US Commission on National and Community Service (1991–1993)

- Governor's Task Force on Ethics in Government (1993)

- Governor's Task Force on Student Aid (1994)

- Governor's Task Force on the Glass Ceiling (1994)

- US Corporation on National and Community Service (1994–1997)

- Governor Jesse Ventura, Advisory Team (1998–2002)

- Ethnic Disparities in Health Initiative Steering Committee, Minnesota Department of Health (2002–2005)

- City of Minneapolis Empowerment Zone Governing Board (2001–2003)

- Minnesota Sesquicentennial Commission (2006–2009)

BIBLIOGRAPHY

Books

Blumberg, Rhoda Lois. *Civil Rights: The 1960s Freedom Struggle*. Boston: Twayne Publishers, 1984.

Branch, Taylor. *Parting the Waters: America in the King Years, 1954–63*. New York: Simon & Schuster, 1988.

Brown, Jeannette E. *African American Women Chemists*. New York: Oxford University Press, 2012.

Clotfelter, Charles T., and Thomas Ehrlich, eds. *Philanthropy and the Nonprofit Sector in a Changing America*. Bloomington: Indiana University Press, 2001.

Cobb, Charles E., Jr. *On the Road to Freedom: A Guided Tour of the Civil Rights Trail*. Chapel Hill, NC: Algonquin Books, 2008.

Cunningham, Michael, and Craig Marberry. *Crowns: Portraits of Black Women in Church Hats*. New York: Doubleday, 2000.

Daniel, Pete. *Lost Revolutions: The South in the 1950s*. Chapel Hill: University of North Carolina Press for Smithsonian Institution, 2000.

George, Bill. "Reatha Clark King: From Cotton Fields to the Boardroom." In *True North: Discover Your Authentic Leadership*. San Francisco: Jossey-Bass, 2007.

Grimm, Robert T. *Notable American Philanthropists: Biographies of Giving and Volunteering*. Westport, CT: Greenwood Publishing Group, 2002.

Guralnick, Peter. *Sweet Soul Music: Rhythm and Blues and the Southern Dream of Freedom*. New York: Harper & Row Publishers, 1986.

Harvey, William B. *Grass Roots and Glass Ceilings: African American Administrators in Predominantly White Colleges and Universities*. Albany: State University of New York Press, 1999.

Karsen, Jill, ed. *Great Speeches in History: Civil Rights*. Farmington Hills, MI: Greenhaven Press, 2003.

Klassen, Don, Arthur Gordon, and Bill Hartfiel. *Diamonds: Eight Key Qualities that Open the Door to the Splendor of Living*. Prior Lake, MN: Century Communications, 2000.

Levine, Arnold. "NASA Manpower Policy." In *Managing NASA in the Apollo Era*. June 1972. https://history.nasa.gov/SP-4102/ch5.htm.

Lewis, John, Aydin Andrew, and Nate Powell. *March: Book One*. Marietta, GA: Top Shelf Productions, 2013.

Margo, Robert A. *Race and Schooling in the South, 1880–1950: An Economic History*. Chicago: The University of Chicago Press, 1990.

Meltzer, Milton. *There Comes a Time: The Struggle for Civil Rights*. New York: Random House, 2001.

Norman, Moses, and George Johnson, eds. *The Panther: Nineteen Hundred and Fifty-Seven*. Yearbook, Clark College, 1957.

Parmet, Robert D. *Town and Gown: The Fight for Social Justice, Urban Rebirth, and Higher Education*. Madison, NJ: Fairleigh Dickinson University Press, 2011.

Partridge, Elizabeth. *Marching for Freedom: Walk Together, Children, and Don't You Grow Weary*. New York: Penguin Group, 2009.

Riesman, David. *On Higher Education: The Academic Enterprise in an Era of Rising Student Consumerism*. Piscataway, NJ: Transaction Publishers, 1980.

Reynolds, Jeannette, and Theodore Matthews, eds. *The Panther: Nineteen Hundred and Fifty-Five*. Yearbook, Clark College, 1955.

Rossiter, Margaret W. *Women Scientists in America*. Vol. 1, *Struggles and Strategies to 1940*. Baltimore, MD: Johns Hopkins University Press, 1982.

Rossiter, Margaret W. *Women Scientists in America*. Vol. 2, *Before Affirmative Action, 1940–1972*. Baltimore, MD: Johns Hopkins University Press, 1995.

Shetterly, Margot Lee. *Hidden Figures: The American Dream and the Untold Story of the Black Women Mathematicians Who Helped Win the Space Race*. New York: William Morrow Paperbacks, 2016.

Sullivan, Otha Richard. *Black Stars: African American Women Scientists and Inventors*. San Francisco: Jossey-Bass, 2002.

BIBLIOGRAPHY

Walker, Eyvaine. *Keeping a Family Legacy Alive: Unforgotten African Americans*. Atlanta, GA: Twins Publishing, 2011.

Warren, Wini. *Black Women Scientists in the United States*. Bloomington: Indiana University Press, 1999.

Weisbrot, Robert. *Marching Toward Freedom: 1957–1965*. New York: Chelsea House Publishers, 1994.

Zinn, Howard. *The People Speak: American Voices, Some Famous, Some Little Known*. Grand Rapids, MI: Zondervan, 2009.

Reports

Acosta, Maureen. *Building a Legacy—The First Forty Years: The History of Giving at Metropolitan State University, 1971–2001*. Metropolitan State University, April 2011.

Armstrong, George T., Defoe C. Ginnings, and R. P. Hudson. "Justification for Performance Rating: Outstanding Performance Rating: Dr. Reatha C. King." US Department of Commerce, June 6, 1967.

Barrett, Diana, and Sheila McCarthy. "General Mills and the Hawthorne Huddle." Harvard Business School Case 303-132, June 2003.

"Construction of Regional Office and Laboratory, Site Specific, Jamaica Site, Queen County: Environmental Impact Statement." Prepared by Edward and Kelcey, Inc. for the United States. Food and Drug Administration. January 25, 1996. https://play.google.com/books/reader?id=F_k0AQAAMAAJ&hl=en&pg=GBS.RA4-SA12-PA3.

Chapter No. 966—HF No. 3137. Minnesota State Senate, 67th Legislature, 1971. https://www.revisor.mn.gov/laws/1971/0/Session+Law/Chapter/966/pdf.

Cultures of Giving: Energizing and Expanding Philanthropy by and for Communities of Color. The W. K. Kellogg Foundation, January 2012. http://www.d5coalition.org/wp-content/uploads/2013/07/CultureofGiving.pdf.

Edwards, Frank, Hedwig Lee, and Michael Esposito. "Risk of Being Killed by Police Use of Force in the United States by Age, Race-Ethnicity, and Sex." *Proceeding of the National Academy of the United States of America* 116, no. 34 (August 20, 2019). https://doi.org/10.1073/pnas.1821204116.

"Founding Documents: The Chancellor's Recommendation to the Board for the Presidency of Minnesota Metropolitan State College." Office of the Chancellor, Minnesota Metropolitan State College, June 28, 1971.

Johnson, Lyndon B. "Report to the Congress from the President of the United States: United States Aeronautics and Space Activities, 1965." Washington, DC: Executive Office of the President, National Aeronautics and Space Council, January 31, 1966.

Karen, David. "The Politics of Class, Race, and Gender: Access to Higher Education in the United States, 1960–1986." In *Bryn Mawr College Sociology Faculty Research and Scholarship*. Bryn Mawr, PA: Bryn Mawr College, 1991.

King, Reatha Clark. *Philanthropy and Public Policy: Working Together to Make a Bigger Difference, Project Summary*. Minneapolis, MN: Hubert H. Humphrey Institute of Public Affairs, 2004.

Klotz, Ann Marie. "The Journey to the Top: Women's Paths to the University Presidency." EdD diss., DePaul University, June 2014.

Messick, Denise P., J. W. Joseph, and Natalie P. Adams. *Tilling the Earth: Georgia's Historic Agricultural Heritage—A Context*. Georgia Department of Natural Resources, Historic Preservation Division. Stone Mountain, GA: New Associates, Inc., 2001. https://georgiashpo.org/sites/default/files/hpd/pdf/TillingTheEarth_0.pdf.

"Minutes of the Meeting of the Board of Higher Education of the City of New York." June 21, 1971. http://policy.cuny.edu/policyimport/board_meeting_minutes/1971/06-21/document.pdf.

Mitau, G. Theodore, et al. *1973–75 Biennial Report to the Governor and the Legislature: A Response to New Realities in the Management of Educational Change*. Minnesota State College Board, 1975. https://www.leg.state.mn.us/docs/2014/mandated/140651.pdf.

Mitau, G. Theodore, et al. "Appendices for 1973–75 *Biennial Report to the Governor and the Legislature: A Response to New Realities in the Management of Educational Change*." Minnesota State College Board, 1975. https://www.leg.state.mn.us/docs/2014/mandated/140652.pdf.

Motycka, Abby E. "White Southerners Respond to *Brown v. Board of Education*: Why Crisis Erupted When Little Rock, Arkansas Desegregated Central High School." Honors project, Bowdoin College, 2017. Bowdoin Digital Commons. https://digitalcommons.bowdoin.edu/cgi/viewcontent.cgi?article=1084&context=honorsprojects.

National Institute of Justice. "Excellence in Problem-Oriented Policing: Winners of the 1999 Herman Goldstein Award for Excellence in Problem-Oriented Policing." Washington, DC: US Department of Justice, 2000.

Pettet, Zellmer R. "Sixteenth Census of the United States: 1940, Agriculture." *United States Department of Commerce*, 1942. http://usda.mannlib.cornell.edu/usda/AgCensusImages/1940/01/28/1940-01-28.pdf.

Ribicoff, Abraham, et. al. *Minority Business Development Administration: Hearing Before the Subcommittee on Intergovernmental Relations of the Committee on Government Operations*. Committee on Government Operations. April 13, 1976.

Saeks, Allen I., et al. *An Urban College: New Kinds of 'Students' on a New Kind of 'Campus': A Proposal for Action in 1971 to Meet Higher Education Needs in the Twin Cities Area*. Citizens League Committee on Higher Education. April 15, 1971.

Schiebinger, Londa. "Women in Science: Historical Perspectives." Women at Work: A Meeting on the Status of Women in Astronomy, workshop proceedings. Baltimore, MD: Space Telescope Science Institute, September 8–9, 1992.

Schmidt, Benno C., Jr., et al. "The History of Open Admissions and Remedial Education at the City University of New York." New York City Records & Information Services, Mayor's Advisory Task Force on the City University of New York, June 7, 1999. http://www.nyc.gov/html/records/rwg/cuny.

Scientific Manpower, 1962. National Science Foundation. Washington, DC: US Government Printing Office, 1962.

"Tanzania Evaluation: P/DP Ampart Reatha King." United States Information Agency, October 1983.

Newspapers and Periodicals

Acker, Elwood B. "Professor Reatha C. King Appointed Natural Sciences Dean at York College." York College news release, September 29, 1970.

Alexander, Michael. "3 Blacks Accuse College Unit of Bias." *Newsday*, March 30, 1977.

Alnes, Stephen. "Metropolitan State University: A Successful Educational Experiment with a Low Profile." *Minneapolis Star*, June 24, 1978.

Apgar, Sally. "Women Finding Place in Boardroom: From the Boardroom to the Executive Suite to the Family Den, Two Generations of Minnesota Female Executives form the Vanguard for Change at Work and at Home." *Star Tribune*, July 28, 1997: 1A.

AP. "37 College Presidents Call for Better Teaching." *New York Times*, September 19, 1987, Section 1: 32.

Austermuhle, Martin. "D.C.'s Black Commercial Districts Came Back From the 1968 Riots, but Many Black Residents Left." American University Radio, April 4, 2018. https://wamu.org/story/18/04/04/d-c-s-black-commercial-districts-came-back-1968-riots-many-black-residents-left.

Bailey, Charles W., ed. "Metropolitan State Has Alumni." *Minneapolis Tribune*, February 12, 1973: 12A.

Benidt, Bruce. "Metro State May Help Fill Educational Void in Cities." *Star Tribune*, January 15, 1989: 1B.

Biano, Tony. "Black Woman Named Head of Metropolitan State 'U.'" *Minneapolis Tribune*, August 17, 1977.

Blair, William G. "Dumont F. Kenny, Retired Educator." *New York Times*, January 3, 1982, Section 1: 28. https://www.nytimes.com/1982/01/03/obituaries/dumont-f-kenny-retired-educator.html.

Bolsta, Phil. "Reatha Clark King: Lifetime Achievement Award." *Twin Cities Business Magazine*. October 1, 2010. http://tcbmag.com/honors/articles/2010/2010-outstanding-directors/reatha-clark-king.

Brettingen, Tom. "Minnesota College to Cater to Urban Students." *Washington Post*, December 19, 1971: 10.

Broaddus, Adrienne. "Minnesota Woman Helped Send Men to the Moon." KARE 11, July 17, 2019. https://www.kare11.com/article/news/local/breaking-the-news/minnesota-woman-helped-send-men-to-the-moon/89-1c47561e-badb-4d1f-b791-0eaa3af9368b.

Bute, Monte. "A Riverboat Gambler's Utopian Experiment." *Journal of Educational Foundations* 30, no. 1–4 (2017): 7–32. https://files.eric.ed.gov/fulltext/EJ1173231.pdf.

Chapman, Reg. "'My People Were Depending on Me': Apollo 11 Scientist Dr. Reatha Clark King Looks Back at Historic Launch." CBS Minnesota, July 16, 2019. https://minnesota.cbslocal.com/2019/07/16/my-people-were-depending-on-me-nasa-scientist-dr-reatha-clark-king-looks-back-at-apollo-11-triumph.

BIBLIOGRAPHY

"Checking In with Some Neighbors: Meet the Prez." *Citizens*, May–June 1978.

Chung, Jeanie. "Burning Ambition." *University of Chicago Magazine* 1121, no. 1 (Fall 2018): 56–59.

Cosgrove, Ben. "Bigotry in the USA: Photos from a Ku Klux Klan Initiation." *Time*, March 5, 2013. https://time.com/3746389/bigotry-in-the-usa-photos-from-a-ku-klux-klan-initiation.

Derickson, Roy. "MMSC: 'A Good Thing for Women.'" *St. Paul Pioneer Press*, August 13, 1972.

Donovan, Lisa. "Community Leader's Voice Lifts Capitol Crowd." *Pioneer Press*, September 17, 2001: A6.

Duchschere, Kevin. "Hands-On Program Makes Kids Want to Read." *Star Tribune*, November 2, 1990.

"Dumont Kenny Resigns for Colorado Post." *Pandora's Box* (The School Newspaper of York College) 4, no. 9 (August 1970). https://archives.york.cuny.edu/pandoras-box/august-1970-pdf.

Egerton, John. "Malcolm-King College: Harlem's Higher Education Volunteers." *Change: The Magazine of Higher Learning* 5, no. 1 (1973).

Engebretson, Jess. "How the Birthplace of the Modern Ku Klux Klan Became the Site of America's Largest Confederate Monument." KQED News, July 24, 2015. https://www.kqed.org/lowdown/19119/stone-mountains-hidden-history-americas-biggest-confederate-memorial-and-birthplace-of-the-modern-ku-klux-klan.

Fairfax, Lisa M. "Some Reflections on the Diversity of Corporate Boards: Women, People of Color, and the Unique Issues Associated with Women of Color." *St. John's Law Review* 79 (February 6, 2006). https://scholarship.law.gwu.edu/cgi/viewcontent.cgi?article=1596&context=faculty_publications.

"First Black Woman: Moultrian Now Heads Minnesota University." *Moultrie Observer*, November 18, 1977: 2.

Folds, Chauntelle. "Getting a Seat at the Table." *Black Enterprise* 37. No. 4 (November 2006): 72–74.

Franklin, Robert. "Agency Gets $2 Million to Fight Child Abuse." *Star Tribune*, September 25, 1992: 10D.

Franklin, Robert. "Honing Skills in the Fund-Raising Game." *Star Tribune*, November 10, 1996: 3B.

Franklin, Robert. "General Mills Grants Include $592,000 for Indian Programs." *Star Tribune*, June 20, 1992: 10C.

Goyal, Rita, Nada Kakabadse, and Andrew Kakabadse. "Improving Corporate Governance with Functional Diversity on FTSE 350 Boards: Directors' Perspective." *Journal of Capital Market Studies*, November 11, 2019. https://www.emerald.com/insight/content/doi/10.1108/JCMS-09-2019-0044/full/html.

Groat, Janet. "East Side St. Paul Chosen for Metro State." *Star Tribune*, January 29, 1988: 1A.

———. "Funding Is Less than Sought, but Metro State Plans New Programs." *Star Tribune*, May 26, 1987: 01B.

———. "Metro State President King Is Known for Hard Work, Sparking School's Growth." *Star Tribune*, November 9, 1987: 1A.

———. "Metropolitan State University Plans 7 Programs to Fill Gap After 'U' Cuts." *Star Tribune*, November 8, 1986: 1A.

———. "Minneapolis Joins Bidding for Metro State Facility." *Star Tribune*, December 11, 1987: 1A.

———. "State University Chief Backs St. Paul Site for Metro State University." *Star Tribune*. January 26, 1988: 1A.

Grumdahl, Dara Moskowitz. "How Philip Brunelle Became the Twin Cities' Song Leader." *Mpls.St.Paul Magazine*, June 18, 2018.

Hall, Jacquelyn Dowd. "The Long Civil Rights Movement and the Political Uses of the Past." *Journal of American History* 91, no. 4 (March 2005): 1233–1263.

Hawkins, B. Denise. "Echoes of Faith: Church Roots Run Deep Among HBCUs." *Diverse Issues in Higher Education*, July 31, 2012. https://diverseeducation.com/article/17259.

"Her Job in a New, Unusual College" (original story: Christian Science Monitor News Service]. *Des Moines Register*, May 31, 1973: 9.

Hevesi, Dennis. "Milton Bassin Dies at 88; Expanded York College." *New York Times*, August 19, 2012, Section A20. https://www.nytimes.com/2012/08/19/nyregion/milton-bassin-88-dies-expanded-york-college-in-queens.html.

Hine, Darlene Clark. "Black Professionals and Race Consciousness: Origins of the Civil Rights Movement, 1890–1950." *Journal of American History* 89, no. 4 (March 2003): 1279–1294.

BIBLIOGRAPHY

Hovis, Kathy. "Alumna's Bequest Supports Young Female Scientists." *Cornell Chronicle*, October 27, 2015. https://news.cornell.edu/stories/2015/10/alumnas-bequest-supports-young-female-scientists.

Impellezerri, Frances Anne. "At Last! Jamaica or Bust, or Both." *Pandora's Box* (The School Newspaper of York College) 6, no. 3 (March 5, 1971): 2.

Inskip, Leonard. "Twenty-Five Years of Helping Minority Business." *Star Tribune*, November 5, 1996: 13A.

Jackson, Sandra, and Sandra Harris. "African American Female College and University Presidents: Career Path to the Presidency." *Journal of Women in Educational Leadership* 3, no. 4 (October 2005). https://digitalcommons.unl.edu/cgi/viewcontent.cgi?article=1171&context=jwel.

James, George. "York College in Queens Gets a Permanent Home." *New York Times*, November 2, 1986: 5.

Johnson, Dirk. "Nice City's Nasty Distinction: Murders Soar in Minneapolis." *New York Times*, June 30, 1996: 1.

King, Reatha Clark. "The Uncharted Territory: My Path to Excellence." *The Chemists Club*. Chicago: The University of Chicago, 2019.

Levs, Josh. "Neil Armstrong's 'Small Step for Man' Might Be a Misquote, Study Says." CNN. June 5, 2013. https://www.cnn.com/2013/06/04/tech/armstrong-quote/index.html.

Lofquist, Vicki, ed. *Metropolitan State University Buzz* 4, no. 1 (Fall 2011).

Lyons, Douglas C. "Corporate Executives Tell: How I Broke through the Glass Ceiling." *Ebony*, January 1, 1993: 102.

Malcolm, Andrew M. "Minnesota College with No Campus, Classrooms or Grades Opens." *New York Times*, February 4, 1972: 33. https://www.nytimes.com/1972/02/04/archives/minnesota-college-with-no-campus-classrooms-or-grades-opens.html.

McCormack, Patricia. "Minnesota's New College or No College." *Cedar Rapids Gazette*. December 19, 1971: 5A. https://crpubliclibrary.newspaperarchive.com/cedar-rapids-gazette/1971-12-19/page-5.

Merrill, Ann. "King Retiring from Foundation." *Star Tribune*, May 29, 2002: 3D.

———. "The Veteran Reatha Clark King." *St. Paul Pioneer Press*, January 31, 1993: 4D.

Molnar, Courtni E. "'Has the Millennium Yet Dawned?': A History of Attitudes toward Pregnant Workers in America." *Michigan Journal of Gender & Law* 12, no. 1 (2005): 167.

Moser, Whet. "Chicago Isn't Just Segregated, It Basically Invented Modern Segregation." *Chicago Magazine*, March 31, 2017. https://www.chicagomag.com/city-life/March-2017/Why-Is-Chicago-So-Segregated.

Murphy, Karen. "It's the Worst of Times for Pavo." *Thomasville Times-Enterprise*, May 2, 2015. https://www.timesenterprise.com/news/local_news/it-s-the-worst-of-times-for-pavo/article_3b0afcde-f0fd-11e4-a1d6-fbe1dcad2c78.html.

Narine, Dalton. "Have Plane, Will Travel." *Ebony*, December 1988: 120.

Nocera, Joe. "Emerald City of Giving Does Exist." *New York Times*. December 22, 2007.

O'Keefe, Kenzie. "Hawthorne Huddle Celebrates 20 Years of Creating a Forum for Positive Change." *North News*, December 6, 2017. https://mynorthnews.org/new-blog/2017/12/6/huddle-celebrates-20-years.

Paine, Bud. "Here's What Happened on Trail of Confessed Killer." *Moultrie Observer*, May 17, 1954.

———. "Tom Williams Confesses Double Murder Here on Saturday Night." *Moultrie Observer*, May 17, 1954.

"Pioneering in Health Services." *Long Island Press*, July 10, 1973.

"President King Welcomes Expanded Role for Metro U." *St. Paul Recorder*, April 18, 1985.

Rani, Bhargav. "Revolution and CUNY: Remembering the 1969 Fight for Open Admissions." *Advocate*, July 30, 2018. https://gcadvocate.com/2018/07/30/revolution-and-cuny-remembering-the-1969-fight-for-open-admissions.

Rao, Maya, and Briana Bierschbach. "Thousands of Minnesotans Gather at Star-Studded Events to Mark MLK Holiday." *Star Tribune*, January 20, 2020.

"Reatha Clark King to Receive Career Achievement Award." *Moultrie Observer*, February 8, 2017. https://www.moultrieobserver.com/news/local_news/reatha-clark-king-to-receive-career-achievement-award/article_ca5829c4-ee6d-11e6-9a09-c3d4a3b648c3.html.

Reynolds, Susanne. "'A Piece of Pavo's Heart' Lost." *Thomasville Times-Enterprise*, May 31, 2014. https://www.timesenterprise.com/

BIBLIOGRAPHY

news/a-piece-of-pavo-s-heart-lost/article_57ba91c7–2c48–599e-bbe2-e93caa53e5e6.html.

Schneider, Kristin, and Pablo Schneider. "The Pioneer: Reatha Clark King." *Latino Leaders*, July/August 2010.

Schumach, Murray. "Dean Stresses York's Citywide Role." *New York Times*, February 10, 1974: 9. https://www.nytimes.com/1974/02/10/archives/dean-stresses-yorks-citywide-role-early-college-desires.html.

Sharkey, Patrick, Gerard Torrats-Espinosa, and Delaram Takyar. "Community and the Crime Decline: The Casual Effect of Local Nonprofits on Violent Crime." *American Sociological Review* 82, no. 6 (October 2017): 1214–1240. https://doi.org/10.1177/0003122417736289.

Small, Andrew. "The Wastelands of Urban Renewal." Bloomberg CityLab, February 13, 2017. https://www.bloomberg.com/news/articles/2017–02–13/how-the-bulldozer-became-an-urban-block-buster.

Smith, Kelly. "Minnesota Is Again No. 1, Topping a List for Most Generous State in the U.S." *Star Tribune*, December 21, 2019. https://www.startribune.com/minnesota-is-again-no-1-topping-a-list-for-most-generous-state-in-the-u-s/566406672.

Smith, Robert T. "Her Car Was Stolen—but She Was Sued." *Minneapolis Tribune*, March 11, 1981: 1A.

Stassen-Berger, Rachel E. "Foundation, Neighbors Huddle Together." *Pioneer Press*, March 29, 1999: 1B.

Stroud, James L., Jr. "Chemist, Professor, Businessman, Pilot and Plane Builder." *Minnesota Spokesman-Recorder*, February 15, 2012. https://spokesman-recorder.com/2012/02/15/chemist-professor-businessman-pilot-and-plane-builder.

"Talmadge Made Defiant Statement." *Atlanta Constitution*, May 24, 1954.

"Talmadge Renews Protest against Court Decision." *Moultrie Observer*, May 21, 1954.

"Talmadge Repeats School Defiance," *Moultrie Observer*, May 24, 1954. https://moultriecoulquitt.advantage-preservation.com/viewer/?k=talmadge%20schools&i=f&by=1954&bdd=1950&d=05011954–05311954&m=between&ord=k1&fn=moultrie_observer_usa_georgia_moultrie_19540524_english_1&df=1&dt=10

"Talmadge Text." *Atlanta Constitution*, May 18, 1954.

"Text of President Bush's 2002 State of the Union Address." *Washington Post*, January 29, 2002. https://www.washingtonpost.com/wp-srv/onpolitics/transcripts/sou012902.htm.

Trimble, Steve. "A Centennial History of St. John's Hospital." *Dayton's Bluff District Forum*, November 2011: 6.

"Vietnam: One Week's Dead." *Life*, June 27, 1969. https://www.life.com/history/faces-of-the-american-dead-in-vietnam-one-weeks-toll-june-1969.

Waterhouse, Benjamin C. "The Personal, the Political and the Profitable: Business and Protest Culture, 1960s-1980s." *Financial History Magazine* 121 (Spring 2017).

Zylber, Adele. "Campus to Be Completed: 197?" *Pandora's Box* (The School Newspaper of York College) 10, no. 2 (February 15, 1973): 1, 4.

Pamphlets, Programs, and Presentations

"Donor Spotlight: Reatha Clark King." *Program: VocalEssence 2019–2020 Season*.

"Reatha Clark King Endowed Scholarship Fund." Metropolitan State University Foundation, 1988.

King, Reatha Clark. "2019 Governor's Civil Rights Legend Award." *The 33rd Annual State of Minnesota Martin Luther King Day Celebration*, 2019, 9.

King, Reatha Clark. "Colquitt County Address to Students." *Moultrie High School Assembly*, Moultrie, GA, March 1, 2017.

King, Reatha Clark. "Excellence in Corporate and Nonprofit Governance: Leading with Brilliance and Courage." Presentation, Women's Corporate Directors: Minneapolis Chapter, Minneapolis, MN, October 7, 2019.

King, Reatha Clark. Curriculum vitae, 2018.

King, Reatha Clark. *Future Challenge for Women in Our Society*. 1983. https://www.worldcat.org/title/future-challenges-for-women-in-our-society/oclc/967334412.

King, Reatha Clark. "Presentation for NIST." Gaithersburg, MD: National Institute of Standards and Technology, 2014. https://www.worldcat.org/title/black-history-month-colloquium-remembering-

nbs-my-gateway-to-a-future-of-service-and-opportunity/
oclc/897990173.

Montague, Stephanie. "Thanks for Time Well Served: A Tribute to Dr. Mamie C. Montague, RN, MS, FNP-BC, CNE, FAAN." *Epistle* 40, no. 3 (April 2019).

"Reflections: Reatha Clark King." Saint Paul, MN: Metropolitan State University, 1987.

"Resolution." General Mills, May 28, 2002.

Zweigenhaft, Richard. "Diversity among CEOs and Corporate Directors; Has the Heyday Come and Gone?" Based on a presentation at the annual meeting of the American Sociological Association, New York City, August 12, 2013. https://www.researchgate.net/publication/288485589_Diversity_Among_CEOs_and_Corporate_Directors_Has_the_Heyday_Come_and_Gone.

Personal Correspondence

Blais, Emily. "Testimonial for RCK Scholarship." September 7, 2020.

Green, Dorothy Clark. "A Tribute Flowing From the Love of a Sister." Poem for Reatha Clark King. April 3, 2004.

King, Kayla. "RCK Biography." Email, October 15, 2020.

King, MacKensey. "RCK Biography." Email, October 7, 2020.

King, N. Judge IV. "RCK Biography." Email, October 9, 2020.

King, Scott. "Qs for RCK Bio." Email, August 26, 2020.

Parker, Jr., George W. "Letter to Reatha Clark King." October 8, 1970.

Tucker, Joe Louis. "Letter to Reatha Clark King." October 7, 1970.

Zilley, Kurt. "Testimonial." April 13, 2020.

Video Interviews, Personal Interviews, Speeches

Baker, Ella. "Bigger than a Hamburger." *Southern Patriot*, May 1960. https://www.crmvet.org/docs/sncc2.htm.

"Corporate Governance Hall of Fame: Reatha Clark King." National Association of Corporate Directors, April 16, 2019. https://vimeo.com/330861467/eade5eaf53.

Danger, Tane. Interview by Kate Leibfried. August 26, 2020.

"Inside the Boardroom: Reatha Clark King." TPT Co-Productions, January 25, 2008. Video, 58:06. https://www.pbs.org/video/inside-the-boardroom-reatha-clark-king.

Kennedy, John F. "Civil Rights: March on Washington, 28 August 1963: Proposed Statement." John F. Kennedy Presidential Library and Museum: Virtual Archive. https://www.jfklibrary.org/asset-viewer/archives/JFKPOF/097/JFKPOF-097-008.

King, N. Judge, III. Interview by Kate Leibfried. March 5, 2020.

King, Reatha Clark. "Accountability in Philanthropy: 'Walking the Talk in Changing Times.'" Tenth Annual James A. Joseph Lecture. Philadelphia, PA: Association of Black Foundation Executives., April 29, 2001.

King, Reatha Clark. "History Center Interview." Interview with Madeline Mitchell and Amrita Jain, August 6, 2016. Transcript.

King, Reatha Clark. "Iconic Voices: Dr. Reatha Clark King's Journey from Jim Crow to the C Suite." Interview by Jeff Cunningham. July 8, 2016. Video, 44:11. https://www.youtube.com/watch?v=kvVkWfiYV1A&t=1863s.

King, Reatha Clark. "Minnesota Philanthropy Partners: Who Inspires Us." Interview by Carleen Rhodes, October 7, 2012. Video, 13:52. https://www.youtube.com/watch?v=y7g6R8ftgv4.

King, Reatha Clark. "Structured Interview for President." Saint Paul Area Chamber of Commerce, June 5, 1986.

King, Reatha Clark. Interviews by Kate Leibfried. November 6, 2019; November 19, 2019; December 4, 2019; January 8, 2020; January 22, 2020; February 13, 2020; March 4, 2020; March 25, 2020; April 22, 2020; July 31, 2020; September 23, 2020; October 5, 2020; March 10, 2021.

King, Scott. Interview by Kate Leibfried. March 12, 2020.

Latimer, George. Interview by Kate Leibfried. August 26, 2020.

McKillips, Nancy. Interview by Kate Leibfried. March 27, 2020.

Montague, Terri. Interview by Kate Leibfried. October 2, 2020.

Perpich, Governor Rudy. "Proclamation: Metropolitan State University Week." June 18, 1986.

Taylor, Glen. Interview by Kate Leibfried. August 26, 2020.

BIBLIOGRAPHY

Online References

"1961–1969: The Creation of CUNY: Open Admissions Struggle." American Social History Project, CUNY Digital History Archive. Accessed July 29, 2020. https://cdha.cuny.edu/coverage/coverage/show/id/23.

"A 1958 Citizenship Test from the Georgia State Voter Registration Act." Digital Public Library of America. 1958. https://dp.la/primary-source-sets/voting-rights-act-of-1965/sources/1387.

Allen, Susie, and Michael Drapa. "When King Made History at UChicago." University of Chicago. January 9, 2012. https://www.uchicago.edu/features/20120109_mlk.

America's Charities. "Facts & Statistics on Workplace Giving, Matching Gifts, and Volunteer Programs." Accessed April 28, 2020. https://www.charities.org/facts-statistics-workplace-giving-matching-gifts-and-volunteer-programs.

Asaro, Salvatore. "Campus Unrest Part I: Queens College in the Spring of 1969." QC Voices. November 5, 2018. http://qcvoices.qwriting.qc.cuny.edu/salasaro/2018/11/05/campus-unrest-part-i-queens-college-in-the-spring-of-1969-2.

Beck, Maya. "Sarah Bellamy: Artistic Director, Penumbra Theatre." Pollen. Accessed May 6, 2020. https://www.pollenmidwest.org/stories/meet-sarah-bellamy.

Boston University. "Reatha Clark King: Woman of Science." Accessed August 21, 2020. https://www.bu.edu/lernet/pathways/bios.html.

Carleton College. "Honorary Degrees." Accessed June 2020. https://www.carleton.edu/honorary-degrees.

City-Data.com. "Pavo, Georgia." http://www.city-data.com/city/Pavo-Georgia.html. Accessed December 5, 2019.

Clark Atlanta University. "CAU History." Accessed July 13, 2020. https://www.cau.edu/history.html.

Clark College. "The Clark College Bulletin: Ninety-Second Annual Catalogue, Announcements for 1959–1960." Clark College Catalogs, Book 57 (1959). http://digitalcommons.auctr.edu/cccatalogs/57.

Cobb, James C., and John C. Inscoe. "Georgia History: Overview." New Georgia Encyclopedia. (original article: University of Georgia). Last modified May 9, 2019. https://www.georgiaencyclopedia.org/articles/history-archaeology/georgia-history-overview.

Cohen, J. Richard, et al. "Ku Klux Klan: A History of Racism." South Poverty Law Center. March 1, 2011. https://www.splcenter.org/20110228/ku-klux-klan-history-racism.

DeFerrari, John. "The Lost Hilltop Home of the National Bureau of Standards." *Streets of Washington.* July 1, 2013. http://www.streetsofwashington.com/2013/07/the-lost-hilltop-home-of-national.html.

Ganzel, Bill. "Farming in the 1950s & 60s: Cotton Harvesting." Wessels Living History Farm. The Ganzel Group, 2007. https://livinghistoryfarm.org/farminginthe50s/machines_15.html.

Giesen, James C. "Sharecropping." New Georgia Encyclopedia (original article: Mississippi State University). Last modified August 28, 2019. https://www.georgiaencyclopedia.org/articles/history-archaeology/sharecropping.

Hatfield, Edward A. "Bus Desegregation in Atlanta." New Georgia Encyclopedia. Last modified December 3, 2013. https://www.georgiaencyclopedia.org/articles/history-archaeology/bus-desegregation-atlanta.

Hatfield, Edward A. "World War II in Georgia." New Georgia Encyclopedia. Last modified September 9, 2019. https://www.georgiaencyclopedia.org/articles/history-archaeology/world-war-ii-georgia.

Hobbes, Dwight. "N. Judge King May 13, 1936–May 26, 2014." *Minnesota Spokesman-Recorder,* June 8, 2014. https://spokesman-recorder.com/2014/06/08/n-judge-king-may-13-1936-may-26-2014.

Johnson, Nick, and Chris Kolmar. "The 10 Most Diverse Colleges in Minnesota for 2020." CollegeSnacks. January 17, 2020. https://www.homesnacks.net/college/most-diverse-colleges-in-minnesota.

Kadinsky, Sergey. "York College-Ashmead Park, Jamaica." *Forgotten New York* (blog). May 28, 2018. https://forgotten-ny.com/2018/05/york-college-ashmead-park-jamaica.

Kridel, Craig. "Introduction to the Secondary School Study." Museum of Education, 2018. http://www.museumofeducation.info/secondary_study_intro.html.

Kridel, Craig. "Moultrie High School for Negro Youth: Moultrie, Georgia." Museum of Education, 2018. http://www.museumofeducation.info/moultrie.html.

BIBLIOGRAPHY

Kridel, Craig. "Progressive Education in Black High Schools: The Secondary School Study, 1940–1946." *Museum of Education*. Columbia, SC: University of South Carolina, 2015. http://www.museumofeducation.info/SSS-4_16.pdf.

Lay, Shawn. "Ku Klux Klan in the Twentieth Century." New Georgia Encyclopedia (original article: Coker College, Hartsville, SC). Last modified July 18, 2016. https://www.georgiaencyclopedia.org/articles/history-archaeology/ku-klux-klan-twentieth-century?amp.

LEAD: LEADership, Education and Development. Home page. Accessed May 6, 2020. https://www.leadprogram.org.

McCollum, Betty. "Honoring the 100th Anniversary of St. John's Hospital." September 8, 2011. https://mccollum.house.gov/taxonomy/statements-for-the-record/honoring-100th-anniversary-st-john-s-hospital.

Metropolitan State University. "College of Nursing and Health Services." Accessed April 16, 2020. https://www.metrostate.edu/academics/nursing-and-health-sciences.

Metropolitan State University. "Key Facts at a Glance." Accessed August 4, 2020. https://www.metrostate.edu/about/key-facts and https://www.metrostate.edu/sites/default/files/2020-02/MetropolitanState_KeyFacts2020_0.pdf.

Metropolitan State University. "University History." Accessed April 16, 2020. https://www.metrostate.edu/about/history.

National Aeronautics and Space Administration (NASA). "Rocket Park: Saturn V." Johnson Space Center. https://www.nasa.gov/centers/johnson/rocketpark/saturn_v.html.

"NASA Budgets: US Spending on Space Travel Since 1958 UPDATED." *Guardian*, February 1, 2010. https://www.theguardian.com/news/datablog/2010/feb/01/nasa-budgets-us-spending-space-travel.

National Center for Biotechnology Information. "PubChem Compound Summary for CID 24547, Oxygen Difluoride." PubChem. Accessed August 10, 2020. https://pubchem.ncbi.nlm.nih.gov/compound/Oxygen-difluoride.

National Institute of Standards and Technology (NIST). "The Founding: Overview." March 8, 2017. https://www.nist.gov/history/nist-100-foundations-progress/founding-overview.

National Park Service. "Building the Memorial." Martin Luther King, Jr. Memorial. Updated June 24, 2019. https://www.nps.gov/mlkm/learn/building-the-memorial.htm.

Penumbra Theatre. "History." Accessed May 6, 2020. https://penumbratheatre.org/history.

Reinhardt, Claudia, and Bill Ganzel. "Farming in the 1940s: Rural Life in the 1940s: Wessels Living History Farm." The Ganzel Group. Accessed December 5, 2019, https://livinghistoryfarm.org/farminginthe40s/life_01.html.

Renfro, Sally, and Allison Armour-Garb. "The History of Open Admissions and Remedial Education at the City University of New York." Archives of Rudolph W. Giuliani, 107th Mayor. June 1999. http://www.nyc.gov/html/records/rwg/cuny/pdf/history.pdf.

Ruff, Joshua. "Long Island in the 1960s: A Visual Essay." Stony Brook, NY: Long Island Museum of American Art, History & Carriages, 2016. https://lihj.cc.stonybrook.edu/wp-content/uploads/2016/12/Long-Island-in-the-1960s-LIHJ.pdf.

Statista. "Rate of Fatal Police Shootings in the United States from 2015 to July 2020, by Ethnicity." July 31, 2020. https://www.statista.com/statistics/1123070/police-shootings-rate-ethnicity-us.

"The State of Louisiana Literacy Test." *Wall Street Journal*. Circa 1964. http://online.wsj.com/public/resources/documents/la-littest-orig.pdf.

Tuck, Stephen. "Civil Rights Movement." New Georgia Encyclopedia (original article: Pembroke College, Oxford University). Last modified September 16, 2018. https://www.georgiaencyclopedia.org/articles/history-archaeology/civil-rights-movement.

Tuttle, Kelly. "For Love of the Lab." Science History Institute. June 2, 2016. https://www.sciencehistory.org/distillations/magazine/for-love-of-the-lab.

US Census Bureau. "Historical Census Information." https://www2.census.gov/library/publications.

Zickuhr, Kathryn. "Discriminatory Housing Practices in the District: A Brief History." DC Policy Center. October 24, 2018. https://www.dcpolicycenter.org/publications/discriminatory-housing-practices-in-the-district-a-brief-history.

BIBLIOGRAPHY

Minor References

"About." *Black Lives Matter.* https://blacklivesmatter.com/about/. Accessed August 18, 2020.

Bird, David. "Marvin Griffin, 74, Former Governor." *The New York Times.* June 14, 1982, D11.

Brandt, Steve. "Metro 'U' Head Lead Firm's Charity: Reatha King Goes to General Mills." *Star Tribune.* September, 10 1988: 1B.

"College Head Here Quits After Strife." *New York Times.* May 19, 1970.

Grossman, Ron. "The University of Chicago Opens." *Chicago Tribune.* December 19, 2007.

King, Dr. Martin Luther, Jr. "Letter From a Birmingham Jail." *African Studies Center.* Philadelphia, PA: University of Pennsylvania, April 16, 1963. https://www.africa.upenn.edu/Articles_Gen/Letter_Birmingham.html.

"Master Plan Ok'd." *Pandora's Box* (The School Newspaper of York College) 10, no. 1. (August 1972): 1.

"Our Story." *Pilgrim Baptist Church.* https://www.pilgrimbaptistchurch.org/history/. Accessed July 24, 2020.

Staff Writer. "Metropolitan State Gets Interim President." *Star Tribune.* September 22, 1988: 3B.

"York College at a Glance." *York College.* https://www.york.cuny.edu/produce-and-print/contents/bulletin/york-college-at-a-glance. Accessed July 6, 2020.